Reflections on American Education

Reflections on American Education

Classic and Contemporary Readings

edited by

JAMES A. JOHNSON
Northern Illinois University

VICTOR L. DUPUIS
Pennsylvania State University

JOHN H. JOHANSEN
Northern Illinois University

ALLYN AND BACON
Boston London Toronto Sydney Tokyo Singapore

Series Editor: Sean W. Wakely
Series Editorial Assistant: Carol L. Chernaik
Production Coordinator: Anne Marie Fleming
Text Designer: Anne Marie Fleming
Cover Administrator: Linda K. Dickinson
Cover Designer: Suzanne Harbison
Manufacturing Buyer: Megan Cochran

A Division of Simon and Schuster, Inc.
160 Gould Street
Needham Heights, Massachusetts 02194

Portions of this book first appeared in *Foundations of American Education: Readings,* Fifth Edition, by James A. Johnson, Harold W. Collins, Victor L. Dupuis, and John H. Johansen, copyright © 1982, 1979, 1975, 1972, and 1969 by Allyn and Bacon, Inc.

Library of Congress Cataloging-in-Publication Data

Reflections on American education: classic and contemporary readings / edited by James A. Johnson, Victor L. Dupuis, John H. Johansen.
p. cm.
Includes index.
ISBN 0-205-12564-6
1. Education—United States. 2. Teaching. 3. Education—Social aspects—United States. 4. School management and organization—United States. 5. Education—United States—History. 6. Education—Philosophy. I. Johnson, James Allen II. Dupuis, Victor L. III. Johansen, John H.
LB17.R43 1991
370'.973—dc20 90-44871
CIP

Printed in the United States of America
10 9 8 7 6 5 4 3 2 1 95 94 93 92 91 90

Contents

PART SEVEN
American Education and the Future *203*

Preface

Reflections on American Education: Classic and Contemporary Readings contains a wealth of educational resources from an impressive array of authorities. The selections represent a cross section of the best articles appearing in professional literature. Many of these essays deal with controversial subjects.

This book can be used as the sole text for an introduction to the foundations of education course. It may also be used as a supplemental reading source with any standard introduction to education/educational foundations textbook. We believe, however, that it will best serve as an enrichment source if it is used with its companion volumes, *Introduction to the Foundations of American Education, Eighth Edition* and the student *Study Guide*.

The essays in Part I introduce the reader to important professional aspects of teaching. The Part II selections examine the school as a social institution and will help you better understand the school's relationship to societal problems and issues. In Part III, you will learn more about the current administrative problems faced by American educators. The readings in Part IV highlight the historical development of education in America and point out the important role schools have played in the development of our nation. We hope that the introduction to the educational philosophy presented in the articles that comprise Part V will assist you to formulate your own educational philosophy and will prompt contemplation of basic questions in education. Various aspects of school curriculum are discussed in Part VI, and the future of our educational system is discussed in Part VII.

We are indebted to the many writers and publishers who so generously gave permission for the use of their material in this book. We are also indebted to our colleagues in teacher education programs throughout the United States who helped to evaluate the materials used in this volume.

Finally, we believe the essays contained in this volume should be read by everyone preparing for a career in teaching. Collectively, they help the reader better understand the traditional and contemporary challenges classroom teachers face. For this reason, we highly recommend them to you.

Reflections on American Education

PART ONE

Professional Aspects of Teaching

Teacher concerns have vastly broadened in the past few years, which further contributes to the complexity of the teaching profession. Topics such as teacher supply and demand, teacher salaries, academic freedom, student rights, tenure, professional liability, professional organizations for educators, and teacher unions are typical concerns that were probably not included in former teacher preparation programs. Part I presents a group of articles that are intended to provide an overview of selected dimensions of the work world of teachers.

The first essay in this book, by Deanna Whitford, is entitled "To Teach or Not to Teach," and discusses some of the advantages and disadvantages of teaching. This article should be of particular interest to college students who are considering teaching as a career.

The second selection, authored by Susan Tifft, is entitled "Who's Teaching Our Children?" This timely essay provides a good deal of information about the teaching profession and also presents vignettes about the events that specific teachers experience throughout the teaching day. The article actually represents a plea for talented young people to enter the teaching profession to provide the help our schools desperately need today.

Mary V. Bicouvaris, in her article "Commitment of 'Public' Vital for Education," points out that schools are only as good as our public wants them to be and as the public is willing to pay for.

The next three articles relate to the subject of teacher supply and demand. In "Back to the Classroom," Melinda Beck points out that people enter the teaching field from a variety of backgrounds. A surprising number of older people who have spent time in other professions decide in midlife that they would like to become teachers. Beck also points out that teachers' salaries are improving rather dramatically, particularly in certain parts of the United States. Future teachers should find this article informative.

Jack E. White, in his thought-provoking article, "Education: Getting What You Pay For," analyzes the relationship between the resources devoted to education in the United States and the quality of our schools. White asserts that our nation simply must find more resources for our educational system if schools are to be improved.

The next selection, "A Closer Look at the Shortage of Minority Teachers," points out the tremendous need for more minority teachers and contains a specific set of recommendations for solving this problem.

The next three articles deal with the outcomes of the current educational reform movement. In "The Futures of Teaching," Linda Darling-Hammond does an excellent job of analyzing the evolution of teacher policy, standards and shortages, and the overall subject of the preparation of teachers for the future. She asserts that it is possible to improve our educational system if we choose the right pathway.

Chester E. Finn, Jr., critically analyzes the current educational reform movement and raises pointed questions about the validity of some of the current reform activity in his essay "Questioning 'Cliches' of Education Reform."

In "Parents Are a School's Best Friends," Anne T. Henderson points out that many studies have shown the value of parental involvement in their children's schools. She advocates that schools develop new and better ways to seriously involve parents in educational activity.

Charles T. Kerchner, author of "A New 'Generation' of Teacher Unionism," has observed that the practices of administrators and teachers suggest a shifting of ideologies and the coming of a new approach to labor relations. Kerchner notes that teacher unionism in the 1990s is taking shape around three important issues in public education:

How can public education retain popular support?
How can union activity aid school effectiveness?
How can teachers become employed professionals?

Those questions might be answered in the 1990s.

The article "The Professionalizing of Teaching" identifies characteristics of a professional: the ability to control one's destiny, to employ one's individual judgment, and to accept accountability for one's actions. Under those criteria, is teaching a true profession? The reasons why teaching is not currently a true profession are presented, along with some ideas for helping it to become one.

Albert Shanker, President of the American Federation of Teachers, in "Partnerships Between Teachers and Administrators: How 'They' Became 'We'," addresses issues similar to those of Charles Kerchner. He then proceeds to provide an example of how labor and school boards can work together.

1

To Teach or Not to Teach

Deanna Whitford

"To teach or not to teach, that is the question." Pardon me, Shakespeare, but that's the way the line appears to me every spring.

I love teaching. It seems as if I was born to teach. But following the hullabaloo of the Christmas season, returning to a hectic classroom schedule always seems uninspiring.

It appears to be at that time of year, also, that some of the well-behaved children decide it's their turn to try a little mischief.

It's usually January when some parent I haven't heard a word from all year has a gripe about something that has absolutely no basis (but causes me lots of worry just the same).

And in January, the principal begins to pass out inventory forms, order sheets, meeting schedules and semester grade lists—all enough to make any teacher ready to pack up her whistle and cardigan sweater and head out the first exit, *before* bus call.

It was at this point, not too long ago, that I began the familiar January activity of browsing through the Sunday want ads to look for possible career alternatives. Many looked attractive, most were much more profitable, but all lacked that attribute most attractive to a working mother—the summer off!

I was still in this unsettled state of mind as I headed to my former school for the basketball homecoming. It was there that I had taught first grade for seven years, and those first graders were now in junior high and high school.

In a small town, the basketball homecoming draws alumni, townspeople and students who may not attend another game all year. It's a wonderful opportunity to see friends, fellow teachers and former students.

The first former first grader I spotted was now a high school football star who was sporting an earring in one ear. As I looked up at him, he smiled and mumbled, "It's good to see you, Mrs. Whitford. I've never forgotten you." That was nice!

I pointed out four of the six cheerleaders to my second grade daughter as some of my former first graders. I told her how those little girls spent many recesses outside practicing cheers. It looked as if their years of efforts had helped. While we were studying the girls, they gave us a shy wave. They remembered me, too!

The girls' basketball team sported seven of my first graders, and two of them were outstanding. Six of *my* boys showed up on the boys' team. I explained to my daughter that I knew two of those boys were going to be good athletes ten years ago. They had that competitive spirit even then.

I was really feeling better about what I had accomplished. My students were succeeding. Could it be that some tiny thing I had taught them had helped them find this success? It was a thought.

The final thrill of that evening came following the games and the crowning of the queen and king (both of whom were *my* kids). Several parents of former first graders came up to say hello, and I heard of other accomplishments of other students.

But then Nathan's mother approached me, and we began talking about Nathan's last day of school with me. That was when the importance of teaching and the significance a teacher has in each child's life became as clear as a bell to me once more.

She told me that Nathan had raced home that day, run to his room, slammed the door and thrown himself upon his bed. His mother remembered hearing sobs erupting from her small son. She grabbed his grade card for a possible explanation for this unexpected outburst. She found nothing but perfect grades, as usual. At that point, she walked into his room to gather her son into her arms and ask what was the matter.

"I passed," he sobbed. "Now I'll never see Mrs. Whitford again."

It breaks my heart to think that my students might have thought I'd be gone to the world after they left my classroom. And I suppose there are some teachers who would like it that way. But I'm the type of teacher who feels a part of me is in every student who has crossed my doorway during the year.

It was the best thing that I could have heard at that moment. I *was* important as a teacher. I *had* meant something to my students. Teaching was a field I was successful in, and I *should* stick with it.

As I left the game that night, I decided to stop worrying about finding another career for myself. At least until next January.

Source: From Deanna Whitford, "To Teach or Not to Teach," *Teaching K–8*, April 1989, pp. 38–39. Reprinted with permission of the publisher Early Years, Inc., Norwalk, Connecticut 06854. From the April 1989 issue of *Teaching/K–8*.

2

Who's Teaching Our Children?

Susan Tifft

Wanted: Men and women with the patience of Job, wisdom of Solomon and ability to prepare the next generation for productive citizenship under highly adverse and sometimes dangerous conditions. Applicant must be willing to fill gaps left by unfit, absent or working parents, satisfy demands of state politicians and local bureaucrats, impart healthy cultural and moral values and—oh, yes—teach the three Rs. Hours: 50-60 a week. Pay: fair (getting better). Rewards: mostly intangible.

With a bachelor's degree from Harvard and a double master's in literature and education from the University of Virginia, New Yorker Carol Jackson Cashion seemed a natural for a high-powered career in publishing or the arts. So last summer when cocktail chatter turned to the inevitable "What do you do?" question, Cashion was prepared for the shocked reaction. She told her companions that in the fall she would begin teaching at Brooklyn's Edward R. Murrow High School. Reports Cashion: "They looked at me as if I had just flown in from Mars."

Americans want their children to *have* good teachers, it seems, but they are not sure they want them to *become* teachers. And perhaps with good reason. Since 1983, when the federally sponsored report *A Nation at Risk: The Imperative for Educational Reform* warned of a "rising tide of mediocrity" in U.S. schools, the country's 2.3 million public school teachers have come in for stinging criticism—some of it no doubt justified.

After all, how else to explain the fact that an estimated 13% of 17-year-olds and perhaps 40% of minority youth are considered functionally illiterate? That less than one-third know when the Civil War occurred? That in a recent ABC-TV-sponsored survey of 200 teenagers, less than half could identify Daniel Ortega (President of Nicaragua) and two-thirds were ignorant of Chernobyl (one guessed it was Cher's real name). Five years after *A Nation at Risk* prompted a flurry of reform, average scores on the Scholastic Aptitude Test (SAT) have risen 11 points. Still, as recently as last spring, former Secretary of Education William Bennett gave U.S. schools an overall grade of no better than a C or a C-plus. To the teaching establishment, and teachers' unions in particular, he issued a sharp rebuke: "You're standing in the doorways. You're blocking up the halls of education reform."

Teachers, of course, are unhappy about the assessment, though it was nothing new. "Over the years, you're constantly bashed," says Kathy Daniels, a Chicago English teacher. "You get it from the principal; you get it from the press. Bennett just topped it all." What particularly rankles is that while accusations are flying, policies debated and remedies proposed, no one has consulted the real experts: those who do daily battle to improve the minds of students. Says Ernest Boyer, president of the Carnegie Foundation for the Advancement of Teaching: "Whatever is wrong with America's public schools cannot be fixed without the help of those inside the classroom."

In their own defense, teachers point out that their job has changed dramatically over the past 25 years. Increasingly, they are asked not only to provide a good education but also to address ever more complex and diverse social problems. Drugs, sex, violence, broken homes, poverty: today's classroom is a mirror of the crises that afflict the U.S. as a whole. Even the children of two-earner, middle-class couples can suffer from lack of attention, if only because neither Mom nor Dad has the time or energy to help with homework or attend PTA meetings.

Add to that the burgeoning population of students from non-English-speaking households, and the teacher's primary task—to convey knowledge—can become nearly impossible. "Society has taken the position that teachers ought to succeed with everybody: the economically disadvantaged, racial minorities, the handicapped," says P. Michael Timpane, president of Teachers College at Columbia University. "No one took those issues seriously a generation ago."

While responsibilities and demands have multiplied, teachers have seen little increase in the financial or moral support they need to do the job. Overcrowded classes, inadequate or outdated equipment and long hours are common. At the same time, in a panicked effort to improve their schools, many states and localities have added new and often burdensome course requirements, typically without input from teachers. "Traditionally, teachers have been treated like very tall children," observes Mary Futrell, president of the National Education Association (NEA), which represents 1.6 million schoolteachers. "We are not perfect," concedes Baltimore elementary school teacher Kathlynn Jacobs. "But people need to walk in our shoes before they criticize."

"It sounds a little bit like English but there are too many 'hochs,' " notes a junior at Chicago's Farragut Career Academy High School.

The subject is the epic poem Beowulf, *which English teacher Daniels has tried to bring to life with a recording in Old English. But the school's tape recorder has an ill-fitting plug, and Daniels cannot get it to start. After several attempts, she asks a visitor to hold the plug in the*

Source: From Susan Tifft, "Who's Teaching Our Children?," *Time Magazine*, November 14, 1988, pp. 58–63. Copyright 1988 Time Inc. Reprinted by permission.

socket. "This is one of the worst things about teaching in the city," she says. "Nothing ever works."

When the guttural words begin to emerge, Daniels, 50, passes around a paper with lines from the poem on one side and the modern English translation on the other. Since there is just one sheet, only a few students see it before the recording ends. An overhead projector would have helped, but the one assigned to the English department is as unreliable as the tape recorder.

Each day teachers cope with working environments that would never be tolerated by lawyers, doctors and other professionals. Copiers, ditto machines, lab glassware and even books, the basic tools of the trade, are battered or nonexistent in many school systems. Teachers are frequently left to fill the gap from their own pockets. Some pay for photocopies; others pick up the tab for educational extras. Every month, for example, Patrice Bertha, a sixth-grade teacher on Chicago's seedy West Side, piles her charges onto a city bus, often paying the fare and admission fee so they can visit a museum or see a play. Many of the children, who are black, would never visit downtown Chicago otherwise. "Their whole world is where they live," she says.

The lack of essentials is symptomatic of a larger problem: inequities in school financing. In most states, schools are supported by a combination of property taxes and state and federal grants. The formula ensures gleaming beakers and well-stocked libraries for schools in wealthier states and neighborhoods but leaves many rural and inner-city schools with peeling paint and leaky pipes. Connecticut, for example, with its tony suburbs, spent an average of $5,900 on each public school student in the state last year; Alabama spent just $2,600.

The physical signs of underfunding are not limited to the inner cities. The roof of one building on the grounds of Tunica Junior High School in Tunica, Miss., collapsed years ago, but the school district—abandoned by whites in the wake of integration—does not have money for repairs. Inside, the wooden desks and textbooks remain, split and rotting: Outside, there is no playground equipment. "The world sends messages to our kids about the importance it places on education," says Robin Gostin, a tenth-grade math teacher in Los Angeles. "Go to shopping malls and see how nice they are. Then look at the desks in our classrooms, and you see nails coming through the bottom of the seats."

Most weekdays, Juan Rodriguez, 46, *roars up to Hartford's Thomas J. Quirk Middle School in his red pickup truck at 7 a.m. and leaves by 3 p.m. In between, he teaches five science classes, grades papers, prepares lesson plans, has two rounds of hall duty, grabs a sandwich at his desk and calls parents to discuss discipline problems or schoolwork. The daytime schedule—which is often followed by two hours of work at home—sounds hectic, and it is. When the last-period bell rang on a recent afternoon, Rodriguez had not yet had an opportunity to go to the bathroom.*

Coffee breaks. A lunch hour. A moment to chat with colleagues. Most workers take these things for granted. But teachers cannot operate that way. Their workweek easily stretches up to 60 hours, including back-to-back classes, lunchroom duty, daily lesson planning, coaching, club sponsorship and conferences.

The frantic pace can take a toll. For 17 years Sue Capie and her husband Ken, of Cupertino, Calif., had a two-teacher marriage. Then in 1981 she fled to a job as a recruiter for Hewlett-Packard. "I had been onstage a long time," she says. "Now I can sit at my desk sometimes and say to myself, 'O.K., you don't have to think about anything for a few minutes.' I have a lot more freedom."

Perched on a stool *at the front of the room, Rochester teacher Michael Pugliese, 30, looks down on a clamorous gaggle of third-graders sitting cross-legged on the floor. After quieting them, he begins reading* Joey, *a book about a Puerto Rican boy whose family moves to New York City. The book's hero has just found needles on the street. Pugliese asks his listeners if they know what kinds of needles the story means. Many of the children do. One boy says he saw two drug addicts in front of his apartment building just the day before. "You all know about* AIDS," *Pugliese says. They nod in agreement. "Well, that's one way you can get* AIDS. *So if you see a needle on the street, don't even pick it up."*

Pugliese is not shocked at the students' familiarity with drugs. In fact, their experiences seem innocent compared with those of the emotionally troubled kids he used to teach in special-education classes. One boy was left alone for days at a time while his mother disappeared into crack houses. A ten-year-old girl had been sexually abused by both her natural and foster parents.

The prim, bespectacled schoolmarm, standing at the head of a well-scrubbed, disciplined class, is a stereotype from a bygone era. Today most high school students have had more experience with alcohol, drugs and sex than she ever could have imagined. Pregnant girls are seen in school corridors; others deposit their babies in school day-care centers. Violence is a regular visitor to the schoolyard. Last year in New York City there were more than 300 instances in which students punched, stabbed or otherwise assaulted public school teachers. Against such corrosive influences, it is increasingly teachers—not parents—who are called upon to function as society's first line of defense. Says Carolee Bogue, dean of students at Fairfax High School in Los Angeles: "Most kids today look to the teachers for the support that they don't get at home."

In urban schools the outcroppings of neglect and despair abound. When Chicago's Kathy Daniels asked her students to write an essay about something that made them angry, one boy described the time his brother was gunned down and died on the front steps of his house. Soon afterward, the boy himself was fatally shot. In poor rural areas, the deprivation can be even more elemental. "I've got kids that have never held a pencil before," says a Mississippi kindergarten teacher. "And last year I had one that had never held silverware." Trying to convey the majesty of Shakespeare or even basic addition and subtraction to such children can be a near impossibility.

Nor is lack of parental involvement limited to inner-city tenements or rural tar-paper shacks.

Kathlynn Jacobs, a 24-year veteran of the Baltimore public schools, vividly remembers one gangly, precocious first-grader, who had been in day care since she was a baby. Both her parents worked, and her life had been rigidly scheduled to accommodate them. "She was the smartest one in the class," says Jacobs, "and she was having a hard day." Jacobs asked her what was wrong. "I'm tired of school," replied the world-weary seven-year-old. "I've been to school all my life."

Home and family life—even in middle-class suburbia—is not what it used to be. With divorce commonplace, youngsters frequently careen back and forth between parents like shuttlecocks. "We used to send one report card home with each student and deal with one set of parents," recalls Kay Grady, a counselor at Hillview Elementary School in affluent Menlo Park, Calif. "Now we send two to two households and sometimes arrange for separate conferences." That is, if the parents have time. Single parents and two-earner couples are often just too fatigued at the end of the day to show much interest in open-house night or Johnny's science project. Students often reflect their parents' indifference. Says Hillview science teacher Ken Capie: "It's like they're always asking themselves, 'Why am I here?' They don't see the need to learn."

"Expectorate—to spit." *Barry Smolin points to one of 20 vocabulary words he has written on the blackboard. The class titters.*

"I had a student last year who used to call his spit 'luggies,'" he tells his tenth-graders. "He could lean out my classroom window and gather enough spit to reach down to the ground and then suck it up again."

"Gross, Mr. Smolin!"

He perseveres, pointing to another word. "Ubiquitous. Sometimes when you are walking around downtown L.A., the police are ubiquitous." Polite laughter. "Resonant. Many opera singers have a resonant quality to their voice." He breaks into a baritone, singing scales with a mock gravity.

Smolin, 27, graduated from Fairfax High himself in 1978. But his classroom reflects a taste for the cultural artifacts of earlier eras. Jimi Hendrix posters keep company with theater reviews from West Side Story. *His unusual methods—using song lyrics to teach literary themes, for instance—are popular with students. But he fears he may soon wilt under the pressure to entertain. "My first year I used to come home hoarse," he says. "I can't keep up five shows a day and not get burned out."*

Burnout. It can happen as easily at the blackboard as in the boardroom. "There are days when I go home with a migraine," says Chicago's Bertha. "It's a stressful job." Especially for those who work with learning-disabled or troubled children. Last spring, after three years of teaching special ed, Michael Pugliese asked to be reassigned to a regular classroom. "When you give your all, and there's no hope—that's too much," he says.

Many teachers do not bother to request transfers; they just quit. Fully half of all new teachers leave the profession within five years. The trend is more pronounced among minorities, who frequently work in schools with the most complex social and academic problems. Given attractive options in private industry, blacks—as well as women—no longer feel forced to endure jobs they consider unsatisfying. "The old days were different," says Chester Finn, former Assistant Secretary of Education. "A lot of our finest teachers were women and minorities who had no other place to earn a living."

Earnings, or the lack thereof, have much to do with the exodus. During the 1970s, while salaries in other fields soared, teachers' pay fell 15% in real dollars. In some states starting salaries remain as low as $13,000. In Mississippi social-studies teacher Jewelie Brown makes only $22,200 after 31 years in the classroom. Californian Ken Capie does better: $41,000 after 30 years, but that is still $3,000 less than his 25-year-old son's starting salary as an engineer.

Belatedly, many districts are rushing to fatten teachers' paychecks. Since 1980 the average teacher's salary has risen 61.7%, from $17,364 to $28,085. The improvement does not dazzle many teachers, who say the increase has yet to make up the losses of the past. But some districts are finding that better pay is a magnet for fresh teaching talent. Since last summer, when it approved a three-year contract providing for salaries of up to $64,000, Dade County, Fla., has received nine applications for every teaching vacancy. "We really have the pick of the crop," exults assistant superintendent Gerald Dreyfuss.

In addition to raising pay, some districts are experimenting with career ladders that allow teachers the opportunity to move up in status without having to abandon the classroom for administrative posts. Others have created "mentor" programs, which help novice teachers by pairing them with talented and experienced ones. Some wealthier schools provide workout centers and time off for stressed-out teachers. New Trier Township High School in suburban Chicago has a wellness program that allows faculty members to exercise on school time, receive personal and career counseling and even reduce their teaching loads without penalty. But such tender loving care is rare. "I don't think burnout is caused by the children," says Tracy Bridgers, a math teacher at Alexander Graham Junior High in Charlotte, N.C. "Usually it is the administration. No one strokes you enough."

At 9:30 a.m. Lillie Rayborn, 43, is already damp with sweat, trying to keep up with her rambunctious first-graders at Tunica's Rosa Fort Elementary School. "All right," she says firmly. "Yesterday we learned the letter l. *Today we will learn the letter* d." *She hands out construction paper "bones." If the word on the "bone" begins with* d, *the child gets to "feed the dog"—a large construction-paper hound with a hole for a mouth. The kids love it.*

Off to one side are about ten "Chapter 1" children—kids who need special attention. Because the district usually requires that everyone complete first grade before being evaluated as learning disabled, kids who have serious problems often limp through the first two years of school behind their more advanced peers.

Eric, for example, has learned to draw a capital E, but cannot write his own name. He is far from the worst case that Rayborn has seen. Once, a child with Down syndrome was enrolled in her class. He was still in diapers and required frequent changing. "I had to run out and buy Pampers," she recalls. "He had never been disciplined. He acted like an animal in the zoo."

If education officials had consulted Lillie Rayborn, a policy requiring learning-disabled children to share classrooms with other kids might never have been written. But decisions affecting schools are still mostly top-down. In Chicago administrators make it clear that students should be held back only once and then promoted to the next grade, regardless of performance. Other kids languish in unsupervised classrooms because the school board underestimates the number of teachers a school needs and will not provide substitutes in the interim. "You can lose total track of the students by the time a board-authorized sub shows up," says English teacher Daniels.

Asked to cope with the consequences of these bureaucratic snafus, teachers feel impotent and bitter. The flurry of educational reforms of the past five years has also been largely imposed from on high. Take, for example, the effort to upgrade the quality and qualifications of teachers. Concerned about an alleged epidemic of incompetency, legislatures in 46 states have enacted tougher training requirements for teachers, including minimum college grade-point averages. While many teachers applaud these changes and hope they will attract higher-caliber people, veteran educators generally give low marks to standardized competency tests such as the National Teachers Examination, now required in 30 states. No multiple-choice exam, they say, can predict success in the classroom.

Last month, in response to such complaints, the Educational Testing Service unveiled plans for a far more sophisticated exam. The new test, which will be in use by 1992, will include two exams—one given during sophomore year in college and a second after teacher training—plus an evaluation of performance in the classroom. Says National Education Association spokeswoman Jane Usdan: "This is a step in the right direction."

Another way of upgrading the quality of teachers, say many veterans, is through a strict peer-review process, in which teachers themselves would help screen and rehabilitate incompetents. "A teacher who is incompetent should have a conference with the principal; then she should get help from a support teacher," says Baltimore's Jacobs. "But if she's still incompetent, then I'm sorry—she has to go." Some take unions to task for protecting poor performers. Says science teacher Rodriguez: "They should not be so closed-minded when it comes to retraining and testing."

In some parts of the country, teachers are being given more say in setting school policies. In Dade County, which includes Miami, 45 of the system's 260 schools are experimenting with "school-based management," which allows teachers and administrators to tackle problems free of the usual bureaucratic constraints. Schools can request waivers from union contracts and from local and state regulations. The result: a palpable boost in morale. At one school, teacher absenteeism is down 50%, saving $7,000 a year in substitute-teacher costs.

It is midmorning when Juan Rodriguez begins to talk about the Egyptian astronomer Ptolemy. The ancients had no idea what the earth looked like, he tells his 24 seventh-graders. The kids cannot believe anyone could be so dumb. "Oh, my God," says one, rolling her eyes.

But one boy is intrigued. "Are we positive that 1,000 years from now, people won't look back and say that we got it all wrong?" he asks. Rodriguez is delighted. "That's a beautiful question," he says. "I love it when my students ask that." Then he leads the class into a discussion of how scientific theories can and must evolve.

The moment the light bulb goes on—that, say teachers, is what they live for. That is why they are teachers and not plumbers or investment bankers. The look in a young person's eye: *I got it! I understand!* In the average school year there may be only a handful of such moments, but to a teacher they are unforgettable.

The ultimate satisfaction comes from the occasional student who, given the right nurturing, suddenly blossoms. Barry Smolin twinkles at the very thought of his "victory student." The Fairfax junior had a mother who was a junkie, a sister who was a prostitute and a father who had long ago abandoned the family. "I gave her a writing assignment, and she was brilliant," says Smolin. "She still had trouble, but she got into college and now she wants to be a writer." What keeps many teachers going is the conviction that somewhere out there, there are more victory students waiting to be discovered.

And there are the small rewards...

***Carol Bowen, 46,** ducks into the teachers' lounge at Harrison Elementary School in Cedar Rapids, Iowa, at 8:40 a.m. for a quick gulp of coffee. Then she heads back to Room 208 to wait for her third-grade students, who have formed two lines outside the red brick building. This particular morning the girls' line enters first. As they file past, one child, Heidi, stops and shyly hands Bowen a slender envelope. Inside is a bookmark. Its inscription: "To my teacher: thank you for taking the time to share what you have learned."*

Despite their frustrations, many teachers are still content with their choice of career. "I love my job," says Rochester's Pugliese. "In the classroom I can have an impact." A Carnegie Foundation survey of 22,000 teachers found that 77% are satisfied with their jobs. "You can make $2 million a year working at some corporation," says Hillview teacher Sue Krumbein. "But who really cares? When you teach, a lot of people care."

Of course, not everyone can have the impact of math teacher Jaime Escalante, the inspiring subject of the movie *Stand and Deliver*. But in small towns and sprawling cities there surely are people like him, each a miracle worker in his or her own way. Teachers say the best of them are born, not made. Perhaps they are right. Several years ago, Patrice Bertha took a sabbatical to see whether she really wanted to spend the rest of her life in the classroom. She wound up tutoring at home instead. "I really missed it," she says. "That's when I told myself, 'You're a teacher forever.' "

3

Commitment of "Public" Vital for Education

Mary V. Bicouvaris

Free public education was established in the United States to aid the development of citizens who are literate, knowledgeable, and equipped with the skills necessary for participation in a democratic society.

In striving toward this goal, American schools and colleges have become the envy of the world. We have made education attainable for all, at any age, from any walk of life.

But something is wrong. Many Americans are not pleased with public education. In addressing their concerns, we must rediscover the meaning of the word "public" in public education: Reforming education requires the commitment of students, parents, and communities as well as teachers.

The list of complaints is long.

Some critics correctly point out, for example, that our students do not test as well in subjects like mathematics, science, and geography as their counterparts in other parts of the world. But the test takers in other countries are often hand-picked, over-tutored, and school-phobic. We don't test in the United States in order to exclude; America wouldn't be America if we did.

If schools intensified their efforts at test preparation, would American parents be willing to send children to be tutored for two to three hours a day, for four to five years, at private expense? When their children returned from such lessons, would parents be willing to supervise several hours of homework every night? That is what most Japanese and many European parents do. Do we want to imitate the Japanese and Europeans or reclaim our own system?

And are American students willing to assume this kind of academic load? Would they give up their minimum-wage jobs—the silent killer of high-quality education?

The truth is that our children are spending more time working, playing, listening to music, and aimlessly wandering the shopping malls than studying, reading, thinking, or pursuing cultural interests. I am afraid we can't blame the public schools for that.

Another common complaint focuses on the fact that some young people never learn to read. This is indeed one of the saddest phenomena in a civilized society. But since our schools teach most students to read, let us be fair about attributing blame for those who don't learn.

Experts say that experiences in the first five years of life have a profound effect on a child's ability to learn. The mind is like a computer: It produces only what it has been programmed to produce. A nonverbal, abusive environment does not help a child store information needed to decode language. But reading is a simple task for a youngster who grows up with verbal stimulation.

A certain percentage of our students drop out of school, the critics point out. Some of these young people have plans, work hard, become worthy citizens, and, in some instances, return to education. There is no need to worry about them.

The others—those we term "at risk"—the country cannot afford to neglect. By "at risk" children, I do not mean only poor, minority, urban youngsters. Another category includes a growing number of middle-class students—average and promising but falling fast in achievement because they choose work before education, pursuing short-term material goals instead of building a strong foundation for academic or vocational competence. If we allow this trend to continue, our educational system is destined to remain mediocre. In Japan and Europe, student labor is unheard of.

Some say that the young lack basic values. While the charge is true for a few, the majority of our young people are solid citizens—sensitive, giving, believing, and ready to defend their country. We should make our judgments on the basis not of the small number who break the rules but of the millions who obey them. And let us remember that values are instilled at home by parents, the first and most important of teachers.

Critics cite drug problems in the schools. In fact, there is a drug problem in American society, and the schools reflect that society. They are trying to keep drugs off their campuses—but how could the schools fare any better with drugs when all the might of the United States, the defender of the free world, cannot stop drugs from penetrating the nation's streets and choking its capital city?

As has been frequently noted, the number of teenage pregnancies is increasing. The statistics are alarming, and they guarantee the continuation of an underclass—and of misery for many—for years to come. But the schools cannot take the blame for this development. Governing bodies must stop short of expecting that jack-of-all-trades, the public-school teacher, to fix this problem.

Education about reproduction certainly has a place in our schools, but it should be conducted by medical professionals and no one else. As for the values of moral decency, respect for life, appreciation for the awesome responsibilities of parenthood—these must be inculcated at home.

Source: From Mary V. Bicouvaris, "Commitment of 'Public' Vital for Education," ***Education Week***, Volume IX, Number 6, October 11, 1989, p. 28. Reprinted with permission from ***Education Week***. Volume IX, Number 6, October 11, 1989. Reprinted with permission from Mary V. Bicouvaris.

And to the contention of some critics that the nation's teachers are not good enough, I would answer that they are the best educated, most dedicated, hardest working, and least honored in the world.

Are our teachers competent? Are they worthy of their charge? I say that they are—in similar percentages as American doctors, lawyers, pharmacists, and other professionals.

We must remember, too, that when a teacher fails, the responsibility must be shared by the teacher, the institution from which he was graduated, the school board that hired him, and the school system that retained him without providing support for success or a passport out of the profession. Likewise, when a student fails to learn, the responsibility must be accepted by the student, the teacher, and the parents.

As a society, we tend to forget that "public" education means education open to all, concerning all, funded by all. It does not mean that recipients are free of responsibility, or that parents can relinquish their duties, or that students will learn and excel simply by showing up at the door of the schoolhouse.

The education of the young requires good teachers, willing students, supportive parents, committed governing bodies, and a citizenry that understands that education in a democracy is society's backbone, the great equalizer, the guarantor of freedom.

And no restructuring of American education will succeed until teachers are set free to teach—free from clerical duties, from issuing forms, from collecting money, from all the bureaucratic slavery that threatens to consume their time and spirit.

Empowered, well prepared, constantly learning teachers who are paid and treated as professionals, and receptive, ambitious students with supportive and informed families are the vital elements for excellence in education.

4

Back to the Classroom

Melinda Beck

Fifteen years ago medicine was the hot field for America's young people. Five years ago it was investment banking. What's attracting attention this year? Ask Oscar Trono, who gave up a $70,000-a-year salary as a chemical engineer to teach eighth-grade science and ninth-grade math in Denver. Or Michelle Cummings, a recent Brown graduate who can't wait to help repair the public schools in her native Louisiana. "The business world is slowing down, and the teaching field is opening up," says Jeff Nadherny, who has enrolled in Harvard's Graduate School of Education after eight years in commercial real estate. "Schools need revamping. It's an exciting time now for teaching."

Teaching? Battered, bad-mouthed and avoided by savvy job seekers for years, the profession is making a comeback. Some school districts report record numbers of candidates for vacant posts; some states have been inundated with requests for teaching certificates. Applications are up—as much as 50 percent—at schools of education. And after a 20-year decline, more college freshmen—particularly women—are once again planning teaching careers, according to the annual survey by UCLA's Higher Education Research Institute. "In 1982 it was down to 1 in 20," says associate director Kenneth C. Green. "Now, 1 in 12 students are interested in teaching."

More important still, the quality of prospective teachers keeps getting better, helping to erase a stigma that has dogged the profession for years. Diane Ravitch of Columbia University's Teachers College vividly recalls giving a speech almost five years ago at Brown, when a student stood up to lament that she had been told she was "too smart to become a teacher." "That kind of gross bias is changing," says Ravitch. "It's very, very encouraging." The typical education student, by one report, now earns a B average during the first two years of college, up from a C-plus five years ago. Well over half the students at Harvard's graduate education school earned honors in their undergraduate years. John P. Ameer, assistant director of Harvard's teacher-training programs, says students "see the stock-market crash, banks closing down and they say to themselves, 'Why not do what I really want to do—teach'."

In many cities, about half the new teachers hired this year are older professionals, switching to teaching from other fields. Programs to help them make the transition are proliferating. George Washington University, for example, is retraining retired military personnel to work as teachers; another GW program qualifies NASA scientists to teach science and math in local high schools. These older career switchers "have a continuing desire to serve—and they see a need," says associate dean Jay Shotel. "I saw the need for strong science teachers in my own children's schools," says 43-year-old Margaret Coppe, who abandoned a career as a research-lab assistant to teach science at Wakefield (Mass.) high school. "When you work for a corporation, you get financial rewards, but you never see the results of all your hard work," says Oscar Trono. "With teaching, you see the results every day and the rewards are immediate."

For all the good news, education insiders are quick to insist that the crisis is not over for the teaching profession. The nationwide shortfall of teachers feared just a few years ago never materialized, some say, because standards simply slipped. Spot shortages still persist in math, science and bilingual education, in inner-city schools and in rural areas. Experts are particularly concerned that the number of minority teachers has fallen from 14 percent to only 7 percent in the last decade. What's more, many working teachers say their morale has fallen since the education-reform movement began five years ago—particularly because politicians often blamed them for the shortcomings of the schools. But that, too, is slowly changing. Says Ernest Boyer, president of the Carnegie Foundation for the Advancement of Teaching: "It's becoming increasingly clear that teachers are part of the solution, not the problem."

Salary boost: The most concrete measure of the new respect is salaries. Average teacher pay—now more than $29,000—has risen twice as fast as inflation in recent years. While compensation still lags behind other careers that require comparable education, "clearly, salaries are no longer a blatant disincentive," says Linda Darling-Hammond of the Rand Corp. According to a recent Rand report, at least 13 states have established across-the-board salary increases for teachers since 1983; 19 states have set up state-wide pay schedules rewarding teachers for advanced degrees and years of experience. Some individual districts have gone further. In Rochester, N.Y., top teachers with 10 years' experience and additional duties such as serving as a mentor to younger teachers now earn as much as $53,900; next year those who qualify could draw nearly $70,000. "People in our recruiting office see long lines of people interested in teaching in our district," says spokesperson Karen Strong.

Even more than salaries, Strong says, the applicants are drawn by new responsibilities that Rochester is giving teachers—including the mentor program and the chance to help develop curricula. A pioneering "school-based management" program in Miami-

Source: From Melinda Beck, "Back to the Classroom," *Newsweek,* October 17, 1988, pp. 74–75. From *Newsweek,* October 17, 1988.

Dade County's 260 schools has also put some budget, salary and personnel decisions in the hands of local councils, composed largely of teachers. "It's a recognition that our voices and input are important," says junior-high school teacher Ann Colman. Her teacher-dominated council must approve all expenditures of more than $1,000 and is currently interviewing candidates for assistant principals. "It's almost like a rebirth," says school superintendent Joe Fernandez, who reports receiving nine applications for every vacancy.

Still, model programs like those in Rochester and Miami are more the exception than the rule. In a recent Carnegie Foundation survey of 22,000 teachers, fewer than half said they helped set standards for student behavior or promotion. Only one in five said they helped determine school budgets and only 10 percent said they helped evaluate teacher performance or select new school personnel. Overall, Boyer says many teachers feel they have merely been "front-row spectators" in the reform efforts. "Others have found that the reform movement has brought a new set of policies that have worsened working conditions, increased their level of paperwork and imposed new constraints," adds Darling-Hammond of Rand.

Back door: The rules for becoming a teacher are also changing—sometimes in contradictory ways. Concerned about faculty quality, many states have toughened standards. According to a Rand survey, 48 states now require applicants for certificates to pass a basic skills test; 18 assess in-class performance before granting full certification, and some have discontinued lifetime certificates, forcing teachers to be periodically reassessed. At the same time, 23 states have established alternative routes to certification, bypassing traditional teacher-training schools. In New Jersey, for example, liberal-arts graduates can qualify as teachers with on-the-job training and as little as 80 hours of course work. Such programs have clearly helped attract older professionals to the field. But some traditional educators see alternative certification as a "back door" that could weaken standards. "We're taking in raw recruits without giving them sufficient training," says Robert H. Koff, dean of the education school at the State University of New York at Albany.

Programs like George Washington's aim to fill that need. And the reform movement has changed the curricula of even standard teacher's colleges; now they emphasize mastery of specific subjects, rather than educational theory. In truth, both trends in teacher education are welcome and necessary. Children of the baby-boom generation are once again swelling classroom enrollments. A large percentage of teachers currently working are set to retire soon. As a result, the nation will need an estimated 1.5 million new teachers by the year 2000, far more than traditional education schools can fill. Experts warn that unless salaries rise still further, and teachers are afforded far more autonomy and respect, quality could slip again—erasing the gains of the past few years. American Federation of Teachers president Albert Shanker agrees: "We've got to make teaching as attractive and prestigious as becoming a lawyer." The teaching profession clearly deserves a grade of "improved"—but it has a long way to go to achieve Shanker's goal.

5

Education

Getting What You Pay For

Jack E. White

An appalling number of America's schools are atrocious.

Study after depressing study confirms what has been painfully obvious to millions of parents, teachers, prospective employers and students. Every year our schools turn out more than a million young adults who cannot keep up with the intellectual demands of an increasingly technological economy or with their counterparts in Western Europe and Japan. In addition to the 700,000 who, despite twelve years of what passes for formal education, have such poor reading skills that they cannot digest a newspaper or fill out a job application, an identical number drop out, forfeiting whatever educational benefits might be osmotically obtained from simply showing up for class.

Far too many inner-city schools are less centers of learning than custodial institutions complete with wardens (principals) and guards (teachers) striving to control a mob of prisoners (students), some so preoccupied with the three Cs—crack, crime and casual sex—that they have no time for the three Rs. But the educational blight is not confined to underclass ghettos and barrios. Despite efforts to upgrade the math skills of U.S. students, a recent survey indicates that nearly half of American 17-year-olds cannot perform simple calculations that are normally learned in junior high school. Other surveys have documented equally dreary student performance in reading, writing and critical thinking. So ill equipped is the current crop of high school graduates that U.S. corporations spend $25 billion a year for remedial training programs for new employees on whom state, local and federal agencies have already lavished $130 billion in an attempt to teach them to read, write and cipher.

As the Department of Education warned in 1983, a foreign power scheming to weaken America could not have concocted a more insidious plot than the debasement of public education. The threat to U.S. security ranges from the fact that nearly a quarter of military recruits cannot understand written safety instructions to the growing shortage of students in science and engineering. At the dawn of a new era of international competition, less than one-quarter of public high school students are currently enrolled in a foreign-language course. The bulk of American students cannot locate the world's most important nations on a map if their lives depend on it, which, in a sense, they do.

Each new revelation of the flunking performance of many U.S. students provokes a loud outcry for tougher standards, better instruction, classroom innovations. So far, all the noise has had shockingly limited impact on what actually goes on in the schools. Most high schools still do not require students to meet widely accepted standards for math and science. On the average, a student takes only 2.3 credits in math and 2 in science to graduate, instead of the 3 credits in each subject recommended by the National Commission on Excellence in Education.

Seldom has there been such a clear-cut case for presidential leadership. But judging by their performances on the campaign trail thus far, Michael Dukakis and George Bush deserve no more than a marginal grade for their proposals for rescuing America's schools. Like Hare Krishnas entrancing themselves by chanting a euphonious phrase, both candidates repeat the frugal mantra of the Gramm-Rudman age: no new taxes, no new social programs, no bold initiatives from the Federal Government. So fearful are they of angering taxpayers that their timid proposals appear more concerned with holding down federal spending than with mounting the comprehensive policies that a solution to the educational crisis demands.

Both Bush and Dukakis have avoided the reality that a huge new investment by the Federal Government is needed to rebuild America's schools because the sums required are beyond the reach of local governments that depend on property taxes or the private sector. There is remarkably little dispute about what is necessary: better textbooks, better facilities and above all restoration of the prestige of teachers by paying them more and improving their working conditions. What remains at issue is how to pay for these worthy objectives and which other goals might have to be sacrificed to raise the required funds.

After loudly declaiming his desire to be known as the "education President," Bush seems to have forgotten the subject. On those occasions when he has proffered specifics, Bush has put forth sound, if not exciting, ideas. He would establish a $500 million program to provide awards of $100,000 to individual schools that show a marked reduction in dropout rates or improvement in test scores. An additional $50 million would be given to states for matching grants to create or support magnet schools, which offer special programs not generally available in other schools. A third program would grant $1 million to each state to experiment

Source: From Jack E. White, "Education: Getting What You Pay For," *Time Magazine*, September 12, 1988, pp. 31–32.

with raising teacher pay, creating a year-round curriculum or allowing parents to enroll their child in any school within the system.

But the Vice President's plans run headlong into a contradiction: although he supports efforts to raise standards for teachers and students nationally, he insists the funds to support such efforts come almost exclusively from state and local governments. He would raise federal expenditures for education less than $1 billion a year—a third of what the Reagan Administration proposes to spend on Star Wars. That is tantamount to fighting a war with local police forces while the U.S. Army sits on the sidelines.

Dukakis has proclaimed his intention to become the "No. 1 advocate for good schools and good teaching." He would create a $250 million national teaching excellence fund to finance the college tuitions of students who become teachers and revive the national teacher corps to give recent college graduates a taste of the classroom. He would establish "field centers" of teaching and learning for veteran teachers, ask businesses to encourage their employees to accept temporary assignments as teachers, and establish levels of teacher competence similar to those that govern doctors and lawyers.

Dukakis has not put a price tag on his educational proposals or stated in detail how he would pay for them. Some of his ideas, moreover, simply do not stand up. Few businesses are likely to permit capable workers to leave their jobs in mid-career for three- to five-year teaching sabbaticals. Dukakis' plan to expand the so-called Boston Compacts and Genesis Programs—in which wealthy individuals and businesses seek to motivate high schoolers by promising a job or college scholarship to each graduate—is doomed to failure in areas lacking either a surplus of good jobs or a willing philanthropist. His notion of asking investment bankers and college administrators to devise investment programs that will allow families to set aside funds today against the cost of their children's college educations will do little or nothing for the poorest Americans.

The rhetoric notwithstanding, neither Bush nor Dukakis has made the conceptual breakthrough that would permit the U.S. to fashion the school system it deserves. While looking through different lenses, both seem to view federal education spending as a frilly, bloated social program rather than as a vital national-security program at least equal in priority to maintaining strong armed forces. During the Reagan years, despite growing concern about huge deficits, the largest peacetime military buildup in the nation's history boosted spending for defense 37% in inflation-adjusted dollars to annual levels of nearly $300 billion. Federal outlays for elementary and secondary education were reduced nearly 20% during the same period. Given that history, perhaps the next President ought to consider assigning the task of shepherding through his education-spending plan to the Secretary of Defense, who has had far more luck in sparing his requests from the budgeteer's ax. There is ample precedent for treating education as a national-defense issue. In the panic that followed the Soviet Union's launch of Sputnik in 1957, Congress passed the National Defense Education Act, which vastly expanded federal support for science, math and foreign-language instruction in public schools.

The U.S. Government's role in education policy, unlike that of its foreign competitors, is strictly curtailed by the Constitution. That encourages innovation at the state and local level, which, in such states as New Jersey and South Carolina, has yielded impressive gains in educational performance. Nevertheless, there are many ways in which the Federal Government can assist financially pressed school systems without unduly intruding into such thorny issues as the exact courses in a curriculum. The objective of federal policy should be to relieve school systems of burdens they cannot manage well while depriving them of excuses for failing to accomplish their stated purpose—the effective education of young people. A number of realistic proposals that go far beyond anything Bush and Dukakis have put forth have been on the table. Among them:

Underwrite the cost of physically maintaining schools. No student can be expected to thrive in a dingy, dilapidated classroom. Yet many school districts, especially the 600 largest, which enroll 40% of all public-school students, lack the ability to raise sufficient taxes or sell enough bonds to keep their schools up to standard. The Federal Government should make no-interest loans available to tear down or rebuild old buildings and replace them with smaller, more attractive units. School systems would not be permitted to pocket the savings but, in exchange for the aid, would be required to shift their current expenditures for maintenance into areas directly related to education—higher teacher salaries and reduced class sizes. It would cost $4.5 billion to renovate every school in New York City.

Expand Head Start and Chapter 1 programs. For the past two decades, the Federal Government has supported Head Start programs, which provide educational and medical services for disadvantaged preschoolers, and Chapter 1, which offers remedial help for those in higher grades. Both have repeatedly been shown to be beneficial and cost-effective. An annual $500 investment in Head Start, for example, makes it less likely that a child will repeat a grade—at an average cost to the community of $3,000. Currently, only one out of five eligible children is enrolled in Head Start, and Chapter 1 programs reach only half of those who qualify. The cost of making them available to every child who needs them: $11 billion annually.

Write off college loans for graduates who go into teaching. No program for reviving public education can succeed until better-qualified students are willing to become teachers. One way to accomplish this would be to forgive the college indebtedness of top students who spend three to five years in the public schools. Academic underachievers need not apply. To qualify, students should be in the upper third of their graduating classes and major in subjects that are most in need of able teachers: math, sciences, computer technology and foreign languages. Annual cost: $500 million.

Obviously, enacting any or all of these approaches would be costly and entail hard choices. But making such decisions is a President's job. For the $3.6 billion cost of one nuclear aircraft-carrier task force, of which the U.S. already has five, the country could pay the full four-year tuitions of 90,000 private-college students. By foregoing one year's cost of living increase in Social Security benefits, the U.S. could raise the average salary of the nation's 2.3 million public schoolteachers by $3,260. The question the next President must decide is which of these expenditures will make the U.S. stronger and do more to ensure its future economic vitality. In answering it, he should keep in mind one bit of folk wisdom: you get what you pay for.

6

A Closer Look at the Shortage of Minority Teachers

Education Commission of the States

In 1980, minorities made up 12% of the nation's teaching force. Estimates are that this will drop to 5% by the year 2000. At the same time, minorities are expected to make up about 33% of the school-age population. This shortage of minority teachers has profound implications, not only for minority students but also for society as a whole. A new economic order influenced by worldwide multi-cultural interaction necessitates that American students be prepared for life and work built on cross-cultural understanding. A deficit of minority teachers will make this difficult.

One explanation for the decline in the number of black and Hispanic teachers is that new college graduates chose to major in disciplines other than teaching during the late '70s and early '80s because they had access to a variety of careers. However, the decline has continued for a decade, and there is no evidence that the displacement of minorities—especially blacks—in the teaching profession can be accounted for by their increased representation in other professions and occupations. On the contrary, the preponderance of evidence shows *insignificant* numbers and proportions of minority students entering a broad spectrum of professions or leaving institutions with degrees, diplomas and certificates.

THE QUEST FOR QUALITY THROUGH QUANTITY

Education reforms have often been built on the premise that more is better. High school graduation requirements and course content requirements have been increased in more than 40 states. In the teaching profession, raised reform standards have contributed to the decline of minority teachers in the public education system:

- 29 states have mandated admissions testing for entry into teacher education programs.
- 33 states require a test for initial certification.
- 10 states deny teacher program approval to institutions if too many students graduate with low test scores.

In the short term, these policies have had the effect of immediately limiting the numbers of students entering and exiting teacher education programs. In the long term, they may discourage institutions from actively recruiting minority students because of the prospect of losing program approval.

A closer look at this problem reveals some interesting patterns. An increasing number of non-minority students cannot perform up to the standards either. Nowhere is this more apparent than in the country's work force, where each year the corporate sector provides newly hired graduates of America's high schools with basic skills training prior to job-specific training.

States want their classrooms staffed with the most qualified teaching force available. However, policies that exclude and deny access to education by pitting excellence against equity do the society a serious disfavor.

Some of these policies and their impacts are:

Federal:

- Limited collection and reporting of data by racial categories has resulted in insufficient and often inaccurate information on which to make policy decisions.
- Reductions in funding of entitlement legislation (Title I, Title II, Title IV) has reduced access to higher education for disadvantaged groups.
- Reduced financial aid for students in higher education has contributed to a decline in the number of minorities attending college.

State:

- Raised entry and exit standards as measured by tests at all grade levels have resulted in the exclusion of a disproportionate number of minority students from higher education and teaching.
- Restrictive publication of certification testing data by racial/ethnic categories and of the number and racial/ethnic breakdown of new teachers employed has resulted in a lack of information on which to plan and design strategies to increase the supply of minority teachers.

Local:

- Children from poorer families often have been placed in the lower tracks where they may not receive equal or high-quality opportunities in schools.
- Teacher placement policies prevent large numbers of minority students from having contact with and exposure to seasoned and experienced

Source: From Education Commission of the States, "A Closer Look at the Shortage of Minority Teachers," *Education Week,* May 17, 1989, p. 29. Reprinted with permission of the Education Commission of the States, 1989.

teachers and, even worse, diminish their ability and self-esteem.

- Ability tracking of students often assumes limited achievement for those students assigned to mid- to low-performance groups. Schools are under pressure to increase the numbers of special education students whenever possible because it is a source of steady income from outside funding.
- Disciplinary policies have resulted in a disproportionate suspension and expulsion rate for certain ethnic groups.

THE NEED FOR MINORITY TEACHERS

Formal, public education is a process through which people are melded into the traditions of their country, learn about common values, attitudes and norms, and gain mutual respect for each other. Public education in America must continue to be the source of shared experiences and common understandings.

Minority teachers provide role models that help build aspirations and raise the self-esteem of minority students who see members of their own racial/ethnic groups contributing to a larger society. Minority students see a place for themselves in the professions and are motivated to work toward that end. They follow the lead of the teacher and increase their performance, set higher goals and see more life choices available to them.

The value of minority teachers is not limited to minority students, however. A diverse teaching force offers all students the opportunity to see a cross-section of people in leadership positions. The contributions of all cultural and racial groups must be included in the school to broaden students' historical perspective.

The consequences of a continued shortage of minority teachers are frightening. Too many minority youngsters lack sufficient academic preparation to enter college or find gainful employment. They are often disproportionately represented in low-ability classes and in the ranks of students at risk of failure, not only in school but also as adults. Minorities' knowledge of the contributions of their own ethnic and racial groups is often scant, and too many members of minority groups are possessed by a growing skepticism that higher education will not result in employment or a changed life.

RECOMMENDATIONS

States no longer can play only a gate-keeping role in assuring a quality teaching force. They must seek solutions to reduce the shortage of minority teachers.

The first mission is to emphasize and focus on the "demand" side of the supply/demand equation. There is wide agreement that the supply of teachers, particularly minority teachers, is dwindling. States must create a sense of urgency and generate a demand for minority teachers. It is in every state's best interest to have as culturally diverse a teaching force as possible, not only for minority youngsters, but for all youngsters. A solution to the supply side of the equation may rest with long-range plans to tap the 33% minority school-age population.

1. Identify what works and why and then transplant these ideas wherever possible. Needed are state and institutional policies that do not exclude so many people in the quest for quality; that minimize competition for the same set of scarce resources; and that value equity and diversity.
2. Identify factors that create an environment in which all youngsters prosper academically. States need to understand the limits of short-term strategies and to work concurrently on installing and following through on long-term strategies, such as early identification of potential teacher candidates.
3. Underscore the connection between the lack of minority faculty in higher education and the shortage of minority teachers in local public schools. State departments of education, the higher education governing boards and the institutions they govern should consider strategies such as:
   - Exchanges between minority and non-minority faculty at predominantly white and black institutions
   - Concurrent course enrollment for students in predominantly white and black institutions within the same cities and general locales
   - Explicit curricular articulation between secondary schools and selected institutions—community colleges and four-year colleges
   - Improved paths of transfers between two- and four-year institutions
   - Improved monitoring and assessment of outcomes (program completion, job placement) for graduates of proprietary schools accepting federal financial aid packages from student
   - Innovative strategies that allow those needing financial assistance to enter college, such as state-funded "work-study" programs permitting teacher education juniors to assist in local school districts
   - Programs designed to attract and encourage the return of college graduates who entered other fields but now may wish to teach
   - The professionalization of teaching to attract more qualified people

The strength and diversity of the teaching force in the nation's schools may hold the solution to this country's domestic tranquility and economic survival.

7

The Futures of Teaching

Linda Darling-Hammond

The teaching profession in America is at a crossroads. Efforts to professionalize teaching in recent years have contrasted sharply with initiatives that, in their form and substance, deprofessionalize the occupation and the act of teaching. In the first category are efforts to improve the knowledge base for teaching and its transmission to teachers, to ensure the competence of entrants, and to create school conditions under which teachers may attend more directly to the needs of their students. In the second category are policies that dilute or truncate preparation for teaching, allow unqualified entrants to be hired, and structure schools so that teachers must attend more to rules, mandates, and procedures than to the needs of students.

Of these two competing forces, the one that proves the more powerful over the next decade will in large part determine the nature of teaching and the character of learning in this nation's schools for many years to come.

BETTER REGULATIONS OR BETTER TEACHERS?

The two very different streams of policy stem from radically different notions of how students learn, how effective teaching is conducted, and how, as a result, education can be improved. In the "assembly line" view, students are raw materials to be "processed" by schools according to specifications defined by schedules, programs, courses, curriculums, and exit tests. Teachers administer the procedures to the students assigned to them using the tools they are given: textbooks, curriculum guidelines, lists of objectives, course syllabi. Administrators translate policies made at the top of the system into rules and procedures that maximize efficiency.

Thus, correctly defining the procedures is the key to educational improvement. If the outcomes are not satisfactory, the solution is to provide more detailed prescriptions for practice and to monitor implementation more carefully. This view assumes that students are standardized, treatments can be prescribed, and standardized rules for practice can be operationalized through regulations, reporting systems, and inspections of performance.

In this view, teachers need not be expert, as most major teaching decisions are handed down through policies and encapsulated in curriculum and teaching materials. It is better that they not be "empowered," as correct implementation depends on a certain degree of uniformity controlled from above.

There is no rationale in this conception of teaching for substantial teacher preparation, induction, or professional development, aside from "in-servicing" designed to ensure more exact implementation of prescribed teaching procedures. There is little use for professional knowledge and judgment, or for collegial consultation and planning. Problems of practice don't exist in this view; the only problems are failures of implementation.

This logic has been extended to its furthest reach in the school policies of the last 15 years. Since the early 1970s, state governments and district central offices have exerted more and more control over the form, substance, and conduct of schooling, producing reform packages that are both teacher-proof and student-proof. For example, in one of the nation's largest city school districts, teachers are supplied with a K–12 standardized curriculum outlining the scope and sequence for instruction in each subject in each grade, complete with a pacing schedule showing how much time teachers should spend on each topic and lesson plans for each day of the school year. Grading standards are also prescribed, showing how much weight teachers should give to each type of assignment (also prescribed), and how they should calculate grades. Promotion standards are determined by standardized tests developed to match the curriculum. The assumption is that marching the students through these procedures is all that is necessary to ensure learning.

It is this logic, too, that has allowed policymakers to avoid investing substantial resources in teacher preparation or teacher salaries. There is no need to provide incentives for rigorous preparation if there is nothing of value to be learned. If we can "fix" teaching by developing better regulations, there is no need to produce better-educated teachers.

An alternative view, which supports the professionalization of teaching, starts from the assumption that students are not standardized and teaching is not routine. Consonant with recent research on learning, this view acknowledges that teaching techniques deemed effective will vary for students with different learning styles, at different stages of cognitive and psychological development, for different subject areas, and for different instructional goals. It posits that, far from following standardized instructional packages, teachers must base their judgments upon knowledge of learning theory and pedagogy, child development and cognition, curriculum and assessment; they must then connect this knowledge to the understandings, dispositions, and conceptions that individual students bring with them to the classroom. The task of teaching is less a matter of "covering the material" than of connecting with the student in whatever ways are necessary to make knowledge

Source: From Darling-Hammond, L. (1988). "The Futures of Teaching." *Educational Leadership* 46, 3: 4–10. Reprinted with permission of the Association for Supervision and Curriculum Development.

the possession of the learner, not just the teacher.

It follows from this view of teaching and learning that teachers must be extremely knowledgeable and highly expert in order to make sound teaching decisions. It also follows that effective teaching procedures cannot be formulated from on high and passed down to teachers to be administered by rote. In this view, education can be improved only by increasing the knowledge base for teaching and ensuring that teachers can use it appropriately in making complex judgments on behalf of their students. This view provides the rationale for the transformation of teaching into a true profession.

In any true profession the emphasis on rigorous preparation, induction, certification, selection, and evaluation is intended to ensure that the knowledge base for practice is transmitted and used. This is part of the bargain that all professions make with society: for occupations that require discretion and judgment in meeting the unique needs of clients, the profession strives to guarantee the competence of members in exchange for the privilege of control over work structure and standards of practice. It is the profession itself that assumes collective responsibility for the definition, transmittal, and enforcement of professional standards of practice and ethnics.

THE EVOLUTION OF TEACHER POLICY

During the 1980s, virtually every state enacted legislation to reform teacher education, licensing, and compensation. In all, over 1,000 pieces of legislation affecting teachers have been developed during the decade, and a substantial number have been implemented. These initiatives represent an important shift in policy focus from earlier decades, attending more to the qualifications and performance of teachers than to changes in programs, curriculums, and management systems. While this new paradigm of educational improvement emerges, however, the old one remains in force, thus pulling the educational system in contradictory directions.

In the last few years, virtually all states have changed their requirements for teacher licensure. Twenty-seven states now regulate admission into teacher education; most have made changes in course requirements for certification; standards for state approval of teacher education programs have also become more highly specified. Forty-one states have imposed tests for initial teacher licensure, and three have imposed tests for continuing licensure. Twenty-five states have created programs for the supervision of beginning teachers, in some cases tied to the acquisition of a continuing teaching license (Darling-Hammond and Berry 1988).

These changes indicate real efforts to regulate entry into the occupation of teaching, one of the important prerequisites for establishing a profession. However, the changes have largely come from legislatures and state education agencies and do not reflect a consensual view either within the profession or across the states of what a prospective teacher ought to know and be able to do. The first generation standards have served political purposes well—imposing screens to justify greater investment in teacher salaries—but have not yet sought to serve professional purposes. For every one of these moves to tighten certification requirements, others have been taken to loosen or waive such requirements, often as a means of counteracting teacher shortages.

Overall, the recent new policies clearly reflect the ambivalence policymakers feel about whether teachers should master a body of knowledge about teaching in order to be licensed to practice, and their subsequent uncertainty as to whether efforts to improve schools should seek to invest in the growth of teachers' capacities or in the development of more exact rules to specify what teachers and students are to do. This ambivalence reflects the historic indecision about whether teachers are semiskilled workers who need only follow procedures, or skilled professionals who apply specialized knowledge to meet the unique needs of each student. As examples of this ambivalence about teaching knowledge, consider the following:

- Virtually all states had provisions for temporary or emergency certification before 1983, but since then a number have created new classes of emergency certificates or have added provisions to allow individuals without preparation in education to teach.

- The number of states now implementing alternative routes to certification jumped from 8 in 1984 to 23 in 1986. Most of these programs require a reduced level of teacher education training—a four- to six-week summer course covering everything from child development to teaching methods often suffices for initial hiring. A few require no specific coursework but do require on-the-job supervision; some appear to have no particular requirements. Although a few states, like New Jersey, eliminated emergency certification when the alternative route was introduced, most have merely added the alternate to their existing array of temporary, provisional, or emergency certificates.

- Many states are specifying more precisely the content of teachers' professional preparation programs; surprisingly, in some cases this has meant actually decreasing the amount of coursework devoted to pedagogy, learning research, and teaching methods. A few states have even placed a ceiling on the amount of education coursework a prospective teacher can take. In contrast, several others are moving to make teacher education a graduate level program.

- The most popular form of testing for licensing teachers is basic skills testing, sometimes supplemented by tests of subject matter knowledge. Testing reading, writing, and arithmetic skills certainly does not establish a sophisticated conception of teaching knowledge. In addition, most existing tests of professional knowledge, including both state tests and the NTE, tap very little of what might be called a knowledge base for teaching, ignoring most of the clinical and research literature in psychology, cognition, and learning theory, and touching only lightly (and simplistically) on matters of child development and teaching methods.

- Requirements for beginning teacher induction programs are often little more than observation systems that prescribe and tally teacher behaviors without regard to their appropriateness or effectiveness. The desire to create systems that are "evaluator-proof" as well as "teacher-proof" has eliminated reflection and judgment from both teaching and its assessment in some states.

It is relatively easy, as we have recently seen, to pass laws requiring more selectivity in entry and more specific coursework for teacher education. However, once the trappings of rigor have been adopted, the basis of confidence in a profession is that these standards can in fact be shown to enhance the knowledge and ability of those admitted to practice.

The limited validity of current teacher tests has been reviewed elsewhere (see, e.g., Haney et al. 1987, Mitchell 1985, Darling-Hammond and Wise 1985, Quirk et al. 1973). Some critics have argued that the current measures, by positing uniform, context-free teaching behaviors and unidimensional responses to simplistic questions, may actually discourage the acquisition and use of professional knowledge that surpasses and should underlie technique (Shulman 1987, Darling-Hammond 1986, MacMillan and Pendlebury 1985). Rather than "legitimizing complexity," as professions must when they seek to establish bars to entry (Starr 1982), these assessment instruments reinforce conceptions of teaching as simple, cookbook-driven work.

It is important to note that not all states are heading in the same direction with respect to teacher policies. While many are creating standards that effectively reduce the qualifications of new entrants to teaching, some—like California, Connecticut, Minnesota, New York, and Washington—are pursuing policies that will ultimately increase the knowledge that teachers bring to the classroom.

Until the content of standards becomes the subject of debate and transformation by members of the profession, standards will serve only short-term political goals. In the long run, if the status and prerequisites of professionalism are to be achieved, professional standards must demonstrate to educators and the public that they do in fact produce improvements in the quality of teaching.

STANDARDS AND SHORTAGES

The apparent schizophrenia about standards for teachers is due, in part, not only to ambivalence about the nature of teaching work, but also to the tensions produced by teacher shortages between raising standards and staffing classrooms.

Shortages of qualified teachers have become apparent in recent years in the growing regions of the South and West, in many urban districts, and in subject areas like mathematics, science, special education, foreign languages, and bilingual education. After years of declining enrollments and teacher surpluses, by 1985 the annual supply of newly trained teachers had dwindled to under 100,000, less than half the number graduated in the early 1970s. These trends are particularly troublesome in light of projected increases in demand for new teachers caused by rising student enrollments and anticipated increases in teacher retirements. These factors are expected to produce nearly 200,000 teaching vacancies annually over the next five years (NCES 1985, Darling-Hammond 1987). The supply of newly graduated teaching candidates is expected to satisfy only about 60 percent of this demand.

Recent attention to teaching has stimulated an increase in the number of college freshmen reporting interest in education as a major or a career (Astin et al. 1987), but their numbers would have to more than double to satisfy the demand for new teachers in coming years. This circumstance leads many to question whether further increases in the educational requirements for teaching, such as those proposed by the Holmes Group, are feasible or realistic.

However, throughout the 20th century, teacher shortages have been an impetus for upgrading salaries and standards within the profession. Shortages following World War I and World War II, and again in the 1960s, propelled substantial real increases in teacher salaries accompanied by increases in the educational requirements for teaching (Sedlak and Schlossman 1986).

The 1980s mirror past experiences with teacher supply shifts and changes in compensation and certification. Following the wage declines of the 1970s, which, along with widely publicized surpluses, dramatically decreased the supply of teachers in training, emerging teacher shortages led to a 40 percent increase in nominal salaries between 1981 and 1986, while certification standards were "raised" by virtue of required licensure tests in most states (Darling-Hammond and Berry 1988). These salary hikes, though helpful, have just returned average teacher salaries to the level they had reached in 1972, following the shortages of the 1960s. Adjusted for the increases in teacher experience and education levels since then, average salaries in 1986 still lagged behind those in 1972 by about 15 percent (Darling-Hammond and Berry 1988).

Thus, teacher shortages have once again created a political climate within which standards and salaries may be raised, but they have also created conditions that work against the continuation of these initiatives. The effect of having standards, however high, with large loopholes available to satisfy demand pressures, is that salaries will always remain somewhat depressed. In the past, although teacher salaries have always increased in times of short supply, they have never reached comparability with those of other professions requiring similar training; and they have tended to slip again when the supply crisis was "solved."

If no substantial improvement occurs in the attractions to teaching, it will be difficult to improve overall teacher quality, since the pool of potential candidates who can meet the standards will not be sufficiently enlarged. In circular fashion, the failure to attract sufficient numbers of well-qualified teachers will lessen teachers' claims for professional responsibility and autonomy and will increase the press for regulation of teaching, thus further decreasing the attractions to teaching for professionally oriented candidates.

It is interesting to note that this process of standard-raising and nearly simultaneous undermining of those standards has occurred over the last century in nearly all occupations that sought to become professions. In those cases, as in teaching currently, the loopholes were created by state governments, and in some cases encouraged by college faculties or employers, who had greater incentives to ensure an adequate supply of students or practitioners than to ensure the quality of that supply (see., e.g., Starr 1982). It was not until members of these occupations organized themselves to promulgate and enforce their own standards through professionally controlled licensure and examination boards that knowledge could be used as a determinant of permission to practice.

Teaching is now alone in the granting of substandard licenses. The American Association of Colleges for Teacher Education Task Force on Teacher Certification has been unable to discover any other state-licensed occupation for which "emergency certification" exists (Bacharach et al. 1985). Only a handful of states have established professionally controlled teaching standards boards and have vested them with sufficient authority to override the judgments of legislatures or other state agencies that standards should be skirted to keep salaries low and classrooms filled.

A related problem is that the public doesn't trust the standards it has set for teachers. Although states have long regulated the content of teacher preparation and the requirements for licensure, there is so little public confidence in these standards that many believe better teachers might be had by eliminating these requirements altogether. Irregular certification procedures are a result of this lack of trust. The curious outcome is that tests that avoid pedagogical problems are seen as a substitute for pedagogical preparation. When the secret gets out that teacher licensure tests don't measure knowledge about teaching, public confidence will only plummet further, reinforcing the cycle of disillusionment, declining salaries, and dwindling supply.

The greatest tragedy of this situation is that the current conditions of teaching create the greatest teacher shortages in those districts that serve the most disadvantaged students. These districts, which often have the least capacity to boost salaries and improve working conditions, must fill many of their vacancies with irregularly certified teachers who have not been adequately trained to teach. Consequently, the students who have the greatest need for well-trained teachers are the least likely to receive them. So it was, too, in other occupations that once had no effective standards for entry. The least advantaged members of society were the most apt to suffer at the hands of the ill-prepared. The quality of service delivery for these groups improved most when professional standards of entry and practice were introduced.

WHICH WAY FROM THE CROSSROADS?

There are two futures at hand. One of these futures maintains the current features of teaching in the face of major demographic and economic changes and expanding expectations of schools. In the year 2000, it looks something like this.

Following a brief and familiar flurry of education reform activity in the mid-1980s, schools settled back down to business as usual. The "education governors" had come and gone; educational leaders were relieved to have the proliferation of commission reports shelved and out of the way. A period of teacher shortages had been addressed by modest salary increases and increased use of emergency and alternative certification provisions. By 1988, teacher salaries had been returned to the levels they had reached in the early 1970s (following the previous teacher shortage), boosting enrollments in teacher education programs enough to allay proposals for radical change. As salaries again leveled off, teacher recruitment remained problematic. Another 20 states joined the 23 that by then had initiated quick routes into teaching through alternative certification. Thus, classrooms, even in the cities, were staffed.

Throughout the 1990s, students in the public education system changed, but schools did not. Great waves of immigration boosted the number of poor, minority, and non-English-speaking children to nearly 40 percent of public school enrollments, and they were increasingly concentrated in poorly funded city school districts. Because a majority of the teaching staffs in these districts had retired, and the large numbers of vacancies were hard to fill, shortages led to larger classes and more emergency hiring. The many teachers whose formal pedagogical preparation consisted of a six-week summer course and two months of supervision on the job desperately wanted to address the learning needs of their students; but their knowledge of child development, language acquisition, learning styles, and alternative teaching methods was too skimpy to provide them with adequate ammunition for the job.

The public's periodic concern for low student performance was assuaged by the enactment of "stiffer" requirements: more frequently administered tests for students to determine promotion, placement, and graduation; more carefully specified grade level objectives and curricular requirements matched to the standardized tests; tighter controls on textbook adoptions; more rigid procedures for tightening school management; more recordkeeping requirements for keeping tabs on administration, instruction, and student progress; and more frequent evaluation and testing of teachers.

Teaching in public schools was increasingly determined by these regulatory requirements rather than by knowledge about teaching and the needs of learners. Teachers taught for the required multiple-choice tests from mandated texts and curriculum packages aligned with the tests. Students no longer read books, wrote papers, conducted experiments, or completed projects in class; their learning was structured instead by worksheets, practice tests, packaged instructional modules, and more practice tests. Scores on basic skills tests remained stable while scores on tests of higher-order thinking continued to decline. More students were held back, and many dropped out. U.S. students continued to perform poorly relative to students in other countries on international assessments.

Earlier enthusiasm for reforms gave way to disillusionment and to lower school budgets, as middle class parents fled to private schools and the general population, composed largely of older citizens without children in schools, voted down tax levies for education. Just as the progressive education initiatives of the 1960s had been replaced in the 1970s by a movement to cap taxes for school support and go "back to the basics," so the restructuring rhetoric of the '80s gave way to technocratic solutions less threatening to established bureaucracies. By the year 2000, public frustration with the schools resurfaced with cries from the business community for employees who could function in an information-based, technological economy. New commissions were born to declare the nation, once again, at risk.

Another future—one that envisions different resolutions of the dilemmas mentioned above—is possible. In this future, teaching continues its progress toward becoming a profession that is both *client-oriented* and *knowledge-based*. In the year 2000, a different public education system has emerged. It looks something like this:

Much has changed since the last "crisis" in education during the 1980s. A second wave of reform impelled new coalitions between teachers, school administrators, and teacher educators, all of whom began thinking of themselves as members of the same profession with common goals. They articulated the first professional definition of teaching knowledge through the National Board of Professional Teaching Standards. This stimulated the creation of analogous state boards, which built upon the new vision to establish meaningful standards for teacher preparation and licensure in the states. Most states established professional internships for clinical training of new teachers following the completion of a master's degree in teaching. A number of states and districts created professional development schools, where all teachers-in-training could be coached by expert mentor teachers. The new cohort of teachers—over a million of them—was better prepared than any that had preceded them.

Teacher shortages were met with higher salaries and differentiated staffing arrangements. These responses also began to change the shape of school organizations and the allocations of school resources. As salaries climbed another 30 percent, to a level comparable with other occupations for college-educated workers, the supply of prospective teachers willing to undergo rigorous preparation programs grew substantially. As the qualifications of teachers increased, the perceived need to spend large chunks of education budgets on massive control and inspection systems diminished. Long hierarchies that had developed to design, regulate, and monitor teaching flattened out. Teachers assumed more professional responsibilities, and schools took on new shapes conducive to professional teaching.

As in other professions, differentiated roles and responsibilities gradually emerged as a means for balancing the requirements of supply and qualifications. Those not fully certified or less extensively trained were limited to performing tasks for which they had been prepared, and they practiced under the supervision of career professionals. Practitioners began to work in teams that jointly assumed responsibility for groups of students. In settings where, for example, three professional teachers and two instructors were responsible for 100 students over several years, many possibilities became apparent for appropriate supervision, for organizing large- and small-group instruction, for consulting about teaching plans and decisions, and for developing strategies for meeting individual children's needs. Not incidentally, such structures promoted the kinds of consultation and peer review of practice that are central to a professional role.

Members of the education profession insisted on selecting and inducting their peers and on collective decision making over the best uses of knowledge and resources to meet students' needs. As serious induction, sustained professional development, and collaboration in problem-solving replaced the sink-or-swim, closed-door ethos of an earlier era, professional knowledge and effectiveness grew.

Instructional practices changed, too. As schools became more learner-centered and teachers more skilled, the assembly line approach to processing students gave way to more varied and appropriate methods of teaching and learning. Lectures and worksheets were no longer the preponderant school activities: cooperative and experiential learning, projects, debates, essays, and exhibitions engaged students of varied learning styles, encouraged students to construct and solve intellectual problems, and created more meaningful and useful ways by which to assess students' progress. A wide variety of more productive approaches to organizing the school day and the school year and to grouping students gave individual teachers and students more time together, reducing the pull-outs, pass-throughs, start-ups, and wind-downs that had stolen teaching time and decreased teachers' capacity to come to know students well.

Incentives to attract the most expert teachers to the profession's greatest needs and challenges also emerged. Following the lead of path-breaking districts like Dade County, Charlotte-Mecklenburg, Rochester, and Louisville, master teachers redesigned inner-city schools as exemplars of professional practice where they coached new teachers, put research into practice—and practice into research—and put state-of-the-art knowledge to work for kids. Equity and excellence became joined with professionalism.

By the year 2000, American education had begun to be transformed. The best American students performed as well as students anywhere in the world. The vast majority of students graduated not only with minimal basic skills but with the capacity to write, reason, and think analytically. Complaints from the business community about the quality of graduates subsided for the first time since World War II. And for the first time since the beginning of the 20th century, a decade was launched without a chorus of commissions crying crisis in the American public schools. The road taken, as it turned out, was the one that finally made a difference.

REFERENCES

Astin, A.W., K.C. Green, and W.S. Korn. (1987). *The American Freshman: Twenty Year Trends*. Cooperative Institutional Research Program, American Council of Education. Los Angeles: University of California.

Bacharach, S.B., et al. (1985). *Teacher Shortages, Professional Standards, and "Hen House" Logic*. Ithaca, N.Y.: Organizational Analysis and Practice, Inc.

Darling-Hammond, L. (Fall 1986). "Teaching Knowledge: How Do We Test It?" *American Educator* 10, 3.

Darling-Hammond, L. (January 14, 1987). "What Constitutes a 'Real' Shortage of Teachers?" *Commentary, Education Week* 6, 16.

Darling-Hammond, L., and B. Berry. (1988). *The Evolution of Teacher Policy*. Santa Monica, Calif.: The RAND Corporation, JRE-01.

Darling-Hammond, L., and A.E. Wise. (1985). *Teacher Testing for Certification: An Overview of the Issues*. St. Paul: Minnesota Higher Education Coordinating Board.

Haney, W., G. Madaus, and A. Kreitzer. (1987). "Charms Talismanic: Testing Teachers for the Improvement of American Education." In *Review of Research in Education*, Vol. 14. Washington, D.C.: AERA.

MacMillan, J.B., and S. Pendlebury. (1985). "The Florida Performance Measurement System: A Consideration." *Teachers College Record* 87: 69–78.

Mitchell, J.V. (1985). *Ninth Mental Measurements Yearbook*. Lincoln: Buros Institute of Mental Measurements, University of Nebraska.

National Center for Education Statistics. (1985). *Projections of Education Statistics to 1992*. Washington, D.C.: U.S. Department of Education.

Quirk, T.J., B. Witten, and S.F. Weinberg. (1973). "Review of Studies of the Concurrent and Predictive Validity of the National Teacher Examinations." *Review of Educational Research* 43, 1: 89–113.

Sedlak, M., and S. Schlossman. (1986). *Who Will Teach? Historical Perspectives on the Changing Appeal of Teaching as a Profession*. Santa Monica, Calif.: The RAND Corporation, R-3472.

Shulman, L. (February 1987). "Knowledge and Teaching: Foundations of the New Reform." *Harvard Educational Review* 57, 1.

Starr, P. (1982). *The Social Transformation of American Medicine*. New York: Basic Books.

8

Questioning "Cliches" of Education Reform

Chester E. Finn, Jr.

American education is awash these days in hoary clichés and trendy maxims thought to be true because they sound so plausible, because we've been hearing them for so long, or because someone we're inclined to trust is uttering them.

But many of these shards of conventional wisdom are unproven. A large number are over-simplifications at best, falsehoods at worst. Some are lightly camouflaged fragments of inertia, self-interest, or wishful thinking.

Yet in these terms the nation's education dilemmas are being framed—and the outcome of our efforts to address the deficiencies of American schooling will be determined to a large extent by how we pose the problems. If you navigate by the wrong stars, pulling hard on the oars still won't get you to the destination.

Especially during this brief quadrennial period of national stocktaking that attends a Presidential transition, we might well examine some of the dustier assumptions on the education-reform shelves.

Most of the commonly accepted notions I discuss here bear on what many educators have persuaded themselves is the epochal choice facing school reformers: "top down" changes—those initiated by state or federal policymakers—or "bottom up" innovations—those designed by local districts and individual schools. But the idea that such a tidy choice can be made—indeed, that it presents "right" and "wrong" options (and you don't have to guess which side most educators line up on)—is itself a dandy example of conventional wisdom that, upon inspection, turns out to be hogwash.

One of the abiding strengths of American education is local control.

Though we still have upwards of 15,000 local school systems, the education action has shifted to the states: For a decade, their share of the nation's public-school dollar has exceeded the local portion. And nearly all the boldest changes in the 1980's—Tennessee's career ladder, South Carolina's comprehensive reform act, California's new curricula, Minnesota's school choice law, New Jersey's "educational bankruptcy" scheme, to cite only a few examples—have been statewide policy shifts.

While local governance and financing of schools worked satisfactorily in an agrarian society, it is less suited to a mobile, megalopolitan nation. Local politics are apt to be petty, given to patronage and favoritism. And reliance on local revenues invites allegations of fiscal inequity. The result has been, and will surely continue to be, ever-greater state dominance of education finance and regulation.

Holding individual schools to account for their performance is a good idea. So is conferring more authority on parents. But the county board of education and town superintendent's office are vestiges of the last century that may not be needed at all in the next one.

Politicians should keep their grimy paws off the schools.

Since the turn of the century, civic wisdom has held that education should be left to the experts—professional educators and lay governing boards, many of them appointed to their positions so as to insulate them from the hurly-burly of electoral politics. Governor and legislator, mayor and selectman—this seedy lot should stick to road building, waste disposal, and law enforcement.

That arrangement got us into the fix we're in. Educators attended mainly to their own interests. The lay boards deferred to their professional staffs, in many places lost the ability to attract first-rate members, and wearied of the interminable meetings and a surfeit of detail. The schools decayed.

Today, education is the largest item in the budget of every state and most localities, and taxpayers have begun to hold elected officials responsible for the effective use of these immense resources. As a result, many governors have made education their issue—and some mayors are starting to do the same.

Though many educators still yearn for the old pattern, practically everybody else now acknowledges that the proper duties of elected officials include—along with finding resources for public education—setting standards, creating accountability systems, and charting policy for schools. The education system, we've learned, is not self-correcting.

Policy-driven reforms of the sort that legislatures enact will not yield authentic improvement in education and may make it worse. What is needed instead is "restructuring"—empowering school "professionals" to make key decisions.

It is true that outstanding schools nearly always display homegrown qualities that cannot be mandated from on high, and imaginative experiments underway in half a dozen communities are modifying timeworn practices in a effort to clone excellent schools.

But with some 83,000 public schools in the land, we cannot suppose that most students would benefit if their "school team" suddenly gained greater autonomy. Too

Source: From Chester E. Finn, Jr., "Questioning 'Cliches' of Education Reform," *Education Week*, Volume VIII, Number 18, January 25, 1989, pp. 38, 29. Reprinted with permission from *Education Week*. Volume VIII, Number 18, January 25, 1989. Reprinted with permission from Chester E. Finn, Jr.

many team members just don't have what it takes, and too few really want to change their ways.

While the capacity for improvement may be nurtured in such schools over time, the best approach is to alter the rules by which the system operates. And that is the proper work of lawmakers.

National standards for education are un-American.

We probably do not want federal regulations to enforce them, but perhaps the single most valuable action that George Bush could take as "education President" would be to catalyze a national consensus-seeking process, meant to settle on some basic education norms for all young Americans.

What is the minimum that a high-school graduate should know and be able to do? Why should Missoula have a different standard from Malden? States, districts, and individual schools may add to the core, but in this mobile society, yesterday's 5th grader in Oregon is apt to be tomorrow's high-school student in Delaware.

Youngsters across the land already watch the same movies and television programs, listen to the same music, read (if at all) the same publications, and chow down in identical outlets of the same fast-food chains. And the school curriculum is already similar in many districts, thanks to education schools, professional associations, textbook publishers, and test makers. Why not turn this creeping sameness into a virtue? Why not have uniform minimum standards, too?

Teaching to the test denatures the teacher-student relationship, paralyzes the curriculum, and turns goals into ceilings.

If a standardized test faithfully appraises the skills and knowledge that the school system seeks to impart—if it is properly aligned with the curriculum—then there is nothing wrong with teaching to it. While schools must not coach students on actual exam items, drilling them on the array of skills and knowledge the test will probe is fine.

The tests do not have to be the multiple-choice, machine-readable variety. As has long been the case with Advanced Placement exams, they can involve analytic essays and complex problem-solving. They can entail subtle computer interactions. They can even be oral. But some means are required to find out whether students have actually learned what the education system sought to teach them. Or else there is no accountability.

At-risk children are the chief problem facing education.

The reigning wisdom holds that the school system is drowning in a demographic tidal wave of immigrant and minority youngsters, children from impoverished, broken, and disorganized families, students with masses of social, economic, medical, nutritional, and emotional problems. In this situation, we are told, "It is unrealistic to think of reading Shakespeare."

To be sure, growing numbers of such children are showing up at the schoolhouse door. And the persistence of an "underclass" is as vexing a social-policy problem as any we face.

But schools as presently constituted have scant leverage over the lives of students, who typically spend less than 10 percent of their time in them, even if they attend faithfully until their 18th birthdays. And schools are good at only a few things: imparting cognitive skills and knowledge and—sometimes—boosting sound values, good behavior, and physical fitness.

The tangled problems of at-risk youngsters have their origins outside the schools and seldom can be solved inside them, though it is legitimate to enlist the schools in whatever policy partnerships are formed. To pretend otherwise is to raise false hopes.

But there is *one* aspect of the at-risk problem that educators alone can do something about and should be held accountable for: the risk of attending a lousy school.

For no one does a first-rate school make a bigger difference than the disadvantaged child. And dozens of schools succeed magnificently, even in the most woebegone locales and with the most challenging of youngsters. Such examples offer plain proof that schools can be islands of order and learning in a tempestuous social sea. What we need are thousands more such places.

The assumption that high standards and a meaty curriculum are bad for disadvantaged youngsters is a recipe for continued second-class citizenship. Anyone who cares about equal opportunity has got to note with alarm that among black and Hispanic high-school graduates in 1987, only 23 and 21 percent respectively had taken a course menu including at least four years of English and three years each of mathematics, science, and social studies. For whites, the figure was 30 percent; for Asians, 52 percent.

Better schools are going to cost more.

The expenditures of American public schools have been rising in real terms for decades and this year are the highest ever—in the vicinity of $4,800 per pupil, or about $110,000 for every classroom. The biggest problem is not that we're spending too little but that the return on this huge investment is too skimpy.

Yes, a few needed changes will demand still more money. Lengthening the school day and year, for example, are big-ticket items. Sophisticated testing methods cost more than the simple kind. But good textbooks cost no more than bad ones; algebra and history are no more expensive to teach than consumer math and family living; at $50,000 a head, enough money is already being paid to high-school principals to hire good ones. And significant sums can be saved—as Chicago may soon demonstrate—by sharp reductions in the bureaucracy of the superintendent's office.

"Choice" is just a code word for vouchers, which portend the end of public education as we know it."

The private-school aid debates of earlier years have nearly vanished from the policy arena; the center-ring event today is choice *within public education*. Such approaches as magnet schools, alternative schools, and schools-within-schools have proven hugely successful in settings as dissimilar, for example, as Spanish Harlem, Cambridge, Mass., and Prince George's County, Md.

Choice is now also expanding to the state level. The Minnesota legislature voted in 1988 to give every youngster in the state the right to attend any of its public schools. New York's commissioner of education, Thomas Sobol, recently proposed that any child in the state should be able to transfer from a bad school to one that works; California's superintendent of public instruction, Bill Honig, is heading in the same direction.

The choice issue illuminates the folly of polarizing the reform debate into "top down" and "bottom up" strategies. As professional teams in individual schools begin to decide what will be taught, how, and by whom, schools will come to differ. It is only right that children and parents be able to select the ones that suite them: The more such "building-level autonomy"—that is, bottom-up reform—is exercised, the more important it is that families be allowed to match the educational needs of their children to the varied offerings of schools in their communities.

Yet replacing involuntary pupil assignments with choice among schools is the quintessential policymakers' decision. However logical a corollary it is to bottom-up reform, the principle of choice cannot be installed from the building level. It needs a gutsy superintendent, a crusading governor, a cadre of bold legislators—and it needs policy control over a lot of schools or it doesn't make any sense at all.

Neither, however, does it make much sense to offer choice in a tightly regulated system of virtually identical schools. What then is to choose?

Only when schools are encouraged to differ—and when educators and officials are willing to live with the certainty that some will thrive and others wither—is choice among schools an authentic reform. This means forging the softer metals associated with bottom-up school improvement on the steel policy anvil of the top-down strategy.

We are not dealing with a neat dichotomy after all. Nor is most of the rest of today's conventional wisdom about education reform more than a collection of half-truths, none of them able to bear much weight until the missing parts are located and firmly joined.

9

Parents Are a School's Best Friends

Anne T. Henderson

Surprisingly little debate about the proper role and responsibilities of parents has surfaced in the current wave of concern over the plight of public education. Has there been a decline in parent involvement in the schools and, if so, is that decline part of the schools' problems? Should parents step in when schools are bad? Should schools that seek to improve themselves reach out to parents for help? What can parents contribute to the education of their children, at home and in the schools?

However interesting the answers might be, these questions are hardly being addressed. Instead, we have assumed that parents are part of the general dissatisfaction with public schools. When they are mentioned at all, as in *A Nation at Risk*, parents are told to let their leaders know that more must be done to improve the schools and to help their children with schoolwork at *home*. Even with adequate support from policy makers, should we expect educators to turn ailing schools around all by themselves, with no direct assistance from parents or other members of the community?

STUDENT ACHIEVEMENT

The national reports and the subsequent reform efforts seem uninformed by a significant body of research on the connection between parent involvement and student achievement. In 1981 the National Committee for Citizens in Education (NCCE) published an annotated bibliography, *The Evidence Grows*, which described 35 studies on the subject. The findings of all the studies were positive: parent involvement in almost any form appears to produce measurable gains in student achievement.

Last year, the NCCE completed an update, *The Evidence Continues to Grow: Parent Involvement Improves Student Achievement*.[1] This time the NCCE found 18 new studies that, together with the earlier research, place the conclusion well beyond dispute. If school improvement efforts are judged successful when they raise student achievement, the research strongly suggests that involving parents can make a critical difference.

The studies show that programs designed with a strong component of parent involvement produce students who perform better than those who have taken part in otherwise identical programs with less parent involvement. Students in schools that maintain frequent contact with their communities outperform those in other schools. Children whose parents are in touch with the school score higher than children of similar aptitude and family background whose parents are *not* involved. Parents who help their children learn at home nurture (in themselves and in their children) attitudes that are crucial to achievement. Children who are failing in school improve dramatically when parents are called in to help. And so on.

The effects persist well beyond the short term. For example, low-income and minority graduates of preschool programs with high levels of parent involvement are still outperforming their peers when they reach senior high school. Some of the major benefits of parent involvement include higher grades and test scores, better long-term academic achievement, positive attitudes and behavior, more successful programs, and more effective schools.

EMERGING AGREEMENT

Despite the way the reform reports avoided the topic, there is far more agreement about the importance of including parents in the educational process today than there was five years ago. For example, the National Education Association has embarked on a major effort to train teachers to work more closely with parents, and the flow of official pronouncements about the need for parents to help their children with schoolwork has increased from a trickle to a steady stream.

Yet it is still not unusual to hear experienced, well-meaning educators say that classroom learning is best left to the professionals. They worry that untrained parents might unwittingly interfere with today's sophisticated teaching techniques or that turf battles between parents and educators might disrupt the learning environment. They also argue that involving parents is a time-consuming "luxury" that places yet another burden on already overworked (and underpaid) teachers and principals.

The general agreement on the importance of involving parents in the educational process tends to break down at the point of implementation. David Williams' research at the Southwest Educational Development Laboratory explains why.[2] After questioning parents, teachers, principals, superintendents, and school board members, Williams

Source: Anne T. Henderson, "Parents Are A School's Best Friends," *Phi Delta Kappa*, October 1988, pp. 148–153. Reprinted with permission from publisher.

[1] Anne Henderson, *The Evidence Continues to Grow: Parent Involvement Improves Student Achievement* (Columbia, Md.: National Committee for Citizens in Education, 1987).

[2] David Williams and John Stallworth, *Parent Involvement in Education Project* (Austin, Tex.: Southwest Educational Development Laboratory, Executive Summary of the Final Report, 1983–84).

found that they all agreed that parent involvement is vital to a child's success in school and that parents and teachers should communicate and cooperate more frequently. But he also found that parents and educators disagree about the value of different parental roles.

Williams found that parents are eager to play a variety of roles at school, ranging from tutoring their children or helping in the classroom to sitting on committees that decide such matters as disciplinary policies or changes in curriculum. While they feel that some activities, such as helping their children with homework, should have a higher priority than others, they feel that all roles are important.

Professional educators are divided on the issue of parent involvement. Williams found that principals and teachers favor more parent involvement in traditional ways (e.g., attending class plays or holding bake sales to benefit the band uniform fund). But a substantial majority of teachers and principals do not view the parental role in educational or personnel decisions as either useful or appropriate. However, superintendents and school board members, who are further away from day-to-day contact with parents, rate parent decision making at the *school* more highly.

The research provides some guideposts that can help keep us on track. First, it is clear that everyone benefits when parents are involved in their children's education. Not only do individual children and their families function more effectively, but there is an *aggregate* effect on the performance of students and teachers when schools collaborate with parents. The research also tells us that parent involvement works better when parents are given a *variety* of roles to play.

In other words, there are no "quick fixes." The particular forms of parent involvement do not seem to be as important as the fact that the involvement is reasonably well-planned, comprehensive, and long-lasting.

THE STUDIES

Although the findings of the research are uniformly positive—NCCE found not a single negative study—the studies vary widely in approach, methodology, and subject matter. Some looked at high-achieving students to see whether their parents tend to be more involved; others compared the relative effectiveness of programs with a standard structure and content but variations in level of parent involvement. Some were confined to a single school district or program over a short period of time; others were massive analyses of nationwide surveys.

For all their diversity, however, the studies tend to examine one of three general approaches: improving the parent/child relationship, integrating parents into the school program, and building stronger connections among schools, families, and the larger community.

1. *Improving the parent/child relationship*. Most of the research has focused on the effects on student achievement of "family process and status" variables. These include such family characteristics as parents' levels of education and income; such family behaviors as whether or not parents read to their children and enforce rules regarding homework and television; such family patterns as whether the parents are married, employed, or part of a social support network; and such family attitudes as self-esteem and expectations for success.

One set of these studies examines the home environments of very young children and the effects of certain behaviors when they later enter school. The other set examines the changes in children enrolled in preschool or early elementary grades when their parents engage in supportive activities at home. While both sets of studies focus on the home environment, the effects are measured in terms of performance at *school*.

These studies show that building a strong learning environment at home—including holding high expectations of success and encouraging positive attitudes toward education—powerfully affects student achievement. Exceptionally gifted students, for example, nearly always have parents who are enthusiastically involved in every aspect of their development, from first toy piano to Carnegie Hall debut.[3] This finding holds true across all social, economic, and ethnic backgrounds.

On the other hand, young children whose backgrounds place them "at risk" of failing or falling behind will out-perform their friends for years if their parents are given training in home teaching.[4] Older children whose performance starts to decline can be straightened out by home reinforcement, especially when parents reward good performance.[5]

It's easy to understand why children would profit from extra attention and help, regardless of the source. But help is most effective when it comes from parents. The key to achievement seems to lie in students' positive *attitudes* about themselves and their control over the environment. And these attitudes are largely formed *at home*, although they are strongly influenced by the myriad interactions between the family and the surrounding community, including the school.[6]

When parents show an interest in their children's education and maintain high expectations for their performance, they are promoting attitudes that are critical to achievement—attitudes that can be formed independently of social class or other external circumstances. Schools can help by encouraging parents to work with their children and by providing helpful information and skills. The studies show clearly that parent involvement—whether based at home or at school and whether begun before or after a child starts school—has significant, long-lasting effects. In fact, these effects vary directly with the duration and intensity of the parent involvement: the more, the better.

It is extremely important to remember that the converse is also true: if schools treat parents as unimportant, if they treat them as negative educational influences on their children, or if they discourage parents from becoming involved, then they promote the development of attitudes that inhibit achievement at school.

2. *Introducing parent involvement in the school*. The second broad approach taken by research studies asks whether bringing parents into a school or into a program within a school improves student achievement. Two reviews of the literature found many examples of programs in which low-income parents have been trained to work with their children.[7] As a result, children improved their language skills, test performance, and school behavior. The studies that were reviewed also turned up important effects on the general educational process. Parents developed better attitudes toward schools and school staff members, helped gather support in the community, became more active in community affairs, and sought more education for themselves. Teachers devoted more time to teaching, were more likely to experiment, and developed approaches that were more student-oriented.

Other studies have looked at the effects of introducing a parent-involvement component into a special program. In government-sponsored programs, such as Chapter 1 and Follow Through, in which parents can play roles as paraprofessionals, decision makers, home tutors, classroom volunteers, observers, or co-learners, student achievement seems to vary directly with the degree of parent involvement.[8] Another interesting

[3]Benjamin Bloom, *Developing Talent in Young People* (New York: Ballantine Books, 1985).

[4]Irving Lazar and Richard Darlington, *Summary: Lasting Effects After Preschool* (Ithaca, N.Y.: Cornell University, 1978).

[5]Richard Barth, "Home-Based Reinforcement of School Behavior: A Review and Analysis," *Review of Educational Research*, vol. 49, 1979, pp. 436–58.

[6]James Coleman, *Equality of Educational Opportunity* (Washington, D.C.: U.S. Government Printing Office, 1966).

[7]Rhoda McShane Becher, *Parent Involvement: A Review of Research and Principles of Successful Practice* (Washington, D.C.: National Institute of Education, 1984); and Hazel Leler, "Parent Education and Involvement in Relation to the Schools and to Parents of School-Aged Children," in Ron Haskins and Diane Adams, eds., *Parent Education and Public Policy* (Norwood, N.J.: Ablex, 1983).

[8]Joan Herman and Jennie Yeh, *Some Effects of Parent Involvement in Schools* (Los Angeles: Center for the Study of Evaluation, Graduate School of Education, University of California, 1980).

study of three performance-contracting programs, which were identical except for their use of parent involvement, found that the one with the most comprehensive involvement produced significantly higher reading gains for students.[9]

3. *Building a partnership between home and school*. The third approach taken by studies of parent involvement examines whether good community relations are related to student achievement and school effectiveness. One way to get at this issue is to ask whether schools with high levels of achievement have more community involvement and support than similar schools with lower average levels of performance. A large national study of high schools concluded that the degree of parent and community interest in the quality of education is "the critical factor" in explaining higher levels of achievement and of educational aspirations.[10] Two studies of large urban school districts reached almost identical conclusions: schools with higher levels of achievement have considerably greater parent involvement.[11]

These studies also strongly suggest that involving parents in their children's education at home, while extremely effective in improving an individual student's performance, is not necessarily sufficient to make a difference for the school as a whole. The average level of achievement of a school does not appear to rise unless parents are involved *in the school*.

Several studies of the Parent Education Follow Through program, which was designed to have a communitywide impact, have documented significant effects on student achievement. In this model, parents play six critical roles: teacher at home, paid school employee, decision maker, adult learner, volunteer, and audience. These roles can be thought of as spokes on a wheel, since they not only influence parents' behavior but also change the community agencies with which parents interact. For the wheel to turn, parents must play *all* the roles. The conclusion of this series of studies is that the better planned, the more comprehensive, and the longer lasting the parent involvement, the more effective the schools in the community become.[12]

QUESTIONS FOR FUTURE RESEARCH

The research to date all points in the same direction: when parents are a basic ingredient in an improvement strategy, students will perform better in school. But parents must be intimately involved; public relations campaigns or dog-and-pony shows are not effective.

There is still far more we need to know. For all the research on low-income and high-risk children, few studies have asked whether parent involvement can help these students achieve at levels expected for middle-class children. Most studies have compared groups of high-risk students receiving special treatment with control groups of their peers. We know that children who graduate from developmental preschool and kindergarten programs score higher on tests than similar children who do not attend. But we don't know whether they perform as well as their middle-class friends.

Herbert Walberg studied inner-city Chicago students whose parents responded to a program modeled after Jesse Jackson's Operation PUSH; the children who took part in the program scored half a grade-equivalent higher than students who did not.[13] In terms of total achievement, however, the participating students made about one year of progress in reading for their year in the program, while those who did not take part gained only about half a year. In other words, the program kept its students from losing more ground. What would it take to boost their achievement to grade level?

Charles Benson examined this question in a series of studies of the use of time in families; his findings were less than encouraging.[14] He found that the amount of time that parents devote to their children and the types of activities in which they engage do make a substantial difference in achievement, but he also found that children from low-income families still tend to perform below average. Parents' efforts *do* improve achievement, but they do not entirely overcome the disadvantages associated with low socioeconomic status.

However, Benson was not looking at the effects of an intensive program to reinforce the mutual efforts of home and school; he was studying family-initiated activities. David Irvine, assessing a developmental prekindergarten program for 4-year-olds, found that the program did have an equalizing effect: the children who benefited most were those who started with the lowest scores.[15]

In Syracuse, New York, Moncrieff Cochran and Charles Henderson designed and studied an intensive, family-oriented intervention program for 3-year-olds that featured home visits and neighborhood-based support groups. While the results varied according to race, income, and family structure, program participation did mean better performance when the children started school—that is, the negative consequences of low income were reduced or eliminated. In addition, the children from the lowest-income families tended to make the largest gains.[16]

In a large and continuing study of high school students in the San Francisco Bay Area, Sanford Dornbusch has found that *parenting styles* produced marked differences in student achievement.[17] Across ethnic groups, family levels of education, and family structures, he consistently found that "authoritarian" styles are associated with the lowest student grades, "permissive" styles with the next lowest grades, and "authoritative" styles (firm but open to discussion and negotiation) with the highest grades. Dornbusch concludes that parenting style is a more powerful predictor of student achievement than ethnicity, family level of education, or family structure. However, he has not yet presented data showing that low-income students from "authoritative" homes do as well in school as middle-class students.

Reginald Clark conducted a much more narrowly focused study of 10 low-income black families and found that those families with a teenager in the top 20% of his or her high school class had "authoritative" parenting styles.[18] His study strongly suggests

[9] Ronald Gillum, "The Effects of Parent Involvement on Student Achievement in Three Michigan Performance Contracting Programs," paper presented at the annual meeting of the American Educational Research Association, New York City, 1977.

[10] Edward McDill et al., *Educational Climates of High Schools: Their Effects and Sources* (Baltimore: Center for the Study of Social Organization of Schools, Johns Hopkins University, 1969).

[11] Susan Phillips et al., *Parents and Schools* (Milwaukee: Study Commission on the Quality of Education in the Metropolitan Milwaukee Schools, 1985). See also Theodore C. Wagenaar, *School Achievement Level Vis-à-Vis Community Involvement and Support: An Empirical Assessment* (Columbus: Ohio State University, 1977).

[12] Ira Gordon, "What Does Research Say About the Effects of Parent Involvement in Schools?," Occasional Papers, School of Education, University of North Carolina, Chapel Hill, 1978.

[13] Herbert J. Walberg et al., "School-Based Family Socialization and Reading Achievement in the Inner City," *Psychology in the Schools*, vol. 17, 1980, pp. 509–14.

[14] Charles S. Benson et al., "Families as Educators: Time Use Contributions to School Achievement," in James Guthrie, ed., *School Finance Policy in the 1980s: A Decade of Conflict* (Cambridge, Mass.: Ballinger, 1980).

[15] David Irvine, *Parent Involvement Affects Children's Cognitive Growth* (Albany: New York State Education Department, 1979).

[16] Moncrieff Cochran and Charles Henderson, "Family Matters: Evaluation of the Parental Empowerment Program," Cornell University, Ithaca, N.Y., 1986.

[17] Sanford Dornbusch et al., "The Relation of Parenting Style to Adolescent School Performance," *Child Development*, vol. 58, 1987, pp. 1244–57.

[18] Reginald Clark, *Family Life and School Achievement: Why Poor Black Children Succeed or Fail* (Chicago: University of Chicago Press, 1983).

that a family's overall cultural style—not the more commonly used variables of marital status, educational level, income, or social class—determines whether or not children are prepared to perform well in school.

In his provocative research on American high schools, James Coleman found that students in private high schools (including Catholic schools) were more successful than comparable students in public schools.[19] The private school students had higher grades and test scores, were more likely to graduate, and were more likely to attend and graduate from college. This effect is easy to explain for independent private schools, where admission can be highly selective. But Catholic schools serve a population similar to that of public schools. Yet they seem to have a greater effect on the achievement of their most disadvantaged students.

Catholic schools are successful, Coleman says, because they have a *different relationship to their community*. Public school educators see themselves as representatives of society; as such, one of their purposes is to help children overcome the deficiencies of their families. Private school educators see themselves as extensions of the families they serve. Catholic schools have the further advantage of acting as agents of a religious community to which many of these families belong. In such circumstances, the continuity of values between home and school reinforces a child's educational experience.

If schools do not make the effort to include parents in the learning process, children can find it difficult to integrate the separate experiences of home and school. If the school and the home are in conflict, the children tend to fall behind and drop out. Coleman points out that public schools *can* increase the sense of community among students' families. The relations of families with one another can be strengthened, for example, so that common standards develop. The structure of high schools can be adjusted, so that students are exposed to fewer teachers over a longer time—thereby allowing stronger bonds to develop between teacher and students and making it possible for parents to work with teachers who really know their children.

Even though the research treats most of the major issues arising from parent involvement, it is far from complete or conclusive. Some of the most important questions still unanswered by the research include:

- What type and intensity of parent involvement will raise the achievement level of low-income and minority children to the level expected for middle-class students?
- What forms of parent involvement are most appropriate for students in middle, junior high, and high schools?
- What resources do parents and educators need to work effectively as partners?
- What are the most appropriate roles for government agencies at all levels in encouraging, nurturing, and expanding parent involvement?
- What can others in the community—such as service agencies, employers, and business and industry—do to help families and schools work together?

AN IMPORTANT QUESTION

What about the effective-schools research? Much of the literature on effective schools implies that educators can do the job alone. Indeed, there are many well-documented cases of schools in which disadvantaged children are learning at levels expected for middle-class students and in which there is no organized effort to involve parents. As a result, many popular lists of characteristics of effective schools do not include parent or community relations.

Although it seems curious that two reliable bodies of research have remained unconnected, there are good reasons. Most of the studies of parent involvement focus on improving the parent/child relationship and on the *individual* child's subsequent progress. The findings regarding the effects of parent involvement on aggregate achievement or on the improved performance of the school as a whole are not as well developed. The research I have discussed above suggests that schools can become more effective if they *do* involve parents, as long as they also do the *rest* of their job.

Ronald Edmonds, one of the founders of the effective-schools movement, made this point in a letter to Yale psychologist James Comer in 1980:

> I believe that the evidence supports me in arguing that schools are responsible for pupil acquisition of minimum competency in basic school skills regardless of the level of parent participation in the life of the school. I also believe that without parent participation, schools cannot move to that excellence that is our ultimate objective in so vital a matter as public education.[20]

While much of the research on parent involvement resonates well with common sense, the major points are worth mentioning again.

- The family, not the school, provides the primary educational environment for children.
- Involving parents in their children's formal education improves the children's achievement.
- Parent involvement is most effective when it is comprehensive, well-planned, and long lasting.
- Involving parents when their children are young has beneficial effects that persist throughout the child's academic career.
- While the effects are particularly strong at the early levels, significant benefits can be derived from involving parents in the intermediate and high school years.
- Involving parents with their children's education at home may not be enough to improve schools; a school's average level of achievement does not appear to improve unless parents are involved in the school.
- Children from low-income and minority families benefit the most when parents are involved in the schools, and parents do *not* have to be well-educated to make a difference.
- Students' attitudes about themselves and their control over the environment are critical to achievement; these attitudes are formed primarily at home, though they can be profoundly influenced by experience at school.

Ultimately, involving parents in education touches on much larger questions than improving reading and math scores. Citizens in our democracy must participate in the governing of public institutions. It is also destructive to the family to shut parents out of their children's experience in school. During the same period in which parent involvement has been on the decline, our children have been falling behind and dropping out in records numbers. This research strongly suggests that there is a connection.

We cannot afford to sequester parents on the periphery of the educational enterprise. Parent involvement is neither a quick fix nor a luxury; it is absolutely fundamental to a healthy system of public education.

[19]James Coleman and Thomas Hoffer, *Public and Private High Schools: The Impact of Communities* (New York: Basic Books, 1987).
[20]Personal correspondence, 18 September 1980.

10

A New "Generation" of Teacher Unionism

Charles T. Kerchner

The signs all around us indicate that a new generation of teacher unionism is emerging. Ongoing changes in the practices of administrators and teachers suggest a shifting of ideologies and the coming of a new approach to labor relations, with educational policy as its center. At issue is the willingness of organized teachers to assume part of the responsibility for winning increased respect for public education, improving the effectiveness of schools, and making teaching a profession.

Administrators and teachers are engaging in labor-relations practices that would be considered heresies under conventional belief systems: peer review, differentiation among teachers, standards setting, problem solving, and self-management. Following years of party-line solidarity, the memberships of union, management, and school-board organizations are vigorously debating what constitutes good labor relations. And, after years of relative quiet, the subject of teachers' unions is attracting renewed public interest.

Among the heretical practices, we find unionized teachers starting to take seriously the idea that teachers should evaluate other teachers. Under conventional ideology the idea that one member of a bargaining unit would evaluate another is a traitorous violation of the "solidarity" norm.

But since 1981 teachers in Toledo, Ohio, have actively engaged in peer evaluation for new teachers and in an intervention program for experienced teachers who are not performing adequately. Though this agreement remains controversial in many quarters, provisions for similar undertakings have found their way into statute in Ohio, and peer-review plans are under study by unions and managements as far away as Lompoc, Calif. In the new thinking, teacher solidarity means self-policing as well as self-protection.

According to the conventional ideology, responsibility for fixing school problems belongs to management. Decisions are management's prerogative; the less involvement with the union, the better, management believes. Labor accepts this turf division. From its standpoint, an offer to make decisions is sucker bait, an invitation to take the heat because management is too weak to make tough decisions. Besides, decisions are complex and messy, and getting teachers involved is a tough job that union officials would rather duck.

Now, in 27 school sites represented by the National Education Association, managers and teachers are engaged in joint planning, goal setting, and redefinition of teacher roles. In Hammond, Ind., members of the American Federation of Teachers bargaining unit are involved in a school-site management plan, and in New York City teachers have negotiated a contract allowing teachers and site administrators to waive work-rule restrictions in the citywide contract in order to restructure their schools.

In conventional labor ideology, the contract encompasses the relationship between union and school district. Although teachers' unions have always engaged in professional development through publications and workshops for members, their official relationship with the school district hinges on the union's standing as the legitimate representative of teacher self-interest through collective bargaining. While the onset of collective bargaining legitimated teacher self-interest and signaled the end to the suffering-servant mentality, the ideology of good-faith bargaining hardened opposition to teacher participation in educational policy.

However, in the emerging belief system, teachers' unions also have a right and a responsibility to speak for the public good. In Pittsburgh and Miami, unions are engaged in practices that "go beyond collective bargaining" into school improvement. In Petaluma and four other California districts, the union and management are establishing a new type of written contract, called a "policy trust agreement," in addition to their regular relationship.

These changes underscore the importance of ideology to labor relations and the extent to which change in unionism is driven by conflict over competing ideas of what unions should do. Labor and management belief systems have progressed through two distinct historical and organizational realities: the first centered around meet-and-confer relationships and the second around good-faith collective bargaining. My research, along with the evidence of recent events, suggests that a third generation of labor relations, with educational policy as its focus, is arriving now.

Because the battles are not simply tugs-of-war about who gets more or less, but ideological struggles over what is good and proper, periods of change between labor-relations generations are particularly tumultuous. The internal tension frequently experienced by national unions and management organizations are reflected in school districts as "radicals" of either the left or the right vie for attention and loyalty with the

Source: From Charles T. Kerchner, "A New 'Generation' of Teacher Unionism," *Education Week,* Volume VII, Number 17, January 20, 1989, pp. 36, 30. Reprinted with permission from *Education Week.* Volume VII, Number 17, January 20, 1989. Reprinted with permission from Charles T. Kerchner.

conventional wisdom. Conflict often becomes public, and in its settlement new leaders emerge: School-board members lose elections, superintendents are sacked, and union officers face defeat at the hands of the members they thought they understood.

It is easy to recall the organizing wars of the 1960's and 1970's as the ideological emphasis of teacher organization changed from participation and consultation through various meet-and-confer mechanisms to self-representation through collective bargaining resulting in written, enforceable contracts. Pitched battles were fought within the N.E.A. over whether collective bargaining was a legitimate undertaking for teachers. The old guard said it would cheapen the profession, and the Young Turks of the N.E.A. Urban Project countered that the current process was a failure. While the A.F.T. had no historic problems with explicit unionism, it had to resolve the battle between its revolutionary and pragmatic wings.

And in thousands of school districts across the country, teachers went through the process of acting out the then-radical notion that they had the right to speak for themselves.

The events we are witnessing now can be seen in this mirror of history. Representatives of the two national unions debate the wisdom and meaning of recent contractual changes, such as the Rochester career-stage plan. The National School Boards Association appoints a commission to study ways of promoting productive, harmonious relationships, but does so in language so provocative that the result is likely to be a clash of wills over unionism itself. U.S. Secretary of Education William J. Bennett castigates the N.E.A. for footdragging on reform issues, to which the N.E.A. replies that Secretary Bennett's idea isn't what it had in mind. Internally, the N.E.A. and the A.F.T. consider radically restructuring. In all these cases, the question being asked is not whether teachers have the right to an economic interest in their jobs, but how the energy and commitment of organized teachers can be brought to bear on problems of school reform.

Although the battle lines have not yet hardened, the struggle for teacher unionism in the 1990's is taking shape around three important issues in public education:

- How does public education retain popular support?
- How can union activity aid school effectiveness?
- How can teachers become employed professionals?

As public education's best-financed and organized interest group, unions play a pivotal role in developing support for public education. The N.E.A., in particular, is a lobbying nonpareil; its members are politically active in virtually every Congressional district in the country. But interest-group representation does not subsume educational politics. The larger perception that public schools are incapable of solving their problems breeds reform movements that either attempt remote control of the schools by close-order certification and testing or seek to disinvest in them by proposing vouchers and other mechanisms that would structurally alter the institution of education in the United States. Unions are hard pressed to come up with credible alternatives.

The next generation of labor relations also faces the problem of making schools effective places for learning. This means that labor, management, and the public must come to terms with a vastly broadened scope of interaction between organized teachers and their employers. Part of the compact that surrounds existing collective bargaining is an assertion that it is possible to cleave between the teachers' legitimate interests in their salaries and working conditions on the one hand and the educational policies of the school district on the other. Elaborate restrictions in the scope of bargaining were supposed to segregate bargaining from school policy.

Of course, nothing of the kind happened. Even in the most restrictive scope of bargaining, establishing the wage-and-salary schedule, transfer policy, and class size for a school district effectively accounts for the allocation of as much as 90 percent of the school's operating budget.

Savvy administrators and union leaders recognized this fact and developed side agreements. Some actually helped one another. But the explicit involvement of unions in school management, and the expectation that such involvement was a central role of unions, not a social service they performed for their members, was not publicly recognized until recently.

Finally, unions face the problem of redefining teaching as a profession. The next decade represents a unique opportunity that the grand hope that a teaching profession can be created will triumph over the grand illusion that one already exists. This decade's teaching-reform movement presages the organizational reform movement of the next. Moreover, it is now recognized that professionals can be employed for wages. Lawyers and physicians more and more commonly belong to large firms that face analogous problems in the clash between professional and bureaucratic authority systems.

For unions, solving the professionalism question means more than muscling control over state teacher-certification boards or winning a chair at the table where the national examination will be drafted. It requires that unions look seriously at the set of policies and practices that define teaching work within school districts. How is employed professionalism defined in school sites? What responsibility are teachers willing to take to define and enforce their own standards? What relationship does the union have to the behavior of teachers in the workplace?

The responses of the unions and management to these issues will significantly influence the shape of teaching in the next decade. As it is currently emerging, the increased involvement of unions in the determination of educational policy will place teachers in roles of greater responsibility: for the public's perception of their status, for the redefinition of their own work, and for the worth of their schools.

11

The Professionalizing of Teaching

A View from the Inside

The Capital Area School Development Association

It is generally agreed that professionals do have certain characteristics in common: the ability to control one's destiny, to employ one's individual judgment, and accept accountability for one's actions. Traditionally, teaching, while being a profession in name, has not been considered a true profession by many, including teachers themselves. Certainly many of the conditions under which teachers operate raise questions about the degree of professionalism they enjoy.

The public often perceives teachers as 180-day-a-year employees who enjoy summers and vacations "off." Teachers' unions, based on an industrial model that appears to be more concerned with starting and ending times than with truly professional issues, have also often contributed to the perception. Unions claim they have been pushed into this factory approach by administrators and boards that have, for many years, been unwilling to accept teachers as participants in the decision making process in schools. It is obvious that both unions and school district management must change if public and self perceptions are to change.

TEACHING IN THE POST-INDUSTRIAL AGE

The changes that need to occur will center around both the ways contracts are negotiated and what is included in them; however, probably the greatest changes must come in the day-to-day management and operation of schools. While recognizing that condition of employment issues such as salary and grievance procedures will continue to be part of the process, other ways for unions, administrators and boards to work together on subjects such as staff development and other professional topics need to be addressed. Schools must move away from the factory model to one that encourages participatory management by those involved. Teachers' unions can become more involved in issues dealing with teaching as a profession, for instance, by developing inservice programs, by heightening legislative awareness to the needs of the profession, and by policing their own members to insure that teachers are all highly qualified and capable and remain so throughout their tenure.

Teachers also need to be more directly involved in the decision making process, particularly in those areas that directly affect how they function in the classroom, such as curriculum, instructional activities, student concerns, and staff development activities. But it is essential that this involvement take place within a context of mutual trust that gives meaningful expression to the decision making process. This can be achieved by providing teachers with real opportunities to participate in activities designed to enhance the educational program. Committees of teachers with clearly established goals and objectives which identify advisory and decision making responsibilities in the overall mission are essential.

Accountability must then follow. Teachers have long recognized the need for accountability but have been understandably cautious about embracing it when they did not have control over how they function in schools. When this is achieved, teachers will welcome accountability.

NEW ROLES FOR ADMINISTRATORS

This approach will also require that school administrators at all levels examine the ways in which they function. They must move away from what is often a totally autocratic style, sometimes accompanied by *pro forma* committees, to one in which they serve more as coordinators and facilitators. All agree that administrators are necessary and desirable. Research reveals, however, that a change in leadership style is necessary to enhance their performance and effectiveness.

Within school buildings an atmosphere must exist that allows for and encourages shared decision making about those issues which affect both the process and the product of education. School district staff, also, must play a role in "opening up" education to the community and parents by encouraging partnerships and other methods of working together.

THE EGG CRATE SYNDROME

Isolationism is yet another inhibitor of the professionalizing of teaching. Most teachers spend most of their time in their own classrooms either working directly with students, planning activities, or other similar tasks. Little opportunity is provided for teachers to work together, to confer, or to participate in mutually beneficial activities. Opportunities must be provided that diminish the feeling of isolation. Grade level meetings, peer coaching teams, conference and visitation days both in house and outside the district,

Source: From The Capital Area School Development Association, "The Professionalizing of Teaching: A View from the Inside," *A Look at National Reports. A Report of the Select Seminar on Excellence in Education*, September 1987.

attendance at local, regional, state, and even national conferences are some ways to assist teachers in achieving the collegiality necessary to the professional.

But teachers are not isolated only from each other. They are also walled off from the community of which they should be a very vital part. Greater communication with the business community, including curriculum development activities and speaking to groups about schools and their programs, must also be encouraged. Schools are very much a part of the community in which they are located and, as such, must be both responsive to community needs and looked to for leadership in directing what schooling should occur.

THE CONSTANT NEED FOR IMPROVEMENT

Teachers, like all true professionals, must be provided with opportunities, not only to maintain skills, but to grow and develop those necessary to a constantly changing career. As more is learned from educational research about what works and what doesn't work in the classroom, and as state mandates and curriculum requirements mount, teachers need increasing opportunities to learn if they are to maintain, much less improve, their effectiveness. And teachers should have a primary role in directing these efforts.

But self improvement alone does not make a professional. True professionals have influence and control over the environment in which they work and opportunities to grow within that environment. Career paths must be established to provide educators opportunities to pursue a variety of activities designed to enhance the profession.

Those students entering teaching should begin the growth process by serving a paid internship under the direction of a mentor teacher. Both should be provided ample time to work together in order to insure that the intern experiences a full range of opportunities. A mentor teacher would be an individual with experience in the profession assigned to work with interns as they begin their careers. Experienced educators desiring to serve in this capacity should have not only the opportunity but also the time to do so. They should be relieved of some classroom responsibilities while mentoring but should resume them upon completion of the mentoring process. Thus, the position is not a rung on a separate career ladder but one that values the expert teacher in both the teaching and mentoring roles.

Another path which educators may choose is that of teacher trainer. These people work with teacher training institutions in preparing teachers. Among their activities are curriculum development, supervision of instruction using a clinical model, and other activities necessary to facilitate the teaching/learning process. Like mentor teachers, trainers would move back and forth between their classroom and training responsibilities.

THE PARAPROFESSIONAL

Another important characteristic of professionals is that they are freed from nonprofessional activities, thus making time available not only to concentrate on the professional act itself, whether filling a tooth or trying a case, but also for the preparation and renewal necessary to maintain growth in the profession. Teachers must be able to call upon paraprofessionals so that they are able to plan, to meet, to share, and to study, both collectively and individually. Support staff should be provided to free teachers from clerical duties, monitoring functions, and other non-teaching activities so that they may engage in more teacher/learner interactions, development activities, parent conferences, etc.

BECOMING PROFESSIONAL

Literally for centuries, teachers have been thought of—and have thought of themselves—as providers of a service at best, "dishing out" instruction to their "customers" in classrooms much as a waiter goes from booth to booth. This perception has been fostered by communities and school boards who may think of "English teacher" or "third grade teacher" as a generic unit; administrators who may see these same people as five-fifths of an instructional unit; and by teachers themselves who may think of themselves as having been trained in their youth (for all time) and then doing much the same thing year after year, with only the students and the salary step changing. And this perception has been further strengthened by union/management focus of concern on salary and working conditions rather than on professional issues.

If teaching is ever to be considered a true profession, major changes must occur not just in classrooms, schools, and communities, but in the minds of teachers themselves. Teachers must *behave* as professionals, both in and out of their classrooms, speaking positively and pridefully about teaching, the school, students and community.

Teaching still has a long way to go to achieve the status of a profession; however, there are definite signs that movement has begun in areas such as those noted above. The term, "professional," may soon be an authentic one that teachers can claim with pride.

12

Partnerships Between Teachers and Administrators

How "They" Became "We"

Albert Shanker

What kinds of roles should teachers and administrators assume at both the school and district levels? We can find an answer to this question, which focuses on what it is teachers and administrators *should* be doing, together and independently, by taking a look at some of the recent changes in American public education—changes that have revolutionized the way teachers teach and students learn across the country.

The changes have started with complaints about quality, leading to finger-pointing. The scenario in most school districts goes something like this: Teachers and their unions usually point at the school and central office administrators and/or the school board as the villains. To school administrators, the bad guys are the district administrators. To the district office, "they" are the school board members and superintendent, and they complete the circle by blaming the teachers' union. The direction of finger-pointing may vary, but in most places, placing blame is a lot more popular than working together—and forming partnerships—to solve school problems.

But this is not the modus operandi in Hammond, Indiana, an economically hard-hit steel town whose 25 schools serve 13,000 students. Because of the School Improvement Process (SIP) negotiated between the Hammond Teachers Federation and the Board of School Trustees, it's now "we" instead of the shadowy and threatened "they." Solving school problems is the shared responsibility of all those with a direct stake in the outcome: teachers, administrators, parents, community representatives, students, the union and school board.

The key concept driving SIP is school-site management. Each school has its SIP committee, or core team, made up of teachers, administrators, parents and students. Subcommittees, or "design teams," involve additional individuals, concerned about a particular school issue. Participants get intensive, ongoing training in communication and group dynamics and learn how to reach consensus on a problem.

It's the core team's job to develop a vision of excellence for its school. Then the design teams work to meet those objectives. Final decisions about school programs are made according to the philosophy that underlies the whole SIP system: Those who are affected by the decision, who are closest to it, who have expertise in the area, who will be responsible for carrying it out, who will be living with the result—those are the ones who should make the decision.

If all of this sounds like a huge effort, it is. Real professional authority involves real responsibility. Because the school staffs in Hammond, unlike most districts, know that their opinions and decisions count, they're eager to embrace that responsibility. And they are held accountable for the results.

As a result, teachers are clamoring for more knowledge to make informed judgments. They want research material on curriculum, school reorganization and teaching practice, the latest journals, books and workshops. They want to know what other districts have tried, what works and what doesn't. Under the old management system, their knowledge, expertise and ideas didn't count. Now that it does, there has been an explosion of creative ideas: reorganized school days and semesters, a revamped kindergarten program, mentor peer evaluation programs, new homework and student attendance policies, a transitional first grade—and a lot more new, innovative programs in the works.

Hammond Teachers Federation President Patrick O'Rourke said, in a recent *American Educator* article, "Now that SIP has been in a few schools for a couple of years and in all schools since September 1985, SIP committees are moving into more and more areas of decision making. I was recently at a meeting of SIP chairpersons where the ideas—and desire to share ideas—were flying left and right." (*American Educator,* Spring, 1987).

Many key partners share the credit for Hammond's success. SIP began as a pilot project assisted by the Charles Kettering Foundation and the Eli Lilly Endowment. The driving forces expanding SIP to the whole school system were Patrick O'Rourke, President of the Hammond Teachers Federation, and David Kickson, the Superintendent of Schools. Their dynamism and leadership coupled with the farsighted attitude of the school board have put Hammond on the educational map.

To those who fear shared decision-making and who say management by committee can never work, the message from Hammond is that the school system hasn't fallen apart. Things are getting better, teacher morale has soared and new ideas are taking hold. Instead of pointing fingers, educators there are joining teachers' hands to help students. History might call it the Great Hammond Pronoun Shift, turning "They won't let us," into "We can do it!"

Source: From Albert Shanker, "Partnerships Between Teachers and Administrators: How 'They' Became 'We'," *Kappa Delta Pi,* Volume 24, Number 3, Spring 1988, pp. 70–73. Printed by permission of Kappa Delta Pi, An International Honor Society in Education.

PART TWO

School and Society

As the decade of the nineties closes out this century, it brings with it a new set of circumstances for the schools of both the current time period and the decades to come in the twenty-first century. Societal diversity has achieved recognition in the culture of the United States. We no longer can look at American culture as the "melting pot" or as preparation for acculturation. Cultural pluralism is the norm as the minority populations of the United States expand their population base with larger families and increased numbers as a result of immigration. Advances in medicine and nutrition have led to longer life spans for all of the population and at the same time have curtailed mortality rates among young children. In addition to these kinds of population demographics, the complexities of value changes and the conflict that accompanies these changes have become regularly occurring phenomena associated with population change. Through all of these societal changes, the school remains the stable social institution that can and does adjust its mission and output to accommodate these changes and expectations.

The teacher has become the filter for the learner as he or she prepares to deal with these changes in the twenty-first century. In order to adequately assist the learner, the teacher, more than ever before, has a greater responsibility to grasp and understand changes in society, interpret them in meaningful ways for the learner, and provide school experiences that aid the learner in his or her preparation to live in a society of cultural diversity. Part II of this text introduces the prospective teacher to a collage of societal issues and their impacts on both the school and the life of the teacher. Further, the articles selected for this part collectively depict the cultural diversity of the society as it must be recognized and attended to if this nation is to continue to grow.

The classrooms of today and tomorrow are filled with a growing assortment of values as they relate to the diversity of the student body. The teacher can no longer just be concerned with the mainstream of a value structure but must also address the "salad bowl" differences as described by James Banks. In "Accepting Others' Values in the Classroom: An Important Difference," Jonathan W. Lambert builds a strong case for the teacher's accepting differing values in the classroom. How the teacher accepts these value differences determines the classroom environment, which in turn has a pronounced effect on the self-concept development of the learner.

Carol Goodstein presents a case for the teaching of race relations in the home and the school in "Educating the Children About Race Relations: The Role of Teachers and Parents." Children come to school with a home-based set of attitudes and perceptions about race relations. The school cannot, by itself, change stereotyped learner attitudes toward race relations. It can, however, in addition to the multicultural offerings in the school, work with parents in suggesting home-based experiences that will lead to greater learner acceptance of cultural differences.

Culture is learned. In "Unstated Features of the Cultural Context of Learning," Edward T. Hall presents a model for examining the cultural differences among ethnic and racial groups. His model addresses teacher classroom performances that take into account work and activity patterns in the learning environment, differences in listening behaviors, individual and peer pressure behaviors, and levels of voice differences in teachers' encounters with learners. He concludes with a set of recommendations for the teacher in training or in practice; these recommendations are intended to assist the teacher in countering what is best described as the bureaucracy culture which is so dominant in the schools of the nation.

The wave of reform that characterized the 1980s had little effect on the schooling of youth. The numerous commission reports did little more than point fingers at schools, accusing the educational establishment of failure. In her essay "Mission Not Accomplished: Education Reform in Retrospect," Mary Hatwood Futrell, past president of the National Education Association, examines the reform movement and concludes that the majority of these reports missed the mark as to what was and is the real problem in education. She offers a shift in the reform movement toward the need to prepare the whole child and builds a case for schooling, not to train students to serve the purposes of others, but to acquire the capacity to question the purposes of others.

The culture of the school dictates the governance issues that direct the daily lives of teachers and students. The rallying cry of the late 1980s and the 1990s has been directed toward teacher empowerment. Kofi Lomotey and Austin D. Swanson examine urban and rural schools, discuss the current state of governance practices in those schools, and offer questions and solutions for improved governance in their article, "Urban and Rural Schools Research: Implications for School Governance." How these kinds of issues are implemented will determine the changing culture of the school and the attitudes that professional staff have toward the program for students.

The sociological problems of the school, varied by type and intensity with different community schools, are examined here in a collage fashion. Although they represent different viewpoints on the issues presented, the prospective teacher can acquire the flavor of issues that he or she must be prepared to deal with during the next decade. In "Racism and the Education of Young Children," James P. Comer presents a thesis on racism in education and its beginning roots in the home. The significance of this article lies in the suggestions for teachers working in a racist society that is growing in diversity by leaps and bounds. Dropout problems still plague learners of low socio-economic status and many of these students come from culturally diverse minority groups. The Native American Indian, for example, experiences the lowest of socio-economic status and also has the highest dropout rate. In "Protecting the Future: A Successful Alternative Program for Dropout Prevention," Larry D. Dorrell presents a program that has experienced moderate success in Mexico, Missouri.

Jonathan Kozol describes what he calls "The New Untouchables" in his article about poor and homeless children. These students in many of our large urban centers are rapidly acquiring the characteristics of illiterates because of a lack of adequate school funding and programs and are caught in a socio-economic web that keeps them from becoming potentially productive members of the society. The number of homeless students in the large urban and suburban centers continues to grow despite the passage of the McKinney Homeless Assistance Act (P.L. 100-77) of 1987. E. Anne Eddowes and John R. Haranitz offer a series of suggestions for working with these students in day care centers, Head Start programs, and the regular programs of the public schools in their essay "Educating Children of the Homeless."

Children at risk and the latchkey lonely child are easily identified as potential dropouts and/or social behavior problems for the school. Jane Brooks Moskowitz and Shirley J. O'Brien discuss the needs of these children and offer program development activities that can be utilized by the school in their respective essays, "A Cry for Help: Children at Risk" and " 'Only the Lonely': The Latchkey Child." As they suggest, there are a variety of activities for both home and school that the school can use to help parents meet the immediate needs of these children.

Many federal intervention efforts have led to compensatory programs supported by the federal government or mounted solely by state mandates and local school districts. A number of the federal mandates for integration of school programs led to the creation of magnet school efforts to meet that need. However, the concept of magnet schools for integration purposes has also led to other magnet school activities to meet the special needs of a particular group of students. One such effort is described in "A Magnet School for the Creative Arts," by Allen Raymond. This New Orleans school is highlighted by the efforts of a dedicated school staff that wants to provide some difference in children's learning.

Special programs for language-minority children, Native American Indian youth, and special education children can again be traced to the federal government's influence in creating the need for compensatory programs for learners with unique needs. In "Educating Language-Minority Children: Challenges and Opportunities," Barbara T. Bowman describes three such programs and gives recommendations for working with language-minority children; in "The Styles of Learning are Different, but the Teaching is Just the Same: Suggestions for Teachers of American Indian Youth," Karen Swisher and Donna Deyhle discuss teaching this population; and in "Computers for Special Populations," Sheila H. Feichtner offers suggestions for using the computer with special education children. The attention given to special groups of students by the authors of these articles provides needed dialogue for teachers who will encounter many different types of learners in their classrooms.

13

Accepting Others' Values in the Classroom

An Important Difference

Jonathan W. Lambert

The economic, social and political dimensions of contemporary life interact constantly. The trade imbalance and the results of surveys have shown that Americans are woefully uninformed about the rest of the world. Senator Fulbright stated in *Newsweek* magazine a decade ago that, in relation to the rest of the developed world's population, Americans are "culturally myopic." Unfortunately, the statement remains true.

The world impinges upon our consciousness, not only through the number of foreign-made products that surround us, but through the myriad of non-English language expressions that have been incorporated into our vernacular. As educators we are faced daily with evidence of the interrelationship of the world community in the heterogeneity of our classroom.

The United States is a nation of immigrants. From its beginnings, through the immigration of Europeans around the turn of this century, to the current influx of Caribbean and Asian peoples, the population of this nation has reflected diverse cultures, religions, and ethnic groups. Early in this century, as immigration into the U.S. increased, public education was charged with the responsibility to teach Anglo-American values and behaviors to newly arrived, potential citizens (Cubberley 1909; 1919). Israel Zangwill's play of 1908, *The Melting Pot,* not only symbolized the impetus toward synthesis but reflected a mainstream social theory that prevailed for more than half a century.

Today the concept of the melting pot has been replaced with what can be referred to as "the salad bowl" (Banks 1977). It is now acceptable to maintain an ethnic group membership and to participate in the larger group culture of the United States. This change in emphasis redefines the socialization task of the educational process. This redefinition creates a new challenge for the professional educator, one that holds tremendous potential for curriculum enrichment and social learning. Students enter the American public school system representing virtually every nationality, ethnic group, and religion of the world. Foreign nationals residing in the United States, newly arrived permanent residents, and first- and second-generation citizens all bring with them the wealth and depth of a cultural heritage that does not necessarily conform to American culture. These students may arrive with differing expectations about curriculum, teaching-learning styles, and appropriate classroom behavior. The functioning of these students in the educational milieu is directly related to the degree of comfort they feel when attempting to participate in classroom learning activities. Here the teacher can be the key.

A major task of the classroom teacher is to develop and maintain a classroom environment that addresses order and discipline, structure, teaching modalities, curriculum content, and classroom ambiance. A major aspect of the ambiance found within a classroom has to do with comfort, not only the creature comforts of desk, chair, heat, windows, and wall coverings but psychological comfort. The degree of psychological comfort each pupil feels in the teaching environment has a direct influence on his or her participation in the teaching-learning situation.

Psychological comfort, to a great extent, is directly related to the perception of threat to one's "self," the core of who one feels that he or she is. This self-concept acts as the center of one's phenomenological world, by which all external things are measured and judged. When one perceives a situation as hostile (a threat to an aspect of the self-image), defenses are raised, and these become psychological barriers between the self and the perceived threat. In a classroom in which there are students from a variety of cultures, the potential for psychological discomfort is high.

Acceptance shapes the learning environment into a place in which the culturally different student can participate. Since the teacher determines what is allowable and acceptable within the classroom, he or she can establish an atmosphere of acceptance: The student who, in response to a question, suggests that there are six cardinal directions (most Americans would say four: north, south, east, and west) might not be wrong. A majority of the people of the world understand six cardinal directions: north, south, east, west, up, and down.

The acceptance of cultural pluralism within the educational mission emphasizes student awareness of cultural and ethnic alternatives. It is important that our teaching

Source: The Clearing House, Volume 62, pp. 273–274, February 1989. Reprinted with permission of the Helen Dwight Reid Educational Foundation. Published by Heldref Publications, 4000 Albemarle St., N.W., Washington, D.C. 20016.

professionals, especially those working in public education, understand that the cultural background of some students has imbued them with ideas and understandings that are different, not wrong.

In addition to acknowledging other ways of looking at facts and ideas, the teacher should understand that social customs might affect the classroom learning process. Interpersonal behavioral taboos can create tensions between teacher and student. Many cultures of Southeast Asia, for example, consider the head to be sacrosanct. A friendly pat on the head by the teacher can be very disquieting to a student. Many cultures consider it taboo to look directly at someone who is older or of greater authority. Thus a student may be uncomfortable looking at the teacher when addressed. These differences can lead to tension.

It is not the intention of this author to suggest that the values and characteristics of American society be eliminated from the classroom, but rather to recognize that American culture is an amalgamation of many world cultures. It is not necessary to reject one's ethnicity or heritage to "fit-in" in America today. Yet it is important that teachers not lose sight of the task of teaching the skills, information, and processes necessary for successful integration into contemporary American society. Supporting the culturally different student not only enriches that student's opportunity to learn, but enhances learning for the native-born student as a global citizen.

The goal of a teacher is to maximize the learning experience of each student, to assist each in recognizing and building his or her potential. As a professional educator, one must work to develop a classroom atmosphere that encourages participation by all students, while assisting them to learn the nuances of American culture. The development of an intercultural classroom environment promises learning for all students and for the teacher.

14

Educating the Children About Race Relations

The Role of Teachers and Parents

Carol Goodstein

April 4, 1968: "Make Room for Father" made room for a special broadcast—Martin Luther King Jr. had been assassinated. I was in fifth grade. At that time his dream was not a part of my curriculum. I learned the basics from Walter Cronkite.

Schools aren't much different today. For the past twenty years they've been abdicating their responsibility to teach students the skills needed to survive in an increasingly pluralistic society.

The neglect has spawned a new wave of racism and violence—Howard Beach, Bensonhurst, Central Park. The police department reports that 70% of all bias incidents in New York City are committed by people under 19, people with no memory of the civil rights struggle. It's not just an issue of black versus white; the victims are Jews, Asians, Hispanics, etc. All told, since 1980, American minority groups have been the target of over 5,000 hate crimes, according to the U.S. Department of Justice.

Within days of Yusuf Hawkins' death, ABC, CBS, and NBC ran specials on the troubled state of race relations. New York endorsed a black mayoral candidate and the public schools announced the introduction of $1 million multicultural curriculum—encouraging news, but then so was integration.

"I think prejudice is something that one has to work on almost forever," says Augustus Trowbridge, director of the Manhattan Country School. "If you relax on those questions, the status quo begins to creep into the attitudes of kids and it's very easy to revert to stereotypic views."

Twenty-four years ago, in an effort to fulfill Martin Luther King's dream, Trowbridge founded New York's only "realistically" integrated private elementary school. In 1966, the average black and Hispanic population enrolled in New York private schools was 3%. He insisted on 30% and today, the student body at Manhattan Country is 50% white; 50% minority, compared with 12.6% in private schools nationally.

Unfortunately, Trowbridge has been in the minority among educators to emphasize race relations in the curriculum. The schools in fact, by reinforcing racial stereotyping, perpetuate racism. Dr. Kenneth B. Clark, the psychologist and New York State regent emeritus whose famous doll study influenced the Supreme Court ruling on school desegregation is pointed in his criticism of the education system; "I think the education decision-makers are either skirting the issue of training American children to respect diversity or are accessories in the perpetuation of racism and segregation in the schools...they seem to permit our children to remain illiterate socially."

Cognitively, bias can be understood as a byproduct of the mind's bent toward categorization. We naturally seek to simplify chaos by fitting like experiences or people into groups.

Once we establish mental categories, we unconsciously seek to support the beliefs and assumptions underlying them—despite evidence to the contrary. In gender for example, it's been found that even little girls who have direct experience with women doctors still connect the career with men—the same is true with racial stereotypes. Once stereotypes are formed, it's difficult to overcome them.

Children become aware of race differences as young as three and four years old. Within a couple of years, they're aware that society places a value on these differences.

Psychologists do not advocate "colorblindness"; instead they suggest recognizing and addressing cultural and ethnic differences in order to inculcate a sense of pride in children.

Ideally, the goal is to build self-esteem by making each child feel special and unique. "In a classroom, we create an environment where we affirm every child and value them as people and for their culture," explains Phyllis Kietha Gagnier, a native American teacher and trainer with bias-awareness programs. "On top of that we create a community in that classroom." She points out that among American Indians, those with the lowest incidence of alcohol, drug abuse and violent behavior are those who have both assimilated and kept their culture.

Psychologists have found that in mixed-race schools, students with the least prejudice and the most mixed-race friends are members of sports teams and bands. Likewise, in the classroom, one of the most successful methods for promoting racial harmony is to divide students into learning teams where, regardless of their race or ethnicity, they cooperate for a common goal. This approach has proven successful in Is-

Source: From Carol Goodstein, "Educating the Children About Race Relations: The Role of Teachers and Parents," *Crisis*, Volume 96, November 1989, pp. 25, 45. Reprinted with permission from the publisher.

rael between students of middle Eastern and European descent, in Canada between Canadians and immigrants and in California between Hispanic and non-Hispanic students.

As the number of Asian and Latin American immigrants in the U.S. grows, children are not only confronted with race differences, but with language and cultural differences, as well. By the year 2000 children of color will be the majority in 53 of the country's largest cities.

"If there were a million me's, this world would come to an end," observed one fifth-grade student.

"It's always better to have more than one religion—you learn other ways," said another.

"My friend May is Chinese. You have to take off your shoes and sit on tatami mats in her house—it's weird."

"I wouldn't consider that weird; you're just not used to it."

Children not only need social skills to function together in a society; they're curious about one another in a classroom. On the whole, schools have not yet found a successful means of coming to terms with pluralistic classrooms—they've adopted tokenisms—Black History month and Pan American Day—they're not talking about kids in the classroom.

In New York State a task force was recently appointed to assess curriculum materials and determine whether they provide sound education in a pluralistic society. Hazel Dukes, president of the New York Conference of NAACP Branches and task force chair, concluded that "the various contributions of the African-Americans, the Asian-Americans, the Puerto Rican/Latinos and the Native Americans have been systematically distorted, marginalized or omitted."

Furthermore, they concluded, just as Dr. Clark had 35 years earlier, that all children suffer from the effects of negative characterizations of minorities.

In New York City where 80% of the public school students are black or Hispanic, a multi-cultural program was introduced this past fall. It has four broad themes: equality; culture and diversity; migration and immigration, and contributions by ethnic groups. Although it's too soon to assess the results, teachers have given it a mixed reception. They feel that no matter what they do, children's feelings about race are largely influenced by their parents.

Child psychiatrist Dr. Alvin Poussaint, offers a few guidelines for parents: he recommends parents take every opportunity to educate their kids without frightening them. "Parents have to be ready to answer their children's questions intelligently and on a level that they can understand without making them fearful, but giving them a balanced answer." For example, if a black child hears news on TV and asks, "Why don't they let black people vote in South Africa?", parents may respond by explaining: "A lot of the whites in South Africa and the people in power don't want blacks to vote and they won't allow them and it's wrong." You can also point out that there are whites who also know it's wrong and are working for change. "You take a moral stand and be very clear about it," suggests Dr. Poussaint.

"Other than explaining, black parents should be raising their kids to feel a sense of comfortableness in being black—in the stories you read to them, the kinds of dolls you buy for them and the sense of self-esteem that you give them...If black parents just go along with what the culture presents to black children, then the black kids are going to feel that white people are powerful, strong, beautiful and better, and that black people are not. All the fairy tales are about white people."

Psychologists also encourage what they term "equal status contact"; getting kids to interact with their socioeconomic equals. Dr. Darlene Hopson, a clinical psychologist in Middletown, CT, explains that one of the drawbacks to bussing for example, is that it introduces kids into a community where they have a lower status. "If white kids see black kids who are so-called lower class, then they're going to assume that most black people are that way." She suggests extracurricular activities; ballet classes, karate classes, and cultural events where children are more likely to come into contact with others from equal status backgrounds.

No matter how well parents and schools educate children, given the nature of our society, at some time they're likely to encounter racism.

"We were in New Jersey at the train station and we were waiting for a taxi," recalls a fifth-grade student. "The taxi driver said he wouldn't take black people. My parents got upset and called another taxi service."

"I would be real mad and then I would write down the taxi cab's number and report him," volunteered a classmate.

Hopson would agree. "I think that children need to see you can be assertive and even if it doesn't get you justice, at least you know that you've made the attempt. And sometimes it does get you justice."

To defend against a verbal assault, Hopson recommends that children use clear, direct and assertive responses; "I don't like it when you say that" and "I wish you would stop calling me names."

There are times however, when children themselves know best how to cope with racism. Every day a black child brought milk to drink with his lunch and every day a white child said to him, "You shouldn't be drinking that, you should drink chocolate milk." The children laughed and the black boy tried defending himself but to no avail. One day, the black child turned to the white child and said, "I don't need to drink chocolate milk—you do—and then you wouldn't need the sun to get dark," and the white boy left him alone.

The child's response was effective because he had a strong sense of self. In the next twenty years, while the institutions are administering their studies, assessing their programs and sorting through their reams of paperwork, individuals can begin to improve race relations by positively affirming, valuing and respecting every individual child.

15

Unstated Features of the Cultural Context of Learning

Edward T. Hall

Some individuals seem to be able to make the best of the worst, but others do just the opposite. In between these two groups, there is a large mass of people for whom what we do can make a difference. Such questions as why some people cannot be kept down, why some are curious and others are not, or why some have a strong drive to learn while others are difficult to motivate remain unanswered. Although the problems faced in the world today are as great as those of any other periods in history, the problem of education is one of the most exasperating in its complexity and proportions. There is no doubt that a world education crisis exists. In spite of this rather stark picture, there do appear to be places where something can be accomplished, some leads that should be followed, and even a few points that are not widely known yet deserve attention. It is to these last that I wish to address myself.

Before I go any further, however, I should mention one thing. In considering education in the intercultural or inter-ethnic context, it is noticeable that much that is written on this subject focuses the attention on the relative accessibility of education to different groups in the world's nation states. In other words, the concern is primarily with who gets educated and *why* or *why not*. The quality of education is measured by the standards of the dominant society, and analyzed in units of the local currency—who gets how much of the standardized educational pie? That these are important, in fact vital, considerations cannot be denied. Nevertheless, this approach sidesteps the equally important issue of the role of education in the formation of ethnic identity. Few people have any notion of how little is really known about the microcultural details of how learning proceeds—the implicit cultural matrix of learning—in different cultures. It is the impact of these microcultural details which I wish to discuss as they contribute to the formation of attitudes in early life. The situation I have spent my life observing is that of the interface between cultures.

MICROCULTURE AND EDUCATION

Immediately following WWII I found myself on the Atoll of Truk as an anthropologist whose task it was to help ease the transition between the former Japanese administration of the islands and that of the Americans. In addition, I felt it my duty to do what I could to bridge the gap between my own culture and that of the Trukese. This was only one of a number of such missions during a long and rather active lifetime. And it is sad to report that while *I* have learned a great deal in the process, my luck in changing the mental habits of my countrymen and women, particularly those who were actively involved with non American-European peoples, has been somewhat less than I would have hoped for. However, my relationship with the Trukese was fruitful and informative because I had formed a close friendship with the Atoll Chief Artie Moses, who used me as a channel of communication to my own government. Trukese expectations were very simple and direct. They were not asking for economic help or technical assistance. What they did want was *education* for their children. Good schools were at the top of their list of priorities. In the course of a half a century of work at the interface between cultures I have found these sentiments consistent for all groups I have had anything to do with. When I worked with the Navajo and the Hopi in the early thirties, I learned that two of my friends, Clare G., a Navajo, and Byron Adams, a Hopi, had run away *to* school as children!

It seems surprising, given the consistent aspiration of all people for *better* education, that the record for public education in the United States has been eroding rapidly, to a point that our schools are now acknowledged to be in a state of virtual collapse. So what is wrong? What can be learned from the study of other cultures, from interface studies, and from microanthropology?[1]

My approach has always been to start by taking a good look at the organism itself, beginning with the question: What is known about the human species in the context of our discussion?[2]

1) Physiologically our species is a learning organism. All one needs to do is to take a look at the size of our brain.[3]
2) One of the first—and I must also say one of the few—things on which anthropologists agree is that our species put its adaptive eggs in the learning basket. Culture is our medium, and culture is first, last, and always, *learned*.
3) It is a common assumption among American-European educators that children must be "motivated" to learn, i.e., offered inducements and bribes to learn. In this these educators are patently wrong—otherwise, how

Source: From Edward T. Hall, "Unstated Features of the Cultural Context of Learning," *The Educational Forum*, Volume 54, Fall 1989, pp. 21–34. Printed by permission of Kappa Delta Pi, An International Honor Society in Education.

is it possible to explain the universal acquisition of both language and microculture with enthusiasm and alacrity? As a matter of fact, while it is not uncommon to find children who do not always like school, young people as a whole love to learn and, when the drive to learn ceases, that is a message to be taken seriously, because it signifies that there is little left in life to hold one on this earth. My own view on this matter is that the learning drive is on a par with the sexual drive. Related in a mysterious and poorly understood way to sex, the learning drive is as varied in its strength as the sexual drive. That is, there appear to be strong and weak learners independent of intelligence. This point is not clearly recognized by those responsible for our school systems, who seem to expect that *all* students are *equally* involved in this remarkable process.

4) According to my colleague Professor Washburn, primates (which include *Homo sapiens*) learn best from their peers.[4] Other studies of warm-blooded animals (including primates) reveal that there is what appears to the American-European cultures an inordinate amount of play associated with the learning of basic survival skills. Perhaps this is one of the places where the American-European educators, being captives of their own culture, stray. Play is something that has its origins inside the organism and that is its *own* reward.[5]

So what else is there, of a more tangible or dramatic nature, to explain the poor showing of American-European education? What is known about the intercultural side of this equation? And is there a contribution that someone like myself can make to the understanding of this process? As is frequently the case in matters of this sort, the most compelling examples frequently are found right under one's nose in one's own back yard. My case is no exception. New Mexico is inhabited by three populations with quite different origins, each with its own language and culture: the Native American Pueblo Indians, the Hispanic Americans, and the Anglo Americans. (There are others, of course, but the numbers are not significant at this time.) The three listed provide a living laboratory that generates a wealth of information for those willing to keep their eyes and ears open.

Bernalillo County schools, for example, serve a large population of Indian students from the nearby pueblos of Santo Domingo, Cochiti, Sandia, San Felipe, Zia, and Santa Ana. There has been some difficulty on the part of educators, even when well motivated, to know what is best for Indians. There are no integrative frames, no acceptable models that bridge the two systems. Recently, at the behest of the governing members of the Pueblos, the Pueblo religious calendar of ceremonies (which require the attendance of virtually everyone in the pueblo) has been integrated with the school calendar. Such an obvious matter hardly required the attention of a specialist. For years, American-European educators have tried to cope with an exodus of Indians from the classroom for a series of important mid-winter ceremonies that occur immediately following the Christmas holidays. For years, American-European educators have clung to a culturally biased school calendar and complained about Pueblo non-participation!

A much more serious problem, which is a matter of record, is that the performance of Native American students is equal to, or better than, that of the other two groups for the first four to six grades. At that point, Native American performance decays rapidly. Until now, there has been no satisfactory explanation. I say "until now" because there *is* an explanation that makes sense to the Indians and makes sense to me in terms of my theories of information processing and storage in different cultures. The explanation is that the school at this point is destroying the unity and integrity of the Indian child's world.[6] Because the conceptual frame is unfamiliar, however, this explanation does not make enough sense for the average American-European educators to do anything with. That is, what seems quite real to one side of this equation is simply an "idea" to the other.

CONTEXT, INFORMATION, AND MEANING

In order to "explain" the explanation, I must digress a minute and talk about some of my most recent work at the interface among such cultures as the American, Japanese, French, and German. This has been a five-year study within all of these cultures, and my partner, Mildred Reed Hall, and I interviewed people with seven or more years' business experience.[7] The study itself originated with a French businessman who found some of my ideas helpful in coping with his own reading of German culture. Mr. Chandel (not his real name) quickly recognized that "high and low context information processing" was not just an idea but a "fact of life" to any Frenchmen working with Germans. These observations are reported in two of my recent books, *Beyond Culture* and *The Dance of Life*.[8] In high context communication, most of the information is stored in the memory of the individuals so that very little is transmitted. In contrast, low context communications are those in which virtually nothing can be taken for granted and in which most of the information is in the transmitted message.

Typical high context situations are found in the communicative patterns of monozygotic (identical) twins, best friends from childhood, and couples who have been married for 25 or more years. Low context situations are found in U.S. legal institutions, government regulations, technology, and computer programming. Low context cultures are those in which there is a widely-shared assumption—and behavior to support that assumption—that the amount of stored knowledge on the part of one's interlocutor is minimal. That is, there is a need to tell everybody everything in great detail (this applies particularly to instructions). An example would be that when one asks directions on how to reach the Four Seasons Hotel in Hamburg, one's informant is not likely to stop at simply providing directions but will also provide gratuitous instructions concerning such matters as being sure to wait for the traffic light to turn green when crossing the intersection near the hotel.

High context cultures like the French in their daily life (but not their intellectual life) take it for granted that their interlocutors will automatically "know" the essentials (even if it is clear that one does not.) In our research we were given examples of Germans who were hired by a French firm and fired a year later because they did not perform. No one told them what to do! The French assumed they would know what to do and the Germans assumed that they would be told what to do![9] In very high context cultures like the Pueblo Indian culture of New Mexico, not only is one expected to know, but if one does not, one is *not* supposed to ask questions. If there is a problem, one is supposed to know what the problem is all about. If one does not have the situation in hand, it is prima facie evidence that one is an outsider and therefore not entitled to know. In matters of this sort, problem solving across cultural lines can become complex.

The principal point to remember concerning high and low context communication is that a considerable part of the message is already encoded in the receiver and that the message itself is frequently little more than an elaborate "releaser." However, one of the significant variables from culture to culture is the *ratio of stored information to transmitted information, both of which must be combined to produce something we call "meaning."* The following figure summarizes the situation.

Furthermore, shifts in the level of context are *meta communications,* which indicate shifts in relationship (e.g., from warm to cool and vice versa). The result is that high context individuals operating in low context cultures constantly feel put down (a problem with many minority individuals in American-European situations). It was one of our French participants who finally realized what bothered him most about the Germans was, as he expressed it, "They were constantly low contexting me. But then after I read what you said I could see that there was nothing personal in it. They did it to each other!"

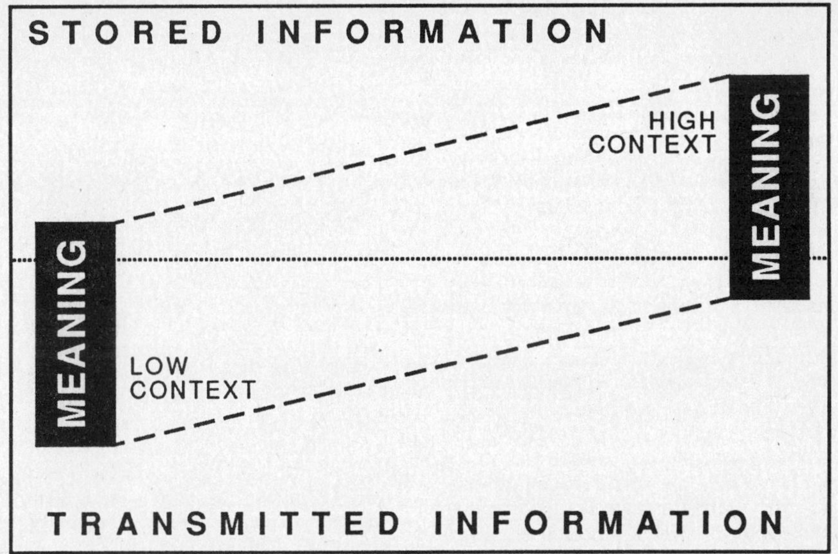

Now, it was a combination of early experiences with the Pueblo and the Navajo Indians, and later repeated contact with the Japanese, that taught me that the two ends of the context scale approached information in very different ways.[10] These different approaches have a deep and abiding effect on the educational process, and they are related to high and low context communicating. Not everyone arrives at "meaning" in an event in the same way. Beginning with the Gutenberg revolution, the Northern European contingent of American-European cultures began to build meaning very much in the way in which one builds a house, a piece of furniture, an organization, an automobile, or a weapon. It appears that Marshall McLuhan was on the right track, that is, meaning is something that is assembled from parts, like words which are themselves meaningful. The meaning of an utterance changes with the selection of the parts as well as their arrangement: "The man bit the dog" vs. "The dog bit the man." This principle is a function of selection and order,[11] and seems to apply to virtually every part of our lives. While there are all sorts of fancy terms that one could apply to this process, the "building block" approach to meaning is descriptive as well as simple.

In sharp contrast, high context peoples like the Pueblo, many of Africa's indigenous cultures, the Japanese, and apparently the Russians, do not construct meaning in their daily lives so much as they "extract it" from the environment and the situation. That is, they inhabit a "sea of information" that is widely shared. This insight would explain the Japanese antipathy to Western logic.[12] The "sea of information" group lives in a unified, very high context world in which all or most of the parts interrelate to make the environment meaningful. It is this fact that has proved to be one of the major (but hidden) stumbling blocks at the interface between American-European education and the culture of my friends, the Pueblo Indians of New Mexico.

You will recall that the Native American in New Mexico did as well or better than whites in the same schools up to the fourth, fifth and sixth grades. The question was, "What then changed?" I discussed this with Gregory Cajete, an educator from Santa Clara Pueblo. He is in the process of putting together a curriculum adapted to the high context "sea of information" world in which Indian children live. I must admit that it came as no surprise when he said: "But, of course, it's a matter of context. When the Indian children had to leave the 'home room' where they were all together with one teacher and take separate subjects with different teachers, the trouble began. All those different teachers held different views. They taught differently, they treated the students differently. They arranged their subjects differently. That's when the world started to come apart." Once this process begins it is apparently irreversible. Like Humpty Dumpty in the nursery rhyme, "All the King's horses and all the King's men could never put Humpty Dumpty together again." A half century's experience in interface research has convinced me that it is matters of this sort—matters of unconscious microculture—that make it so difficult for human beings to carry on meaningful discourses in complex and important fields like education.

SUBTLE YET POWERFUL

What I have just described, much too briefly, is simply a way of talking and thinking about things—a model if you will. It is a model that has enabled me and others of widely divergent backgrounds to relate some things which we were previously not able to include in a single frame. Of course, there are other models and other subjects equally important, equally subtle, and equally difficult to come to grips with. A partial, very incomplete list of such important microcultural topics would include:

1. Rhythm patterns ranging from those at the kinesic level in the classroom, to work and activity patterns for the day, month, and year.[13]

2. Differences in listening behavior that signal attention and deference.

3. Group pressures that result in reluctance on the part of the individual to turn out any performance that exceeds those of the group, a case that is exemplified by many of the rural and ethnic Spanish-Americans in New Mexico.

4. Differences in accepted voice level and kinesics on the part of teachers. At one time, Navajos listening to teachers shouting at children in the Farmington area took their children out of school. The school superintendent could not discover why. When asked, Navajo mothers were evasive. The reason was clear enough except that the Navajo had little luck communicating their idea of proper behavior to the American-European educators. Some rather subtle research revealed what the Navajo parents saw and heard in the Farmington school. Viewed through Navajo eyes and appraised by the standard norms of Navajo behavior, the teachers came across as "deranged." What was worse, the teachers came across as hating the children. Admittedly, a few teachers were prejudiced against Indians, but that is not what we are talking about. Almost without exception, the white teachers all acted the same way that signaled derangement and hate in Navajo behavior codes. This was because the Navajos only raise their voices and shouted if they were either crazy or about to enter that state as a consequence of intense rage. It should be noted in this context that the conversational style of the Navajo includes a voice that is low pitched and soft in comparison to white speech.

There is much more here, of course. Among Navajos the direct gaze is used to punish children. Also, at that time the name was never used as a means of direct address. These two seemingly trivial culture patterns represented hidden reefs in the intercultural sea on which the fragile craft, "Education," frequently floundered. Teachers would ask the children their names and the children, being embarrassed at such outlandish behavior on the part of adults, would hang their heads. At which point, the teachers got impatient because they were getting nowhere, and shouted "Look at me!" or even worse, "Look me in the eye!"[14]

Years later, the gifted father and son team, John and Malcolm Collier, recorded on film the behavior of teachers and children in Eskimo and West Coast Native American classrooms using three different contexts: white teachers, Native American teachers trained in white education schools, and Native American teachers without training in white schools. These films were later carefully studied, using time-motion analyzers. The results were dramatic. Each of the situations was characterized by a particular rhythm. In the first situation the rhythm was somewhat chaotic. In the third the rhythm was slow, almost like an ocean swell on a calm sea after a distant storm. The second was a mixture of the two. Not much is known about rhythms of this sort, except that it appears that they may be as important as almost any single factor in the interpersonal process.[15]

5. Much of the above could fall under the category of unconscious racism or unconscious ethnocentric bias. The problem in using such pejorative terms is that they themselves fall in a class of "releasers," which divert the attention away from what is actually going on and also do little to further the cause of understanding between different groups. Properly labeled and understood, unconscious patterns of behavior (which are inevitably communicative as well as value laden) can aid in understanding the world in which we live and contribute to the reduction of the dreadful tensions the people of the world are experiencing.

Certainly, education should not exacerbate the problems of the world. In fact, just the opposite. Nevertheless, there is inevitably a residue of resentment, even if repressed, associated with negative experiences. I have in mind events that are far from the behavioral differences of the type we have been discussing—for example, the craze for windowless schools in the United States. Much time and effort expended trying to establish a link between learning and the environment has been, apparently, to no avail.[16] This type of development is one of the consequences of a low context culture that is looking for a single cause matched with its own specific, single effect. One of the rationales for the windowless schools was that urban vandals could not break what was not there. But when these very same schools were built out in the wide open spaces of the Navajo reservation, the ultimate absurdity had been achieved. Navajo children who had lived their entire lives in the open with vistas of 100 miles or more were cooped up in an air-tight, sealed environment that was not only stifling but depressing as well.

The cause, if one must have one, apart from the inherent narcissism of most architects, was the compartmentalization of American-European cultures, ignorance of Navajo culture, and an absence of even the slightest knowledge of human physical, psychological, and sensory needs. All this was coupled with a denial of the relationship between human beings and their environments. It is as though school administrators are equipped with an impenetrable set of blinders to keep them from seeing the obvious, as well as with established speech patterns and a mindset that permanently inhibit cerebration. Nevertheless it is not hard to see how these things happen. These people work as cogs in massive administrative machines where it is taken for granted that either "procedures" or power will take precedence over human beings and common sense.

TO SPEAK FOR ONESELF

This brings up another universal point that has a cultural side. I am referring to the incredible inertia of the average bureaucracy. In a well intentioned (though somewhat optimistic) endeavor to do something about the condition of American schools, the dean of a famous school of education at a major university instituted a program specifically designed to create skilled, sympathetic, flexible teachers. And indeed, when they graduated these carefully selected and specially trained teachers could perform as expected and better. The denouement arrived when a follow-up study revealed that the longest expectation for survival of these newly acquired skills was six months in a working school environment. The teachers inevitably became captives of the school system to which they had been assigned. What emerges from the above is that *schools are extensions of the societies of which they are a part*. In McLuhan's terms, the school itself, its staff, its organization, the physical plant, its equipment, the maintenance, and its cultural patterns combine to form a single package that is the medium that is also the message. The message is not only independent of the curricula and the subjects taught, but is also more subtle as well as more powerful in its impact.

Educating is a serious business and a lifetime of experience has convinced me that no society and no culture should force its educational system on another. Furthermore, that children should receive their education from their own group at the primary level, after which point the educational system of the society in which these children are going to have to earn their living could be phased in. Part of my reason for advancing this "bizarre" notion is the need to maintain the following in all peoples: (1) A consistent and coherent core of identity; (2) A continuity with the past; and (3) The preservation of the incredibly rich ethnic variety, which the nations of the world seem to be doing their best to stamp out.

There are other reasons for my position. For one, cultures are integrated wholes, all of the parts interrelate and are reflected in each other. This integrated character of cultures may be one of the results of the holographic nature of memory.[17] It is for this reason that alien educational systems are not easily grafted on. It is not just that each nation-culture must possess its own national airlines but, more importantly, its own educational system that evolves out of the native soil of the country. Early in this century China discovered that sending talented young men and women to Europe and the United States to be educated in medicine was not effective. It was not until they instituted an indigenous system of medical education that progress was made in bringing additional health care to their people. These future doctors had to be trained in the cultural and environmental context in which they would later be practicing.

The Pueblo Indians of New Mexico have just provided another reason for making adaptations of the educational system that are suitable to the very high context Pueblo culture. Their complaint is that any time there is a problem, legal, medical, administrative, etc., involving one of the other two cultures of the region, it is necessary to hire members of the outside groups to represent them because they cannot speak effectively for themselves. The Pueblo people are tired of this and feel that, to be properly represented, they *must* be able to speak for themselves. The Pueblos define the solution in terms of an educational system of their own design that can equip them to do just that, speak for themselves on an equal footing with the surrounding cultures. When and if they can achieve their goal, the ability to translate from high to low context and vice versa, and the ability to move from a sea of information approach to a building block approach, will in most relevant situations constitute a major advance in mental health, peace, and intercultural understanding.

RECOMMENDATIONS FOR EDUCATORS

(a) *Learn about interfaces.* In today's world it is virtually impossible for any society or the members of any culture or group to "go it alone." The matter of interfaces is therefore always present and must be dealt with. Though there is a considerable amount of information on the manifest differences among cultures of the world, the latent, implicit, or hidden cultural differences, particularly those that occur at the cultural interface, are still relatively unexplored and undescribed. Continued interface research is a necessity.

(b) *Evolve indigenous education systems and build on success.* In the United States, because of certain features of organizational structure, it has been virtually impossible for us to take full advantage of our successes when they occur. This is because the heads of organizations, almost without exception, feel compelled to *"place their own stamp"* on the organization. This means dismantling anything a predecessor has put in place. Other countries could learn much from this negative example as they develop their own indigenous educational systems.

(c) *Reward the good teachers.* Just as there are natural students, there are also natural teachers. They need protection, appreciation, and tangible evidence of their value. They are the molders of the future, and much depends on their being able to do their job.

(d) *Study learning styles.* It is commonly believed in the West that normal children all learn the same way. This is not nearly as true as most people think. While there is ample evidence for this, I will cite only two sources, my own research with college students, and the cultural models that have evolved out of my interface research. Both indicate that there are not only different forms of learning for each major division of the brain,[18] but that the high and low context continuum sets up a framework in which there is a wide range in the integration of information.[19] Then there is also the matter of sensory biases within the individual as well as within the culture.[20] The two do not always mesh. It is difficult to estimate the loss to our species due to not knowing enough and failing to implement what is known in matters of this sort.

The media, such as television and the cinema, represent a resource that, if properly used, could add immeasurably to the effectiveness of education all over the world. One cannot ignore the fact that prior to the arrival of television in the mountain villages of New Mexico, Spanish was the only language that was spoken. Following World War II when television was diffused throughout the state, it took no time at all for the older native speakers of Spanish to walk out their doors speaking English. The same method has proved to be very effective for foreign members of the press in Japan. The list is extensive. Over thirty years of teaching students and learning from them have convinced me that no two people learn in exactly the same way. I am also convinced that there are major categories into which learning styles can be fitted.

(e) *Appreciate the importance of the microculture of education.* Culture is the special instrument by means of which the human species has evolved. While correcting differences in the manifest side of cultures poses special problems, the out-of-awareness, implicit dimension of culture is even more difficult to transcend. Matters of this sort are not simply the concern of those working at the cultural interface as, even within the bounds of a single culture, the two levels can get out of phase.

Because cultural "laws" are implicit and operate out of awareness, it is not uncommon that innovations designed to improve something prove to be in direct conflict with the basic and underlying patterns of implicit culture at the microcultural level. As important as the topics mentioned earlier is the necessity for each society to develop its own psychologists and anthropologists. Trained individuals in these fields are needed to produce accurate models of the very things which the culture takes for granted (i.e., the microcultural base on which all interactions rest). Until this happens we are all sailing on seas that are only partially charted.

References

1. "Microanthropology" is the term for cultural anthropology at the analytical level that concentrates on the observation and analysis of very small cultural (*microcultural*) events.
2. Edward T. Hall, *The Silent Language* (Garden City, N.Y.: Doubleday, 1959).
3. Karl H. Pribram, *Languages of the Brain* (Englewood Cliffs, N.J.: Prentice-Hall, 1971).
4. S. L. Washburn, "Primate Field Studies and Social Science," in *Cultural Illness and Health*, eds. Laura Nader and Thomas Maretzki (Washington, D.C.: American Anthropological Association, 1973), pp. 128–134. While there are things that are known about human beings but not widely shared, the knowledge of even the ways in which sensory information is stored and integrated in different individuals as well as cultures is pitifully small.
5. Western educators and those trained in the ways of the Western educator seem to have a problem coping with virtually anything that has not been externalized and which they cannot see or hear.
6. Edward T. Hall, *Beyond Culture* (Garden City, N.Y.: Doubleday, 1976); *The Dance of Life* (Garden City, N.Y.: Doubleday, 1983).
7. The results of these studies have been published in English, French, German, and Japanese and are distributed as a public service by *Stern* Magazine in Hamburg, West Germany.
8. Hall, *Beyond Culture; The Dance of Life*.
9. Sounds trivial, doesn't it? How could any sensible person fail to make connections on matters of this sort? Yet they do, because micro-patterns run deep. Furthermore, many of them are inculcated in the young—not as part of the formal education but in the entire structure and supporting behaviors that go to make up those institutions called schools.
10. Native Americans in their indigenous mode are very high context people. That explains the use of such terms as holistic when applied to their approach to knowledge, society, medicine, education, and religion. Unfortunately, the term holistic, invented by American-European whites, is a label that lacks specificity. And while I could not reject it outright, there was no way for me to integrate it into my work.
11. Hall, *The Silent Language*.
12. Logic, incidentally, predates Gutenberg. It is another story, again.
13. Kinesics is the study of body motion as communication: Ray L. Birdwhistell, *Introduction to Kinesics* (Louisville, Kentucky: University of Louisville Press, 1974): Hall, *The Silent Language*.
14. Edward T. Hall, "To Each His Own—The Manpower Potential in Our Ethnic Groups," *Employment Service Review* 4 (No. 10, October 1967): 24–29. [U.S. Department of Labor]
15. John Collier, *Alaskan Eskimo Education: A Film Analysis of Cultural Confrontation in the Schools* (New York: Holt, Rinehart & Winston, 1973); *Visual Anthropology: Photography as a Research Method* (New York: Holt, Rinehart & Winston, 1973); Hall, *The Dance of Life*.
16. For more information on the transaction between human beings and their various environments, see Edward T. Hall, *The Hidden Dimension* (Garden City, N.Y.: Doubleday, 1969).
17. Dennis Gabor, "Holography, 1948–1971," *Science* 177 (July 28, 1972): 299–313; Paul Pietsch, *Shufflebrain* (Boston: Houghton Mifflin, 1981); Pribram, *Languages of the Brain*.
18. Paul D. MacLean, "Man and His Animal Brains," *Modern Medicine 95* (1965): 106.
19. We have already mentioned the high context, holistic Pueblo Indians and some of the problems they have in low context white schools.
20. Hall, *Beyond Culture*.

16

Mission Not Accomplished

Education Reform in Retrospect

Mary Hatwood Futrell

It was six years ago this month that I became president of the National Education Association (NEA). The education reform movement of the 1980s was still in its infancy. *A Nation at Risk,* the report that started it all, was just four months old.

Our nation had begun a great debate about the quality—and, ultimately, the equality—of public education. But few of us realized at the time that the debate would be so heated, so long lasting, or so fundamental. Few of us realized that education reform in the 1980s held the potential of fundamentally "re-forming" U.S. schools.

That reformation has certainly not occurred in this decade. History will view the 1980s not as the decade of education reform, but as the decade of education debate. We've spent these years arguing, posturing, and traveling well-worn roads. We've only begun to address the basic issues related to schooling in America. For example, we've just begun to redefine the goals of public education. We've just begun to accept the fact that our schools can—and must—offer both educational equity and educational excellence. We've just begun to examine how we teach in light of what we know about how students learn. We've just begun to examine what schools seek to teach in light of what today's (and tomorrow's) students need to know. And we've begun, at long last, to challenge the structure of schooling that has been with us for more than a century and is now obsolete. We are finally arriving at a consensus on the need for meaningful reform of U.S. schools and on the direction which that reform should take.

Education reform from 1983 until very recently was dominated by a coalition characterized by immobility. Educators, politicians, policy makers, teacher unions, child advocacy groups, parents, and business and community leaders argued, bickered, and pulled in a host of contradictory directions. Legislators legislated. Bureaucrats regulated. Commissions wrote reports. And all these groups pointed fingers and accused. The result was an inability to address the real issues of schooling in America.

I believe that our immobility is now coming to an end. We have forged a new consensus on the necessity of providing a high-quality education to all children. We have also come to realize that achievement of that goal will require a radical re-formation of our schools. If we can hold on to this consensus and build around it a new coalition—characterized by mobility—we will finally be ready to undertake the hard work of meaningful education reform.

It has taken us six years to get to this point—to the verge of the fourth wave of the education reform movement of the late 20th century. As we embark on this fourth wave of reform, it is instructive to examine where we have been over the past six years, beginning with the release of *A Nation at Risk.*

That report is a remarkable document. It prefigured, in uncanny fashion, the host of issues that have come to dominate our national dialogue on education reform. It hinted at problems that were only dimly perceived in 1983—but that soon became the focus of the national debate on education. And it touched all the bases:

- illiteracy;
- the decline in graduation standards and in students' mastery of basic skills;
- the specter of a society deeply divided between a scientific elite and a citizenry bewildered by the onrushing advance of technology;
- the challenge of ethnic pluralism and the threat that this poses to the ideal of equity;
- the rising dropout rate and the teacher shortage;
- diluted curricula;
- banal textbooks;
- disciplinary problems;
- problems related to teacher preparation, federal leadership, and parental responsibility; and
- a portrait in miniature of a teaching profession undervalued, underpaid, and under siege.

Though it has many strengths, *A Nation at Risk* is deeply flawed. Despite the breadth and scope of this report, a single paragraph has come to dominate the whole. That paragraph is an analogy, bluntly militaristic, that defines education as an *instrumental* value rather than an *intrinsic* value:

> If an unfriendly foreign power had attempted to impose on America the mediocre educational performance that exists today, we might well have viewed it as an act of war. . . . We have, in effect, been committing an act of unthinking, unilateral educational disarmament.[1]

Source: From Mary Hatwood Futrell, "Mission Not Accomplished: Education Reform in Retrospect," *Phi Delta Kappa,* Volume 71, September 1989, pp. 8–13. Reprinted with permission from the publisher and from Mary Hatwood Futrell.

Those two sentences established the initial tone for the debate over the direction that school reform should take. And those two sentences dictated the direction of all but a few early reform initiatives. For those two sentences defined the mission of education as decidedly utilitarian: education was a weapon. This tenet was seldom challenged, and it became the axiomatic foundation of education reform in the 1980s.

The mission of education was to serve the national interest. The destiny of American democracy, it was argued, demanded what revitalized education alone could deliver: technological might in the service of military security, a rejuvenated economy in the service of reclaimed dominance in the international marketplace, and the social and political integration of waves of new immigrants in the service of national harmony.

With education so clearly "in the service" of national interest, politicians—to no one's great surprise—quickly volunteered for action. Thus was the first wave of education reform born. And thus did this first wave of reform emanate not from the schoolhouse, but from the statehouse. Dictates from on high proliferated. Governors and state legislators swept into action. Their battle cry was, "More!": more tests for students and teachers, more credits for graduation, more hours in the school day, more days in the school year, more regimentation, more routinization, more regulation.

Between 1983 and 1985 state legislatures enacted more than 700 statutes stipulating what should be taught, when it should be taught, how it should be taught, and by whom it should be taught. The clear purpose of this mass of legislation and the bureaucratic mandates that followed was to control and to regulate teachers and local schools.

In a 1985 interview on the state of the reform movement, Ernest Boyer, president of the Carnegie Foundation for the Advancement of Teaching, told the *Christian Science Monitor* that the wave of regulatory intervention was "destroying the spirit of the people in the classroom." He added that working conditions posed the biggest problem, since teachers felt that they had "more responsibilities and less authority, less recognition, less empowerment to do the work."[2]

The mass of regulations imposed by the states usurped the authority that appropriately belongs to teachers, principals, parents, and local communities. The regulations sought to make the curriculum "teacher-proof." In fact, they served to make schools "learning-proof."

It took a couple of years, but the reaction to this top-down wave of legislation and regulation finally arrived. And when it did, it ushered in the second wave of reform.

This second wave sprang from the realization that, if education were to serve as an instrument for social and economical revitalization, the instrument ought to be wielded by educators, not legislators. At the annual meeting of the American Educational Research Association in April 1986, I presented the NEA's thesis that the time had come to reform the reform movement:

> Every attempt at reform that dilutes the authority of the classroom teacher dilutes the quality of instruction in our nation's classrooms.
>
> Teachers cannot hope to prepare students for a world of perpetual flux if they themselves are condemned to static, externally imposed conceptions of effective pedagogy.
>
> Teachers cannot hope to prepare students for the Information Age if they themselves are condemned to organizational structures derived from the Industrial Age.
>
> Teachers cannot hope to ready students for responsibility within a participatory democracy if they themselves are condemned to an autocratic bureaucracy.[3]

Thus did the second wave seek to end educational change imposed from above and to begin to look to local schools, to teachers, and to the teaching profession to lead the educational improvement effort. As the reform movement moved into its third year, a growing body of research argued that the rising tide of regulation had wrenched decision-making authority away from teachers and principals and had produced a web of inefficiency. In 1986 no fewer than five prestigious national reports condemned that inefficiency. Those reports were issued by the Holmes Group, the Carnegie Task Force on Teaching as a Profession, the National Governors' Association, the Education Commission of the States, and the Association for Supervision and Curriculum Development.

Second-wave reform soon rested on a solid, research-based consensus. Theodore Sizer underscored the need to move away from top-down regulation as a means for school improvement when he stated, "The decentralization of substantial authority to the persons closest to the students is essential."[4]

It was during this period that the first steps were taken to win professional recognition and professional autonomy for teachers. Top-down, hierarchical reform was being discredited. Reform from the grassroots—from local schools, local educators, and local communities—became the focus. At last, teacher empowerment was more than an aspiration. In 1985 and 1986 the NEA launched three programs predicated on teacher involvement in decision making: the Mastery in Learning Project, Operation Rescue, and TABS (the Team Approach to Better Schools). Each of these programs gave substance to the principle that effective reform must be defined, designed, and implemented by teachers at the local level, working in concert with the local community. Each was based on the belief that reform must empower local educators and communities, not strait-jacket and stifle them.

The second wave called for reform efforts that brought together teachers, principals, superintendents, school boards, parents, and business and community leaders in collaborative efforts to renew and improve their schools. The local school was seen as the focus of reform initiatives that would be tailored to local needs.

And it was during this period that *equity* began to reclaim a central position alongside excellence in discussions of school reform. Some of us—a small minority that within a couple of years would become the predominant voice in the debate about education reform—persisted in arguing that educational quality must be expanded to cover *all* students in *all* schools. Boyer stated the issue bluntly:

> The harsh truth is that school reform is failing in the inner city because the diagnosis is wrong. Formulas for renewal—more homework, more testing, more requirements for graduation—work best for schools that are already succeeding and for students who are college bound. But to require a troubled student in an urban ghetto to take another unit in math or foreign language, without more guidance or support, is like raising a hurdle in the high jump without giving more coaching to someone who has stumbled.[5]

But while reform through state legislation and regulation was being steadily discredited, the legacy of the movement's first wave continued to shape subsequent reforms. Specifically, the first wave's emphasis on education as a utilitarian rather than an intrinsic value endured. Most reforms, even those that were truly innovative and locally based, continued to claim "the national interest" as their justification.

And so, as the reform movement entered its third wave, the U.S. economy became the focus. Economic imperatives took the place of legislative mandates. Schools needed to produce graduates who could staff American business and industry and reassert this nation's economic preeminence. This economic utilitarianism had more in common with the first wave than with the second wave of reform. The "top"—this time, more economic than political—was again driving the reform agenda.

Hindsight is always extraordinarily clear. So in retrospect it is easy to see that the reform movement lost precious years by failing to ask the basic question: Education for what? We Americans simply accepted the idea that the purpose of education is to serve the national interest, however that interest might be defined at a particular moment in time. I have no doubt that, had we questioned the instrumentalist ideology of *A Nation at Risk* back in 1983, we could have avoided many of the attempts to reform the schools through dictates from on high—attempts that wasted our own and our students' precious time.

But we did not ask the basic question then. In fact, we've only recently recognized the need to reexamine the mission of education, and we've only recently embarked on an effort to define education as *both* an instrumental value *and* an intrinsic one. Indeed, the assumption still prevails that all will be well with the nation if the reform of education is guided exclusively by the goals of catching the Japanese economically and matching the Soviets militarily and politically.

Yet education designed to meet only these goals cannot prepare U.S. students for the world that awaits them today—to say nothing of the world they will inherit tomorrow. That world will demand zealous compassion as much as competitive zeal. Just as surely, it will demand emotional resilience, mental agility, moral stamina, and the creative savvy to improvise effective responses to unforeseen challenges spawned by unrelenting change. These virtues represent the *intrinsic* values of education that, until now, have been all but absent from the debate on reform.

How do we explain this flaw? And how do we prevent it from becoming fatal?

We might start by examining the vocabulary that now dominates the national discussion of education. We are told with increasing regularity that knowledge is a *commodity;* education, an *industry;* learning, an *asset;* research, an *enterprise*. Talk of intellectual *capital* is rife. A stubborn consensus holds that the business of education is business.

Clearly the business community and the education community must work together more closely and more cooperatively. The corporate community may be public education's most valuable ally. But when the language of commerce so thoroughly saturates discourse on education, something is amiss.

In his landmark treatise, *Education and the Next Economy,* which addresses the issue of how to make education a more powerful *economic instrument,* Harvard economist Robert Reich takes care to issue a stern caveat:

> By focusing on education and the next economy, I do not mean to suggest that education's only, or most important, purpose is economic. To the contrary: A truly educated person is motivated by, and can find satisfaction in, a wide array of things that are not traded in markets or that cost very little. A just and democratic society depends on a citizenry educated in civic responsibility rather than in economic aggrandizement.[6]

Reich fortifies his position by quoting—with approval—Horace Mann's eloquent statement to the Boston Board of Education in 1842. Mann summed up his defense of public education with these words:

> [H]owever deserving of attention may be the *economical* view of the subject which I have endeavored to present, yet it is one that dwindles into insignificance when compared to those loftier and more sacred attributes of the cause.[7]

Education is the engine that drives our economy. But it does not follow that our economy ought to be the engine that drives education. In fact, we do a disservice to students if we offer them no more than a curriculum designed to advance economic goals or to serve utilitarian objectives.

During the past two decades we have seen the dangers of designing education to serve narrow, provincial priorities—priorities defined by the crisis of the hour. The graduates of such schooling are skilled but uneducated, short on creativity, incapable of synthesizing new information. They draw a blank when asked what images come to mind when they hear the words *Soweto* and *Gdansk, Managua* and *Phnom Penh, Hiroshima* and *Auschwitz*. But the greatest irony of all is that these graduates are condemned to routinized, dead-end jobs that deprive them of pride and drive them into debt.

It should not surprise us that these students are ill-prepared for both the world we now know and the world we know is approaching. An obsolete curriculum and an obsolete structure of schooling serve neither the ethical *nor the economic* agendas that our nation embraces.

Even when it is defined only as an instrument to advance national goals, education conquers ignorance. But when it is forged with a modicum of attention to its intrinsic value, education has the potential to conquer intellectual myopia. The education that emerges from this broader agenda will not be subservient to parochial interests.

Those parochial interests will persist, of course. And rightly so. Parents will continue to seek an education that offers their children a pathway to fortune or fame. Corporate executives will continue to seek an education that prepares their future employees to increase corporate earnings. Government at all levels will continue to seek an education that prepares students for active and responsible citizenship.

These agendas are beyond reproach; educators must respect them and remain responsive to them. But we can never allow a single goal to define our mission. Educators must accept the premise that the mission of education is defined by a coherent vision of the kind of world we want our children to inherit. More important, the mission of education is defined by a vision of the values that students will need in order to cope with and to flourish in that new world.

As the intellectually demanding and precariously balanced world of the 21st century comes into view, it seems clear that the mission of education must be not to train people to *serve* the purposes of others, but to develop their capacity to *question* the purposes of others. We must bolster students' will to seek wisdom. We must enable them to think creatively about complex issues, to act responsibly, and—when necessary—to act selflessly. We must convince them that the gross national product is not a measure of our worth as a people.

Thus does the fourth wave of reform trace its parentage to what was begun during the second wave. The fourth wave envisions democratic, grassroots reform. It demands a return to schools that are organized to facilitate educational renewal and improvement from the bottom up. Because the fourth wave defines education as both an instrumental value and an intrinsic value, the goals of education become less parochial, more expansive, and less determined by economic forces.

Fourth-wave reform has as its focus an education that prepares tomorrow's adults to meet ethical as well as economic imperatives—that prepares them not only for a life of work, but also for a life of worth. Fourth-wave reform is predicated on the assumption that schools must offer both excellence *and* equity. It envisions schools that will enable *every student*—regardless of race, sex, or socioeconomic status—to reach his or her full potential.

What will schools that are designed to meet these goals look like? We do not yet know. Defining, designing, and constructing these schools is the hard work of the fourth wave of reform. Two years ago, at an NEA-sponsored symposium of educators from three national networks of schools involved in teacher-driven reform, Sizer offered some sage advice:

> Challenge the regularities—the routines and activities that are so familiar they are habitual. We fail to even question them. There are many in school keeping—curriculum, departments, grades, schedules, periods (those 53-minute snippets of time), and particularly the metaphor of giving an education . . . nothing is beyond questioning.[8]

We are learning what questions to ask. And we know who must be involved in the asking. We know that the kind of change that is necessary will entail a restructuring of our schools from the bottom up. We know that we must situate decision making in education where teachers teach and children learn. We know that local educators must be granted the authority, the resources, and the responsibility to design learning environments that meet their students' needs. And we know that we will ultimately succeed in restructuring schools only through cooperative efforts involving educators, school boards, superintendents, parents, students, and business and community leaders.

We possess a strong knowledge base from research and from our experiences with innovative programs and pilot projects begun during the second wave of reform. As the 1980s draw to a close, there is no excuse for believing that educational excellence for all students necessitates a uniform structure for all schools. Solid evidence supports a variety of approaches to teaching, learning, and the structure of schooling—as long as these approaches are forged at the local level. Solid evidence demonstrates that, to educate young people to their full potential, we must legitimate divergent paths to that goal.

Nor will the curricula that emerge from fourth-wave reform be uniform. But if reform in the fourth wave truly becomes less wed to instrumentalist goals, these curricula will share a common feature. Because they will be designed to prepare students for an interdependent, pluralistic world, these fourth-wave curricula will be less deeply rooted in the classics of western civilization. The classics will not be forsaken, nor will traditional curricula be jettisoned. Instead, traditional curricula will be expanded and supplemented.

We can, of course, learn much from the giants of the classical tradition. Pythagoras, for example, offers more than a few lessons for fourth-wave reformers. Indeed, Pythagoras might be characterized as a radical interdisciplinarian. It was he who insisted that the most intimate of all disciplines are mathematics *and* music.

Those who enjoin us to get "back to basics" might wish to give this assertion some thought. In the interest of producing a citizenry (more precisely, a work force) that can read and count, those who advocate for the "basics" all too often define the arts—and especially music—as educational frills. Anyone who believes that education must serve personal human needs as well as economic goals finds this definition unacceptable.

The curricula—and the schools—that emerge from the fourth wave of reform must address both instrumental and intrinsic goals. Fourth-wave education must help America meet its economic imperatives *and* its moral imperatives. Fourth-wave education cannot neglect either artistic or scientific content. If our nation and the world are to be free from pestilence, hunger, and fear, we need scientists, communicators, businesspeople, organizers, technicians—and dreamers.

We need education that serves our *national* interests even as it awakens us to the *common* interests we share with all nations and peoples. Our highest aspirations cannot be achieved without an education in which instrumental and intrinsic values intersect.

The fourth wave of reform has the potential to so transform the landscape of education that, in years hence, the question—Is education an instrumental value or an intrinsic value?—will be incomprehensible. The answer—the one right answer—will be "yes."

When that happens, we will have fulfilled the promise of American education. We will have carried out the mandates of *A Nation at Risk* without yielding to the one-dimensional, instrumentalist ideology of that document. We will have achieved the best of both worlds. That's the promise—and the challenge—of the fourth wave of education reform.

17

Urban and Rural Schools Research

Implications for School Governance

Kofi Lomotey
Austin D. Swanson
State University of New York at Buffalo

American schools range in degree of complexity, from small rural schools serving the countryside and villages to huge urban schools in central cities of large metropolitan areas. In the middle of the continuum are medium-sized suburban schools.

Suburban schools seem to have relatively few problems with respect to academic achievement, discipline, and teacher quality when compared with their urban and rural counterparts; thus, the spotlight of educational reform has focused most sharply on urban and rural schools as the weak links in America's educational system. On the surface it would appear that these two categories of schools are the antithesis of one another. In many respects this is true: the problems of one are not necessarily the problems of the other. In fact, many of the strengths of urban schools are weaknesses of rural schools and vice versa. This leads one to wonder if a comparative analysis might provide useful insights for developing public policies that would help improve the effectiveness of each set of schools. The purpose of this article is to compare the characteristics of urban and rural schools, to look at their strengths and weaknesses, and to consider policy alternatives for improving their effectiveness through restructuring school governance. The implications for the practice of school administration are substantial.

Urban schools are increasingly in a state of deterioration (National Commission on Excellence in Education, 1983; Lomotey, in press). In speaking of this critical state, the Carnegie Foundation for the Advancement of Teaching (1988) concluded that:

> America must confront, with urgency, the crisis in urban schools. Bold, aggressive action is needed now to avoid leaving a huge and growing segment of the nation's youth civically unprepared and economically unempowered. This nation must see the urban school crisis for what it is: a major failure of social policy, a piecemeal approach to a problem that requires a unified response. (p. xv)

Rural education also faces serious problems. The curricular offerings of rural schools are at best limited, and it is difficult to attract well-qualified professionals to work in rural areas. Rural schools are criticized for being too small and too remote from the mainstream of American life to provide a relevant education for those required to attend them. They are viewed as expensive and inefficient. The malady has been diagnosed as smallness; the dominant policy solution for all of this century has been to consolidate rural schools, casting them in the image of their urban counterparts.

Much of the existing scholarship on rural education is unsophisticated (DeYoung, 1987). In recent years, however, research on rural education has become more refined as it has taken into account total cost and socioeconomic status of pupils and included additional criteria such as student achievement, self-image, and success in college. Research into the problems of urban education performed during the mid-1960s through the mid-1970s was not very helpful from the perspective of educational policy since it pointed to the family as the overwhelming determinant of a child's success in school, attributing little influence to the school itself. Recent research on schools has been much more useful. It has found some urban schools that have been unusually successful with "at-risk" children and has concentrated on identifying those characteristics that explain their success (Edmonds, 1979; Weber, 1971; Venezsky & Winfield, 1980; Lomotey, 1987).

RURAL AND URBAN SCHOOLS: AN ASSESSMENT

In this section, the characteristics of typical urban schools, "effective" urban schools, and rural schools will be studied in juxtaposition. The characteristics of special interest are: the nature of the populations served, student achievement, school culture, leadership and decision making, and finance. These characteristics will be considered separately at first; a discussion of their interrelationships will follow.

Nature of Student Population

On measures of socioeconomic status such as family income and education level, both rural and central city communities score low. In central cities, these populations are con-

Source: Kofi Lomotey and Austin D. Swanson, "Urban and Rural Schools Research: Implications for School Governance," *Education and Urban Society*, (Volume 21, August 1989) pp. 436–454, copyright 1989 by Sage Publications, Inc. Reprinted by permission of Sage Publications, Inc.

TABLE 1 Selected Socioeconomic Statistics for the United States, Central Cities and Nonmetropolitan Areas, 1983

Item	*U.S.*	*Central Cities > 1,000,000*	*Central Cities < 1,000,000*	*Non-Metro Areas*
Median family income ($)	24,580	21,858	22,706	20,938
Median Income, family with full-time workers ($)	31,801	30,823	29,706	27,245
% High School grads (persons 18+ years)	73.1	69.1	73.4	67.5
% 4+ years college (persons 18+ years)	16.8	17.5	18.2	12.2

centrated in ghettos and are highly conspicuous. In rural areas, the poor are dispersed, integrated, and frequently "invisible."

Table 1 reports selected socioeconomic statistics for 1983 for the United States at large, for central cities in metropolitan areas with over and under one million inhabitants, and for nonmetropolitan areas. Without exception, nonmetropolitan areas rank below central city and United States medians on measures related to income and education. Central cities in metropolitan areas of over one million inhabitants rank below central cities in smaller metropolitan areas, which rank below the United States at large for every item except percentage of college graduates. Both categories of central cities exceed the national average for the proportion of persons completing four or more years of college. It should be noted, however, that central city populations are mixed, comprising the affluent and the very poor. Since the affluent in central cities often send their children to private schools, the reported statistics probably overstate the wealth and education of parents sending their children to public schools.

Poverty in urban schools tends to be multicultural, while in rural areas the poor are more likely to be of one ethnic group. Forty-six percent of central city students in public schools are African-American, 23 percent are Hispanic, and 5 percent are Asian. Over 100 language groups are represented in urban schools (Council of the Great City Schools, 1987). In contrast, 91 percent of the rural population is white, compared with the national average of 85 percent. This figure is even higher for the northern tier of states, since rural African-Americans and Hispanics are concentrated in the South and Southwest. Ninety-one percent of the nation's 6.4 million nonmetropolitan African-Americans live in the South (Fratoe, 1980). Most of the rural Hispanic population lives in the five southwestern states (Fratoe, 1981). Poverty in rural areas affects all ethnic groups, but the pockets of ethnic poverty are geographically distinct. Rural and effective urban schools (unlike many urban schools) are similar in this respect since both tend to be ethnically homogeneous (Rosenholtz, 1985).

Student Achievement

The achievement level of students attending urban schools is a critical problem. In a recent National Assessment of Educational Progress (NAEP) survey, 17-year-old urban students scored 22 points below the national average. Concurrently, the urban school dropout rate is approaching 50 percent; in the Chicago Public Schools, a system held by some to be the worst in America, 13,000 students drop out of school each year (Council of the Great City Schools, 1987). Student achievement levels in effective urban schools do not compare with those in suburban and rural schools, but they are considerably higher than those seen in typical urban schools (Lomotey, 1989).

Except for African-Americans and Hispanics, the problem is not as severe in rural schools and may even be a source of pride since the achievement of students attending rural schools approximates national and state averages. In New York State, for example, elementary pupils in districts with enrollments under 1,100 (mostly rural) tend to achieve only slightly below the average for suburban districts in reading, writing, and mathematics and well above all categories of cities and the state as a whole (New York State Education Department, 1986). At the secondary level, rural achievement levels are similar to those of suburban districts and exceed those of all city categories and state average performance. This is not an aberration of a single year, but is consistent over the twenty years that the tests have been given (New York State Education Department, 1967). The better achievement of suburban children can be explained in part by the predominance of upper and upper-middle income families in those communities. Research shows that children of these families tend to achieve at higher levels. Socioeconomic differences alone, however, can not explain the achievement gap between rural and urban children. Similar evidence on the success of rural schools in terms of student achievement has been presented (Ward, 1988; Coleman, 1986; Turner & Thrasher, 1970; Sher & Tompkins, 1977; Bidwell & Kasarda, 1975).

All children do not fare well in rural schools, however. Fratoe (1980, 1981) studied the educational status of African-American and Hispanic children in nonmetropolitan areas. The high school completion rate for these populations is not only below the completion rate for whites, but also below that for their counterparts in metropolitan areas. The functional illiteracy rate for nonmetropolitan African-Americans is nearly three times that of metropolitan African-Americans and five times that of nonmetropolitan whites.

School Culture

School culture is the pattern of beliefs and expectations of the members of the school community that guides their predominant attitudes and behaviors. School culture affects everyone's ability to function cooperatively and productively. Differences in student achievement and behavior across schools have been shown to be a function of school culture (Rutter, Maugham, Moritmore, Ouston, & Smith, 1979).

Many urban schools lack purpose and coherence. They are, as one author has suggested, "running" rather than "being run." They often have a negative physical appearance. They are characterized by a lack of coherent instructional programs and regular routines (Carnegie Foundation, 1988; Corcoran, Walker, & White, 1988). Cusick (1983) and others have argued that the high level of ethnic diversity in the student populations of these typical urban schools works against the establishment of consensus on norms and standards within the school, contributing to their characteristic indiscipline. Often, there is no sense of community. In many instances, students are unable to establish meaningful relationships with teachers and are often left on their own to succeed or fail. Furthermore, little or no effort is made to enable students to understand the connection between their schooling and their life outside the school. Many teachers do not believe that inner-city youth can perform adequately. Attitudes and comments of these teachers frequently cause discomfort, fear, and confusion among the students. All of these factors contribute to the low level of academic achievement in urban schools.

Corcoran et al. (1988) found that many urban teachers wanted better relations with their students. The teachers claimed that their efforts were hampered by disciplinary problems, large class size, lack of time for individual interaction, busing policies, and lack of student participation in extracurricular activities. The study concluded that a productive work environment for teachers includes good physical conditions, a supportive administration, and opportunities to work collaboratively to influence policy, curriculum, and instruction.

In those urban schools that have been found to be effective in boosting academic achievement, schools are "being run": There is order and discipline, a positive physical appearance, a coherent structure to the instructional program, and preplanned routines (Venezsky & Winfield, 1980; Weber, 1971). In effective urban schools, there is agreement between school goals, classroom instruction, and test content, and principals and teachers consult regularly to discuss achievement. Instruction is individualized (Jackson, Logsdon, & Taylor, 1983; Lomotey, 1989; Weber, 1971).

The culture of effective urban schools is characterized by a pervasive expectation of high academic achievement (Wellisch, MacQueen, Carriere, & Duck, 1978; Rist, 1970; Jackson et al., 1983). Teachers are supportive and task-oriented, zeroing in on academic deficiencies of students. They set challenging yet attainable goals and encourage all students to do their best. Furthermore, the high expectations are carefully maintained through systematic evaluation of student progress (Brookover & Lezotte, 1979; Weber, 1971; Jackson et al., 1983).

Addressing the issue of the unwholesome culture of many urban schools, the Carnegie Foundation (1988) observed:

> Overcoming anonymity—creating a setting in which every student is known personally by an adult—is one of the most compelling obligations urban schools confront. Young people who have few constructive relationships with adults need a sense of belonging. They need positive encounters with older people who serve as mentors and role models for both educational and social growth. Building community must be a top priority if students in urban schools are to academically and socially succeed. (p. 24)

Rural schools are characterized not only by a strong sense of community within the school itself, but also by a sense of being a part of the larger community and an extension of the family. It is this factor that has been identified as overriding the many admitted weaknesses of rural schools (Barker & Gump, 1964; Coleman, 1986; Newmann, 1981). The fear of losing that sense of community is largely responsible for rural opposition to schemes for school consolidation.

In urban and suburban schools there is great emphasis placed on competitiveness to prepare students for survival in the academic institutions and the harsh economic climate of urban environments. In rural areas, most organizations, not just schools, are small and tend to be quite personal: businesses are frequently family-owned. The warmth of these personal and familial relationships carries over into the schools, where there is a climate of acceptance, cooperation, and mutual support (Skelly, 1988). Indeed, many of the innovations of the current educational reform movement have long been standard features of many rural schools, including individualized instruction, peer tutoring, cross-age grouping, and community involvement (Barker, 1986).

Coleman (1986) hypothesizes that "district ethos" may account for the strong and unexpected negative relationship he found between student achievement and expenditure per student.

> In particular, it [district ethos] seems capable of explaining the unexpectedly strong academic performance of small and rural districts, despite their traditional frugality with public funds. Secondly, it provides a useful linkage between classrooms, schools, and school districts, helping explain relationships known to exist between effective schools and central offices. (pp. 95–96)

Leadership and Decision Making

Leadership in urban schools is in turmoil. This is partly due to the fact that principals have little control over the curriculum, the hiring of staff, and fiscal matters. Most critical decisions are made at the district level, with limited input from the schools. The structure is highly bureaucratic, contributing to many of the problems that arise in these schools. The Carnegie Foundation (1988) observes: "Teachers in urban schools . . . have little control over their work. They are three times as likely as their counterparts in non-urban school districts to feel uninvolved in setting goals or selecting books and materials. They are twice as apt to feel they have no control over how classroom time is used or course content selected" (p. 6).

Lack of a sense of control over school matters also extends to parents. The neighborhood or other designated school is the only option for most parents owing to bureaucratic regulations, although, increasingly, central city districts are permitting some school choice through open enrollment policies and magnet schools. The typical neighborhood school is viewed by members of its immediate community as an alien institution, placed there by an external power and having little to do with the neighborhood itself.

Effective urban schools operate within the same bureaucratic structure as do other urban schools; nevertheless, the principals and teachers, through creative insubordination, have been able to achieve meaningful changes and meet the specific needs of their students. Effective urban schools are characterized by strong leadership, manifested primarily by principals who have assumed control whether or not they have been granted formal authority. Lomotey (1989) has observed that principals of effective urban schools are confident in the ability of their children to learn, are committed to seeing that all of their students receive the necessary tools for success, and have compassion for and understanding of their students and the communities from which they come. The principals of effective schools make an effort to participate in neighborhood affairs and encourage parents to become involved in the education of their children.

Leadership in rural schools has not been studied extensively. Given the fact that rural schools are often training grounds for teachers and administrators in small cities and suburbs, professional leadership often has a fleeting quality and tends to be inexperienced. Program continuity is frequently provided by lay and teaching personnel rather than administrators. Where there is only one school in a district, as is frequently the case in rural areas, school-based decision making and school-based budgeting are long-standing traditions. Decision making tends to be informal, taking into account the uniqueness of each case.

The rural school is seen as an integral part of its community by the educating professionals, students, and other community members. School board members in most rural districts are elected and are readily accessible to any member of the community. Because the school is one of the community's primary social and cultural centers, school activities are given extensive coverage in the local media. School athletic teams receive the attention given to professional teams in urban areas. The school band is an essential element in any community celebration. School plays and musical concerts are frequently the only cultural events taking place in the community.

Curriculum and Staff

The curriculum of most urban schools is very diverse, making available to students an extensive selection of courses in a wide variety of disciplines. This diversity gives the appearance of providing enriched academic experiences not available in rural schools. Without proper guidance, however, this diversity often results in what Powell, Farrar, and Cohen (1985) have referred to as "the shopping mall high school."

Effective elementary urban schools have deliberately limited their curricula, focusing on the basic skills of reading, writing, and arithmetic. The assumption is that once the foundation is laid, students will be more likely to continue in an academically successful pattern. In focusing on basic skills, these schools also give careful attention to intergrade consistency—that is, a given reading or mathematics program is used throughout the elementary grades.

The presumed inferiority of small rural schools is rooted in their limited curricula. This argument may be overblown, however, particularly at a time when greater emphasis is being placed on the development of basic skills. An analysis by Monk (1984) of a random sample of New York State school districts pointed to differences in curricular offerings and teacher qualifications between large and small districts. Opportunities to study science, especially for non-college-bound students, are fewer in small districts; but opportunities to study mathematics and English are unrelated to district size. Opportunities to study a foreign language are greater in small districts. Despite their availability, students in small districts are less likely to enroll in science, math, and foreign languages courses. Opportunities to study advanced subjects are virtually nonexistent in small districts.

In another study, Monk and Haller (1986) report no significant change in class size or in the number of course offerings as school size expands beyond 400 students in grades 9–12. However, they report that "the curricular offerings of the very smallest secondary schools . . . are seriously deficient" (p. 62). They found that although larger schools offer more courses, "never did more than 12 percent of the students enroll in courses that are denied to their peers in the smallest high schools" (p. 59). The greater variety of courses offered by large schools tends to exist only at the introductory level and not at the specialization level. Monk and Haller speculate that this is to avoid small class enrollments. Based on their analysis, they question the wisdom of reorganizing school districts for the sake of offering a richer curriculum. In a much earlier study, Barker and Gump (1964) described similar findings. It should be noted, however, that although small schools may offer a reasonably broad curriculum, individual students experience difficulty in scheduling desired courses because there is usually only one section of each course available, resulting in numerous scheduling conflicts. This is not a serious problem in large schools because of the existence of multiple sections.

Mathematics, English, and foreign language teachers tend to have less training and experience in small districts compared with large districts. There is a greater incidence of first-year teachers in small districts, and teachers are more likely to teach outside of their area of certification. Sher and Tompkins (1976) also observed that highly educated teachers are more likely to obtain a position in a consolidated or larger school system than are teachers with less education.

The Council of the Great City Schools (1987) points to the staffing problems of urban schools, reporting that the shortage of teachers is $2\,^1/_2$ times as great in urban districts as it is for other districts. The shortage is particularly acute for teachers from African-American and Hispanic groups, leaving the increasingly multicultural urban school student population with an inadequate number of culturally similar role models. Moreover, current teachers in these groups report plans to leave the teaching profession at a rate significantly higher than that of white teachers (Lou Harris & Associates, 1988).

Financing

Urban school districts are typically fiscally dependent upon city government, making education just one department among many which must compete for funding. In rural areas, school districts are often organized as special units of local government. As such, they may determine their own programs and budgets, and they levy taxes in support of their operations independently of other local governments. The tax levy of such rural school districts is frequently subject to voter approval, however.

Professional salaries in central cities tend to be competitive with those of most other districts in their metropolitan areas, but working conditions may not be. In addition to school culture considerations, teachers are likely to face very large classes, the only exception being teachers of special education classes. The net result is an overall per student expenditure at about the state average. State/local financing is supplemented significantly by federal categorical aid programs in central city school districts.

Professional salaries in rural districts are low by any standard (Ward, 1988). Class size at the elementary level is about the same as for suburban districts, but classes are much smaller at the secondary level. Rural districts tend to have very narrow property tax bases, severely constraining their ability to raise money locally and making them highly dependent upon state aid for operating revenues. As a result, their per student expenditure is typically well below the average for their state. While the nature of their student populations qualifies them for federal categorical aid programs, it is difficult for them to take advantage of such aid because they do not have specialized staff members to write the proposals.

The discussion of the condition of typical urban schools, effective urban schools, and rural schools is summarized in Table 2. The populations served by urban and rural schools tend to be poor; in urban areas, they also tend to be composed primarily of African-Americans and Hispanics. Urban districts are large, as are the schools they operate; governance is formal and impersonal, epitomizing the bureaucratic tradition. Rural school districts tend to be small, frequently operating only one school serving all grades; governance tends toward the informal and personal with strong community participation. Effective urban schools and rural schools tend to be ethnically homogeneous.

The average achievement of urban children is well below suburban and rural norms. However, some urban schools are more effective than others. Effective urban schools have developed a nurturing school culture that demonstrates care and respect for the individual and sets high achievement expectations, with student progress carefully monitored. The effective urban school establishes linkages with the community surrounding the school and motivates teachers through involvement and example. Strong professional leadership appears to be key to its success.

Strong professional leadership and high expectations are not typically characteristic of rural schools; nevertheless, there are striking similarities between effective urban schools and rural schools (Jacobson, 1988; Reed, 1985). Rural children tend to achieve at or above state averages in spite of the limitations of their curricula. The relative success of rural schools in terms of student achievement has been attributed to their nurturing environment, fostered by smallness and community involvement. Rural schools do not typically have a formal monitoring procedure for student progress, but because of their smallness, children do not get "lost"; their special qualities are well known to teachers and administrators. In rural areas, the prerequisite climate seems to arise naturally out of the rural context; in urban areas, the necessary climate seems to be dependent on professional leadership.

SCHOOL CULTURE, SIZE, AND GOVERNANCE

What size should a school be? Barker and Gump (1964) were not specific, but they provided a useful guide as they concluded their classic work with these words: "The data of this research and our own educational values tell us that a school should be sufficiently small that all of its students are needed for its enterprises. A school should be small enough that students are not redundant" (p. 292). Conant's (1959) study of the American high school was more specific, recommending a school with a minimum of 100 graduates per year. This recommendation agrees with the conclusions of Monk and Haller (1986) cited earlier. Newmann (1981) reports that secondary schools should have between 500 and 1,200 students. Participation in school activities and the quality of general interaction among students are highest in that range; vandalism and delinquency are lowest: "[T]he opportunity that small schools provide for sustained contact among all members is a significant safeguard against alienation. The larger the school, the more difficult it is to achieve clear, consensual goals, to promote student participation in school management, and to create positive personal relations among students and staff" (p. 552).

Goodlad (1984), in his comprehensive national study, *A Place Called School*, observes:

> Most of the schools clustering in the top group of our sample on major characteris-

TABLE 2 Summary of Comparisons of Typical Urban Schools, Effective Urban Schools, and Rural Schools

Characteristics	*Typical Urban Schools*	*Effective Urban Schools*	*Rural Schools*
School and District Size	very large and unwieldly; typically over 1,000	same as typical urban schools	small; most high schools < 400; frequently K–12 configuration
Nature of Pupil Population			
SES of Students	low	low	low
Cultural Diversity of Pupils	highly heterogeneous and increasing	poor and minority	tend to be ethnically homogeneous
Pupil Achievement	well below national average	fair; improving; emphasized throughout school	high, relative to urban schools
School Culture			
Achievement Expectations	low	high	low
Sense of Community	no sense of community; unconnectedness between school and life of students	developing sense of community; nurturing; challenging; compassionate	nurturing; relaxed (laid back); focal point for student and community activities
Achievement Evaluation	traditional teacher evaluation	systematic; emphasized by administrators and teachers	teacher evaluation; report
Discipline	inconsistent and poor; violence; vandalism	good; orderly; preplanned routines	orderly; self-monitored
Leadership and Decision Making			
Leadership	poor; limited power	strong administrators employing creative insubordination	frequently weak and inexperienced; school boards frequently involved in administrative decisions
Decision Making	district level; highly bureaucratic	same as typical urban schools	school board and administrators
Community Relations	very limited; parents feel disenfranchised and no sense of ownership	somewhat greater than in typical urban schools	strong; school is center of social and cultural activities
Curriculum Staff			
Curriculum	very diverse; many offerings	fewer offerings than typical urban schools; emphasis on basic skills	basic skills; enrichment limited; scheduling difficulties
Staff	fair; poor attitudes; no sense of ownership; moderate and increasing salaries	fair; good attitudes; greater sense of ownership; salaries same as typical urban schools	acceptable; many locals; sense of ownership
Financing	moderate	moderate	low

> tics were small, compared with the schools clustering near the bottom. It is not impossible to have a good large school; it is simply more difficult.... What are the defensible reasons for operating an elementary school of more than a dozen teachers and 300 boys and girls? I can think of none. (p. 309)

Concerning secondary schools, Goodlad writes:

> Clearly we need sustained, creative efforts designed to show the curricular deficits incurred in very small high schools, the curricular possibilities of larger schools, and the point where increased size suggests no curricular gain.... The burden of proof, it appears to me, is on large size. Indeed, I would not want to face the challenge of justifying a senior, let alone a junior, high of more than 500 to 600 students (unless I were willing to place arguments for a strong football team ahead of arguments for a good school, which I am not). (p. 310)

Boyer's (1983) report of the Carnegie Foundation's study, *High School,* notes that research over the past several decades suggests that small schools provide greater opportunity for student participation and greater emotional support than larger ones. Acknowledging the difficulty of knowing the exact point when a high school becomes too large, he proposes that schools enrolling 1,500 to 2,000 students are good candidates for reorganizing into smaller units using the school-within-a-school concept. Turning to the issue of the small high school, Boyer asks, "Can a small school provide the education opportunities to match the social and emotional advantages that may accompany smallness? We believe the preferred arrangement is to have bigness *and* smallness—a broad education program with supportive social arrangements" (p. 235).

In summary, there is no clear agreement on the optimum size of a school, particularly at the secondary level, and the criteria for optimally sized schools continue to change. Optimum size is a function of desired standards, available technology, and governing structures. Bigness is no longer automatically viewed as a virtue.

The current school reform movement has set significantly higher academic standards. Standards have also changed because of federal and state policies on affirmative action, education of the handicapped, and occupational education. The need to meet these new standards is often cited as a reason for the consolidation of small schools and school districts.

The creation of regional service units lowered the minimum functional size of school districts by making it possible for many small districts jointly to provide specialized programs and services that none could provide alone. Intermediate units largely provide occupational education and education of the severely handicapped. They also provide certain administrative, instructional, and technological services, e.g., joint purchasing, mainframe computers, staff development, graphics laboratories, curriculum consultants, and hardware and software support groups.

Developments in educational technology have affected the definition of optimal school size in the past and are likely to continue to do so in the future. For example, the policy of rural school consolidation was viable only after the development of the school bus and paved highways. Realization of the full potential of many emerging technological developments, such as teleconferencing and computerized information systems, will occur only through networking at the regional, state, and national levels. School districts, large or small, cannot do it alone. When the supporting infrastructures are built, optimal school size may be greatly reduced.

For decades, the conflict between the ideal of providing for individual needs and the practice of standardization has plagued the educational community. School district consolidation has assumed that individual needs can be met only by providing an increased number of standardized programs. Studies of size have generally assumed that the variety of programs identified by separate classes truly measures diversity of opportunity for learning. This can be a fallacious assumption. Compare, for example, the one-room schoolhouse to the comprehensive urban high school. In the one-room schoolhouse, one teacher served 30 or more students at different grade levels and taught a variety of subjects. Older children helped younger children, and much learning was done independently. Program diversity derived simply from the diversity of the children and the flexibility of the teacher. It cannot be said, however, that because one teacher served a group of 30 children, only one program existed.

The comprehensive urban high school assumes that the greater the number of program offerings, the richer the program for the student. Yet, just the opposite may be true. With size comes specialization and more rigidly defined curricula. Teaching becomes compartmentalized into departments and special topics or courses within departments. Once size forces departmentalization and specialization within programs, organizational constraints do indeed require a greater number of programs to provide enrichment. A large school may offer more "pieces" of an educational program; but if the pieces are standardized, they may also be fragmented. When education is fragmented, building understanding of a broader picture requires more fragments. In this context, a greater variety of "programs" might be necessary for "quality" education, but the availability of a greater variety of fragments by no means guarantees a quality education for individual students.

Both rural and urban schools are finding it difficult to meet the higher standards of the current school reform movement. The bureaucratic nature of urban schools and school districts, derived primarily from their large size, appears to be a major impediment to reform for all but the most stalwart. On the other hand, the smallness of rural schools severely limits their options in providing new curricula. A nurturing school culture and community involvement seem to be achieved more easily in small schools than in large ones; however, it is easier to provide diversity in large schools than in small ones.

In the past, providing diversity in curriculum and support services at an affordable cost were the primary justifications for large urban schools and rural school consolidation. Now, the disadvantages of bigness and the virtues of smallness have been well documented. Additionally, technological advances characteristic of the "Information Age" have made it possible for any individual in almost any location to access curricular diversity easily. These developments combine to impel a reassessment of the large-school policies of central cities and state school consolidation policies.

Smallness facilitates, but does not assure, the nurturing school climate desired. Strong leadership with staff and community involvement is also necessary. The single-building district is the epitome of school-based decision making and can serve as a model for urban schools. On the other hand, rural schools are not noted for strong professional leadership, high expectations for their students, or careful monitoring of academic progress. Despite their success in teaching the basic skills to poor white populations, their record with poor African-American and Hispanic populations is abysmal. In these respects, rural schools can learn much from effective urban schools.

Schools of any size, but especially small schools, require support services which they cannot provide themselves in a cost-effective manner. In rural areas, such services increasingly are being provided through intermediate districts. This trend needs to be greatly accelerated if rural schools are to keep up with modern demands. In enlarging the domain of decision making at the building level, and in reducing the domain of decision making at the district level, central city districts may begin to take on the characteristics of intermediate districts.

It is interesting to note that the state of Illinois has made radical changes in the governance of education in Chicago. In the fall of 1989, the functions of the present board of education will be altered, placing much of the control of schools in the hands of school councils consisting of six parents, two local residents, and two teachers. Day-to-day authority will be in the hands of principals, who will be selected by the councils. The councils will also have the authority to set the budget and to dismiss incompetent teachers on 45 days' notice (Snider, 1989). This may be a precursor of things to come.

School building administrators will be responsible for many of the functions formerly associated with central offices, such as budgeting, community relations, and personnel selection. Traditional responsibilities of building principals will continue, although they may be shared to a greater extent with teachers. Discretion over curriculum and programs will increase at the building level. The type of shared decision making envisioned will require a substantially different orientation from the authoritarian, bureaucratic style characteristic of administrators in most urban and many other schools today. The role of the principal of the future is likely to be cast in terms similar to that of today's rural school superintendent. The role of the big-city superintendent is likely to focus on strategic planning and policy development.

Programs preparing teachers and school administrators will have to adjust their curricula to prepare professionals appropriately for these newly defined roles. Teachers will require some orientation toward traditional administrative concerns such as group decision making and organizational development. Principals will continue to need to be experts in curriculum development, but they will also need a fundamental understanding of school business functions and community relations. Superintendents will have to master skills and concepts related to strategic planning, policy making, and negotiations relying heavily upon the disciplines of political science and policy studies.

18

Racism and the Education of Young Children

James P. Comer
Yale University

In the child's development, when and how does the concept of race arise? How can primary and secondary caregivers help a child in a racist society develop a positive self-image and achieve a healthy understanding of racial and cultural diversity?

A four-year-old black child slapped her doll and said, "Shut up, you black bitch!" Her white teacher, horrified and confused by the incident, retreated without a response. In a second situation, several white classmates of a black child spoke to her in racially derogatory ways. Her mother complained to her teacher and to the principal. They both acknowledged the incidents but indicated that the children intended no harm. The principal did eventually agree to move the child to the classroom of a second white teacher at the same grade level. Several days later the child sent her mother a card on which she had drawn a big red heart with a note that read: "Thank you, Mommy, my teacher touched me [an affectionate hug] today."

In the first case, the child and her family were victims of long-standing societal racism that had been institutionalized and internalized, and was being prepared for transmission to the next generation. Because the pervasiveness and multiple manifestations of racism have not been acknowledged, nor adequately addressed, the teacher was not in a position to help minimize its harmful effects. In the second situation, overt racism was acceptable, harmful, but limited in the case of this particular child largely because of the action of her mother. Because of racism and its pervasiveness, however, its victims are unable, disproportionately, to limit its effects and ancillary problems.

Racism interferes with the normal development of those children subjected to it. It hampers their ability to function at their full potential as children and, later, as adults. This contributes to their greater involvement in social problems such as poor school learning, juvenile delinquency, teenage pregnancy, and substance abuse. These problems decrease our human resources, drain our financial resources, and intensify intergroup relationship problems. They permit and promote harmful assumptions that, in turn, interfere with the development and functioning of majority-group children, adults, and institutions.

It is estimated that by the early 1990s minorities will make up one-third of our work force.[1] Unless minority children are fully prepared to participate in the job market of tomorrow, the economy will be adversely affected. Unless minority and majority children are prepared to function adequately in an open society, our quality of life will be lowered and our democratic ideals will never be realized. Once racist attitudes, values, and ways are established in individuals, change is difficult. Thus, prevention in early childhood is extremely important, yet early childhood education has not given adequate attention to this matter.

In this article, I will discuss the ways that racism affects child development. Then, I will briefly discuss the historic racial experiences and reaction to them that have made it difficult for us to address racism. Third, I will discuss the implications of racism and its history in this country for the preparation and practice of early childhood professionals.

RACISM AND CHILD DEVELOPMENT

Because of the dependent nature of the child, the parent or caretaker must provide for essential needs. In the process, the relationship needs of child and caretaker are met and lead to an emotional attachment or bond between them. This enables the caretaker to influence the development of the child along multiple growth pathways, five of which are critical to school learning: social-interactive, psycho-emotional, moral, speech-language, and cognitive-intellectual-academic. Interactions between parent and child in almost every setting—from a bedtime story to discussing safety precautions, or a trip to the grocery store—provide the content and context for growth and development.

The child needs the guidance, protection, and approval—and resulting security—the caretaker provides. This need motivates the child to behave more often than not in an adult-satisfying manner. A cycle of generally acceptable performance and approval is set in motion. Approval gives the young child a sense of acceptance and belonging and a related sense of well-being. Disapproval, rejection, and neglect are sources of anxiety.

Source: Reprinted by permission of the publisher from Rust, Frances O'Connell and Williams, Leslie, THE CARE AND EDUCATION OF YOUNG CHILDREN: EXPANDING CONTEXTS, SHARPENING FOCUS. (New York: Teachers College Press, © 1989 by Teachers College, Columbia University. All rights reserved.), "Racism and the Education of Young Children" by James P. Comer.

The parents are the first members of the larger society in the life of the child. They are members of a social network that may or may not be a part of the social mainstream. They bring their particular skills and the social network attitudes, values, and ways to the task of child care and rearing. Because of the extreme dependency of the child and the important role of the caretaker, the attitudes, values, and ways of the caretaker greatly influence those of the young child. This allows the caretaker to mediate the child's experiences—to give them meaning and to establish their relative importance.

Also, the psychosocial status of the child is derived from that of the parent. The education, economic condition, religion, and belief system of the parents all affect the quality of care the child receives from them. The social status and race of the parent often affect the expectations of the child by parents and others alike. When the child enters a larger network of social contacts, his or her behavior and skills elicit a positive or negative reaction. Frequent success and approval deepens and enlarges a child's previously gained sense of well-being and confidence. A positive sense of self begins to emerge, but it is highly vulnerable. Adults must be able to protect the young child from experiences that undermine his or her sense of well-being, adequacy, and confidence.

Cognitive development around three years of age permits a child to become aware of racial difference and it is here that he or she can first directly experience the effects of racism. It is here that caretakers should be able to help children feel positive about their own racial group and that of others. Positive feelings about race can enlarge a child's overall desirable sense of self. Negative feelings about race can plant seeds of self-doubt even among children who are developing well otherwise.[2]

There is a more subtle and serious problem for many minority children. Race-related social conditions, past and present, have put a disproportionate number of minority parents under stress. Many are not able to provide their children with the kind of developmental experiences that will prepare them for school or elicit positive responses from others. Some are underdeveloped along critical developmental pathways. Some display attitudes, values, and ways that are different from those of the mainstream.[3] This was the case for the four-year-old who slapped her doll in the vignette above. Such behaviors are sometimes believed to be due to the race of the child. Even when this is not the case, caretakers—for reasons described below—are often not able to respond appropriately. Negative racial feelings and behaviors are maintained. The child's behavior reinforces adverse expectations and behaviors of even the most empathetic caretaker. Reactions from guilt through avoidance to pity and permissiveness are as harmful as overt racial antagonism.

Majority children, and more fortunate minority children, interacting with minority children from families under stress often gain racial perceptions that are harmful to themselves and to minorities. For example, two six-year-old first graders—one black, one white, and both from middle-income families—were walking to school. They encountered a group of black children from a housing project who attended the same school. The white child said to her black friend, "Hold my hand, here come the black kids, and they fight." From her point of view, her black friend was not "black." Such perceptions are harmful to all involved.

Adequately functioning minority parents usually help their children understand such perceptions, and show them that the problem or shortcoming is with the person who displays misperceptions or outright racial antagonisms, not in themselves. Such parents usually teach their children to manage overt racial antagonisms in ways that minimize the frequency of such attacks, and their psychosocial damage. When minority parents are comfortable with their own racial identity, their children have a good chance of acquiring the same level of comfort. They acquire their racial and ethnic culture from their parents and the experiences they expose them to in a natural and positive way. For many, however, this is not the case. Often, as in the case above, child-care workers are not able to protect children from the negative effects of racism, even when they would like to do so. As in the second case above, the caretakers—teachers and principals—are sometimes the source of the racist attitudes, or make no effort to protect the black child. Again, many black parents are victims of racism to the point that they cannot protect their children from its negative effects.

The effects of racism begin to impact children more directly after eight or nine years of age. Somewhere between eight and twelve children begin to "place" themselves and their families in the social status structure that they have begun to observe. They begin to internalize the attitudes about themselves held by powerful individuals in their environment—parents, teachers, others—and they often act on or react to these expectations in a self-fulfilling manner. School curricula, television programs, people and practices, regularly convey messages about race that can be troublesome to minority children.

Many minority children have no way to understand the inequities in the society as anything but deficits within their own group. This can be troublesome even for black young people who are developing reasonably well overall, creating outright racial identity problems for many during adolescence. Without a mechanism to counter the negative messages about themselves transmitted in the larger society, some associate problem behavior with their minority identity. Among some, school achievement or high-level aspirations become nonminority activities. Some successful minority young people who are uncomfortable with their identity attempt to distance themselves from their group. For example, the first black valedictorian at a suburban high school in Ohio said, "I'm tired of hearing all this stuff about being the first black; I'm an individual and that's the only thing that counts." Such attitudes and behaviors among the most able minority students limit the peer support available to undermine the effects of racism in this country, and in turn permit racism to interfere with the development of black children in the next generation.

HISTORY, RACISM, AND CHILD DEVELOPMENT

We have reacted to our historical racial experience in ways that make it extremely difficult to overcome its contemporary adverse effects on child development. Many Americans—black and white—would prefer to end past race-based inequities and injustices and try to create a more just society without fully considering the effects of the past. We are embarrassed, guilty, and ashamed of the treatment of blacks, Native Americans, and Hispanics in particular. Many see no political, economic, or social benefit for themselves in fully considering the adverse effects of the past on these groups. Because our society has avoided, denied, and rationalized the more difficult and more troublesome outcomes of our historical racial experience on these groups, we have facilitated race-based public policy and practices that victimize these groups even more.

The textbooks and curricula in most schools inadequately address our racial history. Some do not address it at all. Schools of higher education are only slightly better. Even the social and behavioral sciences and social services give inadequate attention to historical public policy and social context issues that focus more on the affected groups and individuals. Most relevant here, many schools of education give little attention to the way in which minority students have been disadvantaged, and what to do about it. As a result, some of the most educated people in America—policymakers and trend setters—do not have the knowledge base necessary to understand and address race-based problems. Thus, it is not uncommon to hear even well-meaning people say, "We [their ethnic group] made it, why can't the blacks—or browns?"

Without an understanding of the fundamental difference between the European and Asian immigrant experience and that of blacks, we cannot understand and interpret the forces of racism in the society in general, and in early childhood education in particular. Racism's most serious damage was done by disrupting the organizing aspects of the culture of victimized groups.[4] This resulted in adverse effects on institutional life, particularly family life, and in turn on child development. I will briefly review the European and Asian experience in this regard, and while the underlying problem is the same for other minority groups, I will confine my discussion in this paper to the experience of blacks.

All immigrant groups experienced hardship, but most also experienced a reasonable degree of continuity. They were able to continue their religion, language, and other aspects of their culture in the new country. Many came in groups, voluntarily, from the old country and settled together in the new country. These circumstances often created a fair degree of cohesion within immigrant groups.[5]

Most immigrants were able to vote within a short period of time. This facilitated the acquisition of political power in one generation and, in turn, brought economic and social power. Usually a few members of a group either brought or had access to wealth from the old country. Political, economic, and social power within the mainstream of the society created networks of contacts, ties, and information that first served to decrease the antagonism toward their group, and then to pull many other families into networks of mainstream opportunity. These developments made education available and important. As a result, immigrants were able to undergo in three generations development that paralleled economic development in this country. Our most massive immigration occurred before 1915. Before 1900 it was possible to earn a living without an education and to create the level of family stability that would enable children to participate in a job market between 1900 and 1945 that required a moderate level of education and training. Families able to participate in the job market of this period were in the best position to enable their children to acquire the high level of education and skills necessary to participate in the economy between 1945 and 1980, and so on into the postindustrial economy after 1980. While there were psychosocial casualties due to the dislocation and hardships related to immigration, there were fewer among these immigrant groups than among groups that experienced more traumatic social histories.

The black beginnings—as Americans—were marked by cultural discontinuity, rather than continuity. Blacks experienced the loss of their organizing institutions—political, economic, and social. In West Africa, these institutions were providing adaptive attitudes, values, and ways. The culture of slavery that was imposed broke this influence. Slavery was a system of forced dependency and inherent inferiority, without hope of a better future. Slave parents were not preparing their children for a prideful place or greater opportunity in the new culture. These conditions produced severely negative psychosocial consequences for many. Some made adaptive responses that protected them from the most adverse effects of slavery, and some lived under less harsh conditions of slavery. A black church was created out of the aesthetic remnants of African culture and the Protestant religion of slavemasters.[6] Some slaves were able to identify with the best aspects of their masters and the new culture. Even these adaptations, however, left the slaves vulnerable to negative identifications as a racial group. In fact, they were not a single and cohesive ethnic group. All of these conditions made cultural cohesion during and after slavery extremely difficult.

After slavery, violence and subterfuge were used to deny most blacks the vote.[7] As a result, blacks were closed out of mainstream political, economic, and social power. They had no access to wealth. Without power, the group could not decrease the high level of racism and the denial of opportunity. As a result, in the eight states that had 80 percent of the black population right into the 1930s, educational expenditures for white children were four to eight times those for black children. In some places the disparity was as great as twenty-five times or more.[8] The same disparity existed in higher education. As late as the mid-1960s, the combined endowment of two prestigious white women's colleges was equal to one-half that of a single Ivy League college serving white males; and the one-half endowment of the latter was greater than that of the more than one hundred black colleges put together.[9]

Even educated black people were closed out of the economic mainstream. In order to facilitate segregation, a black leadership group, serving blacks, was allowed to emerge in religion and the professional areas only. These conditions denied blacks the contacts, knowledge, and experiences of mainstream political, economic, and social institutions, and the ability to pull families into them, or to make education possible and meaningful to the widest number of people. Despite this, the supportive and adaptive nature of rural culture and the black church enabled many families to do reasonably well until the 1950s. As late as the 1940s, only slightly over 20 percent of all black families were single-parent families; now the statistic is around 50 percent. Most black communities were reasonably safe through the 1950s.[10] Around 1945, however, education became the ticket for admission to living-wage jobs. Blacks, closed out of the educational mainstream during the period when most Americans were gaining the education needed to participate in the last stage of the industrial era and beyond, were most hurt.

Exclusion from the primary job market, combined with urbanization and the significant decline of black church influence, put a large number of families under great stress. Many families that once functioned well began to function less well in urban areas north and south. After 1945, well-functioning families from all groups began to have fewer children, except where there were religious reasons. This was not the case for poorly functioning families, of whom, for historic reasons, a disproportionate number were black.

Because of racist policies, practices, and structural changes, blacks were not able to undergo the same degree of the three-generational movement as other groups. Nonetheless, there were three generations of development among many black families. It is this group that has been able to take advantage of opportunities created by the elimination of the legal structures supporting racism. Those families most victimized by past conditions of racism and structural changes are least able to take advantage of new opportunities. These constitute the group that American institutions have not brought into the mainstream of society.

American institutions made an inadequate adjustment to structural changes after World War II. We did not develop the kinds of housing, health, and educational policies that could have interrupted the residual effects of racism and related poverty, that could have reduced the stress on black families. Today, many families under stress are unable to give their children the kinds of experiences that can prepare them to succeed in school and in life. Even many functioning reasonably well are excluded from the mainstream of the society to the point that they often do not know how to provide their children with experiences that can enable them to succeed.

The black community has been preoccupied with trying to reduce racism without having access to the traditional mainstream power base. It has not had the cohesion and power needed to positively affect the lives of its most victimized families. As a result, too many underachieve, and behave in troublesome ways. Racism allowed many to accept the academic underachievement and troublesome behavior of many children from the most victimized black families as evidence of their lack of ability and undesirability, rather than as consequences of exclusion from the societal mainstream. This has resulted in school failure and other social problems rather than the social mainstream success that was, and is, possible for most Americans.

The black experience described above permits a black child to slap her doll and say, "Shut up you black bitch"; permits some white school personnel to ignore racist intimidation of black children, or to participate in it; permits black children to experience conditions and pick up information that contributes to negative racial identities; permits white children to make inaccurate assumptions about blacks, and their own racial group; and, finally, permits our institutions, even those preparing teachers to help children grow and learn, to ignore the past effects of racism to the point that they cannot help children avoid the adverse consequences of it.

IMPLICATIONS FOR EARLY CHILDHOOD EDUCATION: TRAINING AND PRACTICE

In 1968 our Yale Child Study Center team—a psychiatrist, a social worker, a special education teacher, and a psychologist—went into two inner-city schools that were troublesome expressions of our nation's racial policy. The students were 99 percent black, and almost all were poor. In 1969, the achievement level of the fourth graders in these schools was thirty-second and thirty-third out of thirty-three schools. These students were nineteen and eighteen months behind in language arts and mathematics. We terminated the program in one school after five years because both staff and parents there were comfortable with the changes that had been made and were unwilling to proceed further. We entered a second school with a similar profile to that of the school we had been serving. The majority of students in the new school were also drawn from a housing project. By 1984, the two schools, without any changes in socioeconomic makeup, were tied for the third and fourth highest level achievement on the IOWA Test of Basic Skills. One school was a year above, and the second was seven months above grade level. Attendance and behavior in these schools were among the best in the city. These outcomes were achieved by using our knowledge of history, child development, and human-system interactions to understand the behavior of parents, staff, and students in school. With this understanding, we were able to create mechanisms, programs, and practices in the school that overcame those effects of racism and poverty that limited the school performance of staff and students, and school support among parents.

A major task was to overcome partially race-based assumptions among staff and parents about the ability and troublesome behavior of the students. Through an understanding of the historical experience of blacks, the staff came to appreciate how many of the students were prepared for life in the nonmainstream social network of their families, but were not prepared for the mainstream experience and expectations of the school. This led to a project entitled "The Social Skills Curriculum for Inner City Children." This curriculum involved parents and integrated the teaching of basic skills, social skills, and appreciation of the arts. It included an appreciation of black culture. This program facilitated positive home-school relationships, greater student growth and development, and a positive racial identity among the students. It also resulted in significantly improved achievement and social behavior.

None of the teachers had had the kind of preservice training that would have enabled them to work in the ways needed with the children, parents, and each other. In-service activities had to be provided. This should not have been necessary in a multicultural society committed to providing children from all socioeconomic backgrounds with the kind of education that allows them to achieve at the level of their ability. Preservice programs—in and outside the discipline of education—should provide all students with an understanding of how structural forces, policies, and practices impact communities, groups and families, and child development.

Race has been a central issue in American life. The ways in which it has affected child development must be considered in preservice programs. Teachers should have an opportunity—both in pre- and in-service training—to learn the ways in which their behavior can either facilitate or interfere with the development of children. They should be prepared to address the race-related needs of minority children. Because of the power of early childhood educators to influence child development, it is critically important that their educational training provide them with the knowledge, skills, and sensitivity to protect children from racial attitudes and conditions that interfere with development. Early childhood educators must be prepared to promote the development and learning of children who are attempting to grow and learn in spite of race-based obstacles to their success.

REFERENCES

1 "Here They Come, Ready or Not," *Education Week*, Special Report, May 14, 1986, p. 31.

2 James P. Comer and Alvin F. Poussant, *Black Child Care* (New York: Simon & Schuster, 1975).

3 James P. Comer, *School Power: Implications of an Intervention Project* (New York: Free Press, 1980).

4 James P.Comer, *Beyond Black and White* (New York: Quadrangle/New York Times Books, 1972).

5 Marcus Lee Hansen, *The Immigrant in American History* (Cambridge: Harvard University Press, 1940).

6 E. Franklin Frazier, *The Negro Church in America* (New York: Schocken Books, 1963).

7 John Hope Franklin, *Reconstruction after the Civil War* (Chicago: University of Chicago Press, 1961).

8 David T. Blose and Ambrose Caliver, *Statistics on the Education of Negroes, 1929–1932*, Bulletin #13, U.S. Office of Education (Washington, D.C.: Department of the Interior, 1936).

9 Council for Financial Aid to Education, *1964–65 Voluntary Support of America's Colleges and Universities* (New York: Council for Financial Aid to Education, 1967).

10 U.S. Bureau of the Census, *Statistical Abstract of the United States* (Washington, D.C.: U.S. Department of Commerce, 1951 and 1987).

19

Protecting the Future

A Successful Alternative Program for Dropout Prevention

Larry D. Dorrell

The administration of the Senior High School in Mexico, Missouri, like most public secondary school administrations, was concerned about the number of students dropping out of school. During the decade of the eighties, the national high school dropout rate has been between 25 and 28 percent (Beck and Muia 1980; School Dropouts 1983; School Dropouts 1985; High Schools 1986; Thompson 1986; Fine 1983) and the rate in Missouri has remained around 25 percent (Ashcroft 1988). While Mexico's dropout rate, at 20 percent, was not as high as the state or national average, it was still too high (Mongler 1988). The loss of even one student from the educational environment was a reason for concern to these administrators.

To find alternative programming for those students at risk for failure, the school administration began discussions with the special services director at the building and district levels. A decision was made to organize an advisory committee from the school and community. As a result of the deliberations of the advisory committee, an alternative program to aid the at-risk student was developed. Potential dropouts entering the ninth and tenth grades in the 1983–84 school year were identified. Participants were students who

1. failed to pass the reading and/or math subtest of the Missouri Basic Essential Skills Test;
2. scored below the 28th percentile on the reading, total language, and/or total math subtest of the Iowa Test of Basic Skills; or
3. had a cumulative eighth grade grade point average of 1.0 or less.

Thirty-five students from each grade, seventy in all, entered the program in the fall of 1983. The new alternative program became known as the Career Exploratory Program (CEP) and contained three important aspects: identifying potential dropouts, providing those students with a greater opportunity for success in the educational environment through prevocational education, and providing a greater opportunity for successful completion of a secondary education.

It was the mission of the CEP to provide an alternative educational environment for the at-risk student. Those students who were identified for the program were provided remediation in the core skill areas of math, reading, and English. They did not take the regular communications skills or math classes during their freshman and sophomore years. Rather, they received individualized attention through the Related Occupational Communications and Related Occupational Math classes.

In support of remediation in math and English, each student took a course entitled Occupational Orientation/Assessment. That class was taught by the director of the CEP program and was an attempt to motivate the at-risk student while providing assessment and information to the student on occupational choices and opportunities.

With remediation in math, reading, and communication skills and a program director to provide support and motivation, school officials assumed that at-risk students would have a greater chance at educational success. Many high school dropouts leave school because they believe that school is not for them, a result of the students' failure to achieve any success in the educational environment (Mann 1986; McDill, 1985; Solorzano 1986). The CEP program was designed to provide opportunities for successes and to motivate the at-risk student to remain in school.

Many secondary school educators are aware that, at the high school level, elective courses give the at-risk student a greater opportunity for success, but most of these classes are available only to juniors and seniors through area vocational schools. Many at-risk students who can survive the required courses at the freshman and sophomore levels and then qualify for vocational classes will remain in school. It is true that the at-risk student has a higher success rate with the elective prevocational and vocational course offerings (Batsch 1984; The Forgotten Half 1988). But, as indicated, the problem arrives before the student has the opportunity to elect classes.

The pressure for the at-risk student to drop out is often greatly increased when those students enter their third year of high

Source: The Clearing House, Volume 62, pp. 259–262, February 1989. Reprinted with permission of the Helen Dwight Reid Educational Foundation. Published by Heldref Publications, 4000 Albemarle St., N.W., Washington, D.C. 20016.

school if they are still struggling to master the required classes and are not eligible for vocational education. The Mexico CEP therefore provided early remediation to help students meet graduation requirements. The program also provided the at-risk student with the opportunity for hands-on, prevocational courses at the freshman and sophomore levels. Course options in the prevocational area for the CEP students included exploratory classes in business/computer literacy, home economics/health care, auto body repair, automotive and small engine mechanics, building trades, and metal trades.

As a result of these new prevocational offerings, at-risk students found a reason to stay in school—hands-on education. Their day was broken up with some nontraditional classes that the students elected and enjoyed, and which were designed to provide greater opportunities for success.

How successful was the CEP program? The grade point average of the pool of students from the class of 1988 who were eligible for the CEP program provided some evidence. Thirty-five students were accepted into the program and nineteen others who were eligible were not. The grade point average of those who did not enter the program was 1.48 at the end of the eighth grade and increased to 1.87 in the tenth grade, an increase of 21 percent. The thirty-five CEP students' grade point averages increased from .95 in the eighth grade to 1.92 in the tenth grade, an increase of more than 100 percent. The CEP students had lower eighth grade averages, but by the tenth grade their averages were higher than those of the non-CEP students who had been eligible to enter the program (tables 1 and 2). One hundred percent of the sophomores who entered the program in 1983 were strong candidates for dropping out of school. Yet by 1986, 50 percent of the students had graduated, and 25 percent were still in school.

Mexico Senior High School's Career Exploratory Program was successful because the at-risk students had the opportunity to experience educational success. Nothing brings about success more than success itself. Those students who had experienced failure began experiencing success. Their attitudes towards school, teachers, and their fellow students improved. Many experienced the feelings of accomplishment and acceptance in school for the first time in years. Those positive experiences carried over into other areas. Attendance at school improved among those students. Referrals to the office by classroom teachers for discipline decreased.

The CEP students were not only experiencing success in the elective prevocational course offerings, but also in required classes. The restructuring of the freshman and sophomore classes required by the state or district for graduation enabled the students to succeed. In fact, teachers of the required math and English classes had to reevaluate their methods of instruction. Teachers identified teaching techniques that worked with their at-risk students. Lesson plans were organized into short, competency-based units, which required students to demonstrate mastery of each unit. The at-risk students were better able to demonstrate mastery with the short units, because many of them had short attention spans. Classroom teachers began to present material in shorter segments. For example, a full page of math problems might have resulted in students' giving up because there seemed to be no end to the work. So teachers began to give students the same work, but in smaller segments.

The CEP teachers discovered that teaching aids often considered inappropriate for

TABLE 1
Changes in Grade Point Averages of Students in CEP, Eighth Grade to Tenth Grade

Class of 1988 CEP students	*First semester eighth grade GPA*	*First semester tenth grade GPA*
1	1.00	3.056
2	1.25	2.833
3	.75	2.722
4	.75	2.667
5	1.50	2.665
6	1.00	2.556
7	1.50	2.444
8	2.25	2.444
9	1.00	2.389
10	1.25	2.389
11	1.00	2.333
12	1.00	2.222
13	.75	2.167
14	.75	2.167
15	1.25	2.056
16	.75	2.056
17	.25	1.994
18	.50	1.889
19	.25	1.889
20	1.25	1.833
21	1.25	1.722
22	1.25	1.667
23	1.50	1.667
24	.75	1.556
25	1.00	1.556
26	1.00	1.556
27	1.25	1.556
28	1.50	1.444
29	.75	1.389
30	.25	1.384
31	1.00	1.333
32	.25	1.1111
33	0.00	.944
34	.50	.889
35	1.00	.778
Average for 35 CEP students	.95	1.920
Average percentage of increase 102%		

Note: Four-point grading scale.

TABLE 2
Changes in Grade Point Averages of Students Not in CEP, Eighth Grade to Tenth Grade

Class of 1988 non-CEP students	*First semester eighth grade GPA*	*First semester tenth grade GPA*
1	1.50	2.833
2	2.00	2.777
3	2.25	2.611
4	1.25	2.555
5	2.00	2.166
6	1.25	2.166
7	1.50	1.944
8	2.25	1.944
9	1.25	1.888
10	1.50	1.833
11	1.50	1.777
12	1.50	1.777
13	1.25	1.722
14	1.25	1.666
15	1.00	1.666
16	1.25	1.166
17	.25	1.166
18	2.00	1.111
19	1.50	1.055
Average for 19 non-CEP students	1.48	1.870
Average percentage of increase 21%		

Note: Four-point grading scale.

regular students were of great benefit for the at-risk student. Hand calculators were made available in the math classrooms for simple math problems. The calculators proved to be aids to success. The math teachers began to understand that those students who were learning to operate a calculator, and thus gaining the ability to solve math problems, were gaining a valuable survival skill. If these students could use such aids effectively, they were better prepared to operate in society. When calculators were not used, and students did not attempt to solve problems, then none of the valuable math calculating skills could be gained.

In communication skills classes, writing assignments were also given in short segments to allow for success. Likewise, the teachers of the CEP students turned to unusual methods to retain the attention of students. Guest speakers from within the school and community were used to change the routine of the instructional period. Teachers allowed students to communicate their ideas and thoughts during a sharing time. At that time, students talked about their experiences, friends, problems, and school. They were not allowed to use the names of others if they were being critical, but they were allowed to express their concerns. Students were encouraged to share. That activity created a bond between teacher and student, which enhanced the holding power of the school. The teachers' sincere caring for students was a strong force in encouraging them to stay in school. The at-risk student, who is often not accepted by peers, is in great need of acceptance by his or her teachers.

The CEP teachers began to give rewards for completion of assigned work. Eventually that resulted in improvement of grades, and improved grades began to motivate the students. But first the students needed to experience success. When assignments were completed, the students were offered free time, allowed special passes outside the classroom, given candy bars, and so on.

The CEP teachers also directed the required math and communication skills course work toward subjects of interest to the students. The at-risk students had great interest in obtaining a car, with its symbolic independence and status. So, CEP teachers taught such things as percentages in relation to car loans. Bank loan officers and insurance representatives came to the classroom as guest speakers. In the communication skills class, students completed job applications and heard guest speakers from local businesses that employed high school students. A connection was made between school work, employment, and subjects of interest to the at-risk student.

The CEP teachers developed awards and certificates of accomplishment. The at-risk students were thus able to receive recognition like other students. Likewise, the CEP teachers made every attempt to brag about their students and their accomplishments. For some of the students, it was the first time in years that anyone had complimented them to their parents and others.

Opportunities for the students to pass the required classes for graduation, to experience prevocational classes, and to develop a bond with their teachers were basic to the success of the program. The teaching staff was also integral to the program. Teachers were able to demonstrate a caring concern for their students that resulted in positive action on the part of the students.

The Career Exploratory Program is an alternative program for the at-risk student that works. It has made it possible for the Mexico public schools to protect part of the city's future.

20

The New Untouchables

Jonathan Kozol

On an average morning in Chicago, about 5,700 children in 190 classrooms come to school only to find they have no teacher. Victimized by endemic funding shortages, the system can't afford sufficient substitutes to take the place of missing teachers. "We've been in this typing class a whole semester," says a 15-year-old at Du Sable High, "and they still can't find us a teacher."

In a class of 39 children at Chicago's Goudy Elementary School, an adult is screaming at a child: "Keisha, look at me . . . Look me in the eye!" Keisha is fighting with a classmate. Over what? It turns out: over a crayon, said The Chicago Tribune in 1988. Last January the underfunded school began rationing supplies.

The odds these black kids in Chicago face are only slightly worse than those faced by low-income children all over America. Children like these will be the parents of the year 2000. Many of them will be unable to earn a living and fulfill the obligations of adults; they will see their families disintegrate, their children lost to drugs and destitution. When we later condemn them for "parental failings," as we inevitably will do, we may be forced to stop and remember how we also failed them in the first years of their lives.

It is a commonplace that a society reveals its reverence or contempt for history by the respect or disregard that it displays for older people. The way we treat our children tells us something of the future we envision. The willingness of the nation to relegate so many of these poorly housed and poorly fed and poorly educated children to the role of outcasts in a rich society is going to come back to haunt us.

With nearly 30 percent of high-school students dropping out before they graduate—60 percent in segregated high schools—it is not surprising that illiteracy figures have continued to grow worse. The much publicized volunteer literacy movement promoted for the last six years by Barbara Bush serves only 200,000 of the nation's estimated 30 million functional illiterates. Meanwhile, the gulf in income between rich and poor American families is wider than at any time since figures were recorded, starting in the 1940s. The richest 20 percent received 44 percent of national family income; the poorest 20 percent got only 4.6 percent. More than 5 million of the poorest group are children.

Disparities in wealth play out in financing of schools. Low-income children, who receive the least at home, receive the least from public education. New Trier High School, for example, serving children from such affluent suburbs as Winnetka, Ill., pays its better teachers 50 percent above the highest paid teachers at Du Sable, by no means the worst school in Chicago. The public schools in affluent Great Neck and White Plains, N.Y., spend twice as much per pupil as the schools that serve the children of the Bronx.

Infant-mortality figures, classic indices of health in most societies, have also worsened for poor children and especially for nonwhite children. The gap between white and black mortality in children continues to widen, reaching a 47-year high in 1987 (the most recent year for which data are available). Black children are more than twice as likely to die in infancy as whites—nine times as likely to be neurologically impaired. One possible consequence: black children are three times as likely as whites to be identified as mentally retarded by their public schools.

Federal programs initiated in the 1960s to assist low-income children, though far from universally successful, made solid gains in preschool education (Head Start), compensatory reading (Chapter I) and pre-college preparation (Upward Bound), while sharply cutting the rates of infant death and child malnutrition. Limited funding, however, narrowed the scope of all these efforts. Head Start, for example, never has reached more than one of five low-income children between its start-up in the '60s and today.

Rather than expand these programs, President Reagan kept them frozen or else cut them to the bone. Living stipends paid to welfare families with children dropped to 35 percent (adjusted for inflation) below the 1970 level. Nearly half a million families lost all welfare payments. A million people were cut from food stamps. Two million kids were dropped from school-lunch programs. The WIC program (Women, Infants, Children), which provides emergency nutrition supplements to low-income infants, young children and pregnant women, was another target of Reagan administration cuts, but Congress successfully fought them off. Despite their efforts, the WIC budget is woefully inadequate, and has never been able to provide services to even half of the children and women who meet the eligibility requirements.

Federal housing funds were also slashed during these years. As these cutbacks took their tolls, homeless children were seen begging in the streets of major cities for the first time since the Great Depression. A fivefold increase in homeless children was seen in Washington, D.C. in 1986 alone. By 1987 nearly half the occupants of homeless shelters in New York City were children. The average homeless child was only 6 years old.

The lives of homeless children tell us much of the disregard that society has shown for vulnerable people. Many of these kids

Source: From Jonathan Kozol, "The New Untouchables," *Newsweek, Special Issue*, Winter 1989, pp. 49–53. First appeared in Newsweek, printed by permission of the author.

grow up surrounded by infectious illnesses no longer seen in most developed nations. Whooping cough and tuberculosis, once regarded as archaic illnesses, are now familiar in the shelters. Shocking numbers of these children have not been inoculated and for this reason cannot go to school. Those who do are likely to be two years behind grade level.

Many get to class so tired and hungry that they cannot concentrate. Others are ashamed to go to school because of shunning by their peers. Classmates label them "the hotel children" and don't want to sit beside them. Even their teachers sometimes keep their distance. The children look diseased and dirty. Many times they are. Often unable to bathe, they bring the smell of destitution with them into school. There *is* a smell of destitution, I may add. It is the smell of sweat and filth and urine. Like many journalists, I often find myself ashamed to be resisting the affection of a tiny child whose entire being seems to emanate pathology.

So, in a terrifying sense, these children have become American untouchables. Far from demonstrating more compassion, administration leaders have resorted to a stylized severity in speaking of poor children. Children denied the opportunity for Head Start, sometimes health care, housing, even certified schoolteachers, have nonetheless been told by William J. Bennett, preaching from his bully pulpit as U.S. Secretary of Education under Reagan, that they would be held henceforth to "higher standards." Their parents—themselves too frequently the products of dysfunctional and underfunded urban schools—have nonetheless been lectured on their "lack of values." Efforts begun more than 10 years ago to equalize school funding between districts have been put on the back burner and are now replaced by strident exhortations to the poor to summon "higher motivation" and, no matter how debilitated by disease or hunger, to "stand tall." Celebrities are hired to sell children on the wisdom of not dropping out of school. The White House tells them they should "just say no" to the temptations of the streets. But hope cannot be marketed as easily as blue jeans. Certain realities—race and class and caste—are there and they remain.

What is the consequence of tougher rhetoric and more severe demands? Higher standards, in the absence of authentic educative opportunities in early years, function as a punitive attack on those who have been cheated since their infancy. Effectively, we now ask more of those to whom we now give less. Earlier testing for schoolchildren is prescribed. Those who fail are penalized by being held back from promotion and by being slotted into lower tracks where they cannot impede the progress of more privileged children. Those who disrupt classroom discipline are not placed in smaller classes with more patient teachers; instead, at a certain point, they are expelled—even if this means expulsion of a quarter of all pupils in the school. The pedagogic hero of the Reagan White House was Joe Clark—a principal who roamed the hallways of his segregated high school in New Jersey with a bullhorn and a bat and managed to raise reading scores by throwing out his low-achieving pupils.

In order to justify its abdication, the federal government has called for private business to assist the underfunded urban schools. While business leaders have responded with some money, they have also brought a very special set of values and priorities. The primary concern of business is the future productivity of citizens. Education is regarded as capital investment. The child is seen as raw material that needs a certain processing before it is of value. The question posed, therefore, is how much money it is worth investing in a certain child to obtain a certain economic gain. Educators, eager to win corporate support, tell business leaders what they want to hear. "We must start thinking of students as workers," says the head of the American Federation of Teachers, Albert Shanker.

The notion of kids as workers raises an unprecedented question. Is future productivity the only rationale for their existence? A lot of the things that make existence wonderful are locked out of the lives of children seen primarily as future clerical assistants or as possible recruits to office pools at IBM. The other consequence of "productivity" thinking is an increased willingness to make predictions about children, based almost entirely on their social status. Those whose present station seems to promise most are given most. Those whose origins are least auspicious are provided with stripped-down education. IQ testing of low-income babies has been recently proposed in order to identify those who are particularly intelligent and to accord them greater educational advantages, although this means that other babies will be stigmatized by their exclusion.

A heightened discrimination in the use of language points to a dual vision: we speak of the need to "train" the poor, but "educate" the children of the middle class and rich. References to "different learning styles" and the need to "target" different children with "appropriate" curricula are now becoming fashionable ways of justifying stratified approaches. Early tracking is one grim result. A virtual retreat from any efforts at desegregation is another: if children of different social classes need "appropriate" and "different" offerings, it is more efficient and sensible to teach them separately.

A century ago, Lord Acton spoke thus of the United States: "In a country where there is no distinction of class a child is not born to the station of its parents, but with an indefinite claim to all the prizes that can be won by thought and labor. It is in conformity with the theory of equality . . . to give as near as possible to every youth an equal start in life." Americans, he said, "are unwilling that any should be deprived in childhood of the means of competition."

That this tradition has been utterly betrayed in recent years is now self-evident. The sense of fairness, however, runs deep in the thinking of Americans. Though frequently eclipsed, it is a theme that stubbornly recurs. A quarter century ago, it took disruptions in the streets to force Americans to question the unfairness of de jure segregation. Today it is not law but economics that condemns the children of the very poor to the implacable inheritance of a diminished destiny. "No matter what they do," says the superintendent of Chicago's public schools, "their lot has been determined."

Between the dream and the reality there falls the shadow of the ghetto school, the ghetto hospital, the homeless shelter. Appeals to the pocketbook have done no good. Black leaders have begun to contemplate the need for massive protests by poor people. Middle-class students, viscerally shocked by the hard edge of poverty they see in city streets, may be disposed to join them. The price may be another decade of societal disruption. The reward may be the possibility that we can enter the next century not as two nations, vividly unequal, but as the truly democratic nation we profess to be and have the power to become. Whether enough people think this outcome worth the price, however, is by no means clear.

21

Educating Children of the Homeless

E. Anne Eddowes and John R. Hranitz

Millions of American citizens are homeless. Families whose members once held good-paying jobs and owned homes are joining ever-increasing numbers of the nation's *invisibles,* the homeless (McLuckie, 1988). These are the "... disheveled men slumped in doorways, the 'shopping bag ladies' poking their heads into garbage cans ... men, women, children sleeping in public parks, bus and train stations ... [and] evicted families who huddle together in an armory or other shelter" (Hope & Young, 1986, p. xi). Since the early 1980s, there has been a substantial increase in homelessness with estimates up to 3 million. More than one-third of the total are families with children, and at least one-third of that group are families with both parents who are trying to stay together (Children's Defense Fund, 1988a).

Generally, homelessness is defined as including anyone whose night residence is either in a shelter, on the street or in another public place (LaGory, Ritchey & Mullis, 1987). It is a complex problem with no easy solutions. The decreasing supply of older low-income housing is often cited as the primary reason for the increase in homelessness. For example, in Washington, DC, from 1977–82, thousands of apartments were converted into condominiums and cooperatives (Hope & Young, 1986). Also, since 1980 there has been a 70% decrease in federal funding for new low-income housing units (Children's Defense Fund, 1988b).

While the number of jobs has increased during this period, many of them pay minimum wage ($3.35 per hour) and have no health or sick-leave benefits. One parent must work 40 hours per week at $5.40 per hour for 52 weeks in order to earn $11,200, the current poverty line for a family of two adults and two children (National Coalition for the Homeless, no date). The decrease in federal funds for day care has compounded the problem, making affordable child care very scarce. With the rising costs of food, clothing and transportation, the plight of the homeless becomes more desperate with each day (McLuckie, 1988). Clearly, decent low-income housing, affordable day care and jobs paying more than the minimum wage (with basic benefits) must be a part of the complex formula to help the many homeless families.

PROBLEMS OF HOMELESS PARENTS AND CHILDREN

It has been said that families must learn to balance their priorities when trying to meet individual physical, personal and social needs (Hranitz & Eddowes, 1987). This is surely a mandate for all families, whether or not they have a home. When there is no home, however, the task of keeping things in balance may be next to impossible.

Maslow (1970) has described a hierarchy of human needs, beginning with bodily requisites and moving upward through several levels to self-actualization (Figure 1).

The typical homeless family today finds that the lowest level needs for shelter, adequate food and clothing are not being met. In addition, the family has little security (Level 2). Living in a car or on the streets is certainly not very safe. Even publicly supported shelters can be dangerous and unhealthful places to live (Kozol, 1988). This creates situations in which emotions inherent in trust, hope and achievement are replaced by mistrust, apathy and despair.

Moving is a way of life for homeless families. Sometimes it is done with the false hope that things will be better somewhere else. At other times it may be due to shelter rules. Most shelters won't allow people to stay longer than 30 days. Others may provide shelter only at night, forcing people to leave during the day (Children's Defense Fund, 1988a). Although the families try to provide a sense of love and belonging (Level 3), constant moving and lack of extended family support mean there are virtually no personal belongings to provide for tradition or a sense of being rooted in a culture or group (Kozol, 1988).

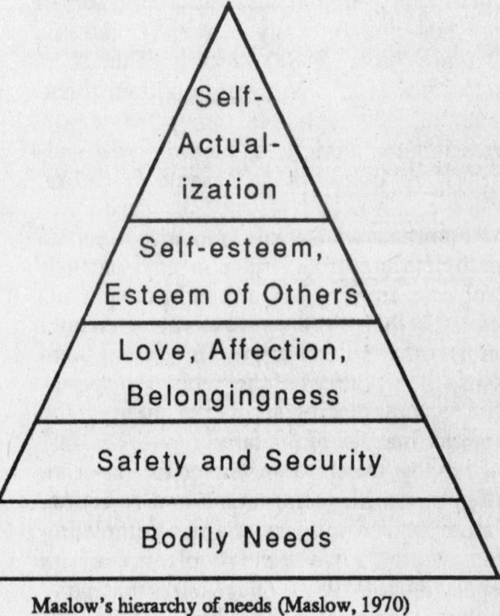

Maslow's hierarchy of needs (Maslow, 1970)

Source: From E. Anne Eddowes and John R. Hranitz, "Educating Children of the Homeless," *Childhood Education*, Volume 65, Summer 1989, pp. 197–200. Reprinted by permission of the Association for Childhood Education International, 11141 Georgia Avenue, Suite 200, Wheaton, MD.

Parents, no matter how poor, want to provide for the needs of their children. When this is impossible, the loss of self-esteem and the accompanying stress result in perceptions of failure and helplessness (Level 4). Homelessness itself is very stressful, as are the conditions leading to the loss of a home: loss of a job, eviction and marital problems (LaGory, Ritchey & Mullis, 1987). One can easily understand that few, if any, of these people reach the highest level of Maslow's hierarchy, self-actualization.

Homelessness is devastating to children, taking a toll on health and emotional well-being. Homeless children have no place to call their own; few personal belongings; and no intellectual support such as books, games, crayons or other materials. They continually leave behind any friends they may have made. The most critical problem many of these children face, however, is the denial of an education (National Coalition for the Homeless, 1987).

EDUCATIONAL PROBLEMS OF HOMELESS CHILDREN

Traditionally, homeless children have been excluded from the nation's public schools because of state and local enrollment requirements. In some communities, roadblocks include residency status, proof of age, immunization and health records, and proof that the child has attended school. For most homeless parents, getting their children enrolled is a feat that goes beyond their resources.

A survey completed by the Child Welfare League of America found that 43% of homeless children were not enrolled in any school program. In numbers, this translates into 4 out of every 10 homeless children of school age not attending any school (Children's Defense Fund, 1988a). A study of the characteristics of 156 homeless children found that "... developmental delays, severe depression and anxiety, and learning difficulties were common" (Bessuk & Rubin, 1987, p. 279).

Families whose children are fortunate enough to be enrolled in school find that their problems are only beginning. Many parents learn that their children are to attend a school on the other side of town. This forces them to use the resources of the public transportation system, placing another drain upon the limited finances of the family.

Finally, the children who go to school are often met with jeers, taunts and rejection. Falling asleep in class and not completing homework are two of the problems teachers report (Kozol, 1988). The result is that many drop out. Progress is short-lived for the children who *can* cope and do well in school, because the family is soon on the move again. The repeating cycle makes it easier to stay out of school.

NEW FEDERAL LAW

Congress passed the Stewart B. McKinney Homeless Assistance Act (P.L. 100-77) in July 1987. It was the first piece of comprehensive national legislation that addressed the problem of homelessness. As a part of the Act, states are now required to ensure that homeless children be guaranteed access to education. Grant funds were made available to assess the needs of homeless children in each state, and to designate a coordinator to assist in the design and implementation of programs (National Coalition for the Homeless, 1987).

Although the legislation was passed and funds appropriated almost two years ago, the Coalition for the Homeless reported a wide variation among the states in their compliance with the law. States such as New York have had a coordinator for two years and are moving ahead with their programs. Other states were proceeding more slowly, and at least one had not yet designated a coordinator (David Blaver, personal communication, November 14, 1988).

WHAT SHOULD CHILD CARE AND EDUCATIONAL SYSTEMS DO?

Educating the children of homeless families has created a national crisis. New York City, for example, has found that its streets may contain as many as 6,000 pupils requiring additional expenditures (Barron, 1987). New York City is not alone. It joins the ranks of such cities as Seattle, Philadelphia and Washington, DC. Recent studies have reaffirmed that one-third of all homeless families have children under 6 years of age (Mathews, 1988) These data suggest that child care agencies and the schools must begin to deal with the homeless, the "... country's No. 2 problem" (Mathews, 1988, p. 57).

A first priority of any program designed to meet the problems of homeless children is to establish a multidisciplinary task force composed of parents, school personnel, and leaders from all areas and strata of the community. The task force should study the homeless problem in the community, particularly as it relates to education. *More effective lines of communication must be created between the service-providing agencies and the schools.*

Networking among agencies at different levels has been found successful in promoting articulation between groups (Hutchison, Searight & Stretch, 1986). Joint inservice training of community agency and school district personnel would further increase communication. Training should emphasize the nature of the problems faced by homeless families and their children, and include a tour of shelters to promote a deeper understanding of the problems with which children must cope after school (Gewirtzman & Fodor, 1987). Some other elements to consider:

• *Greater accessibility to the nation's schools.* When fully implemented, the new law should make public school programs more accessible to homeless children. Residency requirements would be more flexibly interpreted, enabling schools to accept and enroll children more easily. The law states:

> Each homeless child shall be provided services comparable to services offered to other students in the school ... including educational services for which the child meets the eligibility criteria, such as compensatory educational programs for the disadvantaged, and educational programs for the handicapped and for students with limited English proficiency; programs in vocational education; programs for gifted and talented; and school meals programs. (Stewart B. McKinney Homeless Assistance Act, 1987, p. 527)

To be most effective, schools must reach out to shelters and inform all community agencies and law enforcement officials that there are educational programs for homeless children. Schools serving these children must open earlier and close later than regular school hours. Breakfast, lunch and an after-school snack should be provided. A place to do homework assignments (complete with a tutor) might help to improve school achievement. Funds should be available to help families with additional transportation and extracurricular expenses.

• *Greater accessibility to day care programs.* Families with preschool children form a large segment of the homeless population. Most of these families would meet the income requirements for federally supported day care provided by the states (Title XX) and Head Start programs. With dwindling Title XX funds, however, as few as 7% of eligible children are being served in those day care programs. Current Head Start funding provides for only 16% of eligible children nationwide. Both types of programs may have long waiting lists (Children's Defense Fund, 1988a).

Generally, no provisions are made in either program to serve children on a short-term basis. If parents in homeless families are to resolve their stress-laden problems, good day care for their young children must be available. Some shelters have worked with other community agencies to provide child care in or near their facilities (Kozol, 1988). Child care is only one aspect of the support system necessary to assist homeless families, however. Counseling, medical, nutritional and educational support are also necessary for effective long-term change to occur (Hutchison, Searight & Stretch, 1986). To provide for continuity, there should be an information "tracking and sharing" network between agencies and school systems. If families cross state borders, lines of communication should be in place to assist agencies in the receiving state.

• *Greater support for an individualized educational program.* In successful programs (National Coalition for the Homeless, 1987), school districts have worked with social agencies to solve educational problems. Sometimes schools are maintained on shelter premises. When this is not feasible, social agencies work with schools in arranging placements.

Research shows that homeless children may experience difficulty with language, sustained attention to task and physical coordination (Bassuk, 1987), as well as developmental delays and severe depression or anxiety (Bessuk & Rubin, 1987). Children without homes have no "place" in their lives to call their own. These children need "... a structured, stable, non-threatening environment in the classroom" (Gewirtzman & Fodor, 1987, p. 243).

Individualized programs have worked well in both Salt Lake City, Utah (National Coalition for the Homeless, 1987), and Santa Clara, California ("Against Odds," 1988). In both programs, children are of mixed grade levels in a classroom; the teachers structure the work at each child's level. Teachers must be skilled at diagnosing and planning for homeless children's needs. Since there is no guarantee that a child will ever return to the school, the most must be made of each instructional day. This kind of program requires teachers who are experienced, resourceful and flexible—who understand the homeless child's plight. The "one-room school" model, with its emphasis on peer teaching, may be the best answer to supplying the necessary support.

IN CONCLUSION

The educational problems faced by children of homeless families cannot be solved entirely by an influx of federal dollars to schools. Children need decent housing, adequate nutrition and medical care. Their parents need jobs that include health and sick-leave benefits. Schools and community agencies must believe that they can make a difference in the lives of homeless children. Permanency will enable many of the families to keep things in balance. All homeless families should receive the clear message that education is still one of the best paths to achieving life's goals. To regain a sense of one's self-esteem gives one hope that tomorrow will be a brighter day, filled with the promise of better things to come!

22

A Cry for Help

Children at Risk

Jane Brooks Moskowitz

Jenny, a doe-eyed, slight child with a mass of dark curls, stood in the far corner of the playground at the center of a group of other second grade girls, and in a soft hush recounted how her mother had fallen down the steps the night before. Her mom was okay she assured her friends as she saw the frightened expression on their faces. It wasn't the first time it had happened. Her mom had just had too much wine for dinner. There was a silence as the girls took in this forbidden information, unsure of what to do with it. Jenny always had these threatening stories to tell.

Two days after this incident occurred on the playground, Clovis Dorney, the guidance counselor at Jenny's elementary school, received a phone call. It was the mother of one of Jenny's friends calling. She was very concerned and upset about the stories her own daughter was bringing home. "Is it true?" inquired this parent. "Isn't there something you can do? My daughter is quite upset."

For Clovis Dorney, the call signaled a red flag. She began to take a close look at Jenny, observing her behavior in the classroom and on the playground. Jenny had never been a problem, but it became evident upon observation that something was going on. She often appeared tired and tense. She frequently attracted attention by telling these stories about her mother. And so Dorney called Jenny in "to talk."

What Dorney learned verified what she had suspected. Jenny's mother was probably an alcoholic. And if that were so, then Jenny herself was "at risk" since children of alcoholics typically live in emotional chaos and frequently grow up to have an alcohol or addiction problem. During the talk with her guidance counselor, Jenny revealed that sometimes she and her sister would go shopping and their mother would leave them to go get a drink. They would worry as they waited for mom to return. Would she be alright? Would she remember to come back for them? And, then when she finally did return, she would be drunk, and the girls were afraid to get in the car for fear she'd have a driving accident.

Clovis Dorney's next step was more difficult. She had to confront the mother with her suspicions. Confrontation with parents was often difficult because the parents frequently denied their own problems or resented the school's interference. But when Dorney spoke to Jenny's parents, they agreed that the mother would go for an evaluation at a local alcoholic treatment facility. That was all that Clovis Dorney could do. In later meetings with Jenny, it became apparent that the home situation was better. Jenny's stories had stopped. The guidance counselor continued to monitor Jenny.*

Jenny, whose troubled home situation was manifesting itself socially at school, could be considered a child "at risk." The term "at risk" is used to describe those children whose behavior appears to be potentially problematic for academic success. In general, a student defined as "at risk" is one who, because of either social or academic problems, may not graduate from high school in the traditional manner. In this country, and in many foreign countries, educators and mental health practitioners have been proactive in their efforts to deal with potentially troubled children. Some feel that with societal pressures being what they are today, all of our children are "at risk." Alcohol and substance abuse, while not the only type of "at risk" problems, are pervasive in our high schools and middle schools and, even more alarmingly, in some elementary schools.

Our schools are responding to these societal problems—drugs, alcohol, teen pregnancy, depression, suicide—with programs and resource material that not only provide intervention but are also preventive in nature. The availability of federal and state monies has been a tremendous boost to the advent of these intervention and prevention programs.

Variations on these programs are many. While some school districts have brought in special personnel to head up programs or created new positions to deal with the ever-increasing problems that vie for counselors' time, other districts have retrained existing personnel and set up teams within the schools.

According to Larry Newman, executive director of ComSAP in Chester, Pennsylvania, and a consultant to school Student Assistance (SA) programs designed to deal with alcohol and substance abuse, "student assistance programs aim for early identification of 'at-risk' kids and for subsequent referral to treatment." Newman emphasizes that one of the key elements of such a program is the team approach. Typically, the program has a core team. The team's central administrator, a guidance teacher, usually a nurse or health science teacher, and one or more classroom teachers undergo intensive

Source: From Jane Brooks Moskowitz, "A Cry for Help: Children at Risk," *Media Methods*, Volume 25, January–February 1989, pp. 27–36. Reprinted with permission.

*Jenny's and Dorney's names are fictitious but the incident is not.

workshop training that is both content- and process-based. The team works together within the school to identify and refer kids who are "at risk." Some programs include local police and parent liaisons.

Most administrators are quick to point out that a successful program to deal with the visible behaviors of children "at risk"—drug and alcohol abuse, truancy, depression and suicidal depression, appetite disorders—require several components including a solid community network. Linda McCloskey, a substance abuse prevention specialist with the Boise, Idaho, Public Schools comments, "The problem of alcohol and substance abuse permeates society. . . . We have to get the entire community educated and involved."

Most student assistance programs include a student leadership component. This component calls for a group of student leaders to be trained to identify and deal with their peers who are having problems. These leaders are students who have a high profile in the school, are respected and can be influential. In essence, they serve as role models and liaisons between the students and the team. Student leaders, known as peer educators in some programs, are encouraged to talk to other students about drug and alcohol problems and to let them know that they are available for support.

Generally, in addition to the student leadership component and the community network, a school system must have established policies regarding absence, behavior, drug and alcohol use, with stated sanctions for violations; a parent education component; and a curriculum for prevention. Prevention programs use a variety of materials to get their messages across. The "Here's Looking at You 2,000" curriculum out of Seattle, Washington (developed for CHEF, Comprehensive Health Education Foundation by Robert Fitzmahem, Inc.) is currently being used in all 50 states and some seven foreign countries. It is a comprehensive self-contained prevention-oriented program for K through 12 that includes filmstrips, videos and computer software. At each level, the curriculum has three components—(1) informational (2) social skills and (3) bonding.

The first component offers alcohol and drug information. The second, social skills, goes beyond "just say no" to how to say "no" without alienating peers and how to select friends wisely. The bonding component encourages the students to bond with one another and with pro-social groups that preclude the use of drugs or alcohol or undesirable behavior. At certain levels, take-home activities are provided to involve the parents.

Until recently, most children "at risk" were not identified until they were already having problems. Intervention and prevention were done at the high school level. But as the numbers increased, it was apparent that it was critical to look at our younger children and to begin to provide help at an earlier age. Dr. Fred Muck, administrative assistant to the superintendent of the Davidson County School District in Lexington, North Carolina, explained that "'at risk' children don't become that way overnight. We've got to begin looking for some kind of long term comprehensive therapy." So many problems—teenage pregnancy, AIDS, drug and alcohol abuse, drop-outs—vie for prevention and education monies and curriculum time that "we should be centralizing these programs that are basically duplicating each other in order to reach the same population," continues Dr. Muck. "The programs all have the same general goals of teaching problem-solving and decision-making skills, better communication skills and increasing self-esteem."

Those three goals—decision-making skills, good communication skills, and positive self-esteem—constitute the basis of most prevention programs designed to help children "at risk." Previously, skills that were taught in high school prevention programs are now being taught in elementary schools throughout the country, beginning with kindergarten.

In southern Connecticut, RYSAP (Regional Youth Substance Abuse Project) serves six municipalities and six school systems, offering a K through 12 prevention program and providing regional support for substance abuse programs. In the schools, teams are usually headed by an administrator who is already employed by the school and is trained in alcohol and substance abuse. John Higgins-Biddle, director of RYSAP, stresses that his organization is working to limit the responsibility of the schools to handle drug and alcohol abuse through a system of early identification and intervention that would refer the student to treatment.

Prevention programs in the primary years are frequently incorporated into the regular curriculum. In the Boise (Idaho) Public Schools, with some 22,000 students placing it among the 100 largest school systems in the United States, an introduction to life skills with the emphasis on recognition of individual differences at the kindergarten level lays the foundation for later techniques in decision making and problem solving. Drug and alcohol information is introduced in science and in language arts. The Boise schools have developed their own curriculum that draws from substance abuse prevention research. Selected supplemental teaching materials such as activity books, videos and software are incorporated into the curriculum.

Some schools have introduced even more proactive components into their prevention and intervention programs. The Methacton (Pennsylvania) School District has begun an "Adopt an At-Risk Student" program, according to Joye Schrager, crisis prevention counselor. With this program, each teacher on the student assistance team works specifically with one student. When a student has been identified as having a problem, then there is a teacher available for that student. "We have to be careful to separate those behaviors that are normal for an adolescent," explains Ms. Schrager "and not to misinterpret normal adolescent experimentation for the real behavioral changes that are evident with a student who is at risk." Although her position was initially developed in response to a local tragedy involving the murder of two children in the community, Ms. Schrager's job goes beyond crisis intervention. She works very closely with the student assistance teams. Prevention has been worked into the curriculum with a single topic being introduced for an entire week. A cadre of selected student leaders head follow-up class discussions.

Student assistance programs are aimed at fostering recovery within the schools. According to Ann Walsh, health educator and curriculum developer at Prevention Resources in Needham, Massachusetts, one of eight regional centers in Massachusetts, primary prevention takes care of the straight kids, but intervention is necessary for the kids already engaged in risky behavior who don't respond to prevention information. Recognizing the undeniable influence of peers, the schools in Walsh's region train high school students to work as "peer educators" with fifth through eighth graders. The peer educators are trained on a decision-making model (refusal skills) that they can use to teach and to influence younger kids. Listening exercises, improvisational theater, role play, team building activities as well as some videos and commercially produced materials are all used in the curriculum.

Sandy Knecht, the guidance counselor at Arrowhead Elementary School in Collegeville, Pennsylvania, emphasizes that in her school, prevention is not just aimed at children "at risk." Knecht explains that effective education helps children to develop those life skills that will give them better self-esteem and alternatives to choices that might put them "at risk." Students at Arrowhead learn stress reduction techniques—relaxation exercises, proper deep breathing techniques, positive self-talk, and even some biofeedback—beginning with the kindergarten on up through the fifth grade. One aspect of her job that she enjoys is the work she does with small groups. Kids who demonstrate evidence of problems are identified and sometimes placed into groups that meet for eight weeks with Knecht. Thus, kids whose parents are separated or divorced, those with peer relationship problems, those with low self-esteem or poor social skills, get support in groups that meet during the school day.

Some schools offer more than just prevention and intervention referrals. In Ozone Park, New York, Neil Rothberg, executive director of the Aspects 27 program, explains that in his district's program, the focus on "at risk" is, like that of most schools, two-fold—primary prevention and intervention. The major difference here is that family counseling is a major part of the program. A counseling intern program that utilizes counseling interns from various local colleges, ie; Columbia, Yeshiva, and Hofstra, provides free intensive family counseling services to the school community.

In fact, his school's family counseling program could be the only one of its kind anywhere, says Rothberg. Not only is free family counseling available from early morning into the evening hours to accommodate working parents, but there is a summer program as well.

A sound school board policy on drugs and alcohol and behavior, student assistance programs, student leadership programs, community networks, and timely resource material—these are all the components of programs that deal with children "at risk."

Dramatic increases in referrals, particularly from the students themselves or from their peers, are the most valuable evidence that the programs are working. More children than ever before are reaching out for help. We, as educators, must be there to respond. And now, more than ever before, we must begin working with parents, with the community, and with the children to quiet the cries when they are merely whimpers, to maximize the chance that our children will never be "at risk."

23

"Only the Lonely"

The Latchkey Child

Shirley J. O'Brien

Robin is a 10-year-old girl who calls *Kid-Talk* almost every day. She checks in with the phone volunteer at 3:30 p.m. to tell the latest joke and discuss events of the day. The volunteer helps her to decide what snack to prepare for her brother and, most important, how to spend the time until their parents come home at 6:00 p.m. Robin has been taking care of her 8-year-old brother after school since he entered 1st grade two years ago.

Joey is an 11-year-old boy who often needs help with his math. He calls *Kid-Talk* with a math division problem he cannot solve. Since he does his homework while his Mom is still at work, he calls *Kid-Talk* for assistance. Charles, a *Kid-Talk* phone volunteer, works through the problem with Joey and has him complete several more to make sure he grasps the concept. When they are finished, Joey thanks Charles and promises to call again tomorrow.

Robin and Joey are typical of many latchkey children in thousands of communities across the U.S. Statistics in the Arizona Casa Grande *Kid Talk* phone-in program indicate that well over half of the after-school calls come from children who are lonely or bored.

Although no one is sure just how many children take care of themselves on a regular basis, it is safe to assume that a large percentage do so occasionally. As more and more parents enter the labor force, a growing number of children spend an hour or more after school without adult supervision. The best guess of experts is that these numbers are growing every day.

Let's dream together for a moment! If this were an ideal world, all children would come home to a loving parent or another caring adult. There would be long conversations about the child's ups and downs of the school day and some wonderful activity to fill the afternoon hours before dinner-time—such as baking cookies, raking leaves, taking walks and doing homework together.

For a majority of families, the ideal isn't possible. Some may wonder if it is really necessary, since many children seem to do just fine when left home alone. In fact, most experts agree that in many cases the latchkey life actually helps children develop desirable skills and abilities.

On the other hand, some children have a hard time coping with the responsibility of being home alone. Indeed, a great deal of responsibility is associated with being home alone. For example, personal protection is ranked as one of the highest fears children have when left alone. What will happen if someone rings the doorbell or calls on the phone? What are the funny noises in the basement (attic, next door, next room)? What will happen if I start a fire or cut myself? Who will help me if I get in trouble?

These questions may seem trivial to an adult. To children, however, such situations are like monsters waiting to attack the minute they look the other way or let down their guard.

Call-in latchkey hotlines have filled a community void by providing a friendly voice, calm reassurance and suggestions for time-fillers. These programs have helped numerous children in times of crisis as well. Phone volunteers have even saved lives by detecting serious personal injury and dispatching emergency services.

A concomitant benefit has resulted in researching these programs. We have been provided a new look at the developmental stages of young children and their age-level needs for human contact and supervision. Based on what we have learned in the Arizona program, apparently a child can be perfectly safe in a home, but not feel safe. It is the feeling of safety that parents must help foster if the latchkey experience is to be successful.

Parents can take several steps to help children have a feeling of safety if they are alone in the home. The first step is to establish a contact person who may be either the parent or another adult who cares about the child. This contact person might be a neighbor the child visits or telephones each day, a friend or relative across town, or even someone in another city. If necessary, the contact person might be the latchkey hotline volunteer. The idea is to establish a consistent contact for the child at the beginning of the afternoon hours.

Susan, a secretary in our office, asked her 10-year-old son Brian to call her each day when he arrived home. She wanted to be Brian's contact. If she had to leave the phone for an errand around 3:45 p.m., she designated some other secretary to be Brian's contact. Another idea Susan developed was to set a radio timer that went off at 3:30 p.m. Between the dog and the radio, Brian was greeted quite royally on his homecoming.

Many parents agree that providing the child with structured activities or routine chores is vital for curing the "lonely/bored" feeling. Making a large chart of these duties is the best way to keep them straight. Some

Source: From Shirley J. O'Brien, "Only the Lonely: The Latchkey Child," *Childhood Education*, Volume 65, Summer 1989, pp. 231–232. Reprinted by permission of the Association for Childhood Education International, 11141 Georgia Avenue, Suite 200, Wheaton, MD.

tasks and activities might need to be done every day and others on certain days each week. For example:

1. Call contact person.
2. Turn on the heat/cooling.
3. Let the pet out/in.
4. Give the pet food and fresh water.
5. Do homework.
6. Turn on oven/put pre-prepared dish into oven.
7. Set the table.

Monday
Draw new picture for family "Art Gallery."
Tuesday
Write letter to a grandparent.
Wednesday
Hide 5 items for after-dinner treasure hunt.
Thursday
Read library book.
Friday
Practice piano.

(There might be a rule that after tasks are completed the child may watch a favorite after-school television program.)

My secretary-friend Susan said that general safety rules were important for answering the phone and the door. Susan even wrote out words on a poster above the phone: "My mother can't come to the phone right now. Please give me your number and she'll call you later." Susan purchased some pink "While You Were Out" pads so Brian could easily fill in the important information from the phone calls.

Many experts caution parents against leaving a child under age 10 completely alone after school. After age 10 children have more resilience and independence to cope with their near environment. Above all, whatever the arrangement, parents must listen carefully to their children. If the latchkey situation is not working well, then other arrangements must be made. If the children do not *feel* safe, then closer supervision is a parent's next step.

Although many latchkey children may be lonely or bored, latchkey life is here to stay. In fact, the numbers will greatly increase in the next decade. Our goal should be to reach out and provide phone contact for these children—even as neighbors, co-workers and friends. In this way, we are all helping to provide young children with the feeling of being safe and secure in their growing-up years.

24

A Magnet School for the Creative Arts

Allen Raymond

Three in one . . .

This article should really be three *articles. The first would talk about the economic climate in Louisiana that makes educational funding so traumatic for so many.*

The second article would be about the New Orleans School System, from the Orleans Parish School Board to the superintendent and on to the teachers and support staffs. For the most part they are, we believe, a proud, professional group of individuals bent on getting the last drop of educational blood from every nickel available to them.

The third article would be about the principal and staff at Gentilly Terrace Elementary School. It would begin by digging deeply on how the principal has inspired so many to create such a special school.

It would then bring you a picture of each teacher in action—and we took those pictures. It would tell you about what happens in each of those teachers' classes, for we visited them all, or most of them. It would share with you the ideas of all those teachers, because all of them are professionals who know how to teach. We know, because we were there.

It would talk about the support staff, those unsung individuals who do everything from cutting the lawn to polishing the floors to cooking the food.

We'd write about all of those things if we could but, unfortunately, a magazine is like a teacher's day—divided into segments, most not long enough for the task at hand.

"We'll be in New Orleans tomorrow," we said on the phone to Rose Drill Peterson, Director of Information and Community Services for the New Orleans Public Schools. "May we come by for a visit?"

The next day—Friday, April 28, at 3:00 p.m.—we were in her office looking through a list of 81 elementary schools in New Orleans.

We spotted something we'd never heard of before—*a magnet elementary school for the creative arts.* That sounded good to us and, after a quick phone call to the school's principal, we jumped into our car. Led by Ms. Peterson in her car, we raced around corners and through intersections and by 3:30 we were in the office of Dr. Juanita Schroeder, principal of Gentilly Terrace, a K–6 elementary school.

Dr. Schroeder has been principal of the school for 12 years, taking over when its enrollment was 260 and the school was in danger of being closed. Today it would take a shoehorn to squeeze in one more kid. The school is at capacity—550 students.

How did it all happen? Some say it was the emphasis on the creative arts.

Maybe. However, if one spends time at the school it's easy to discover that's not the whole answer and, in fact, Gentilly Terrace is in only its second year as a magnet school for the creative arts.

The emphasis on the arts helped, of course, and it was Dr. Schroeder's goal to create such an emphasis from the day she set foot in Gentilly Terrace.

"I wanted to bring the arts to the school." Dr. Schroeder said. "I knew it would make a difference. If the children could express themselves in creative ways, if they could see they had other talents, I knew it would help them feel better about themselves.

"As we gradually brought in more arts programs, I began to visit with neighbors, telling them about our school. I also urged parents to let others know, by word of mouth, that good things were going on at Gentilly Terrace.

"My objective was to tell everyone, 'Hey, there are exciting things happening at this school—*and we have room!*' "

Thus did the wheels begin to turn and the enrollment begin to climb. And, giving credit where credit is due, Dr. Schroeder reminded us that the schools' growth came not just from the emphasis on the arts, but from the efforts of many people, especially the staff.

In fact, as we walked the halls on the following Wednesday and visited classrooms—we were sad we could not visit them all, and that our visit could only last one day—she demonstrated her pride in the teachers by saying frequently, as we'd leave one room and enter another, "That's a dynamite teacher," or "You're about to see another dynamite teacher."

Gentilly Terrace serves two constituencies. One is the local neighborhood; children living within the school's district boundaries are automatically accepted if they wish to attend.

The second constituency is those kids who attend because it is a magnet school for the creative arts. They come because they *want* to come and, quite literally, they come from all over New Orleans.

Source: From Allen Raymond, "A Magnet School for the Creative Arts," *Teaching K–8*, Volume 20, August–September 1989, pp. 58–61. Reprinted with permission of the publisher, Early Years Inc., Norwalk, Connecticut 06854. From the August/September 1989 issue of *Teaching/K–8* magazine.

One could easily conclude—but one would be wrong—that, because of the economic climate in Louisiana, it is not always comfortable to be a professional educator in the state or in its best known city, New Orleans.

Yes, the state and the city are rich in history, culture and beauty, but the economy, to put it mildly, is not robust.

As a result, in spite of the strong support of the schools by most of its citizens and a huge proportion of large and small businesses, statistics about school funding are sobering indeed.

The State of Louisiana ranks 44th among all 50 states in per-pupil expenditures. In New Orleans in 1988 the starting salary for teachers was $17,665; the top was $29,412. Per-pupil expenditure in the city for the 1988–89 school year was $2,866.

But we said it would be wrong to conclude that it is uncomfortable for professional educators to be working in New Orleans. It is not uncomfortable, it is exciting.

The teachers and administrators are proud of their schools and proud of their accomplishments. They point to rising test scores, to growing enrollments, to national recognition being given to the schools in New Orleans. They point to the cultural programs available in the schools, to the wide diversity of the educational opportunities.

And yes, they wish more schools were air conditioned, that there was more money for textbooks. As one teacher said to us, "There's not enough available for these kids. I feel like I had more in the 6th grade, 30 years ago, in terms of materials, than these kids have today."

But stringent financial restraints don't seem to dampen either the creativity or enthusiasm of the professionals we met who seemed to be giving so much to the kids of New Orleans—and enjoying it.

Gentilly Terrace describes what it offers its kids as "... a comprehensive arts program integrated into the total academic program. Instruction is provided in visual arts, vocal and instrumental music, drama and creative writing."

Also, "... computer-designed instruction is used to promote critical thinking skills and creative writing, as well as to reinforce basic skills."

Dr. Schroeder, who has taught English and Journalism at the high school and junior high level, turned to anyone who could help her build the school's emphasis on the arts. Her biggest boost came when, about seven years ago, the New Orleans school system introduced the Arts Connection Program.

Each school may become a part of the program if it meets certain requirements. Those include a $600 annual commitment, plus a .5 staffing position. When a school meets those goals, it receives a halftime artist-in-residence.

New Orleans, as a city, has a heritage rich in cultural programs, of course, and the schools are no exception. Their Cultural Resources Program brings performing artists from all over the country to perform for the children.

At Gentilly Terrace all students receive one hour of vocal music per week. The 4th through 6th grades have a choir. Beginning in 2nd grade students may receive instruction on stringed instruments—the violin, viola and cello.

There is a school band, there are two halftime artists-in-residence—one for visual arts, the other for drama—and the school has even managed to entice children's author Natalie Babbitt, who lives in the northeast, to spend time at the school when she is visiting a friend in New Orleans.

The business community of New Orleans is an active supporter of the schools through "Partners in Education." Over 300 businesses and other organizations—such as the University of New Orleans—have established partnerships with 122 schools and 19 administrative departments of the schools. The resource these businesses offer is mainly people; they share their talents.

And speaking of talents, our day visiting the classrooms of Gentilly Terrace demonstrated that teaching talent is in abundance. As Dr. Schroeder said of her staff, "They're wonderful, very creative, nothing is too much for them. If someone comes up with an idea that sounds good, I can count on them to always say, 'Sure, we'll do that!'"

As 6th grade teacher Joyce Flaxbeard said, "the whole concept of a magnet school is to draw people into the public schools. I'm a firm believer in public schools. Over the years parents have picked private or parochial schools because of the programs schools had to offer.

"Finally public schools woke up, and we can offer something, too. We can give parents options. *A magnet school is a strong school,* it pulls the faculty together because we're all working toward a common goal.

"It's good for the public to see the variety," she added. "When we have more variety, when we have more to offer, we have a better program. It's good for teachers, too, because we can choose where our strengths lie.

"My strength," she continued, "is in math and science, but I'm also good in music and art. That satisfies me, because I can put art into anything—into science, into math.

"I feel real at home here. Dr. Schroeder lets us teach the best way we can, using different teaching methods, different teaching styles, a variety of teaching methods.

"When a kid finishes here, after having gone through the 6th grade, that kid can go to any school anywhere, and make it!"

She said, of her hopes for the kids, "My main goal in the 6th grade is to prepare these kids for life. I don't really want to prepare them for 7th grade; that's going to happen anyway.

"I want to teach them such things as standing in line, not cutting in line. I want to teach them to deal with problems."

Joyce has a good sense of humor, which she says has carried her through lots of difficult times. She told us she tries "... to teach the whole child, which (and here she took a long pause) is a good trick, especially when it's 90 degrees and the air conditioning hasn't been installed.

"I try to begin and end the day happily," she said. "One of the rules we have is to leave our problems behind when we come through that classroom door in the morning.

"And at the end of the day, no matter how bad it went, when kids walk out of this room they've had a hug, or they've had something enjoyable happen to them."

25

Educating Language-Minority Children

Challenges And Opportunities

Barbara T. Bowman

Why can't all Americans just speak standard English? This plaintive question reflects the distress that many citizens feel about the linguistic diversity that has become a source of divisiveness in society and a source of failure in the schools. In many school districts, the number of languages and dialects spoken by children and their families is staggering, as the languages of Central and South America, Africa, and Asia mix with various American dialects to create classrooms in which communication is virtually impossible. Across America, language-minority children are not learning the essential lessons of school and are not fully taking part in the economic, social, and political life of the country.

And the problem will soon become even more serious. Over the next decade or two, language-minority children will become the *majority* in our public schools, seriously straining the capacity of those institutions to educate them.

In a nation that is increasingly composed of people who speak different languages and dialects, the old notion of melting them together through the use of a common language is once again attractive. Requiring all children to speak the same language at a high level of proficiency would make the task of educating them a good deal easier. Unfortunately, what seems quite simple in theory is often difficult to put into practice. One of the most powerful reasons in this instance is the interrelationship of culture, language, and the children's development.

CULTURE, LANGUAGE, AND DEVELOPMENT

Christian men show respect for their religion by removing their hats but keeping their shoes on in church, while Muslim men show similar respect by keeping their hats on and removing their shoes in a mosque. But differences in how groups think and act are more than a matter of using different words or performing different actions for the same purposes. Differences in culture are more substantial than whether members of a community eat white bread, corn pone, or tortillas. The behavior of people varies, and the beliefs, values, and assumptions that underlie that behavior differ as well. Culture influences both behavior and the psychological processes on which it rests; it affects the ways in which people perceive the world—their physical environment, the events that surround them, and other people. Culture forms a prism through which members of a group see the world and create "shared meanings."

Child development follows a pattern similar to culture. The major structural changes in children—changes that arise from the interaction of biology and experience, such as language learning—are remarkably similar in kind and sequence across cultural groups. However, the specific knowledge and skills—the cultural learning—that children acquire at different ages depend on the children's family and community.

Learning a primary language is a developmental milestone for young children and is, therefore, a "developmentally appropriate" educational objective. Moreover, the informal, social method by which children learn their primary language is also "developmentally appropriate." However, the specific uses to which that language is put are determined by the culture.

As the ideas from a child's social world are brought to bear through the guidance of the older members of the community, children come to know, to expect, and to share meanings with their elders. Children acquire *scripts* (sequences of actions and words) for various interactions with people and things, and the adults in their families and communities structure these scripts for children to help them learn. Gradually, children internalize the adult rules for "making meaning."

Classroom discourse presents a challenge to children to learn new rules for communication. The use of formal language, teacher leadership and control of verbal exchanges, question-and-answer formats, and references to increasingly abstract ideas characterize the classroom environment, with which many children are unfamiliar. To the extent that these new rules overlap with

Source: From Barbara T. Bowman, "Educating Language-Minority Children: Challenges and Opportunities," Phi Delta Kappa, Volume 71, October 1989, pp. 118–120. Reprinted with permission from the publisher and from Barbara T. Bowman.

those that children have already learned, classroom communication is made easier. But children whose past experience with language is not congruent with the new rules will have to learn ways of "making meaning" all over again before they can use language to learn in the classroom.

When teachers and students come from different cultures and use different languages and dialects, the teachers may be unaware of the variations between their own understanding of a context and that of their students, between their own expectations for behavior in particular contexts and the inclinations of the children they teach. When children and adults do not share common experiences and do not hold common beliefs about the meaning of experiences, the adults are less able to help children encode their thoughts in language.

Children are taught to act, believe, and feel in ways that are consistent with the mores of their communities. The goals and objectives presented, the relationships available, and the behavior and practices recommended by family and friends are gradually internalized and contribute to a child's definition of self. Language is an integral part of a group's common experience. Speaking the same language connects individuals through bonds of common meaning and also serves as a marker of group membership; it is the cement for group members' relationships with one another. The shared past and the current allegiances of the group are the bedrock for the "common meanings" taught to children through language.

TEACHING CULTURALLY DIFFERENT CHILDREN

The idea of a developmentally appropriate curriculum is inherently attractive. It evokes a vision of classrooms in which experiences are synchronized with each child's levels of maturity and experience, so that what is taught is consistent with the child's capacity to learn.

But teachers facing the challenge of teaching children from different cultural communities find themselves hard pressed to decide what constitutes an appropriate curriculum. If the children speak different languages and dialects, how should teachers communicate with them? If children from some groups are hesitant to speak up in school, how can teachers organize expressive language experiences? If children from some groups are dependent on nonverbal cues for meaning, how can teachers stress word meaning? If different groups have different ways of expressing themselves, how can teachers know what children mean to say or what children understand of what teachers and other children say? How can teachers test for mastery of the curriculum if children do not speak a standard language or use the same styles of communication? Cultural diversity makes it hard for teachers to assess each child's developmental status, to find common educational experiences to promote further growth, and to measure the achievement of educational objectives.

Given the complexity of the interaction between culture and development, is it possible to design a developmentally appropriate curriculum at all? If that question implies that the same curriculum can be used for all children, the answer must be no. Children who have been socialized in different worlds will not understand material in the same ways. On the other hand, recognizing a few developmental principles can provide a conceptual framework for the culturally sensitive teacher. The following list of principles is not meant to be exhaustive; it merely provides a beginning for teachers who are trying to bridge the gap between children's cultural backgrounds and the school's objectives.

First, teachers need to learn to recognize developmentally equivalent patterns of behavior. Before they come to school, all children have learned many of the same things—a primary language, categorizing systems, interpersonal communication styles. Although these developmental accomplishments may look quite different, they can be said to be developmentally equivalent. There are a number of "equally good" ways to shape development. When a child does not respond to the social and cognitive expectations of the school, the teacher should look first for a developmentally equivalent task to which the child will respond. For instance, a child who does not talk in the classroom can be observed on the playground or at home. A child who does not separate buttons correctly can be asked to sort car logos or other personally relevant artifacts. A child who does not listen to stories about the seasons may be spellbound by a story about a basketball player.

Teachers who have doubts about the development of culturally different children should assume that the children are normal and look at them again, recognizing that their own vision may be clouded by cultural myopia. By assuming the developmental equivalence of a variety of tasks, adults can begin the search for the mismatch between their own and a given child's understanding of a situation or of a task to be performed.

Second, it is essential not to value some ways of achieving developmental milestones more highly than others, because young children are particularly sensitive to the ways in which adults view them. Asa Hilliard and Mona Vaughn-Scott point out that, because the behavior of African-American children is so different from that of their white peers, such children are often judged to be deficient in their development, rather than just different. The result is that normal, healthy children are sometimes diagnosed as sick or retarded.*

Speaking a common language is the cement that binds individuals to groups. Thus young children who speak languages other than English (or nonstandard dialects) are reluctant to give up this connection to the members of their own group. When such children find that the way they talk and act is not understood or appreciated in school, they are apt to become confused or disengaged. And their rejection by the school presages their rejection of school.

Third, teachers need to begin instruction with interactive styles and with content that is familiar to the children. Whether this entails speaking in the child's primary language, using culturally appropriate styles of address, or relying on patterns of management that are familiar to and comfortable for children, the purpose is to establish a basis for communication. While fluency in a child's primary language may not be an achievable goal for many teachers, they can nonetheless become more adept at understanding, planning, and implementing a culturally sensitive curriculum. Such a curriculum must encompass more than tasting parties and colorful ethnic costumes; it must be more than shopworn introductions to the odd and amusing practices of people from different nations or different racial groups. In order to teach such a curriculum, teachers must have come to grips with their own ethnocentricity and must be able to deal with themselves and others fairly; teachers must know the difference between style and substance.

Fourth, school learning is most likely to occur when family values reinforce school expectations. This does not mean that parents must teach the same things at home as teachers do in school. However, it does mean that parents and other community members must view achievement in school as a desirable and attainable goal if the children are to build it into their own sense of themselves. This means that interpreting the school's agenda for parents is one of the most important tasks for teachers.

Fifth, when differences exist between the cultural patterns of the home and community and those of the school, teachers must deal with these discrepancies directly. Teachers and children must create shared understandings and new contexts that give meaning to the knowledge and skills being taught. The challenge is to find personally interesting and culturally relevant ways of creating new contexts for children, contexts in which the mastery of school skills can be meaningful and rewarding. Learning mediated by teachers who are affectionate, interested, and re-

*Asa Hilliard and Mona Vaughn-Scott, "The Quest for the Minority Child," in Shirley G. Moore and Catherine R. Cooper, eds., *The Young Child: Reviews of Research*, Vol. 3 (Washington, D.C.: National Association for the Education of Young Children, 1982).

sponsive—teachers who are personally involved in the lives of young children—has greater "sticking power" than learning mediated by an adult who is perceived as impersonal and socially distant.

Sixth, the same contexts do not have the same meanings to children from different racial and ethnic groups. The meanings of words, of gestures, and of actions may be quite different. The assessment of learning outcomes presents a formidable problem when children misunderstand the meaning of the teacher's requests for information and for demonstrations of knowledge and skills. The same instructional materials and methods may take on meanings different from those that the teacher intended. Formal assessment should be delayed until teachers and children have jointly built a set of new meanings, so that the children understand the language and behavior called for in school.

A developmentally appropriate curriculum can never be standardized in a multicultural community. Thoughtful teachers, however, can use the principles of child development to make the new context of school meaningful, to attach new kinds of learning to what children have already achieved, and to safeguard the self-image and self-confidence of children as their knowledge and skills expand. It is not easy, but it is the only workable system.

26

The Styles of Learning are Different, but the Teaching is Just the Same

Suggestions for Teachers of American Indian Youth

Karen Swisher
Donna Deyhle

Our Indian students feel inferior. They are passive in the classroom. A white kid can ask a question in the classroom. The Indians cannot ask questions because they don't understand. And they don't learn as much (Navajo counselor, personal communication, 1984).

For decades, educators and educational researchers have attempted to understand reasons for the high rate of academic failure among minority youth. Genetic characteristics, racial segregation and discrimination and/or cultural deprivation were offered as explanations for low achievement. Some researchers viewed the school as a panacea for bringing about educational equity; others viewed it as not making a difference.

In the late 1960s and early 1970s, the cultural-difference hypothesis was presented as an alternative explanation for low achievement. This hypothesis attributed poor academic performance to differences between children's home learning methods and environments and those of the school. Researchers such as Ramirez and Castenada (1974) and Philips (1972) suggested that the school culture was alien and often in conflict with the home culture, and that by creating a congruence between the school culture and the home culture, ethnic minority youths would be helped to make gains in their academic and emotional growth. Researchers in the mid-1970s also began to look at classrooms ethnographically to investigate the interactional structure of schooling; that is, the interactional context in which students from different minority group cultures prefer to learn and demonstrate what they learned.

In addition to the examination of cultural differences affecting the learning process in the 1970s, a powerful theoretical model emerged (Ogbu, 1978) which looked outside the schools to historical factors that formed and shaped minority responses to schools. According to Ogbu (1978, 1987), minority school achievement must be examined in relationship to the groups' experiences in the post-school opportunity structures (job market) and their responses to the perception of dismal future opportunities. This is not to ignore language and cultural differences, for it is within the context of the larger structural factors that language and cultural differences become persuasive and enhanced as oppositional cultural responses within the classroom. We agree with Ogbu's theory, but for the purpose of this paper, we focus on the in-school factors that teachers can effect and change in their interaction with their students.

In the 1980s, educational researchers and practitioners are continuing to search for instructional methods which will address the relationship of how children have "learned to learn" and the ways in which they are expected to demonstrate learning in the classroom. The purpose of this paper is to illustrate with specific classroom examples, learning style and interactional style differences of various groups of American Indian/Alaskan Native youth. Each example is followed by a summary of the literature, including research studies, concerning different cultural patterns of behavior. The paper concludes with suggestions for teachers to consider as they adapt their teaching styles of learning and interaction that students bring with them to the classroom.

Source: From Karen Swisher and Donna Deyhle, "The Styles of Learning are Different, but the Teaching is Just the Same: Suggestions for Teachers of American Indian Youth," *Journal of American Indian Education*, Special Issue Volume, August 1989, pp. 1–13. Reprinted with permission from the publisher.

LEARNING STYLE: THE ACQUISITION OF KNOWLEDGE AND HOW IT IS DEMONSTRATED

It is our premise that people perceive the world in different ways, learn about the world in different ways, and demonstrate what they have learned in different ways. The approach to learning and the demonstration of what one has learned is influenced by the values, norms, and socialization practices of the culture in which the individual has been enculturated. In this section we will present and discuss differences and similarities in learning to learn and the demonstration of learning among several American Indian groups.

LEARNING TO LEARN

> When I make an assignment, my Indian students are reluctant to finish quickly or to correct other peers' papers. My Anglo students are quick to jump into the task. The Indian students seem to need time to think about things before they take action on their assignment. It is almost like they have to make sure they can do it before they try. Or, on the other hand, they seem to just not care about doing their assignments (Teacher, personal communication, 1987).

It is generally accepted in the literature that the ways in which children have learned to learn prior to entering the formal education environment are influenced by early socialization experiences (John, 1972; Philips, 1972; Cazden, 1982). Different sociocultural environments result in behaviors that differ from culture to culture.

Differences between the home learning style and the school learning style are often manifested when an Indian child goes to school. Wax, Wax, and Dumont (1964) have described one such conflict situation in which performance does not precede competence:

> Indians tend to ridicule the person who performs clumsily; an individual should not attempt an action unless he knows how to do it; and if he does not know, then he should watch until he has understood. In European and American cultures, generally, the opposite attitude is generally the case; we "give a man credit for trying" and we feel that the way to learn is to attempt to do so (p. 95).

Werner and Begishe (1968) presented evidence from the Navajo to illustrate how home culture affects styles of learning. They reported that Navajos seem to be unprepared or ill at ease if pushed into early performance without sufficient thought or the acquisition of mental competence preceding the actual physical activity. This philosophy, according to Werner and Begishe (1968), suggests "If at first you don't think, and think again, don't bother trying." In contrast, the Anglo approach, which stresses performance as a prerequisite for the acquisition of competence, is summed up in the philosophy of "If at first you don't succeed, try, try, again" (pp. 1–2).

Longstreet (1978) also reported the different ways in which Navajo children have learned to learn. She stated that Navajo children observe an activity repeatedly before attempting any kind of public performance. They do not have an adult close by helping and correcting them; instead, they observe and review the performance in their heads until they will perform the task well before presentation in front of an audience.

Brewer (1977), in describing learning at home and school for Oglala Sioux children said that observation, self-testing in private, and then demonstration of a task for approval were essential steps in learning. "Learning through public mistakes was not and is not a method of learning which Indians value" (p. 32).

In pointing out how culturally influenced styles may conflict with one another, Appleton (1983) reported differences found in Yaqui Indian learning style and that in the typical public school classroom. Using information from a report titled *Culture: A Way of Reading,* Appleton (1983) reported that Yaqui children avoid unfamiliar ground where trial and error or an inquiry method of reasoning is required. Yaqui children instead come to school believing that a respectful attitude toward any task includes doing the task well. For Yaqui, the activity done according to recommended or correct form is as important as the purpose or goal of the activity and if it cannot be done well, there is little reason to engage in the activity at all.

The above citations from the literature present examples from various tribal groups, i.e., Navajo, Oglala Sioux, and Yaqui, regarding the home socialization practices which influence the respective ways children learn to learn. They prefer to learn privately—competence precedes performance. Although each group is different and distinct from the others in language and in other aspects of their particular culture, a similar approach to learning seems to be prevalent.

EXPERIENCING THE WORLD: A VISUAL APPROACH TO LEARNING

> I study like this. The teacher lectures and then I take notes. And then I read them over, I study them. And then when I take a test I see the study notes in my mind (her hands quickly outline a rectangular shape). I see the paper and then I know where the answers are when I see the paper in my mind (Navajo student, personal communication, 1988).

Within the last two decades, researchers have investigated the visual approach that many Indian groups use as a method by which they come to know or understand the world. John (1972) suggested that there is considerable agreement among social scientists, educators, and others "that the Indian children of the Southwest are visual in their approaches to their world" (p. 333). Impressions formed by careful observation and looking are lasting impressions. John (1972) reported that Navajo children learn by looking. "They scrutinize the face of adults; they recognize at great distances their family's livestock. They are alert to danger signs of changing weather or the approach of predatory animals" (p. 333). Appleton (1983) in describing Yaqui children, said they are encouraged to learn by watching and modeling; "learning the correct way to do a task by watching it being performed repeatedly by others is highly reinforced" (p. 173).

Indian children of the Northwest also exhibit the same sort of visual strength in how they view their world. For example, Kwakuitl children apparently have learned to learn by observation (Philion & Galloway, 1969; Rohner, 1965; Wolcott, 1967). Rohner (1965) pointed out a possible conflict situation in that Kwakuitl children learn by observation, manipulation, and experimentation in their homes, but in school the learning experience is limited to verbal instruction, reading, and writing. Philion and Galloway (1969) in their research with Kwakuitl children and the reading process stated that the children displayed remarkable ability in visual discrimination. By imitating the behavior of others, very young children (ages four or five) were able to follow complicated sets of directions without verbal directions.

Kleinfeld (1973) described the extraordinary accuracy of Eskimos in memory of visual information. She reported that their figural and spatial abilities enabled them to draw maps of the terrain which were accurate in significant detail and in spatial arrangements.

The visual strength of Indian children in the Southwest has also been the subject of reports by Cazden and John (1971) and John-Steiner and Osterreich (1975). Philips (1972) added to the literature on observations of visual strength from her work with Warm Springs, Oregon, Indian children. When viewed as cultural strengths and not weaknesses or deficiencies, the natural skills and abilities of Indian children contribute to providing a total picture of a child's learning style.

FIELD-DEPENDENCE/FIELD-INDEPENDENCE: THE INFLUENCE OF CULTURE

> Yea, when I think about this field dependent/independent stuff, my Indian students seem to be more field sensitive. They do better when they understand the total picture (Teacher, personal communication, 1988).

Although field-dependence/independence is the most thoroughly researched dimension of cognitive style (Cazden & Leggett, 1981), there are few reports devoted to study of this dimension with American Indian students. The work of Ramirez and Castaneda (1974) with Mexican-American children has provided a framework for looking at the impact of culture on learning styles of Indian children. Ramirez and Castaneda (1974) have examined field-dependence/field-independence in light of cultural differences among Mexican-Americans and postulate that Mexican-American youth tend to grow up in a culture in which family organization tends to produce primarily field-dependent or, as they term it, field-sensitive learning styles. Conversely, children reared in formally organized families that promote strong individual identity tend to be more field-independent (Cohen, 1969). It has been speculated that Indian children viewed from this paradigm tend to be more field-sensitive. However, in one study of field-dependence/independence in Navajo children, Dinges and Hollenbeck (1978) found that their Navajo sample scored significantly higher in a field-independent direction than the Anglo sample. Their findings are in contrast to previous research and hypothesized results which suggested that there is a direct relationship among family organization, cultural isolation, and field-dependence/field-independence for cultures of the United States and in other cultures of the world. They attempted to determine that a similar relationship also holds for American Indian groups, but found contrasting data. They suggested a multi-factor explanation comprised of genetic, environmental, experiential and linguistic factors unique to the Navajo to account for the outcomes.

In summary, the body of research which examined learning styles of American Indian students, although small, does present some converging evidence that suggests common patterns or methods in the way these students come to know or understand the world. They approach tasks visually, seem to prefer to learn by careful observation which precedes performance, and seem to learn in the natural settings experientially. Research with other student groups has clearly illustrated differences in learning style, whether they be described as relational-analytical; field-dependent/field-independent; or global/linear, can result in "academic disorientation." It is not clear where Indian students fit on this continuum. However, what is clear from the research summarized in the previous section is that American Indian students come to learn about the world in ways that are different from mainstream students.

SHOWING COMPETENCE: PUBLIC AND PRIVATE TALK

> I have noticed that when I asked a question, the (Pima) students would not respond; there was dead silence. But when I made a comment without questioning, they were more likely to respond a join in the discussion (Teacher, personal communication, 1988).

The way in which people prefer to demonstrate learning is an important corollary to the way in which they prefer to learn. It is as Mehan (1981) has described:

> To be successful in classroom lessons, students must not only know the **content** of academic subjects, they must know the appropriate **form** in which to cast their academic knowledge. Although it is incumbent upon students to display **what** they know during lessons, they must also know **how** to display it (p. 51).

There is evidence that the ways in which children acquire and demonstrate knowledge are influenced by accustomed cultural norms and socialization practices (Cohen, 1969). The classroom context dictates an interactional style often in conflict with the interactional style of the home and/or community.

A body of recent research on minority children has produced studies that show different reactions to cooperative vs. competitive situations, questioning techniques, classroom pacing, and classroom organization. Included in this research is considerable ethnographic evidence on children's responses to different interactional situations in school and in their home and community.

In examining the issue of interactional styles or the demonstration of knowledge in classroom studies on Indian children, a focus has emerged which centers on the continuity/discontinuity spectrum as it relates to the child's home environment and the environment of the schools in which they are participants. Situations have been reported in which the interactional style of the home environment is at conflict or interferes with the interactional style required for successful participation in the classroom (Cazden, 1982; Dumont, 1972; Erickson & Mohatt, 1982; Philips, 1972, 1983; Van Ness, 1981).

In particular, recent studies point to the different cultural orientation Indian children experience when participating in classroom learning. One of the most extensive studies was done by Philips (1972) in which she examined participant structures and communicative competence with children from the Warm Springs Indian Reservation in Oregon. Philips (1972) observed that Indian children were reluctant to participate in structures that required large and small-group recitations. However, they were more talkative than non-Indian children in the last two structures when they initiated the interaction with the teacher or were working in student-led group projects. She noted a failure of Warm Springs Indian children to participate verbally in their classrooms because the norms for social performance in their community did not support public linguistic performance, whereas, the school environment demanded this form of interaction. Philips' study revealed that observation, careful listening, supervised participation and individualized self-correction or testing are modes of learning in the Warm Springs Indian community. Philips (1972) concluded that this process of acquisition of competence may help to explain a reluctance of Warm Springs Indian children to speak in front of their classmates. An incongruency exists in that the process of acquisition of knowledge and demonstration of knowledge in the classroom are "collapsed into the single act of answering questions or reciting when called upon to do so by the teacher, particularly in the lower grades" (p. 388).

Other ethnographic research suggests that the communication difficulty experienced by the Warm Springs Indian children when participant structures are teacher-dominated and require public recitations may be generalized to other groups of American Indian children as well as other minority group children. Dumont (1972) found a similar situation in a study which contrasted two Cherokee classrooms. In one classroom, teacher-dominated recitations were a predominant structure and the children were silent. In the other classroom, the children were observed to talk excitedly and productively about all of their learning tasks because they had choices of when and how to participate and the teacher encouraged small-group, student-directed projects. The landmark research conducted by Philips (1972) and Dumont (1972) present frameworks for analyzing the interactional structure which exists in schools attended by children from other tribal groups. Their research indicates that some Indian children may be more apt to participate actively and verbally in group projects and in situations where they have control in volunteering participation and less apt to perform on demand when asked a question individually in a large group.

COOPERATING AND COMPETING: THE INDIVIDUAL AND THE GROUP

> You put them out on the basketball court and they are competitive as can be. But in the classroom they don't want to compete against each other. I can ask a question and when a student responds incorrectly no other student will correct him. They don't want to look better than each other or to put another student down. The Anglo students are eager to show that they know the correct answer. They want to shine; the Indian students want to blend into the total class (Teacher, personal communication, 1988).

There is evidence of the predisposition of Indian children to participate more readily in group or team situations. While much of the evidence on cooperation/competition is anecdotal, Miller and Thomas (1972) and Brown (1980) conducted studies with Blackfoot and Cherokee Indian children, respectively, using the Madsen Cooperation Board in which cooperative and competitive behaviors were examined. Miller and Thomas (1972) found dramatic differences between Blackfoot Indian children and white Canadian children while playing a game which permitted competitive or cooperative behavior, but rewarded cooperative behavior. White children behaved competitively even when it was maladaptive to do so, while Blackfoot children cooperated. Brown (1980) found Cherokee children to be more cooperative and less competitive than Anglo-American children. In Brown's (1980) study, he found a negative relationship between the cooperative behavior of Cherokee children and their school achievement. In other words, cooperative behavior produced lower achievement. Brown (1980) explained that in Cherokee classroom society, children closely follow traditional Cherokee norms such as maintaining harmonious relations, but more important is the norm which requires children "to hold fast to group standards of achievement that all of the children are capable of meeting" (p. 70). High ability students who do not want to violate this norm, keep from displaying their competence and the result, according to Brown (1980), is lowered achievement for many members of the classroom society.

The implications of this research are that if Indian children have learned to learn in a cooperative way, they may experience conflicts when they enter the competitive world of the classroom. It also confirms the findings of ethnographic studies that suggest that many Indian students avoid competition, which they view as unfair in its composition (Dumont, 1971; Wax, Wax & Dumont, 1964).

It is apparent that many Indian children tend to avoid individual competition, especially when one individual appears to be better than another. In fact, in many Indian societies the humility of an individual is something to be respected and preserved. Havighurst (1970) observed that "Indian children may not parade their knowledge before others nor try to appear better than their peers" (p. 109).

In looking at competition and the peer society of Indian youth, Wax (1971) stated that:

> It has frequently been observed that Indian children hesitate to engage in an individual performance before the public gaze, especially where they sense competitive assessment against their peers and equally do not wish to demonstrate by their individual superiority the inferiority of their peers. On the other hand, where performance is socially defined as benefiting the peer society, Indians become excellent competitors (as witness their success in team athletics) (cf Dumont & Wax, 1969, p. 85).

What the literature suggests is that for Indian children from certain groups, public display of knowledge that is not in keeping with community or group norms may be an unreasonable expectation. It may be an experience that often causes Indian children to withdraw and act out the prototype of the "silent Indian child."

TEACHING STYLE: ADAPTATION TO LEARNING STYLE

The teaching style or method one chooses to transmit learning can have a significant effect on whether students learn or fail. As John (1972) suggested:

> Styles of teaching are, in part, an expression of the goals of education. When working with Indian children, educators choose methods of instruction that zero in on what they wish to accomplish instead of methods that reflect the developmental stages of children or respond to the specific features of tribal life (p. 332).

In choosing methods for a particular situation, there are many variables to consider that will lead to optimal learning. Only recently has the culture of the learner been considered among those variables, other than as a deficiency to be remedied. As Burgess (1978) pointed out, "Unfortunately, many instructors ignore culture and its impact on learning both in 'content' and 'style,' rather than devising methods and techniques through which culturally diverse individuals approach problem solving" (p. 52).

Leacock (1976) provided a strong rationale for understanding culture and its influence on instruction. She believed that "true cultural insight" enables one to look beyond differences that are superficial and socially determined to the integrity of the individual; it prevents misinterpretation of behaviors which do not follow an accustomed pattern. Leacock (1976) cited as an example teachers' misinterpretation of the pervading "cooperative spirit" in Indian societies and a reluctance of Indian children to compete with peers as a lack of desire and motivation. In essence, Leacock was saying that cultural differences are often misinterpreted and the lens through which the teacher views the behavior is colored by atypical behavior used as prototypes in the teacher training process. For example, "timidity" is often interpreted as lack of initiative, motivation, or the competitive spirit. If the behavior were viewed through a more culturally relativistic lens, the timid behavior might reveal a reluctance to compete with one's peers, or a reluctance to display learning in a way incongruent with the child's lifestyle. Wax, Wax and Dumont (1964) reported similar conflicts when teachers misinterpret cultural behavior. They concluded that:

> When Indian children err, their elders "explain" which as we understand it means that they painstakingly and relatively privately illustrate or point out the correct procedure or proper behavior. However... teachers in school do not understand this. Their irate scolding becomes an assault on the child's status before his peers. At the same time, the teacher diminishes his own stature, inasmuch as respected elders among Indians control their tempers and instruct in quiet patience (p. 95).

Mohatt and Erickson's (1981) study of cultural differences in teaching styles in an Odawa school supports the differences between participant structures Philips (1972) found in Warm Springs and illustrates that teachers who have viewed cultural differences as strengths have been able to create the type of atmosphere which motivate learning. In this study, an Odawa Indian and a non-Indian teacher were observed to see if there were differences in their teaching styles. Although both teachers were effective and experienced, they varied as to the strategies used with students. The Odawa teacher's strategies reflected Odawa cultural patterns of what is appropriate in ordinary social relations between adults and children and was manifested in pacing of classroom activities and interactions with students.

In most classrooms there is a tendency for teachers to introduce almost all new concepts and give all instructions verbally (Rohner, 1965; Appleton, 1983). This teaching style conflicts with the traditional cultural patterns reinforced in many Indian communities where visual strengths are encouraged. As John (1972) speculates, "If the description of the ways in which young Navajo children learn is correct, that is, that they tend to approach their world visually and by quiet, persistent exploration, then a style of teaching stressing overt verbal performance is alien to such a child" (p. 338). This is not to say that Indian children should not be expected to respond to verbal instructions nor perform verbally; rather, this information suggests that new concepts can be presented through alternative modes or teaching styles, and Indian children can display their learning in alternative interactions. For example, Cazden and Leggett (1981) recommend that because children differ in sensory modality strength, their learning may be depressed in overly verbal environments and schools should deliberately plan more multisensory instruction. While Cazden and Leggett were referring to children in bilingual classrooms, they do not use the term "bilingual classrooms" to refer to any classroom where minority children are present. Their recommendation makes sense for teachers of Indian children.

IN THE CLASSROOM: THE APPLICATION OF THEORY INTO PRACTICE

The premise of this paper is that although Indian students come to school with an approach to learning which is culturally influenced and often different from students of mainstream America, the styles which teachers use to deliver instruction are essentially the same for everyone. Philips (1983) capsulized this attitude when she said:

> Surprisingly little attention has been given to the teaching methods used in teaching ethnic minority students in this country. Particularly when the notion of culturally relevant curriculum materials has been around as long as it has. It is as if we have been able to recognize that there are cultural differences in what people learn, but not in how they learn (pp. 132–133).

The best research intentions are often challenged by teachers with the "But what do I do on Monday morning?" syndrome. Translating theory into practice is an enigmatic situation with which educators have wrestled for years. Teachers who are empathetic and want to change, do not do so simply because they have not had the time to reflect, research, and restructure their teaching style. Embedded throughout this paper are implications for teachers of Indian students. In addition, the multicultural literature is replete with general suggestions and guidelines which should be considered when implementing learning style aspects to teaching. Bennett (1985) encourages teachers to know their own teaching and learning styles and determine how far they can stray from these strengths and preferences and still be comfortable. She cautions teachers to build classroom flexibility slowly, adding one new strategy at a time. Her encouragement to use all modes (visual, auditory, tactile, and kinesthetic) when teaching concepts and skills is compatible with Cazden and Leggett's (1971) suggestion that teachers plan for multisensory instruction.

Cox and Ramirez (1981) recommend the use of direct observation and classroom experience for assessment and planning in addressing goals related to learning styles. They have summarized a field-tested process into six points:

> 1. Assess students' preferred ways of learning and the way(s) in which student behaviors change from situation to situation.
> 2. Plan learning experiences that address conceptual goals or skills or other objectives that incorporate the student's preferred ways of learning, using teaching methods, incentives, materials, and situations that are planned according to student preferences.
> 3. Implement the learning experiences that were planned.
> 4. Evaluate the learning experience in terms of attainment of conceptual or other goals as well as in terms of observed student behaviors and involvement.
> 5. As the year progresses, plan and implement student participation in learning experiences that require behaviors the student has previously avoided. Incorporate only one aspect at a time of the total experience from the less familiar behaviors—focusing on only the reward, the materials, the situation, or the task requirements—so that the student utilizes what is familiar and comfortable or motivating as support for the newer learning experience aspects.
> 6. Continue to provide familiar, comfortable, successful experiences as well as to gradually introduce the children to learning in new ways (pp. 64–65).

Following this process, teachers can implement specific methods and strategies which will communicate to Indian students an attitude of understanding and caring while demanding high performance. Kleinfeld (1979) has referred to this type of teacher as a "warm demander;" in other words one who can balance humanistic concerns with high expectations for achievement. The suggestions which we have outlined are distilled from many sources. Certainly, the authors whose work we have reviewed are to be given credit, but there are countless numbers of teachers in workshops who have shared workable ideas and, unfortunately, will remain nameless and unrecognized for the purposes of this paper. The following suggestions have special significance for teachers of Indian students:

- Discuss students' learning style with them; help them to understand why they do what they do in the learning situation;
- Be aware of students' background knowledge and experiences;
- Be aware of the "pacing" of activities within a time framework which may be rigid and inflexible;
- Be aware of how questions are asked; think about the discussion style of your students;
- Remember, some students do not like to be "spotlighted" in front of a group;
- Provide time for practice before performance is expected; let children "save face," but communicate that it is "okay" to make mistakes;
- Be aware of proximity preferences; how close is comfortable;
- Organize the classroom to meet the interactional needs of students; provide activities which encourage both independence and cooperation;
- Provide feedback that is immediate and consistent; give praise that is specific.

We urge teachers to use our selected references. No one source can provide the answers to the complex questions facing teachers of Indian students. The community in which one chooses to teach will provide the most comprehensive resource for perplexing sorts of questions. Teachers must become participants in the community; they must observe and ask questions in such a way that genuine caring and concern is communicated. Teachers must let students (and their parents) know that they, too, are learners. An excellent source of guidelines generated by beginning teachers of Indian youth can be found in a program operated by the Division of Teacher Education at Indiana University. In this program, student-teacher volunteers over several years have been placed on Indian reservations in the Southwest. Their observations were organized into an article which emphasized that "anyone attempting to teach children of another culture should be as fully aware as possible of the language, customs, traditions, and taboos of that culture so that he or she can avoid classroom and community understandings and become an effective teacher" (Mahan and Criger, 1977, p. 13).

CONCLUSIONS

In summary, it seems appropriate to end this paper with an observation by a historian who participated in a conference about multicultural education and American Indians:

> Schools, in general, can never hope to perfectly mirror the society they represent. Likewise, American Indian society, philosophy, and life (sic) can never be a perfect instrument within the format of the schools which came to us from Europe. But, the schools can do a lot more than they have done in the past! Furthermore, the time for them to do that something has long since passed" (O'Neil, 1979).

EPILOGUE

The typist of this paper is a Muskogee-Creek. She read the paper as she typed it and commented about the relevance of its content to understanding how she approached learning. She indicated that she had many of the "aha!" moments in which she was enlightened about her own learning style. She provided validity to our paper. We are happy that we were able to do this for her.

27

Computers for Special Populations

Sheila H. Feichtner

The full integration of the computer into the vocational classroom will initiate a new era for students with special training needs. When that day comes, the computer will empower them as learners, enrich their learning experiences, and enable them to access information as readily as others do. Already, computer technology is having a major impact on the assessment necessary for educational placement of special populations.

The students targeted for special educational services come to vocational education with a variety of learning needs. Some perform significantly below grade level in reading or computing; some know very little English; some are handicapped physically, mentally, or emotionally; some have not learned how to learn or are rusty at learning; some have personal pressures which take precedence over learning. Many have damaged self-concepts, lacking the sense of self-worth that is as important to learning as the possession of basic skills.

The computer can help special needs students who have come to expect failure to experience success. Computer instruction can be tailored to an individual's needs—even to the native language of the learner. Computer instruction is self-paced. It focuses the student on one task at a time and allows mistakes to be made in private. By providing positive reinforcement, it motivates the student to continue learning.

With appropriate software, the computer can empower learning through:

- word processing programs, which ease the physical burden of writing and revising, helping students to write better,
- instructional programs that train students to break down problems into component parts and set strategies for their solution, thus promoting the development of higher-order thinking skills,
- simulations that help students understand abstract concepts in vocationally specific content areas, and
- data base programs that help students manipulate data, and so understand relationships among ideas.

Computer instruction can also be used as an end in itself for target populations, providing them with marketable skills in programming, data processing, or word processing.

If the computer offers so much promise, why is it that computers are not used more widely in the instruction of special needs students? The problem is threefold: equipment is expensive, educational software is minimal, and teachers feel inadequate or anxious about using computers in instruction.

The U.S. Office of Technology Assessment recently reported (1988) that the vast majority of those teaching or planning to teach have had little or no computer education or training. As for the reported prevalence of computers in the classroom, the average public school has one computer for every 30 students. Moreover, access to computers is significantly less in the poorer school districts, black students have less access than white students, and limited English proficient (LEP) students have the least access of all.

Integrating the computer into instruction requires that teachers and students have access to a critical mass of computers. Computers cost. They require a large initial outlay and continuing expenditures for maintenance, repair, updating equipment, and purchasing software. While funds for buying computer hardware and software for target populations are available from a variety of public and private sources . . . , there are bound to be additional costs for school districts serious about full-scale integration of computers. Districts that have been able to develop computer capability have done so by seeking multiple sources of funding.

SPECIAL EQUIPMENT

Computer users have to be able to perform three kinds of activities: *input* (entering information into the computer's memory), *process* (doing something with the information), and *output* (producing the information for use outside the computer). Since computers are a visual and tactile medium, all three steps have been problems for would-be computer users with certain physical disabilities.

Good vision and manual dexterity would seem to be essential for keyboarding (input), working with data (processing), and reading printouts (output). In recent years, however, technological innovations have enabled users with disabilities to perform these activities through specialized or adapted equipment. For those who are blind or visually impaired, there are Braille keyboards and printers, optical scanners, screen displays in very large print, and synthesizers that convert computer output into speech. For those unable to use a standard keyboard, there are touch-sensitive screens, oversize keyboards, and adapted keyboards that can be operated with one finger or a joystick. More severely disabled users can manipulate on-screen data by speaking, blowing or sucking on a plastic tube, aiming a light-pointer attached to the head, or moving the eyes.

In fact, with special devices available today, anyone who has control of a single

Source: From Sheila H. Feichtner, "Computers for Special Populations," *Vocational Education Journal*, Volume 64, March 1989, pp. 36–37, 51.

muscle in his or her body can control a computer—and even a robot that receives its commands from the computer. . . .

SOFTWARE CONSIDERATIONS

Learners with special training needs need instructional software that is pedagogically sound and designed with students in mind. Good software will be accurate, clear, and logical. It will integrate content with previous knowledge and will be free of stereotypes (Harte, 1987).

Even good software can pose problems for people who have mental deficits, who can't read, or can't read English well. Some of these problems can be alleviated through software adapted to specific needs.

Special education teachers recommend the use of software that allows a teacher to control some aspect of the instructional process. Because instruction must be tailored to the individual, "good programs let the teacher make some of the instructional decisions: whether the sound is on or off, what difficulty level the student should begin with, how many problems the student should attempt, and so on" (Lewis, et al., 1987).

Unfortunately, although excellent software is available to teach reading, none of it is written for vocational education, and much is inappropriate for secondary students and adults. Some teachers have gotten around this problem by requiring older students to use the software to teach younger students the writing and problem-solving skills that both need to learn (Harte, 1987).

The picture is much brighter for software to correct deficiencies in mathematics skills. A large amount of commercial software is designed to teach math, and a significant amount applies basic math in particular vocational content areas.

Commercial software is also available for helping LEP secondary students and adults, although none of it is specifically designed for the vocational classroom. Some of the software provides an auditory response in a foreign language as the English words appear on screen. Other software helps improve English pronunciation by a visual display of speech patterns. Some software helps the LEP learner understand the grammatical idiosyncrasies of the English language.

Software now under development will translate English input into a foreign language output. One day, this software will enable vocational teachers to provide LEP students with vocational instructional materials in the student's native language.

Computers are like books, pencils, and chalkboards. They are just another tool for teaching the existing curriculum, albeit a powerful tool that promotes equity, adds excitement, increases student options, minimizes some administrative chores, and eases classroom discipline problems. (As one teacher said, "If the kids have their hands on a keyboard, they don't have their hands on each other.")

Because the computer is just another instructional tool, the same principles of teaching target populations apply to the computer that apply to any instructional process, teaching material, or piece of equipment. Some students will need additional time to complete an assignment, some will need some of the adaptive equipment discussed above, and some will need tutoring as they work through a piece of software (Sarkees, 1985).

Mastering anything new takes time and energy, and learning to use the computer to teach is a time-consuming task. Teachers need to learn enough about computers so that they can teach students to operate equipment. Teachers need to learn enough about software that they can make judgments about when and how to use it. Hardware can be mastered through coursework, inservice training, or instruction from a computer dealer. What works in software and in the classroom is best learned from teachers who are already integrating computers into their curriculum.

Finally, computers can help in the management of the classroom. They can be used to track student progress, maintain an inventory of equipment and supplies, produce grade reports, generate tests, and maintain files. They are able assistants in the performance of the many everyday housekeeping chores that keep teachers from their primary task—working with students.

PART THREE

Governance, Organization, and Support of American Education

All three levels of government—federal, state, and local—have important roles to play in the governance, organization, operations, and financing of education in the United States. The United States Constitution makes no specific references to education; however, the Tenth Amendment provides that "the powers not delegated to the United States by the Constitution, nor prohibited to it by the States, are reserved to the States respectively or to the people." Therefore, public education is a legal function of the respective states.

Historically, local school districts have had great latitude in organizing and operating their own schools in the fashion they desired. In recent years, however, both the state and the federal governments have played a much stronger role. This change has resulted from a number of factors—among them are federal court decisions; state and federal legislative mandates; and student, teacher, and parental rights, along with educational reform activities.

The role of the judiciary has been significant in recent years in altering the balance of federal, state, and local governance of American education. Education in the United States must be conducted in accordance with the United States Constitution, specifically those provisions having to do with guaranteed individual rights. The interpretations of the First and Fourteenth Amendments by the United States Supreme Court have had decided effects on the governance, organization, and operations of education at the local level. The Fourteenth Amendment reads in part: "No State shall make or reinforce any law which shall abrogate the privileges or immunities of citizens of the United States; nor shall any State deprive any person of life, liberty, or property without due process of law; nor deny to any person within its jurisdiction the equal protection of the law." The First Amendment, "Congress shall make no law respecting an establishment of religion nor prohibiting the free exercises thereof" has been made applicable to education within several states by the Fourteenth Amendment.

The financial support of education is closely related to the governance, organization, and operation of education. All three levels of government contribute to that support. Historically, financial support came from local sources, namely the property tax. The trend in the past few years has been to increase state support. The federal government's contributions are very small, less than 10 percent, compared to the local and state contributions. The trend toward more state funding is in harmony with the recommendations of recent studies and court rulings in the area of school finance, which in essence, are directed toward achieving equal educational opportunity.

The first three articles deal with parental, teacher, and student rights. Lisa Jennings, in "Open Records: A Legitimate Public Interest?" describes one woman's crusade to gain access to the records of her son's teacher. The issues focused on the delicate balance between a school employee's privacy and the public's right to secure protection for its children and to insure accountability from the system. In "Schoolhouse Speech," David S. Tatel and Elizabeth Heffernan provide insight into teacher rights and the First Amendment. Teacher rights seek the proper balance which will accommodate teachers' protected speech and school administrators' needs to ensure the smooth operation of the school system. In "Reasonableness—The High Court's New Standard for Cases Involving Student Rights," Lowell C. Rose addresses the proper balance between the rights of students and the schools' need to "maintain an environment in which learning can take place."

The topics in the second series of articles include the First Amendment and religion, secular humanism, and the status of Black Americans. In "Public Schools and the Road to Religious Neutrality," Daniel A. Spiro proposes that Separationists and Fundamentalists share common goals: to establish true religious neutrality in the schools and to eliminate the stranglehold of the American Civil Religion. Christy Macy and Ricki Seidman, in "Attacks on 'Secular Humanism': The Real Threat to Public Education," describe and discuss the alarming increase in the censorship of books and curricula in our schools. In "Outlook is Bleak for Many Blacks, Study Concludes: Council Says Progress Has Lagged Since 70's" Peter Schmidt reports that the National Research Council has concluded that despite gains in recent decades, blacks still face formidable barriers in their struggle to achieve educational parity with whites.

The topics of the third series, improving the preparation of school administrators and redefining the roles of principals are significantly different from any of the previous topics mentioned. The next essay, authored by Malen, Ogawa, and Kranz, discusses the status of "Site-Based Management." In his article "Policy Board Proposals Ignore Real Problems," Willis Hawley challenges the viability of the proposals of the National Policy Board for Educational Administration. Ann Bradley notes in "School-Restructuring Efforts Forcing Principals to Redefine Their Roles" that participatory decision making is challenging the traditional definitions of principalship and of central office leadership.

The last series of articles deal with financing the schools. Accountability is an important issue. Michael Newman, in "School Financing in Texas is Ruled Unconstitutional," provides detailed information that addresses the issues of the wide disparities in funding between the rich and the poor districts. In "In Finance Arena, A New Activism Emerges," Nancy Mathis notes that equity concerns are resurfacing across the country both in litigation and in vigorous debates over school-financing systems in nearly half the states. In a more practical vein, in "Budgeting for the 1990s" Harry J. Hartley describes the steps in developing school budgets. He notes that in many cases the annual budget is the best statement of values a school system makes.

The governance, operations, organization, and financial support of American education are intertwined, not only with one another but also with our political processes. As our society has changed, so has our educational system.

28

Open Records

A Legitimate Public Interest?

Lisa Jennings

When Madonna Tibor asked school officials in the small town of Hebron, N.D., to let her see the records of her son's teacher, she had no idea she was launching a freedom-of-information crusade that would send her first to the courts and then to the state capital.

That was in 1987, when she and about 40 other Hebron parents were concerned over problems their children were having in a business-education class at the town's only school. They wanted to know whether any complaints about the teacher had ever been lodged with the school district.

As a city worker, Ms. Tibor knew that the records of public employees were open in North Dakota, so she simply asked for the teacher's files.

"If the district had given us the information then" she says, "it would have done away with a lot of rumors and suspicion."

But the district refused, citing the privacy rights of the teacher.

Ms. Tibor has since won a victory in the North Dakota Supreme Court and a gubernatorial veto of legislation exempting teacher records from the state's open-access law. And she remains firm in her conviction that taxpayers deserve to know all there is to know about those who teach their children.

She is not alone. The Hebron case is one of several nationwide this year to focus attention on the delicate balance between a school employee's privacy and the public's right to secure protection for its children and accountability from the system.

Lawsuits over access to school personnel records have also been filed in Colorado, Connecticut, Texas, and Washington State.

Teachers' unions in those states have argued that because educators have already met certain minimum requirements when becoming certified and are continually being evaluated, their files contain more personal data than those of other public employees and should be accorded a different status under open-records laws.

But freedom-of-information advocates counter that open records are particularly important in education, where "accountability" has become the latest reform catch phrase.

Gov. George Sinner of North Dakota expressed these sentiments in his veto message on the teacher-exemption bill last month.

"Teachers, administrators, school boards, and students need to be held accountable to parents and to the public for their performance—or lack of performance," he said. "Open records help assure such accountability in North Dakota."

'SUNSHINE' LAWS VARY

Every state has a law similar to North Dakota's. Often called "sunshine" laws, they determine whether and when public meetings or records will be open to citizen scrutiny.

Every state also has exemptions to these laws, usually to protect medical records, family information, and other personal facts not deemed of "legitimate public interest," according to a 1986 report on state sunshine laws by the Council of State Governments.

But in many states, the personnel records of school employees have remained largely unexamined—either because teachers' unions have successfully argued the issue of privacy rights, or because parents and other citizens have remained unaware of their rights under sunshine laws.

Peggy Portscheller, president of the North Dakota Education Association, says privacy was the key concern when her union took the position that the Hebron case amounted to little more than a "witchhunt."

"Our main bone of contention was the access to teacher evaluations," Ms. Portscheller says, noting that state law requires two such evaluations each year. "In order to protect the integrity of that process, we believe those records are best kept between employer and employee."

When Ms. Tibor's lawsuit reached the state supreme court in February 1988, the judge agreed with lower courts that teacher records could be inspected by anyone under the North Dakota law, because the legislature had failed to pass any laws exempting them.

That ruling, and the intense lobbying by the N.D.E.A. that followed it, prompted lawmakers to take immediate action to close school files.

A bill adopted by a wide margin in both houses of the legislature early this year restricted access to the records of teachers, administrators, and higher-education faculty members, to supervisory administrators and school-board members. The proposal would have allowed those officials to discuss information in the files with parents.

But in his veto message, Governor Sinner said he saw no need for such confidentiality.

"The records are, after all, not 'personal' files, but 'personnel' files" he wrote.

Source: From Lisa Jennings, "Open Records: A Legitimate Public Interest?," *Education Week*, Volume VIII, Number 33, May 10, 1989, pp. 1, 20. Reprinted with permission from *Education Week*.

"Given the critical role of education and the high percentage of public money expended on it, this bill moves in exactly the wrong direction."

Ms. Portscheller, who says she was "disappointed" by the veto, predicts that the action will "water down" the teacher-evaluation process. "Administrators will be reluctant to put anything substantial down in writing," she says, "and that is certainly not in the best interests of the public."

Ms. Tibor disagrees. "The evaluations won't be watered down if you have an honest administrator," she says. "He'll keep the truth in those files." She and her allies argue that, if the district has nothing to hide, there is no reason to close the files.

TRANSCRIPTS ISSUE IN TEXAS

Parents and newspaper editors in Texas have contended in access battles there that school districts may in fact have something to hide.

Last year, the *Houston Chronicle* reported that at least five, and possibly as many as 25, administrators in the Houston Independent School District had purchased mail-order doctoral degrees from an unaccredited California institution.

When the newspaper sought to obtain the academic records of district personnel, however, the school system filed suit to block the request.

A county judge ruled in the district's suit last August that the newspaper lacked legal standing to seek an order forcing the disclosure of the records. The *Chronicle* has appealed that ruling.

The newspaper's own suit, meanwhile, was merged last year with a class action filed by a group of parents seeking the academic records of teachers in the Klein Independent School District.

The cases were split again last month. Litigation in the Klein case is expected to continue for another year or more, but late last week a state judge ruled in the Houston case that such documents should be made public. He gave the district 21 days to release the transcripts, but agreed to allow a lawyer to review each one for personal data that should not be disclosed. The district plans to appeal.

Although teachers' records are generally considered open under Texas sunshine laws, Houston school officials have maintained that academic transcripts are protected by legal precedents established in 1987 covering such personal information as parents; address and religious affiliation, often included in college transcripts.

Lawyers for the district have also pointed out that educators are the only public employees that have their transcripts on file, submitted as part of the certification process.

But Tony Pederson, managing editor of the *Houston Chronicle*, sees the dispute as an instance of schools seeking to avoid their accountability to the public.

"It is impossible to accurately judge the competence and qualifications of those who make decisions in public schools without public access to those records," he says. "It's simply a matter of discovering flaws in the way the Texas Education Agency watches over the backgrounds of its employees."

Darah S. Headley, a lawyer representing the Klein district, agrees that accountability may be an issue in both cases.

"But we feel that using academic transcripts is a flawed measurement of an administrator's qualifications," she says. "And there is a lot of personal information included in those records that is unrelated to their course of study."

Attorney General Jim Mattox last month issued an opinion stating that academic records should be considered public information, according to his spokesman, Ron Dusek.

The opinion is based on court decisions, Mr. Dusek said, particularly a 1987 ruling by the state supreme court that the federal Family Educational Rights and Privacy Act—known as the Buckley Amendment—does not cover an administrator's academic records.

Mr. Mattox had delayed his decision, however, to give the Texas legislature time to work on a measure that would specifically exempt sections of school employee's academic records, such as grades earned, from the sunshine laws.

Variations of the bill have passed both houses of the legislature, but lawmakers had not reached an agreement as of late last week.

Meanwhile, the Texas Education Agency has adopted a policy requiring all school administrators to have degrees from an accredited institution, according to Ms. Headley.

Superintendent Joan Raymond of Houston has also offered the newspaper a list of the system's administrators, with the college they graduated from. But this has apparently not satisfied the newspaper, which plans to pursue its lawsuit.

CHILD-ABUSE PROTECTION

School officials in Washington State have made similar attempts to appease a group of newspapers seeking information on 89 former teachers who voluntarily surrendered their teaching certificates or had them revoked by the state.

Cowles Publishing Company, publisher of the *Seattle Spokesman-Review* and the *Spokane Chronicle*, requested the records from the state superintendent of public instruction in January 1988. The newspapers were investigating reports that teachers who had been accused of sexual misconduct with students had been allowed to leave the system quietly, unpunished and unreported.

"It's important for the public to know how these investigations were pursued," says Duane M. Swinton, a lawyer representing Cowles.

Last summer, a state judge ruled that the records should be released, with the students' names deleted. (*See Education Week, Aug. 3, 1988.*)

But lawyers for Frank B. Brouillet, the former state superintendent, have appealed that decision and sought a temporary injunction to block release of the records.

Ralph E. Julnes, the superintendent's legal counsel, argued that the files contain much information considered confidential under state statutes, such as student records, psychological profiles, and inter-office communications.

Release of this kind of information, he argued in a legal brief filed last month, would hinder school officials' ability to investigate child-molestation charges because witnesses would be less likely to testify for the public record.

The Washington Education Association, which has intervened in the suit on the superintendent's side, contends that teachers falsely accused of molestation are also included in the files, and the release of such information without due process could be seriously damaging.

This year, the W.E.A. lobbied for a bill that would have restricted access to school employees' disciplinary records, says Robert D. Fisher, the union's legislative liaison.

The bill died, however, after a series of amendments to stiffen penalties for child molestation were proposed. Last month, the legislature adopted a bill that would bar from public-school teaching anyone convicted of killing, injuring, or sexually assaulting a minor.

Lawyers on both sides of the Washington case say they will appeal to the state supreme court if the appeals-court verdict is not in their favor.

CONNECTICUT DISCLOSURE STYMIED

In Connecticut, open-records advocates say their experience suggests that state high courts, whose justices often have a political background, may not always be sympathetic to open-access issues.

"Our supreme court is psychopathically opposed to freedom of information," charges Chris Powell, managing editor of the *Journal Inquirer of Manchester*, which has been fighting for years to gain access to personnel records of local school-district administrators.

Last month, the Connecticut Supreme Court refused to rule on a lower-court order in the case that would have required school officials to publicly disclose job-performance records of teachers.

The judges instead asked the state's Freedom of Information Commission—an independent, five-member panel representing citizens' access interests—to reconsider the facts of the six-year-old suit in light of a 1984 statute exempting teacher evaluations and records from Connecticut's access requirement.

Although many states have agencies that handle freedom-of-information complaints, Connecticut's commission is the only one with the authority to mediate complaints and represent citizens in court.

Mitchell W. Pearlman, executive director and general counsel for the commission, said the supreme court's action probably would force the newspaper to drop its request, because pursuing the dispute could take another six years.

The newspapers first requested the documents from the Somers School District in 1983, after a citizens' group complained that the district administration was top-heavy.

The newspaper has contended that knowing the basis on which the administrative promotions were made is an accountability issue, and lower-court judges agreed that the records should be made public.

But the high court concluded that the commission, in its initial finding, had not adequately weighed the balance between privacy interests and the public's right to know.

Mr. Powell of the *Journal Inquirer* complains that the 1984 law has been applied retroactively. But the high-court judges said in their opinion that the law merely clarified what was already legal intent—to close the records to the public.

The newspaper editor charges that the exemptions for teachers were not legal clarifications, but the result of "powerful lobbying" by the Connecticut Education Association.

UNIONS ON BOTH SIDES OF ISSUE

Teachers' unions are not always on the side of nondisclosure, however.

In Colorado, the state affiliate of the National Education Association last week said it planned to file suit in the second round of a legal battle over a list of minority teachers employed by the Denver Public Schools.

Both the Denver Classroom Teachers Association and the Colorado Education Association have sought to obtain the list, whose existence has become the subject of heated debate in the city. The unions want it, officials say, as a means of alerting minority teachers to special programs, such as training for administrative positions.

But district officials have denied in court that such a list exists. Last month, in fact, a state court of appeals upheld a district court's decision that the school system could not be forced to disclose a "non-existent" list.

The *Rocky Mountain News*, however, has reported that it was able to obtain a copy of a list of minority school employees—and that sources within the school system maintain such a list was available in 1987.

Jan Erskine, the Denver union's president, charges that the district also has a list specifically of teachers "with their ethnicity identified."

"The district just does not want to be cooperative," she says. "They want to maintain an adversarial relationship with the unions."

According to Marti Houser, chief attorney for the Colorado Education Association, the unions have obtained a list of black teachers from an unnamed source but still need a list of other minorities.

"It defeats the purpose of open-records laws if your request for information is blocked because you haven't used exactly the right buzzword," Ms. Houser says.

Ms. Erskine maintains that the union should have special access to such records. "We're not just anyone off the street asking for information," she points out.

According to a spokesman for the district, officials had sought not to infringe on employees' privacy rights. Colorado laws exempt most school personnel files from the public record.

POST-WATERGATE REACTION?

Mr. Pearlman of the Connecticut freedom-of-information commission suggests that legislative attempts to weaken open-records laws with exemptions for school employees may be part of the cyclical move toward nondisclosure that has followed the public-right-to-know high of the Watergate era.

But such statutes, he insists, are an example of "what is bad for education in this country."

Others note that the continuing drive toward professionalization of teaching will more than likely harden the divided positions on the issue of records disclosure, as teachers trade greater certification rigor and accountability standards for more pay and autonomy.

Against this backdrop, Ms. Tibor in North Dakota may represent the public's determination to keep its own watchful eye on teaching standards.

"You can't trust a lot of school boards to keep watch," says Ms. Tibor, who has finally obtained at least some of the information she sought but has paid a heavy price in legal fees and time away from her family for the victory. "Only about 1 percent are incompetent, but you've got to be able to watch that 1 percent."

29

Schoolhouse Speech

David S. Tatel
Elizabeth B. Heffernan

A school's ability to control what a teacher says decreases when the teacher voices opinions outside the classroom. Though school officials may not discipline a teacher merely for expressing views, publicly or privately, on issues regarding school policies or other matters of public interest, they need not tolerate insubordination.

In the landmark case of *Pickering v. Board of Education,* 391 U.S. 563 (1968), the local school board attempted to dismiss a teacher who had written a letter to a local newspaper criticizing the school board's handling of revenue proposals and allocation of financial resources.

The U.S. Supreme Court stated that although the school administration had interests as an employer in regulating the speech of its employees to promote efficient schooling, a balance must be struck between the need for orderly school administration and the constitutional right of the teacher as a citizen to comment on public matters.

This balancing takes into account several factors: the need for harmony in the workplace; whether a close working relationship has deteriorated between the teacher and the superiors against whom the statements are directed; the context in which the speech arose, including the degree of public interest involved; and whether the comments impeded the teacher's ability to perform his or her duties.

In *Pickering,* the Court overturned the teacher's dismissal, concluding that the teacher's statements related to matters of public concern and presented no questions of faculty discipline.

On occasions when a teacher expresses a personal grievance over internal office policy or personally confronts an immediate superior, school officials may take disciplinary action to deal with insubordination without violating the teacher's First Amendment rights.

In *Roberts v. Van Buren Public Schools,* 773 F. 2d 949 (8th Cir. 1985), the school faced a challenge from two elementary school teachers who claimed that the school had failed to renew their contracts in retaliation for their exercise of First Amendment rights. The teachers had filed grievances with the principal criticizing the school's "inequitable" funding of a class trip to the state capitol and the inadequacy of classroom supplies.

The court ruled that the speech involved subjects of public concern. The court held, however, that the speech was not protected under the First Amendment because the matters it raised, while previously open to active discussion, had been settled and approved through the school's proper channels. Because the First Amendment did not shield these teachers' speech, their action amounted to insubordination directed at school officials.

DISRUPTION THREAT

A teacher enjoys a constitutionally protected right to comment on matters of public interest not only outside the schoolhouse, but also inside the classroom. School administrators should develop appropriate guidelines concerning expression of opinion on controversial subjects at school and should not limit teacher's speech in these circumstances unless the speech would disrupt the educational process.

In *Tinker v. Des Moines Independent Community School District,* 393 U.S. 503 (1969), the Supreme Court stated that teachers, as well as students, possess First Amendment rights on school campuses, although school administrators still retain substantial discretion in controlling the school system.

In First Amendment cases addressing speech in the classroom, courts balance the school's interests in maintaining and promoting the discipline necessary to the proper functioning of schools against the teacher's interest in exercising fundamental rights of individual expression.

To justify any limitations on the teacher's constitutional rights, the school must show a reasonable basis for concluding that the teacher's conduct threatens to disrupt classwork or interfere with the operation of the school.

In *James v. Board of Education,* 461 F.2d 566 (2d Cir. 1972), *cert. denied,* 409 U.S. 1042 (1972), for example, the Court held that a school could not dismiss a high school teacher solely because he wore a black armband in class in silent protest against the Vietnam War, where his symbolic expression did not disrupt classroom activities or interfere with his teaching obligations.

In a related vein, in *Russo v. Central School District,* 469 F.2d 623 (2d Cir. 1972), *cert. denied,* 409 U.S. 1042 (1972), the court ruled that school officials could not dismiss a high school teacher who respectfully refused to pledge allegiance to the flag during class ceremonies, even though school regulations required her to participate. The court observed that the teacher did not attempt to prevent her students from reciting the pledge or to proselytize her students.

Local school authorities traditionally have been granted broad discretion by the courts to prescribe curriculum content, set

Source: From David S. Tatel and Elizabeth B. Heffernan, "Schoolhouse Speech," *The School Administrator,* May 1989, pp. 40, 41, 43.

classroom standards, and evaluate the speech and conduct of teachers in light of the special characteristics of the elementary and secondary public school environments.

But the courts have also recognized that safeguarding the First Amendment guarantee of free speech requires a balance to accommodate both the teacher's protected speech and the school administrator's need to ensure the smooth operation of the school system.

Weighing these competing interests in any particular conflict does not yield any formulaic answers. By developing appropriate policies in accordance with established legal principles, however, school administrators can help ensure that their regulation of teachers' speech will be constitutionally permissible.

If school authorities determine in accordance with such policies that teacher discipline is an appropriate response in a particular case, they will be in a favorable position to defend their action against any subsequent legal challenge.

30

"Reasonableness"—The High Court's New Standard for Cases Involving Student Rights

Lowell C. Rose

The Supreme Court of the United States is applying a new legal standard in court actions involving the constitutional rights of students. The change has increased the discretion of school officials in such areas as search and seizure, student publications, and student expression. In establishing the new standard, the Court seems to be giving school officials broad latitude in structuring an environment in which students can both learn and develop "socially appropriate behavior."

The cases in which the Court enunciated the new standard—though they involve different areas of student activity—all grew out of situations in which the actions of school officials were viewed by students as violations of their constitutional rights. The first case, *T.L.O. v. New Jersey* (1985), involved an assistant vice principal's search of a student's purse. The student had been accused of smoking in violation of a school rule and had denied all involvement. The search uncovered marijuana and related items that implicated the student in marijuana dealing.

The second case, *Bethel School District #403 v. Fraser* (1986), involved a speech by a student placing another student's name in nomination for an elective office in the high school. The student giving the speech was subsequently penalized for using sexually explicit language in violation of the school's "disruptive conduct rule."

The third case, *Hazelwood School District v. Kuhlmeier* (1988), grew out of a high school principal's decision to prevent the publication of two pages of a student newspaper. The decision was made because the principal felt that two articles, one on student pregnancies and the other on the effects of divorce on young people, were inappropriate.

In each of these cases, the Supreme Court held that the constitutional rights of students had not been violated and upheld the actions of school officials. More important than the decisions, however, is the fact that in each case the Court applied a standard different from the one previously used in such cases. (The choice of standard is, in the legal arena, often *crucial* to the outcome since the various sets of facts are measured against that standard.) The result of the three recent decisions is that, in judging the facts in cases involving student rights, courts at all levels will be applying a standard that seems to make court intervention less likely. Before moving to consideration of the new standard, it may be helpful to review the situation as it was prior to this change.

The landmark case in the area of student rights has been *Tinker v. Des Moines Independent Community School District* (1969). The decision in that case established the fact that students have constitutional rights that must be protected in school. The Court did recognize that these constitutional rights were different in schools but still found that these rights could not be removed except when their exercise would "substantially interfere with the work of the school or impinge upon the rights of other students." The burden for demonstrating that the standard of "substantial interference" was met rested on school officials. By selecting this standard, and by placing the burden of proof where it did, the Court required that schools make a fairly strong evidentiary showing before abridging student rights. This was the standard that was applied by the courts from 1969 until 1985.

In the three most recent cases, however, the Supreme Court has established a different standard, the key to which appears to be *reasonableness*. A closer examination of the three cases will demonstrate the significance of this change and show how the Court applied the new standard.

The student in *T.L.O.* had been accused of smoking in a school rest room. She denied the charge and even denied that she smoked at all. The assistant vice principal pursued his investigation by asking to see her purse. On opening the purse, he found a package of cigarettes and rolling papers of the kind associated with the use of marijuana. He then proceeded with a search that uncovered marijuana, a pipe, plastic bags, a fairly substantial amount of money, and two letters, the contents of which connected the student with marijuana dealing.

The issue the Supreme Court ultimately chose to deal with was whether the search had violated the student's rights under the Fourth Amendment. The Court first established that the standard needed to justify a student search in school would be different

Source: From Lowell C. Rose, " 'Reasonableness'— The High Court's New Standard for Cases Involving Student Rights," *Phi Delta Kappa,* Volume 69, Number 8, April 1988, pp. 589–592. Reprinted with permission from the publisher.

from the standard that applied in other settings. It then found that the legality of a student search should be based, not on "probable cause," but simply "on reasonableness, under all the circumstances, of the search." Using this standard the Court held that school officials have the right to search when there is a "reasonable suspicion" that the student "has violated or is violating either the law or the rules of the school."

In *Fraser* the offending nominating speech was given at a voluntary assembly held during school hours as part of a school-sponsored program in self-government. School officials felt that the student who delivered the speech referred to his candidate "in terms of an elaborate, graphic, and explicit sexual metaphor." The student was subsequently suspended for three days, and his name was removed from the list of candidates for graduation speaker. The student contested the penalties, alleging that his First Amendment right to freedom of speech had been violated.

In *Fraser* the Supreme Court reiterated the position it had previously taken in *T.L.O.*, holding that the rights of "children in public school" are different from those enjoyed by adults in "adult public discussion." The Court specifically found that it is appropriate for the public schools "to prohibit the use of vulgar and offensive terms in public discourse." The Court fixed no specific standard for determining what speech is appropriate, however. Instead it found that the determination "of what manner of speech in the classroom or in school assembly is inappropriate properly rests with the school board."

The *Kuhlmeier* case involved two articles that were to appear in the first two pages of a school-sponsored newspaper. One of the stories dealt with the pregnancies of three teenage girls and the other with the experiences of students whose parents had gone through a divorce. The principal found the two stories objectionable and, under the pressure of time, opted simply to delete the two pages in which the stories appeared. He subsequently indicated that he had acted to protect the privacy of students and parents, to avoid any appearance that the school endorsed the sexual mores of the pregnant girls, and to protect younger students from what he felt was "inappropriate material."

The Supreme Court was asked to determine whether censoring the two articles violated the First Amendment free speech rights of the student editors. The Court first disposed of the contention that the student newspaper was a public forum. It ruled that school facilities can be found to be public forums only in the event that school officials "have 'by policy or practice' opened those facilities for indiscriminate use by the general public." The Court then upheld the principal's actions on the ground that in schools school officials may "impose reasonable restrictions on the speech of students, teachers, and other members of the school community." In reaching this decision, it applied a standard of reasonableness to the specific actions of the school principal and found that his actions at each step met this test.

Thus in these rulings the Court has fixed the reasonableness standard as the one that school officials must meet. A search will be upheld if it is reasonable in nature. Restrictions on student expression will be upheld if they are reasonable in nature.*

With this standard firmly in place, we can turn our attention to what constitutes reasonableness. A starting point would be the factual situations in the cases in which the Court established the standard.

In the Court's judgment, T.L.O. involved two distinct searches—with the first, the search for cigarettes, providing the basis for the second, the search for marijuana. The Court found that the initial search for cigarettes was reasonable because finding cigarettes "would both corroborate the report that T.L.O. had been smoking and undermine the credibility of her defense to the charge of smoking." In the Court's opinion, the fact that the student's purse "was the obvious place to find [cigarettes]" gave the assistant vice principal the reasonable suspicion needed to justify the search. This justification would almost certainly have been inadequate if a probable cause standard had been used.

The discovery of "rolling papers" during the first search "gave rise to a reasonable suspicion that T.L.O. was carrying marijuana in her purse." This justified the further search, including the search of a separate, zippered compartment in which further items implicating T.L.O. in drug dealing were found. The Court used a step-by-step test of reasonableness, finding that the results at each step justified the further intrusion.

In *Fraser* the Court did not deal with what constitutes a standard for inappropriate speech. Instead it chose to leave that determination to the school board. The Court did, however, accept the school board's finding that the speech in question constituted "an elaborate, graphic, and explicit sexual metaphor." The text of that speech follows:

> I know a man who is firm—he's firm in his pants, he's firm in his shirt, his character is firm—but most of all his belief in you, the students of Bethel, is firm. Jeff Kuhlman is a man who takes his point and pounds it in. If necessary, he'll take an issue and nail it to the wall. He doesn't attack things in spurts—he drives hard, pushing and pushing until finally he succeeds.
>
> Jeff is a man who will go to the very end—even to the climax, for each and every one of you.
>
> So vote for Jeff for ASB Vice President—he'll never come between you and the best our high school can be.

In *Kuhlmeier* the Court found that it was reasonable for the principal to censor the two articles he found objectionable. Once again, it may be instructive to look at the specific content of these articles. The article on pregnancy included three personal accounts by Hazelwood East students who had become pregnant. All three were similar, and, though the fact was not a subject of specific comment in the decision, each gave a rather positive report of the experience. None of the accounts contained language of a sexually explicit nature. A verbatim reporting of one of the accounts follows:

> I didn't think it could happen to me, but I knew I had to start making plans for me and my little one. I think Steven (my boyfriend) was more scared than me. He was away at college and when he came home we cried together and then accepted it.
>
> At first both families were disappointed, but the third or fourth month, when the baby started to kick and move around, my boyfriend and I felt like expecting parents and we were very excited!
>
> My parents really like my boyfriend. At first we all felt sort of uncomfortable around each other. Now my boyfriend supports our baby totally (except for housing) and my parents know he really does love us, so they're happy. After I graduate next year, we're getting married.
>
> I can talk to my mother about anything but I could not face her and tell her I was pregnant. I never thought it could happen to me.
>
> My boyfriend and I have a beautiful relationship and it's been that way ever since three years ago. Therefore, I really do think that the future looks good for baby Steven.
>
> Steven takes care of my baby. We have a bank account for him (baby) and while he's away at school I get money out as I need it.
>
> I want to say to others that it isn't easy and it takes a strong, willing person to handle it because it does mean you give up a lot of things. Secondly, if you're not willing to give your child all the love and affection around, you can't be a good parent. Lastly, be careful because the pill doesn't always work. I know because it didn't work for me.
>
> This experience has made me a more responsible person. I feel that now I am a woman. If I could go back to last year, I would not get pregnant, but I have no regrets. We love our baby more than anything in the world (my boyfriend and I) because

*The lower courts have already begun to apply the standard of reasonableness as it is spelled out in *Kuhlmeier*. See Kirsten Goldberg, "Censorship Decision Is Rapidly Coloring Other School Cases," *Education Week*, 17 February 1988, pp. 1, 24.

we created him! How could we not love him??? . . . he's so cute and innocent . . .

The second objectionable article in the *Kuhlmeier* case dealt with the impact of divorce on young people. Among the comments attributed to students in the school were the following:

> My dad didn't make any money, so my mother divorced him.

> My father was an alcoholic and he always came home drunk and my mom really couldn't stand it any longer.

> My dad wasn't spending enough time with my mom, my sister, and I. He was always out of town on business or out playing cards with the guys. My parents always argued about everything.

> It stinks! They can, afterwards, remarry and start their lives over again, but their kids will always be caught in between.

The last two quotes were attributed by name to specific students.

The court found the principal's decision to censor these two articles to be reasonable. It would be an error, however, to limit the significance of the Court's ruling to the specific situations in these cases. These three decisions (and especially *Kuhlmeier*) appear to have a much greater scope. The language of the *Kuhlmeier* decision specifically embraced "theatrical productions and other expressive activities." The Court also included any school-sponsored activity that the public "might reasonably perceive to bear the imprimatur of the school."

Where then do the recent court decisions leave school officials? The Court clearly expects school officials to exercise broad authority and seems to be placing its reliance on their judgment, requiring only that "their actions are reasonably related to legitimate pedagogical concerns." This is what might be termed, at law, a "minimum scrutiny" standard.

If one considers *T.L.O.* and the search that was involved, the highest standard the Court could have established for validating the search, and the one most often used in Fourth Amendment cases, would have been the standard of "probable cause." A middle-level standard might have required a "substantial basis" for the search. The Court chose, instead, the even lower standard of "reasonableness." By establishing this standard, the Court is placing considerable confidence in school officials. It is also placing on these officials a major part of the responsibility for maintaining a proper balance between the legitimate constitutional rights of students and the school's equally legitimate need to "maintain an environment in which learning can take place."

31

Public Schools and the Road to Religious Neutrality

Daniel A. Spiro

Normally, when national leaders are moved to passionate debate over an educational issue, all of society benefits. Once that debate becomes polarized, however, and is carried on in an atmosphere of mutual distrust, the opportunity for progress will be lost. Unfortunately, it is in such a climate that our leaders have been grappling with the question of how best to insure that students in public schools are free from religious indoctrination.

In one corner have stood the Separationists, who stress the need to separate church and state. Applying this policy to the public schools, the Separationists defend the status quo, arguing that avoiding the subject of religion as much as possible in the schools is the necessary alternative to Fundamentalist domination. In the other corner have stood the Fundamentalists, who claim that, by keeping all references to theology out of the classroom, the public schools promote the religion of secular humanism.

If, as many Separationists contend, *religion* refers only to Judaism, Christianity, and other well-known theistic belief systems, secular humanism should not even be called a religion, let alone the religion of the public schools. I will argue in this article, however, that the narrow definition of religion that the Separationists commonly use is inaccurate. As properly defined, religion is such a broad concept that schools cannot separate themselves entirely from religious issues and still provide a decent education.

I will also argue that the Fundamentalists are incorrect in concluding that schools currently promote the religion of secular or atheistic humanism. It is more accurate to say that the schools promote what I call the "American Civil Religion"—a coherent hybrid of scientism, a brand of American nationalism, and Christianity.

I hope to persuade the Separationists that the public schools, far from being religiously neutral, promote a particular religion. Perhaps they will then negotiate willingly with the Fundamentalists to find a means of establishing true religious neutrality in the public schools—a goal that I believe will be achieved only when the schools present various religious points of view impartially and allow the students to choose for themselves which perspectives to adopt.

In recent months, a movement has emerged among a broad group of organizations calling for the public schools to reform the way they address religion. This article echoes the call for reform and attempts to explain the extent to which the reform movement must succeed before the schools can truly become religiously neutral.

THE FIRST AMENDMENT AND RELIGION

While the question of how the schools should address religion raises a multitude of social and political concerns, the debate in the courts has become a battle over the meaning of the First Amendment, which guarantees freedom of thought and the dissemination of a wide range of ideas. With respect to religion, the First Amendment states, "Congress shall make no law respecting an establishment of religion, or prohibiting the free exercise thereof."

To determine whether the public schools currently engage in religious indoctrination in violation of the First Amendment, we must first define the scope of the word *religion*. Historians agree that James Madison and the other authors of the First Amendment understood religion to refer solely to the worship of a Supreme Being.[1] The Supreme Court continued to use this narrow, 18th century definition of religion throughout the next century. Indeed, in 1890 in *Davis* v. *Beason,* the Court explicitly enunciated that definition, stating that "the term 'religion' has reference to one's views of his relations to his Creator, and to the obligations they impose of reverence for his being and character, and of obedience to his will. . . . With man's relations to his Maker . . . no interference can be permitted."[2]

More recent Supreme Court pronouncements on religion reflect major changes in our society since Madison's time, such as the increased number of religious sects in America and an enhanced tolerance for religious dissent.[3] A new wave of Supreme Court decisions, beginning in 1947 with *Everson* v. *Board of Education,* stressed that the First Amendment protects equally those who do and those who do not believe in God.[4] In 1961 in *Torcaso* v. *Watkins,* the Court explicitly broadened the First Amendment definition of religion to include Buddhism, Taoism, ethical culture, and secular humanism—all of which espouse nontheistic doctrines.[5]

The Court once again had to define *religion* when, in *United States* v. *Seeger,* it evaluated the right of three conscientious objectors to receive exemptions from the

Source: From Daniel A. Spiro, "Public Schools and the Road to Religious Neutrality," *Phi Delta Kappa,* Volume 70, Number 10, June 1989, pp. 759–763. Reprinted with permission from the publisher and from Daniel A. Spiro.

military draft during the Vietnam War.[6] Although none of the defendants claimed to believe in God, each based his argument on a federal statute that exempted those opposed to participation in war on "religious" grounds. The statute defined religion solely by reference to a belief in a Supreme Being. Nevertheless, the Court consulted eminent theologians and religious bodies in order to find a definition of religion that embodied the spirit underlying the statute.

After consulting the experts, the Court sided with the conscientious objectors, holding that their opposition to war, though nontheistic in origin, reflected sincere and meaningful religious beliefs. According to the Court, "religious beliefs" for purposes of the statute in question included any sincere and meaningful belief occupying "the same place in the life of the [conscientious] objector as an orthodox belief in God holds in the life of one clearly qualified for exemption."[7]

In 1970 in *Welsh* v. *United States*,[8] another case involving a conscientious objector, the Supreme Court confirmed the concept of religion that it had used in *Seeger*. More recently, the Court has implied that sincerely held views on issues of societal importance may be secular rather than religious in nature.[9] However, not since the cases involving conscientious objectors has the Court offered an explicit definition of religion for purposes of either the First Amendment or any related statute. It is clear then, that the modern Court has broadened the scope of religion for First Amendment purposes. It is also evident that the modern religious community consulted by the Court in *Seeger*, construes the concept of being "religious" so broadly that it embraces many who do not believe in God and who hold other unconventional beliefs on fundamental issues.

I suggest that the Court consider a coherent framework for resolving issues of fundamental ethical and metaphysic significance as a religion protected by the First Amendment. This view grants equal protection to those who hold minority points of view. For example, humanists and naturalists may possess the same reverent state of mind traditionally associated with religion, even though for them the sacred realm is inhabited solely by certain moral principles and not by transcendent beings.

Most important, however, construing religion to include all coherent frameworks for resolving fundamental ethical and metaphysical issues recognizes the reality that popular religions, whether theistic or humanistic, are generally based on a particular approach to just such issues. While the popular religions may focus most centrally on questions about God and how individuals can live full, virtuous lives, they also provide strong guidance on how individuals should interact in society. We need only examine the lives of those prototypically religious individuals—the Biblical prophets—to see that all traditional western religions are profoundly concerned with fundamental social, political, and economic questions. According to the eminent Jewish philosopher Abraham Heschel, the prophets were so consumed with the horrors of social injustice that they depicted God himself as ruminating upon such matters instead of contemplating ethereal ideas.[10]

THE AMERICAN CIVIL RELIGION

If educators were to agree on the broad definition of religion suggested above, they would probably concede that public schools cannot ignore religion altogether. At the very least, they would have to admit that schools already confront religious issues in much of their curricula. For example, students receive training in such fields as the natural, physical, and social sciences, which address such fundamental questions as: How did life begin? What are the proper and improper forms of social behavior and social governance? Do absolute standards of right and wrong exist, independent of an individual's subjective opinions?

To try to exorcise discussions of these and other central religious issues from the classroom would be disastrous from an educational standpoint. It would deprive students of opportunities to study some of the most fascinating and important questions and would thus confirm the suspicion of many children that classroom learning has little relevance to their lives.

The Separationists, employing a narrow definition of religion, have generally denied that the schools currently address religious questions. To their credit, the Fundamentalists have stressed that public schools do address religion and must continue to do so. The Fundamentalists are also correct in questioning the intensity of the commitment by the public schools to true religious neutrality. It appears to me that those who control our schools have simply been too preoccupied with other matters to concentrate on religious neutrality. They have been content merely to avoid the explicit promotion of Christianity—traditionally, the religion of the majority. Thus, in a literal sense, they separate church from state.

To achieve true religious neutrality, however, educators must undertake an affirmative effort to insure that *no* religious points of view are promoted above any others. Educators must neither avoid discussing religious issues altogether nor present such issues in a one-sided manner. From this, it follows that, to be religiously neutral, educators must impartially present *diverse* points of view whenever patently religious issues are discussed. In so doing, educators would best enable students to choose for themselves how these issues should be resolved. Of course, it is impossible to instruct students on every conceivable religious point of view. Yet, so long as a few diverse perspectives are taught well, students will have the opportunity to exercise a measure of choice.

Ideally, then, the public school would become a free marketplace of religious ideas. The mere sound of this phrase resonates with the spirit of the First Amendment. Indeed, as the Supreme Court stated in 1969 in *Red Lion Broadcasting Co.* v. *FCC*, "It is the purpose of the First Amendment to preserve an uninhibited marketplace of ideas in which truth will ultimately prevail, rather than to countenance monopolization of that market. . . ."[11] Unfortunately, such a marketplace does not exist in the schools of today.

In my view, the failure of our schools to accept the obligation to teach differing perspectives on religious questions has resulted in the indoctrination of students in a single religion: the "American Civil Religion," an amalgam of scientism, American nationalism, and Christianity. An examination of the three components of the American Civil Religion will help demonstrate why change toward a freer marketplace of religious ideas is urgently needed.

1. *Scientism.* Generally understood to be an exaggerated faith in the power of the natural sciences to explain social, psychological, or physical phenomena; to solve human problems; and to provide a comprehensive picture of the cosmos, scientism is at the heart of the approach to knowledge promoted by the public schools. Human reason, as manifested through the scientific method, is viewed as the primary tool for attaining truth and social progress. This is perhaps the foremost principle of scientism.

Our schools fail to set forth either philosophy or theology as a reasonable alternative to scientism, despite the influence of those two disciplines on the great minds of the past. Consider the case of philosophy, a discipline that has moved both scholars and world leaders throughout human history. No one dares question philosophy as a discipline that offers valuable approaches to the search for truth. Nevertheless, the curricula of American public schools virtually ignore this discipline.

No rational basis exists for excluding philosophy from the public schools. To argue that the subject is inherently too complex to be a useful learning tool for children simply demonstrates a misunderstanding of the nature of philosophy. The lucid writings of such philosophers as Plato, Nietzsche, and Mill are readily accessible to young minds. Furthermore, philosophy can also be taught by using novels written expressly for students. The Educational Testing Service, for example, has conducted highly successful philosophy courses for elementary and middle school students who form a community of philosophical inquiry based on the study of novels for children.[12] Indeed, anyone familiar with the discipline understands that, like mathematics, philosophy can be taught at various levels of complexity and that children can comprehend many profound philosophical concepts.

Why, then, is philosophy so notably absent from our public schools? This is a question with strong First Amendment implications. As a young scientist inadequately exposed to philosophy or theology, a student will inevitably form a microscopic—rather than a macroscopic—approach to learning. Moreover, because his or her work has been primarily empirical, this young scientist will be led to assume that humans and nature—the objects of study—are of central importance. In comparison, abstractions—even God—appear remote and irrelevant to daily affairs.

By steeping students in empiricism while neglecting to consider, for example, pantheistic or theistic alternatives, public schools are directly assaulting the First Amendment. The student, trained as a crude empiricist, tends to believe in the existence of only what he or she can clearly and distinctly perceive: namely, discrete life forms, evolving into higher and higher entities and culminating in human beings as the crown jewels of the universe. By contrast, followers of various Buddhist and Hindu faiths believe that living beings may *appear* to be discrete, autonomous entities, when they are actually interrelated parts of a single creative and transcendent essence that infuses all reality. That such a concept seems alien to the conventional American mindset is a testament to the power of the American Civil Religion in our society.

2. *American nationalism.* The second component of the American Civil Religion deals with our perspectives on society. Public schools extol the manner in which American society is organized—politically, economically, and socially. Moreover, the values that underlie our social ordering are scarcely questioned. Just as scientism suggests ways to resolve questions of metaphysics, so lionizing the American way of life suggests a one-sided approach to social ethics.

Educators readily admit that a fundamental purpose of the public school in our nation of immigrants is to "Americanize" our youth. Certainly, this is a legitimate goal insofar as it increases opportunities for children of immigrants and of poor families to obtain special instruction in the language, culture, and institutions of our society. However, as practiced in the public schools, Americanization consists of political indoctrination, the effect of which is to minimize dissent in future generations.

Students learn at an early age that we live in a "democracy" ruled by a government consisting of three independent parts. Alternative forms of political organization are given brief, superficial treatment—or none at all. For example, students are rarely told that we do not live in the most democratic society possible. Ours is a "representative democracy" in which individuals select leaders to formulate national policy; in a "participatory democracy," on the other hand, policies derive more directly from the citizenry, through the frequent use of such mechanisms as popular referenda.

Furthermore, public schools expose students to classical capitalist theory and to the history of capitalism in our nation, but they generally ignore alternative forms of economic production, distribution, and exchange. For example, little class time is devoted to such economic systems as the Swedish mixed economy, Yugoslavian socialism, or the Israeli kibbutzim. More to the point, teachers fail to show students that social scientists and theoreticians throughout the world are combining the best features of existing institutions with their own creations to construct alternatives to the American and Soviet systems. As a result, the students have no reason to believe that critical examination of American political and economic institutions can ever lead to exciting and useful discoveries.

Just as the public schools promote America's national governmental and economic systems, so they generally fail to examine critically the values associated with these systems, including the faith in the market as a means of distributing societal resources and of expanding the economic pie; the stress on individual, rather than group, achievement; the association of material wealth with individual success and the successful society; the tolerance for severe inequities in the distribution of wealth; and the adherence to pragmatism, rather than ideological consistency, as an ethical guideline.

Moreover, public schools repeatedly praise America above all other countries and lead students to identify themselves with the nation, rather than with local or world communities. From American history and civics classes, students can come to view Americans as some sort of "chosen people." They learn that they belong to a nation with a noble, clearly delineated beginning; an imperfect but basically upstanding past; and a momentous destiny. They are taught to associate America with such virtues as courage, diligence, and independence—virtues that their ancestors needed in order to be socially productive pioneers. They also learn to revel in the fact that, unlike other empires in history, the American empire has withstood the test of time.

Hence, in Americanizing our children, public schools subject them to the traditional approach to social issues, without also opening their eyes to competing points of view. As a result, many students blindly adhere to the majority's values, which is precisely what the First Amendment is designed to avoid. Equally tragic is the apathy and boredom experienced by students when they study social theory. In exposing students to but one approach to social issues, we deprive them of the excitement and enrichment that stem from examining differing perspectives and freely choosing among them.

3. *Christianity.* The dominant traditional religion in our society is the third and final source of principles underlying the American Civil Religion. In American history courses, students learn that early America (after the European colonization) was almost entirely Christian and that many early American heroes, whom they have been taught to revere, derived considerable strength from their Christian faith. Literature courses, which focus on America and (Christian) Europe, further affirm the relevance of Christianity. Students are inevitably informed in these courses about various aspects of the Christian faith. They are told that Christianity espouses such sublime goals as peace and love for one's neighbor. They are not so often told, however, that all the great religions of the world preach such goals.

To some extent, it is inevitable that any nonsectarian school system located in a primarily Christian country would promote Christianity. What offends the First Amendment, however, is the minimal exposure given to other religions, and, worse yet, the explicitly Christian nature of such joyous public school holidays as Christmas and Easter. For public schools to associate these occasions in any way with celebrations of Christianity only strengthens the identification of Christianity with the full, wholesome life. Other religions do not receive the benefits of such an association.

I am not contending that public schools make the figure of Jesus or the Christian God the focus of their curricula or that they promote a devout faith in the specific tenets of Christianity. Rather, what emerges is a diluted Christianity that makes the American Civil Religion more palatable to children and that functions as a supplement to a completely empirical scientism. Christianity can play an uplifting role because the schools expose students to a belief in an omniscient, omnibenevolent deity and to the inspiration that can arise from such a belief, without stressing the Christian faith's restricting commandments and principles for the human race. In essence, students are provided with a brand of Christianity that serves as a source of hope and joy, without severely restricting their daily actions and beliefs, as would the *devout* practice of any of the well-known religions.

The demands on public school students to think in a rigid scientistic manner are immense. Recognizing the human need for a supplement to such scientism makes clear the powerful role that Christianity plays in the religion of the public schools.

TOWARD RELIGIOUS NEUTRALITY

We can't eliminate schoolhouse indoctrination in a day—or, for that matter, in a decade.

The public schools simply do not have sufficient resources to enable teachers, administrators, curriculum specialists, and textbook companies to begin teaching every student in a religiously neutral manner in the foreseeable future.

As difficult as it will be to eliminate classroom indoctrination, however, the way to begin is clear. We must encourage those who control the curricula of the public schools to introduce courses explicitly designed to compare and contrast diverse points of view on religious issues. While the addition of these courses will do nothing to prevent indoctrination in other courses, they may at least provide a springboard to allow many students to understand the beauty of religion and the richness of a life freely and intelligently chosen.

According to a 1985 survey, more than 80% of public school systems offer no courses that specifically examine the Bible or other teachings of popular world religions.[13] Religious groups, as well as such organizations as the National Educational Association and the American Federation of Teachers, recommend that the public schools place greater emphasis on studies in comparative religion. Nevertheless, it remains to be seen how urgent these mainstream education organizations consider this issue, compared with other priorities. At present, the public schools continue to devote only minimal resources to instituting or improving courses in comparative religion.

Furthermore, to give our children a full opportunity to examine religious issues through a multicolored lens, an additional subject must be inserted into public school curricula. That subject is philosophy. It is indeed sad that apathetic students slumber through hour after hour of indoctrination while timeless philosophical works gather dust on library shelves. If Plato's *Republic* does not awaken these students, surely Nietzsche's diatribes against democracy and theology would arouse them. If the Holy Scriptures fail to convey truth or meaning to some students, perhaps Spinoza's unorthodox view of God may ignite their enthusiasm for monotheism. It did for me.

COMMON GROUND

Separationists and Fundamentalists should share common goals: to establish true religious neutrality in the schools and, in particular, to eliminate the stranglehold of the American Civil Religion. Including more courses in comparative religion and philosophy in public school curricula would go a long way toward achieving these goals.

As we lobby those who control education's purse strings, we must keep in mind the value of instruction in comparative religion and philosophy, apart from its contributions to religious neutrality. Teaching these subjects sends a clear message to students: you can fnd meaning in life if you know where to look. It is the job of educators to show students various paths to wisdom. It is the job of students—as thinking, feeling human beings—to choose the best paths to walk and to take responsibility for the paths they choose.

References

1. See Elwyn Smith, *Religious Liberty in the United States* (Philadelphia: Fortress Press, 1972), p. 249; Richard Morgan, *The Supreme Court and Religion* (New York: Free Press, 1972), p. 23; and Joseph Story, *Commentaries on the Constitution of the United States*, 2nd ed. (Boston: C.C. Little and J. Brown, 1851), pp. 593–95.
2. *Davis* v. *Beason*, 133 U.S. 333 (1890), at 342.
3. See Daniel A. Spiro, "Creating a Free Marketplace of Religious Ideas," *Alabama Law Review*, Fall 1987, pp. 28–30.
4. *Everson* v. *Board of Education*, 330 U.S. 1, 18 (1947).
5. *Torcaso* v. *Watkins*, 367 U.S. 488, 495, n. 11 (1961).
6. *United States* v. *Seeger*, 380 U.S. 163 (1965).
7. Ibid., at 184.
8. *Welsh* v. *United States*, 398 U.S. 333 (1970).
9. See *Wisconsin* v. *Yoder*, 406 U.S. 205, 215–16 (1972).
10. Abraham Heschel, *The Prophets* (New York: Harper & Row, 1962), pp. 3–5.
11. *Red Lion Broadcasting Co.* v. *FCC*, 395 U.S. 367, 390 (1969).
12. "How Philosophy for Children Sharpens Thinking Skills," *Thinking: The Journal of Philosophy for Children*, vol. 7, 1987, p. S4.
13. Richard Dierenfield, "Religious Influence in American Public Schools," *Religion and Public Education*, Summer 1986, p. 44.

32

Attacks on "Secular Humanism"

The Real Threat to Public Education

Christy Macy
Ricki Seidman

Public education is facing a major challenge today. Recent studies show that writing and critical thinking skills are low, and students in other industrialized nations are out-scoring their American counterparts in both science and math. Responding to the challenge, the Carnegie Commission, the National Governor's Association, and others have made dramatic proposals for how to improve both the teaching and learning environments of our schools.

While the national debate is focussing on these various proposals for reform, however, little attention is being paid to an important factor in the ongoing debate: the alarming increase in censorship of books and curricula in our schools. The groups and individuals who have "dumbed down" textbooks, tried to prevent schools from teaching critical thinking, and attacked the very concept of public education are now more numerous and active than ever.

A recent study by People for the American Way revealed that censorship incidents in schools and libraries nationwide have increased 35% over last year, and have doubled over the past four years. Perhaps more alarming than the rate of increase is the dramatic change in the nature of censorship. Almost 60% of the incidents reported this year were attempts to censor ideas, information and teaching methods in the classroom, and almost half were organized by groups such as Phyllis Schlafly's Eagle Forum, Pat Robertson's Freedom Council, Beverly LaHaye's Concerned Women for America, and the National Association of Christian Educators. To understand how these groups and individuals want to change the public schools, and what they want to censor out of the classrooms, one must understand their unifying slogan: Rid the classrooms of "secular humanism."

The now familiar phrase comes in part from "humanism"—a philosophy which originated during the intellectual awakening of the Renaissance in Western Europe, in which the classic Greek and Roman texts were rediscovered, and the study of man and science flourished. Humanism does not necessarily mean unreligious. Prominent religious leaders from St. Thomas Moore to the present day have described themselves as humanists. However, by tacking on "secular" to the word "humanist," the religious right has created a catch-all phrase to describe what they see as a "godless" religion which is taking over the country. According to them, "secular humanism" is the root cause of most of the ills of our society—from teenage pregnancy to suicide, from the decline of academic standards to the erosion of the traditional family.

Textbook censors Mel and Norma Gabler, for example, describe "secular humanism" as a faith "that promotes situation ethics, evolution, sexual freedom (including sex education courses), and internationalism." Jerry Falwell refers to its "satanic influence" and warns: "It advocates abortion-on-demand, recognition of homosexuals, free use of pornography, legalizing prostitution and gambling, and free use of drugs, among other things." A pamphlet from the Pro-Family Forum says secular humanists believe in equal distribution of wealth, control of the environment, and "disarmament and the creation of a one world, socialistic government." The pamphlet is entitled, "Is Humanism Molesting Your Child?."

The hotbed of "secular humanism," according to these groups, is the public schools. According to television evangelist Jimmy Swaggart: "the greatest enemy of our children today in this United States, whether you know it or not, is the public school system. It is education without God; education without morality; education without the Bible." Pat Robertson, in a recent speech announcing his presidential ambitions, further explains the threat to our society: "We have taken the Holy Bible from our young and replaced it with the thoughts of Charles Darwin, Karl Marx, Sigmund Freud, and John Dewey."[1] According to those on the religious right, if public education doesn't include religious right, if public education doesn't include religious instruction, then it is tantamount to indoctrination in "secular humanism."

Emerging out of this debate about indoctrination and public education, however, is a growing national consensus: today's textbooks often in fact do shy away from coverage of religion and its influence in our society. Three textbook reviews were published in 1986—one commissioned by the Department of Education, and two by groups often critical of that Department, People for the American Way and Americans United

Source: From Christy Macy and Ricki Seidman, "Attacks on 'Secular Humanism': The Real Threat to Public Education," *Kappa Delta Pi*, Volume 23, Number 3, Spring 1987, pp. 76–80. Printed by permission of Kappa Delta Pi, An International Honor Society in Education.

for Separation of Church and State—and all found that textbooks did not offer adequate coverage of either the role of religion in our society, or the influence religious groups and individuals have had throughout American and world history.

Yet the groups and individuals who warn against the ills of "secular humanism" go far beyond this point, criticizing books, courses and teaching methods that they don't agree with, and that don't conform to their sectarian worldview. If they disapprove of something in the school curriculum—whether it's learning about the theory of evolution, historic tragedies like the Holocaust, or literary classics from Homer to Shakespeare—then they simply call it "secular humanism" and claim it must be thrown out.

The first known claim that "secular humanism" was being taught in the schools took place in Kannawha County, West Virginia in 1974, when a member of the state textbook selection committee objected to a series of English textbooks. The dissenting committee member launched a public campaign against the books, claiming that they were anti-Christian, anti-American, anti-authority, and depressing. Petitions were distributed stating that while it was unconstitutional for public schools to promote religious belief, "we hold that it is equally unconstitutional to promote religious disbelief."

Although the Board of Education voted to purchase all of the disputed materials except for 8 supplemental texts, the controversy widened, with groups boycotting and picketing the schools, and violence spilling out into the streets. In November of that year, the school board adopted strict textbook guidelines, which required, among other things, that "textbooks . . . shall recognize the sanctity of the home . . . must encourage loyalty to the United States . . ."[2]

Since that incident, the Far Right has used the hoax of "secular humanism" to justify censoring a wide range of books, courses and teaching methods from the classroom. Sex education, literary classics, the teaching of evolution, the use of personal diaries, open-ended discussions, and textbooks that reflect social, political or cultural change have all been accused of promoting "secular humanism" and thus targeted for organized attacks. Even Shakespeare's *Romeo and Juliet* and *The Diary of Anne Frank* have been criticized. Sources ranging from a guidance and counseling program in Corvallis, Oregon, to an award-winning novel, *The Learning Tree* in Washington state, to a health textbook in Florida have been criticized for promoting "secular humanism." In People For's most recent study of censorship efforts nationwide, "secular humanism" was used to criticize, among others, a K–6th grade drug abuse prevention course in California, a sex education unit in Maine, English books in Florida, and journal writing in North Dakota.

An underlying theme of many of the objections based on "secular humanism" is the fear of students learning how to think critically, to analyze, to make decisions. Thus courses that encourage students to develop decision-making skills, such as drug and alcohol abuse prevention courses, are targets of constant criticism, as are open-ended classroom discussions. For example, a superintendent in Cobb County, Georgia, restricted nine topics from classroom discussion because of parental objections that they promote "secular humanism." The topics included religion, evolution, values, and sex education.

This past year, two textbook trials have brought into sharp relief the religious right's agenda to make public school curricula conform more closely to their sectarian beliefs, and in the process to keep out of the classroom books and courses they find objectionable. One trial, dubbed "Scopes II," took place in Hawkins County, Tennessee, and involved objections to a K–8th grade reading series published by Holt, Rinehart, and Winston. The plaintiffs, backed by Concerned Women for America, a national far right group, listed over 400 objections to the reading series, claiming that taken together, the stories constituted a violation of their religious beliefs. Although the term "secular humanism" was barely mentioned during the proceedings, the objections to the books came directly out of that tradition.

The theory of evolution was an obvious target. Thus stories in the reading series concerning prehistoric animals, or events that took place millions of years ago, were found objectionable, due to their evolutionary nature. Also criticized were stories that portrayed the modern roles of men and women, and were "favorable . . . about the women's rights movement."[3] Stories dealing with international concerns such as pollution and overpopulation, and which stressed the need for international cooperation, were also objectionable. Even well-known folk and fairy tales, including the *Wizard of Oz,* were criticized for encouraging the imagination "beyond the limitation of scriptural authority." A story about the Renaissance was objected to, on the grounds that it promoted "the idea that the human mind has unknown capabilities for imagination, intelligence, and creativity."

Mel and Norma Gabler, two of the pioneers of the secular humanist conspiracy, testified at the trial in support of the plaintiffs, and against the reading series. The Gablers had appeared in Church Hill, Hawkins County, in 1983, and the original complaints against the text were promoted by their exhortations.

In October, the Judge ruled that while the plaintiffs could not be given a separate reading curricula as they had requested due to "an excessive entanglement between the state and religion,"[4] their children would be allowed to opt out of reading class, to be taught that subject at home. Although the ruling was immediately appealed, it is causing great concern within the educational community. Teachers and schools boards across the country are worried the decision opens the door to any sect to demand their children be excused from classes which contain information or ideas that they don't agree with. They worry that a "cafeteria" style education will develop, one in which students will pick and choose the books or courses they want to take on the basis of sectarian beliefs. Michael Farris, lawyer for CWA, has already claimed that the ruling could apply to opting out of sex education courses.[5]

Another major concern within the educational community is the effect this decision will have on textbook publishers, which have historically shied away from controversial topics, and "dumbed down" textbooks so as not to offend anyone. The publicity surrounding the Tennessee trial, and the judge's ruling, will only add to the publishers' fear of controversy, and will encourage them to publish safer, less challenging textbooks.

In the Tennessee case, "secular humanism" was the subtle underlying theme that provided the basis for many of the objections to the reading series. The plaintiffs in a trial now in progress in Mobile, Alabama, however, are not mincing their words.

The Alabama case is the most ambitious yet of the religious right's efforts to censor textbooks and inject sectarian beliefs into public school curricula. Charging that state-approved textbooks advance the religion of "secular humanism" and do not conform to their beliefs, the plaintiffs want a federal court to declare the books unconstitutional. This case, backed by Pat Robertson's National Legal Foundation, arose out of an earlier school prayer case that reached the Supreme Court in 1985.

At the trial stage in the original school prayer case, the judge had allowed over 500 individuals to intervene in support of prayer in schools. The intervenors introduced an additional claim that the public schools were unconstitutionally promoting the religion of "secular humanism." The judge ruled that the Bill of Rights did not prevent Alabama from sanctioning prayer in public schools, and did not reach a decision on the secular humanism issue. In an unusual ruling, he left open the possibility that, if reversed at the appellate level, he would reopen the case to rule on the intervenors' claim. The judge wrote, "If this Court is compelled to purge 'God is great, God is good, we thank him for our daily food' from the classroom, then this court must also purge from the classroom those things that serve to teach that salvation is through one's self rather than through a deity."[6] He further noted that the curriculum was "rife with efforts at teaching or encouraging secular humanism—all without opposition from any other ethic."

. . . The Supreme Court reversed the trial judge. In August 1985, he issued an order reopening the case to decide the "secular humanism" issue. By February 1986, both Governor George Wallace and the Mobile County Board of School Supervisors signed a consent decree authorizing the judge to set standards for the selection of public school textbooks (an ironic endorsement of federal intervention by the same governor who "stood in the schoolhouse door" to prevent federally mandated desegregation of the University of Alabama). The State Board of Education resisted intense political pressure and mounted a strong defense at the trial, along with a group of parents who intervened in support of the curriculum with the help of People for the American Way and the American Civil Liberties Union.

The plaintiffs contend that textbooks approved for use in Alabama public schools unconstitutionally promote the religion of secular humanism and that they fail to include appropriate references to contributions of Christianity, Catholicism and Judaism to American and world history and society. The claims they presented at trial were narrower than their original charges which had earlier addressed the curriculum of the schools, without indicating any specific aspect of the curriculum.

Their experts "analyzed" textbooks and isolated the passages they deemed objectionable in six home economics books used for an elective course at the high school level. They also singled out thirty-nine history and social studies texts which they claimed included inadequate references to religion. Among other things, they contended that passages in the home economic books about divorce and one-parent families offended their notions about "traditional" families. According to one expert, divorce is a "manifestation of sin" and must be discussed as such. They also objected to sections in the books about decision-making, careers, and recognizing values.

The plaintiffs are, in effect, asking a federal court to censor textbooks line-by-line and passage-by-passage. This blue-pencilling would excise any passages that are inconsistent with their sectarian beliefs and would rewrite history and social studies texts to conform to their world view. They seek a result that would turn the court into textbook writer, editor and curriculum developer. In fact, a ruling that orders Alabama textbooks to be rewritten according to the sectarian criteria of the plaintiffs would constitute state-sanctioning of religion that violates the Constitution.

Prior to the trial, the judge granted a class action motion allowing the plaintiffs to represent every taxpayer in Alabama who is or may be the parent of children in public schools, so the result in the case will affect every public school classroom in Alabama. The trial lasted for three weeks in October and a ruling is expected in the first half of 1987.

The trial in Mobile, and the decision in Tennessee, are just the latest in a prolonged effort by the religious right to censor a wide range of books and ideas from the classroom, and impose sectarian demands on the public school curriculum. People for the American Way has responded to the resulting threat to quality education in a number of ways. Over the years, we have publicized the dramatic rise of censorship incidents in our schools and libraries, using films, speakers, publications and op-eds to alert the public and the media. Every year, People For publishes a survey of censorship incidents, which documents such efforts state-by-state, and also charts national trends in the censorship movement. People For keeps in contact with a growing network of concerned parents, teachers, and school administrators, providing them with information and resources to defend against censorship, and to push for stronger, more challenging schools in their communities.

Since the quality of textbooks is at the heart of the debate over educational excellence, People For has initiated a textbook review series. The series, which includes reviews of the major textbooks in the fields of biology, American history, and most recently civics and U.S. government, is intended to provide local school authorities and state textbook committees information about specific books which will allow them to make more informed decisions in textbook selection. The purpose of the reviews is also to encourage textbook publishers to improve their products by providing constructive criticism.

In light of the recent trend in textbook lawsuits, People For began to build legal defense fund, designed to defend local school boards and teachers in their efforts to promote quality education. In that capacity, People For provided pro bono legal counsel for the defendants in the Hawkins County case, in addition to providing legal and financial assistance for parents who intervened in defense of the public schools in the "secular humanism" trial in Mobile.

In addition to these activities, People For is continuing to search for new ways to build a consensus within the educational and religious communities that will promote the kind of quality, non-sectarian public education that every student deserves.

References

1 Speech entitled "A New Vision for America," delivered at Constitution Hall, Washington, D.C. on September 17, 1987.

2 See "Inquiry Report: Kanawha County, West Virginia. A Textbook Study in Cultural Conflict," by the National Education Association, Teacher Rights Division, Washington, D.C., February 1975.

3 See official Transcript of Proceedings of *Bob Mozert, Et. Al. v. Hawkins County Public Schools, Et. Al.*

4 See decision of *Bob Mozert, Et. Al. v. Hawkins County Public Schools, Et. Al.*, No. Civ-2-83-401, filed in the United States District Court for the Eastern District of Tennessee, Northeastern Division, October 24, 1986.

5 *New York Times*, October 25, 1986.

6 See *Ishmael Jaffree v. Wallace*.

33

Outlook is Bleak for Many Blacks, Study Concludes

Council Says Progress Has Lagged Since 70's

Peter Schmidt

In what is being called "the most comprehensive assessment of the status of black Americans to date," the National Research Council has concluded that, despite gains in recent decades, blacks still face formidable barriers on their path to educational parity with whites.

"Segregation and differential treatment of blacks continue to be widespread in elementary and secondary schools," says the report by a distinguished panel of scholars in the social and behavioral sciences. And though black children on average enter schools with substantially greater socioeconomic handicaps, "the schools do not compensate for these disadvantages."

The report warns, moreover, that progress in education, as in other areas examined in the massive four-year study, has slowed dramatically since the economic downturn of the early 1970's.

"Barring unforeseen events or changes in present conditions—that is, no changes in educational policies and opportunities, no increased income and employment opportunities, and no major national programs to deal directly with the problems of economic dependency—our findings imply several negative developments for blacks in the near future," it concludes, "developments that in turn do not bode well for American society."

Released here last week, the 600-page study, *A Common Destiny: Blacks and American Society,* reviews the social and economic gains of the past 50 years and assesses the effectiveness of policies designed to bring about greater racial equality. It represents, its authors say, a distillation of available studies, including new research commissioned by the N.R.C.'s 22-member Committee on the Status of Black Americans.

"A striking theme that emerges from many bodies of evidence," said the Cornell University sociologist Robin M. Williams, chairman of the committee, at a press conference here, "is the importance of the legacy of the past—that is, the massive influence here and now of past segregation and disadvantage."

"Equally striking," Mr. Williams said, "is the evidence that many white Americans today—contrary to the facts—seem to believe that the civil-rights era of the 1960's removed all barriers to equal opportunity."

The report concludes that while the overall well-being of both blacks and whites has advanced greatly over the past five decades, black Americans remain "substantially behind whites" on almost all statistical measures of socioeconomic status.

Blacks made great economic strides in the 1940's and the 1960's, it says, but "since the early 1970's, the economic status of blacks relative to whites has, on average, stagnated or deteriorated."

This has been accompanied by a widening of the status differences among groups of blacks, the study adds, complicating any overall assessment of the quality of life for blacks as a whole.

NO 'CULTURE OF POVERTY'

The N.R.C. initiated the $2.7-million research project, Mr. Williams said, because it felt there had been no comprehensive study of blacks in society since the Swedish economist Gunner Myrdal published his groundbreaking work, *An American Dilemma,* in 1944.

The 1968 *Report of the National Advisory Commission on Civil Disorders,* or "Kerner report," had a significant impact on public policy, he said, but its authors "were under the gun" to make recommendations and did not have adequate time to address race relations in great depth.

The N.R.C. committee focused its attention on six primary areas: participation in the political process, economic status, schooling, health, crime and criminal justice, and the well-being of children and families.

One of its most significant findings was that the data and analyses it examined did not support the commonly accepted notion that a self-perpetuating "culture of poverty" exists in the black community.

"The chronically poor are a minority of poor people in general, including blacks; attitudes toward work and the desire to succeed are not very different among the poor and nonpoor," the report says.

The panel found instead that racial barriers and disadvantages "persist in blocking black advancement."

Nevertheless, it pointed to troublesome recent developments in black family life:

Source: From Peter Schmidt, "Outlook is Bleak for Many Blacks, Study Concludes: Council Says Progress Has Lagged Since 70's," *Education Week,* Volume VIII, Number 40, August 2, 1989, pp. 1, 29. Reprinted with permission from *Education Week.*

- While the proportion of black families with incomes above $35,000 was rising between 1970 and 1980 from 18 percent to 22 percent, the proportion with incomes of less than $10,000 was growing from about 26 percent to 30 percent.
- Black female-headed families were 50 percent of all black families with children in 1985, but had 25 percent of total black family income; 70 percent of black family income was received by black husband-wife families.
- In the course of their childhood, 86 percent of black children are likely to spend some time in a single-parent household; the comparable figure for white children is 42 percent.

"The greater inequality between family types among blacks," the report warns, "has important consequences for the welfare of future generations."

EDUCATION FINDINGS

In its examination of schooling, *A Common Destiny* reports signs of both progress and continuing roadblocks. It notes, for example, the impact of federal programs in early intervention and compensatory education, saying that Head Start and Chapter 1 have had "overall positive (although sometimes short-term) effects on the academic achievement of disadvantaged students."

But it also points to the continuing segregation of many black students—both within schools through tracking and ability grouping, and by their assignment to various schools.

"The pace of school desegregation has slowed," the study asserts, "and racial separation in education is significant, especially outside the South . . . Residential separation of whites and blacks in large metropolitan areas remains nearly as high in the 1980's as it was in the 1960's."

Almost two-thirds of black students in public elementary and middle schools in 1980, the study found, attended schools with minority enrollments exceeding 50 percent.

"Standards of academic performance for teachers and students are not equivalent in schools that serve predominantly black students and those that serve predominantly white students," the report stresses. "Nor are equal encouragement and support provided for the educational achievement and attainment of black and white students."

Blacks have made small but consistent gains on tests of academic achievement, the study confirmed, and have experienced dramatic increases in rates of high-school completion. But the college-enrollment rates of high-school graduates declined after 1977.

"The odds that a black student will enter college within a year of graduation from high school are less than one-half the odds for a white student," the report asserts.

SCHOOLS MAKE A DIFFERENCE

One factor in such disparities, the study suggests, may be the inability of many black children, particularly those in impoverished circumstances, to view education as a viable avenue to future success.

But the authors conclude that "the large differences in socioeconomic background between blacks and whites are perhaps the most significant factors in accounting for these black-white disparities in educational status."

"When background differences are combined with such factors as residential separation of blacks and whites," it continues, "the impact is very great."

Nevertheless, the report stresses that "what schools do substantially affects the amount of learning that takes place."

"Much research on between-institution differences," it says, "has focused on a limited number of the most tangible inputs to the schooling process, such as expenditures per pupil and teacher-test scores. Other between-school differences that are related to within-school practices do matter."

"These differences," it says, "are closely tied to teacher behavior, school climate, and the content and organization of instruction."

The National Research Council is the principal operating agency for the National Academies of Sciences and Engineering. Funding for *A Common Destiny* was provided by the Carnegie Corporation of New York; the Pew Charitable Trusts; the Ford, Robert Wood Johnson, Andrew W. Mellon, Rockefeller, and Alfred P. Sloan Foundations; and the National Research Council fund.

Copies of the report are available for $35 each, prepaid, from the National Academy Press, 2101 Constitution Ave., N.W., Washington, D.C. 20418; (202) 334-2000.

34

Site-Based Management

Unfulfilled Promises

Betty Malen
Rodney T. Ogawa
Jennifer Kranz

Among the many reforms in education today, site-based management is one of the hottest.

Numerous commissions, task forces, organizations, and individual leaders are advocating site-based management as a viable approach to education reform. A number of state legislatures and local districts are experimenting with versions of this reform.

Due to the keen interest, we analyzed evidence regarding the ability of site-based management to achieve its stated objectives and highlighted the implications of this analysis for educators and policy makers.

From our review of nearly 200 documents describing current and previous attempts to use site-based management in the United States, Canada, and Australia, we must conclude site-based management in most instances does not achieve its stated objectives.

While there may be exceptions, in most cases a variety of factors prevents site-based management from fulfilling its proponents' promises.

LIMITED EVIDENCE OF OPERATION

While we reviewed a large number of documents, evidence about the actual operation of site-based management plans is limited in several ways.

First, there are only eight systematic studies of site-based management programs. These studies rely on the experiences of a relatively small number of elementary and secondary schools (from six to 32) located in such diverse settings as California, New York, Utah, Florida, Minnesota, and Australia. They examine different versions of site-based management and focus on its different dimensions.

Second, most writings on site-based management are either project descriptions, status reports, or advocacy pieces. These sources tend to rest on the impressions of a single individual and emphasize the exceptional cases, such as the achievements attained in a small number of the most successful pilot schools.

Despite these limitations, the available information is instructive. It provides a basis for assessing the ability of site-based management to achieve its stated objectives and a basis for identifying issues that warrant special attention as educators and policy makers consider this reform option.

We attempted to summarize the major conclusions and implications that can be drawn from the documents reviewed.

DEFINING TERMS

Basically, site-based management is a form of decentralization. It identifies the individual school as the primary unit of improvement and relies on the redistribution of decision making authority as the primary means through which improvements might be stimulated and sustained.

While site-based management plans vary, the general approach can be characterized in the following manner:

- Some formal authority to make decisions in the central domains of budget, personnel, and program is delegated to the school site.
- The formal authority to make decisions may be delegated to the principal or distributed among principals, teachers, parents, and others. In most cases, the authority is broadly distributed.
- A formal structure (council, committee, team, board) often composed of principals, teachers, parents, and, at times, students and community residents, is created so these actors can be directly involved in school-wide decision making.
- The formal authority granted site participants may be circumscribed by existing policies, procedures, contractual agreements, or accountability provisions, but site participants are afforded substantial discretion.

Although site-based management is advanced as a robust remedy for a wide range of problems, the rationales rest on several sets of assumptions regarding the manner in which site-based management engenders school improvement.

Essentially, proponents contend site-based management will improve schools because it:

Source: From Betty Malen, Rodney T. Ogawa, and Jennifer Kranz, "Site-Based Management: Unfulfilled Promises," *The School Administrator,* February 1990, pp. 30, 32, 53–56, 59.

- Enables site participants to exert substantial influence on school policy decisions,
- Enhances employee morale and motivation,
- Strengthens the quality of school-wide planning processes,
- Stimulates instructional improvements,
- Fosters the development of characteristics associated with effective schools, and
- Improves the academic achievement of students.

For a number of reasons, site-based management does not succeed in meeting its objectives.

POLICY UNTOUCHED

Proponents suggest principals, teachers, and parents should be able to exert significant influence on matters of budget, personnel, and programming through a transfer of authority from the central office.

This promise is rarely realized. Although site-based management creates opportunities for site participants to be involved in school-wide decision making, they rarely exert substantial influence on school policy decisions. Three themes illustrate this assessment.

First, site participants rarely address central, salient policy issues in their school council or committee meetings. Teachers and parents frequently characterize the subjects councils and committees consider as "routine," "blasé," "trivial" or "peripheral."

Council members do address topics related to the operation of the building or the implementation of district directives.

For example, council members develop procedures for handling disruptive student behavior, set times for parent conferences, adjust school schedules, sponsor fund-raising projects, make facility improvements, and augment extracurricular activities. They also determine how reduction in work force directives might be implemented or how utility costs might be reduced.

But even on the more tangible, tangential matters, council members typically characterize their involvement as "listening," "advising," "endorsing the decisions others have already made," taking "rubber stamp" or "token" action.

Second, on councils composed of teachers and principals, teachers do not exert meaningful influence primarily because principals control council meetings. By virtue of their position in the school, principals are inclined to protect their managerial prerogatives and able to use low cost, routine strategies to control interactions.

In most instances, principals control the agenda content, meeting format, and information flow. The principals' capacity to exert control is enhanced by the tendency of teachers to defer to the principal. Even when teachers identify issues they would prefer to discuss, they permit the principal to set the agenda.

During discussions, teachers tend to "accept the boss's opinion" or "take the principal's lead." When responses are selected, teachers often "approve what the principal wants."

In short, the propensity of principals to protect their prerogatives and the reluctance of teachers to challenge this dynamic allows principals to fundamentally control decision processes and thereby decision outcomes.

Third, on councils composed of principals, teachers, and parents, professional-patron influence relationships are not substantially altered primarily because principals and, at times, principals and teachers control council meetings.

Since professionals can set the agenda, manage the meeting time, disperse the information, and shift potentially contentious issues to more private arenas, they essentially control decision processes and ultimately control decision outcomes.

Parents are reluctant to challenge this dynamic. As a result, the traditional pattern wherein administrators make policy, teachers instruct, and parents provide support is maintained.

PARTICIPANTS HANDCUFFED

Several factors combine to restrict site-based management from increasing the influence of teachers and parents on school policy decisions.

One set of factors relates to the composition of councils. Councils tend to be, at least on demographic dimensions, relatively homogeneous groups.

Members bring information-service expectations to the group. They tend to view participation in councils as an opportunity to acquire information and provide service, not an opportunity to redefine roles and make policy.

A second set of factors relates to norms. Schools have deeply ingrained norms, well-established unwritten rules that guide and govern behavior.

Even though site-based management plans stipulate that teachers and parents can affect decisions in the central domains of budget, personnel, and program, ingrained norms dictate that district officials and school administrators set policies, teachers deliver instruction, and parents provide support.

Site-based management plans grant participants the formal right to challenge and change this presumption. But well-established norms nullify that option.

A third set of factors relates to the nature of site-based management provisions. Site-based management plans often are ambiguous. They also frequently are circumscribed by the need to keep council decisions consistent with existing policies.

As a result, it's difficult to determine what decision-making authority site participants have been given and how that differs from prior arrangements.

Given these conditions, site participants are uncertain of the parameters of their formal power. They are unconvinced they have been given greater power. They become skeptical of the new arrangements and inclined to accept decision-making roles that conform to familiar practice.

A fourth set of factors relates to capacity. While school systems do delegate formal decision-making authority, they tend not to address participant capacity. Sponsoring systems rarely infuse councils with critical resources (e.g., time, technical assistance, independent sources of information, continuous, norm-based training, funds to assess current programs or develop new programs).

In addition, sponsoring systems rarely redistribute existing resources in ways that might balance the positional advantages of principals vis-à-vis teachers or the positional advantages of professionals vis-à-vis parents.

MORALE BOOST FLEETING

Proponents claim site-based management will improve the morale and motivation of school employees primarily because principals and teachers are given greater opportunity to be involved in and exert influence on school policies and operations.

Site-based management appears to have an initial, energizing impact on some participants. While individuals often are skeptical and workplace tensions clearly are present, some principals are excited by the prospects.

Some teachers are eager to tackle the important issues facing schools. Some teachers feel "truly professional."

However, the initial, energizing effects of site-based management often are offset by factors such as the:

- Time-consuming character of the process,
- Confusion, anxiety, and contention as site participants and district employees attempt to define their new roles,
- Dissonance created as committee demands compete with teaching responsibilities,
- Complexity of the problems site participants are supposed to solve,
- Resentment generated if site participants perceive they have only modest influence on marginal matters, and
- Frustration produced by fiscal constraints.

PLANNING UNAFFECTED

Proponents claim site-based management will improve the quality of planning because it capitalizes on the expertise of site participants and the benefits of group interaction.

While site-based management may direct attention to aspects of school-wide planning in some settings, there is little evidence it stimulates interest in or enhances the quality of that process in a significant number of settings.

Various factors prevent site-based management from improving the planning process. In most instances, site participants simply do not have the time, technical assistance, or logistical support to carry out the full range of planning activities in a substantive and coordinated fashion.

As such, there is a pronounced tendency to go through the recommended or required procedural motions (e.g., surveying the faculty or parents to assess needs, writing a plan, preparing reports, and rehearsing presentations for review team visitations).

INNOVATION LACKING

Proponents claim site-based management will foster the implementation of instructional improvements for two reasons.

First, site participants are free to design innovative instructional programs that meet the unique needs of students in their schools.

Second, since they are involved in designing these programs, they will be more likely to implement them.

While site-based management precipitates a wide range of activities, such as student recognition programs, discipline policies, workshops, and newsletters, there is little evidence that it stimulates the development or enhances the implementation of major instructional changes.

Site participants rarely address subjects central to the instructional program in their school council or school committee meetings. Where instructional program issues are discussed, it often is difficult to see how the plans depart from or improve upon existing practices.

Where instructional changes are proposed, they rarely are implemented in classrooms. Where teachers incorporate the recommended adjustments, they tend to "drift back to conventional practice" in a fairly short period of time.

Moreover, in some cases the move to site-based management impedes the development and installation of instructional improvements. It diverts attention from teaching and learning as site participants take on activities and responsibilities that only remotely are related to instruction.

Various factors restrict the ability of site-based management to produce substantial improvements in instruction.

At times, teachers are prone to define instructional improvement as an individual responsibility rather than a collective pursuit. Thus, they are reluctant to address or assess the school's instructional program.

In some cases, district and/or state requirements are viewed as so extensive or confining that site participants focus more on compliance than improvement. In most instances, site participants lack the time, technical assistance, requisite skills and supplemental funds to develop major changes.

In many cases, these conditions prompt site participants to develop plans to "keep their day-to-day operations intact."

Even where instructional innovations are proposed, they rarely are implemented for many of the same reasons. The initial enthusiasm gets "outstripped" by the gaps in knowledge (i.e., how to translate enthusiasm into action, how to convert interesting ideas into teaching behaviors) and the failure to recognize that change is "a costly process." Sizable and stable financial allocations to procure instructional materials and provide training experiences and professional development programs are required to sustain substantial instructional improvements.

LIMITS TO AUTONOMY

Proponents argue that because site-based management grants schools greater autonomy, it facilitates the development of characteristics associated with effective schools.

While these characteristics seem to be more pronounced in schools with considerable autonomy, there is no clear evidence that greater autonomy will produce these characteristics.

Some studies indicate when site participants are asked to develop school improvement plans which address the elements of effective schools, their efforts are constrained by state and/or district regulations, priorities, and pressures.

Other studies demonstrate that where these constraints are relaxed and site participants have both considerable latitude and extensive involvement in designing plans (albeit not formal authority for determining those plans), the features of effective schools do not become more pronounced.

These studies suggest if the objective is to engender the characteristics of effective schools, factors related to capacity (e.g., number and types of demands on the system, technical assistance, staff development, time to discuss and develop alternatives, funds for new program costs, district response to requests for assistance) are at least as important as factors related to autonomy.

ACHIEVEMENT UNAFFECTED

Proponents maintain site-based management can improve the academic achievement of students. Their arguments often rest on the ability of site-based management to fulfill the promises already discussed.

Yet again there is little evidence that site-based management improves student achievement. Although some documents claim site-based management produced improved scores on achievement tests, the requirements for making these causal claims are not met.

First, these sources do not address the issue of temporal order. They fail to establish that gains in achievement followed the move to site-based management and in some cases, acknowledge achievement scores already were improving before site-based management was in place.

Second, these sources do not address the issue of rival explanations: They fail to demonstrate that site-based management is a contributing factor, let alone the critical factor affecting student achievement.

The fact that achievement gains occur in only a small number of select pilot schools over a short period of time is a sign that site-based management is not the critical factor. If it were, one would expect achievement gains to be more widespread and more stable.

Only two systematic studies examine the relationship between site-based management and student achievement. While there are exceptions on both ends of the spectrum (a few schools improve and a few schools decline), these studies conclude that most schools maintain their previous level of performance. Student achievement does not appear to be either helped or hindered.

ISSUES NEEDING ATTENTION

Since there is little evidence site-based management plans achieve their stated objectives, several issues warrant attention. Educators and policy makers may want to pay particular attention to the following:

- The viability of site-based management as a reform strategy,
- The conditions necessary for site-based management to be successful, and
- The need for continuous, systematic assessments of site-based management programs.

Educators and policy makers need to carefully consider whether they wish to invest in a reform strategy that has not been able to achieve its objectives in most settings where it has been attempted.

Perhaps site-based management simply is not an effective approach to education reform. However, it is also possible site-based management has not been given a full or fair test.

It may be premature to dismiss site-based management on the basis of only eight systematic studies, particularly when some of these studies indicate isolated instances where site-based management appears to be approaching, if not achieving, its stated objectives.

Policy makers and educators may need to give site-based management a more complete test by designing plans that attend to those inhibiting factors. Perhaps if these factors were addressed, site-based management could become an effective approach to education reform.

WHAT ARE THE STEPS TO SUCCESS IN SITE-BASED MANAGEMENT?

Precise prescriptions for addressing the various factors that hamper site-based management cannot be derived from the available literature. However, general guidelines can be identified.

The guidelines relate to the content and specificity of site-based management plans, the provision of resources, and the development of strategies for changing participant orientations and organizational norms.

First, site-based management plans must specify what authority is delegated to site participants, how that authority is distributed, and the manner in which the discretion of site participants is conditioned and constrained by contractual agreements, by district, state or federal policies, procedures, and/or accountability provisions.

Without this detail, site participants have no basis for determining what they can and cannot do. They have no basis for determining whether they have greater discretion or greater opportunity to make policy decisions.

When site participants are not clear on the parameters of their power or when they are not convinced that they have been given greater power, they become frustrated by the ambiguity, skeptical of the new arrangements, and inclined to adopt decision-making roles that conform to familiar practice.

Second, site-based management plans must provide site participants adequate resources, namely time, training, technical assistance, and supplemental funds. Without these critical resources, site-based management plans do not achieve their intended objectives.

Third, site-based management plans must recognize the orientations of site participants and the norms of schools can nullify the impact of formal policy provisions. Site-based management plans must address these factors.

These factors can be addressed in several ways. Plans could include provisions that school council membership reflect the diversity of the school community and incorporate strategies to enlist participants with different backgrounds, orientations, and points of view.

Plans also could include provisions for training programs that address individual attitudes and school norms. Such training could redefine the roles administrators, teachers, and parents play in decision making and the development of skills needed to carry out these new roles.

Continuous, systematic assessment is essential. While the existing literature on site-based management identifies factors that impede the ability of this reform to achieve its stated objectives, there are no guarantees site-based management will fulfill its promises even if some or all of these factors are addressed.

Therefore, continuous, systematic assessments of site-based management programs must be conducted to determine the conditions under which site-based management might be able to achieve its objectives and improve the performance of schools.

Given the widespread interest in and reliance on site-based management as a reform strategy, those interested in site-based management have both the opportunity and the responsibility to carry out these assessments.

35

Policy Board Proposals Ignore Real Problems

Willis D. Hawley

The recent report of the National Policy Board for Educational Administration, "Improving the Preparation of School Administrators: An Agenda for Reform," is a devastating attack on much of what goes on in higher education in the name of preparing school administrators.

Although few will challenge the report's attack of the status quo, there is good reason why most of the report's recommendations should not be implemented.

In order to reinvent the way school administrators are prepared, and to do so in ways that promise to improve the quality of our schools, at least four questions require answers:

- What are the things school administrators do that contribute meaningfully to student learning?
- What must school administrators know and be able to do in order to perform those tasks that facilitate student learning?
- How do school administrators learn the knowledge and skills that enhance their effectiveness and what are the implications of the answer to this question for the respective roles of university-based and inservice education?
- How should people with leadership potential be recruited, inducted, and nurtured professionally?

The report does not address these fundamental questions and many of its proposals are unconvincing and vulnerable.

WHOSE PROBLEMS ARE THESE?

The report's critique of the preparation of school administrators identifies problems with educational administration programs rather than problems with the way schools are administered. No case is made for the contributions advanced study can make to improving schools.

Thus, one might conclude, after being convinced doctoral programs for school administrators are a mess, there is little reason to invest more money in higher education to improve degree programs.

In the absence of a vision of what we need from our educational administrators and a case for how advanced education will address these needs, the recommendations of the report could be interpreted as little more than an effort to enhance the resources and status of higher education.

CANDIDATES FOR TRAINING

The report argues that better efforts can and should be made to recruit and select able people to serve as school administrators. The report urges that recruitment and selection focus on people who are "the brightest," have strong analytic ability, have strong administrative potential, and are successful teachers.

The report proposes to measure the first two of these characteristics by a standardized test. What reason would anyone have to believe that a valid test of administrative potential could be developed?

We cannot develop a test or tests of potential until we are clear about the knowledge and competencies that school administrators need to be effective. The report offers no such clarity.

But the worst is that the report recommends that only those who pass in the top quartile of test takers be eligible to pursue the doctoral degree which the report argues should be a requirement for all full-time administrators, except business managers.

The report gives considerable attention to the need to ensure that large proportions of blacks and Hispanics are in the pool of trainees—but its proposals would have an opposite effect. As any analysis of the relative performance on standardized tests of different races and ethnic groups will show, those who "pass" the test will be disproportionately white and Asian.

With respect to the argument that all school administrators must be successful career teachers, there are at least two important questions.

How will we measure teacher success? More fundamentally, is there any evidence to support the assumptions upon which this old convention is based? And why must one have a master's degree in teaching, as the report proposes, to be an effective teacher?

In order to facilitate effective teaching, school-level administrators need to understand what is required by teachers and students if both are to be effective. But aren't there other ways this can be learned than by extensive teaching experience?

QUALITY FACULTY

The report calls for higher quality faculty in programs for training school administrators and argues that quality be assured by reducing faculty-student ratios to those seen in other professional schools and by increasing the number of school administration professors.

Source: From Willis D. Hawley, "Policy Board Proposals Ignore Real Problems," *The School Administrator*, Volume 46, Number 10, November 1989, pp. 8–11, 14–15.

What professional schools did the authors have in mind? There are enormous differences between the faculty-student ratios in medical schools and law and business schools, where most courses are taught in large classes.

The report proposes that there be at least five full-time faculty in educational administration departments. Why five?

Why would it be desirable for a professor assigned to a department of educational administration to teach courses (which the report recommends to be taught) on cognitive development, effective teaching, policy analysis, social and cultural influences on learning, ethics, and qualitative and quantitative analysis?

Most likely, faculty in other departments and schools would be better qualified to teach these courses. While this report seems aimed at discrediting programs taught largely by faculty who are part-time or unqualified to teach advanced courses, it is an inefficient and inappropriate mechanism that might be seen as a full employment program for professors of school administration.

REQUIRED DOCTORATES

The report proposes that no one should administer a school, much less a school system, who does not have a doctorate in educational administration.

There is absolutely no evidence to support the view that having a doctorate makes one a better administrator.

No such assumption is made about the leaders and managers of our largest corporations, the military, or other public bureaucracies.

FULL-TIME STUDY

The report urges that the doctoral degree, required for school administrators, be awarded only to those engaged in both a full-time residency on campus and a year-long internship at a site which participates in a carefully designed, ongoing collaboration with a particular university.

Since it is unlikely that most of the candidates for the doctorate will work in the districts involved in a collaborative relationship with a university, the report's recommendations, if taken literally, would require most prospective administrators to take two years out of their lives with no pay or benefits.

This has the effect of placing a $60,000 to $90,000 price tag on the license required to engage in school administration.

But why chide the report's authors for being ambitious? Perhaps because the report is unbending in its insistence that high cost or not, individuals must pay the price because "the trade-off in learning has been too great."

What evidence is there of a trade-off? Are there really no theoretically defensible alternatives to full-time study?

For example, what about a system of distributed learning that integrates work and study, that provides for full-time study for short periods that would not require leaving one's job, and that uses advances in learning technology?

If the concern being addressed by full-time versus part-time learning is the quality of potential administrators, why is the report unwilling to trust in the tests of knowledge and competence it proposes and in the selection processes used by the school districts?

THE CURRICULUM

The report proposes a curriculum that emphasizes what is to be learned rather than how learning is to occur. In their choices regarding the curriculum, the authors of the report appear to have opted for breadth rather than depth.

What we know about learning is that this is not the way to develop understanding or higher order thinking and learning skills. Of all the things we want school administrators to learn from their university education, understanding complex issues and acquiring higher order thinking and learning skills should be at the top of the list.

TOWARD ANSWERS

It is, of course, much easier to attack a proposal than to hammer out the compromises necessary to bring forth a positive set of proposals for change. Now, I will address the four questions I raised at the start.

STUDENT LEARNING

The success of efforts to reform the preparation of school administrators seems inextricably linked to the opportunities such reforms create for dramatically enhancing the quality of our schools.

Developing a concept of how improvements can be made in administrators' preparation to create new possibilities for our children might start with evidence from recent research on learning.

This research supports the idea being promoted by Philip Schlechty and others that students are "knowledge workers" who must—if they are to acquire knowledge and skills to develop the confidence and will to be self-directed learners—actively engage in the construction (production) of knowledge and their own learning capacity.

Teachers then become managers and facilitators of instruction who attend not only to the content and methods of student learning, but to parents, administrators, and other teachers to ensure that students are motivated to work and have the necessary resources to be productive.

Seeing schools this way, first focuses attention on the central importance of what administrators do to motivate teachers, ensure that teachers have the resources and learning opportunities they need, and create conditions within schools that allow students and teachers to use their motivation and capabilities to be productive learners and managers.

Second, this view places a premium on administrators' capabilities for integrating life inside the school with life outside the school and, therefore, puts school administrators at the heart, rather than at the margins, of community, state, and national policy making.

KNOWLEDGE AND ABILITY

The knowledge and capabilities school administrators need to have in order to facilitate the ability of teachers to manage students' production of knowledge and learning capacity include:

- what is known about student learning and the implications of this for instruction,
- how to facilitate both incidental and formal learning by teachers, and
- the essentials of group dynamics and how these shape and sustain school cultures.

The knowledge school administrators need to have and be able to use in order to link schools with the needs and resources in their environments include:

- how to communicate with and effectively involve parents in the education of their children, and
- what resources are available in other agencies and institutions that will help teachers and students.

This short list of topics only emphasizes a few priorities associated with some key functions administrators must perform. Clearly what an administrator must know to be effective varies both with the local situation and the administrator's particular role.

A heavy and perhaps terminal investment in university-based training for administrators before they become principals means that much of what is learned that would be useful in administrative roles, especially those attained well after the doctorate was earned, would be outdated and, in any case, unused.

HOW DO THEY LEARN?

We can assume that:

- school administrators construct knowledge by combining what they experience with what they already know and value,
- the transfer of what is learned in one context to a new situation or problem requires acquiring specific capabilities

and mental processes that are not intuitive, and
- knowledge about how one learns is a powerful learning resource.

These assumptions have significant implications and possibilities including:

- advanced educational opportunities should be part of a continuing interaction between intensive work and intensive study,
- much of what is learned and how it is learned should aim at developing the capacity to learn—especially in the context of a university—and to evaluate what one assumes one knows,
- it is better to study a few things in depth than to cover all the topics one can imagine school administrators might need to know and be able to do, and
- theory learned independent of applications that do not have meaning to the learner will be soon forgotten or dismissed as irrelevant; and lessons learned absent a theory are likely to go unused or be misused when one concentrates on solving problems on the firing line.

The importance of focusing greater attention on the way school administrators learn seems critical. How can we expect to develop a curriculum without understanding the social, organizational, and cognitive factors that influence how the curriculum will be learned?

One way is to begin researching the topic. But this will not yield short-term answers. Until then, the issues I have raised here and others might be productively explored in discussions about what administrators can learn best on the job, what they can learn best in university-based learning opportunities, and how these two sets of experiences can be practically and productively interrelated.

SET OF BARRIERS

The report illustrates why having no conventional paths for movement through different types of leadership roles is problematic.

Without career paths, the report recommends for administrators the same curricula, regardless of the role they play or are likely to play. Because the report wants to concentrate all of one's doctoral-level education at a particular point in time, the report calls for curricular breadth that is likely to result in neither academic rigor nor practical relevance.

Inevitably, universities with educational administration programs will view such curricula as superficial. And just as surely, those "preparing" to be administrators will view a general purpose, all-at-once curriculum to be unuseful.

Moreover, because of its breadth and its gate-keeping functions, the proposed selection criteria and curriculum will be seen as a set of barriers to be hurdled in the quest for status and position rather than a set of learning experiences that are intellectually enriching.

This, in turn, will lead many would-be administrators to seek out the lowest barriers and encourage state agencies and legislators to tie certification and advance professional education together in ways that standardize and trivialize what is learned in doctoral-level training and that discourage innovation in universities.

RECRUITING AND NURTURING

Why not experiment with ways of recruiting, inducting, and nurturing that target men and women who have demonstrated leadership potential by their achievements in college, business, the military, or civic activity?

Such ways should include preparation for teaching and service as teachers but would, very early in their educational careers, provide these persons with opportunities to learn about administration and demonstrate their leadership capacity. Those who demonstrate such a capacity would receive opportunities for further education and training for an administrative career.

WHERE'S THE RESEARCH?

I am perplexed that many educational researchers who advocate educational reform (those who drafted the report were all researchers) do not call on research in making their proposals or for the careful evaluation of alternatives before changes are mandated.

Not only should the authors have made use of existing research, but they should have identified significant questions about what research was needed and should have encouraged the design of alternative approaches for preparing school administrators that would be evaluated in terms of their effects on teachers and children.

It would be possible and desirable to move quickly and decisively to address many of the issues raised by the report without taking the more dubious steps it proposes. For example, if state education agencies, universities, and professional associations cannot put the doctorate of education scams out of business through collaborative action, they surely cannot pull off the more ambitious actions called for in the report.

Many other reforms could be encouraged and facilitated without the costly and untested solutions proposed by the report.

The report asks colleges and universities, states, and school systems to commit major time and resources to change the ways school administrators are prepared. Only a critical need justifies such commitments.

The crisis we need to address is not the embarrassing character of so many of our degree programs for potential school administrators.

The real danger is that our schools will not have the leadership they need to better educate the millions of disadvantaged children, and to change fast enough to keep pace with the increasing complexity of the workplace and the growing needs of individuals to problem-solve and adapt to raise their children, sustain their families, and get along with others.

PROPOSALS OF THE POLICY BOARD

Sharply critical of the "deteriorating quality" of administrator preparation programs in U.S. colleges and universities, the National Policy Board for Educational Administration laid out a nine-point agenda for improvement last spring.

"Improving the Preparation of School Administrators: An Agenda for Reform," issued in May, is the work of the representatives of 10 major national educational organizations. According to Terry Astuto, the Policy Board's associative executive secretary, the report's intent was to spur debate and action on the national level about reform and recommend ways to raise standards in educational administration preparation programs.

At a meeting convened by the National Policy Board and attended by 100 national representatives of all levels of school administration in May, "there was lots of discussion about the proposals," said Astuto.

"Concerns were raised over certain recommendations such as the recruiting of minorities and potential conflicts in using standardized testing; the problems of those professionals unable to undertake full-time study; and if the doctorate in educational administration is a level of training that should be required of all school administrators," she added.

"The heart of the issue right now is whether real reform is possible or whether reform will be stalled by focusing solely on efforts to reach consensus on these specific proposals. No one would argue that these proposals could be implemented overnight. I believe that emphasizing consensus building will prevent real reform since obviously we're not going to get all people to agree on these proposals," Astuto explained.

Here's a summary of the report's nine overall recommendations for improving school administration educational programs:

1. Vigorous recruitment be mounted to attract the brightest and most capable students of diverse race, ethnicity, and sex with a minority enrollment at least comparable to the region's minority public school enrollment.
2. Entrance standards be raised significantly to ensure all candidates possess strong analytic ability, high administrative potential, and demonstrated success in teaching.

3. The quality of faculty be ensured by:
   - strengthening faculty recruitment, selection, and staff development programs,
   - maintaining at least five full-time faculty members,
   - providing the bulk of teaching, advising, and mentoring through full-time faculty who have demonstrated success in teaching, clinical activities, and knowledge production in the field, and
   - having a student-faculty ratio comparable to other graduate professional degree programs on campus.
4. The doctorate in educational administration (Ed.D.) be a prerequisite to national certification and state licensure for full-time administrators who are in charge of a school or school system.
5. One full-time year of academic residency and one full-time year of field residency be included in the Ed.D. preparation program. Modifications in the type or duration of the clinical residency be permitted for candidates with full-time administrative experience in education.
6. The elements of the curriculum be developed to transmit a common core of knowledge and skills, grounded in the problems of practice.
7. Long-term, formal relationships be established between universities and school districts to create partnership sites for clinical study, field residency, and applied research.
8. A national professional standards board consisting primarily of practicing school administrators be established to develop and administer a national certification examination and that states be encouraged to require candidates for licensure to pass this examination.
9. National accreditation of administrator preparation programs be withheld unless the programs meet the standards specified in this report and that criteria for state accreditation and program approval include these standards.

The National Policy Board consists of representatives from these organizations:

- American Association of Colleges for Teacher Education
- American Association of School Administrators
- Association for Supervision and Curriculum Development
- Association of School Business Officials
- Council of Chief State School Officers
- National Association of Elementary School Principals
- National Association of Secondary School Principals
- National Council of Professors of Educational Administration
- National School Boards Association
- University Council for Education Administration

The next meeting of the Policy Board, to be held this month, will address the concerns surrounding these proposals and a plan to secure funding for establishing a national professional board for educational administration.

For more information, please contact Terry Astuto at 804-924-0583 or write: National Policy Board for Educational Administration, University of Virginia, Curry School of Education, Ruffner Hall, Room 183, 405 Emmet St., Charlottesville, VA 22903-2495.

36

School-Restructuring Efforts Forcing Principals to Redefine Their Roles

Ann Bradley

Robert J. Holzmiller, principal of Hopi Elementary School in Scottsdale, Ariz., is not ashamed to admit that his school's foray into site-based decisionmaking this fall has left him feeling scared.

The district has provided few guidelines on how teams in its five pilot schools are to go about the process of changing school governance, he said.

In the absence of such advice, Mr. Holzmiller has decided to try to involve parents, teachers, other staff members, and students in decisions he previously might have made by himself.

"Everything I get, I channel to a committee," Mr. Holzmiller said. "I don't know if that's right or wrong."

Mr. Holzmiller is not alone in his feelings of uncertainty. The growing movement to restructure schools through participatory decisionmaking is challenging the traditional definitions of the principalship—and of central-office leadership.

As teachers, parents, and even students take on added responsibility, principals across the nation are seeking to redefine their roles and their relationships with others in their schools and districts.

But that task is complicated, principals and others agree, by a lack of agreement among educators about what constitutes "school-based management." And the problem is exacerbated, in some cases, by a feeling among principals that teachers are pushing too hard and too fast to increase their decisionmaking authority.

"People started by focusing on teachers, and the notion was restructuring and teacher involvement," said Stephen Mitchell, vice president of Organizational Analysis and Practice, an educational consulting firm in Ithaca, N.Y.

"But you're starting to see them say, 'Wait a minute. If we're going to do that, we have to pay more attention to the principals,'" he said, "and the principals are saying, 'You're asking us to do this, but you're not paying attention to what the demands are on us.'"

'FACILITATORS' NEEDED

Mr. Mitchell and others believe that principals must become 'facilitators" who share ideas and information with their school teams and guide them toward consensus, rather than traditional managers or the sole decisionmakers in their schools.

But to do so effectively, they warn, principals must be supported—not directed—by their district offices.

"The principal is often [told], 'Fix it by this afternoon,'" said Peter Bucholtz, principal of Miami Palmetto Senior High School in Dade County, Fla. The school has adopted site-based management.

"Now, I can't always fix it by myself," he added, "and sometimes the person [in the central office] wanting it to be fixed doesn't understand that."

The skills needed to be effective in working with a team made up of a diverse group of teachers, community members, parents, and students are quite different from the skills most principals were taught, noted Dale Mann, a professor at Teachers College, Columbia University.

"All the bets are off," Mr. Mann said. "They can no longer be old-style [chief executive officers]. Is their new role clear? Not at all."

At a recent conference in Phoenix, approximately 200 educators from across the country engaged in a wide-ranging exploration of how central offices can support site-based decisionmaking.

The meeting was sponsored by the American Association of School Administrators, the National Education Association, the American Federation of Teachers, and the National Network for Educational Renewal.

The discussion centered around the concept of recasting the central office into a role in which it serves the school buildings, rather than prescribing a set of rules and regulations for teachers and principals to follow.

The concept of central offices as "enablers" is receiving increased attention in many restructuring projects, educators at the conference and elsewhere confirmed.

"The central office, as we know it, is going to be the third wave of reform," predicted Robert Hasson, assistant superintendent of the Wells-Ogunquit Community School District in Maine.

Mr. Hasson is planning a project for the N.E.A.'s Mastery in Learning program that will examine how principals' roles change in schools that are engaged in restructuring.

Source: From Ann Bradley, "School-Restructuring Efforts Forcing Principals to Redefine Their Roles," *Education Week*, Volume IX, Number 9, November 1, 1989, pp. 1, 12. Reprinted with permission from *Education Week*.

The project has received a grant from the Danforth Foundation.

MORE JOB SATISFACTION

Mr. Hasson said his experience with the N.E.A. program, now in its fourth year, has shown that principals who feared they would lose authority to site-based decisionmaking committees actually feel more powerful in the restructured schools.

Indeed, principals engaged in shared decisionmaking say its rewards are considerable, once initial barriers are crossed.

For instance, if a parent complains about a textbook, "You can't say, "They made me do it,"' noted Woody Norwood, principal of Wright Elementary School in Tulsa, Okla. He said he did not realize not blaming others would be nice "until I got out of that mode."

Elaine Dodd, who teaches at a magnet elementary school in Tulsa, said she enjoys an "enormous sense of freedom" because her principal "isn't intimidated or threatened by very bright teachers."

"I've worked for many principals, and I have found that I am not nearly as good a teacher when I feel confinement or restraint about what I can be involved in," she said.

'UNION JUGGERNAUT?'

Despite a degree of agreement on the new roles for central-office personnel and principals in reconfigured schools, a strong theme at the Phoenix conference was confusion over exactly what "restructuring" means.

What was considered shared decisionmaking in one district—advisory panels of teachers, parents, and students, for example—was far different from the formalized process in another district in which the teachers' contract spells out who will sit on the team and how it will make decisions.

Several principals noted that they have always made it a practice to involve teachers in decisions. Theirs is a perception shared by Scott Thomson, outgoing executive director of the National Association of Secondary School Principals.

"This is where restructuring gets so fuzzy," Mr. Thomson noted. "Good management anywhere involves a lot of involvement of the staff. I will argue that good principals have always done that."

"Where we part company with the two teachers' unions," Mr. Thomson added, "is that they are interpreting empowerment and restructuring as a committee of teachers in effect managing the school."

The perception that the teachers' unions are driving the restructuring movement has put some principals and central-office administrators on the defensive. In some areas, teachers' unions have called for the elimination of central-office jobs to redirect limited resources to the schools.

Gene Geisert of St. John's University in New York characterizes the teacher-empowerment movement in an article in the August issue of *The Executive Educator* as a "union juggernaut" that will "severely limit management's ability to function."

Ted Elsberg, president of the American Federation of School Administrators, agrees that principals may have their hands tied: "What you have is a situation in which the person delegated with responsibility, and who will take the blame if it doesn't go well, is left hanging out to dry."

URBAN UNREST

In large urban districts where systemwide restructuring is occurring, principals' associations complain that their members' concerns are being subordinated to the demands of teachers during collective bargaining.

In the wake of a teachers' contract instituting site-based management in Los Angeles, principals will take a vote early next year on whether to explore forming a union, according to Roger Johnson, deputy director of the 1,500-member Associated Administrators of Los Angeles.

"Administrators were concerned that the concept of shared decisionmaking was negotiated without their input," Mr. Johnson explained. "They don't feel their opinions are sufficiently solicited."

The Los Angeles contract established "school leadership councils," half of whose members are teachers. The principal has one vote on the council, and no power to veto its decisions.

Principals' organizations in Chicago and Rochester, N.Y., have unsuccessfully sought to block restructuring efforts in the courts.

In Chicago, a council at each school will decide every four years whether to renew a principal's contract, which will spell out performance goals. And in Rochester, teachers have taken on a function traditionally reserved for principals through a mentoring program for teachers who have received unfavorable evaluations.

Richard Stear, president of the Association of Administrators and Supervisors of Rochester, said his union feared that mentor teachers who were released from the classroom for the program would assume "quasi-administrative positions."

"Administrators are licensed and certified to evaluate," Mr. Stear said. "If an administrator loses that function, you lose the job."

And the principals' union in New York City already is at odds with Joseph A. Fernandez, the city's newly appointed schools chancellor, over his intention to challenge their tenure in school buildings as a prelude to school-improvement efforts.

ROLES EXPANDED

In contrast to the experiences of principals in large urban areas, principals in Prince William County, Va., have been given significantly more authority under the suburban district's new site-based management program, which will take effect next July.

Last month, the school board approved a sweeping plan that will allocate a lump sum to each school based upon calculations of how much it costs to educate each student, explained Richard Neal, director of school-based management.

Teams of faculty members, parents, and students at each school will determine how best to spend the money, with the superintendent's approval.

"The principal is held accountable under the close scrutiny of a collaborative relationship," Mr. Neal said. "It's a very serious change. When we transfer the money in a lump sum, that's not talk. That's as much power as you can transfer."

The shift in the way the school system's budget will be spent will remove power from the central office and give it "a consulting and advisory role," Mr. Neal said.

With the additional responsibility, each principal will be held more accountable, he noted.

"If somebody gets fired, it's not going to be the advisory council," he added. "It's going to be the principal."

ATTITUDES SURVEYED

In New Jersey, state officials quickly identified the high level of anxiety among principals as an issue that deserved special attention after a pilot site-based management program was created in 1987, said Jeffrey Graber, coordinator of the Cooperative Relationships Project.

The education department received a grant last year from the National Governors' Association to examine the role of the principal in site-based decisionmaking.

Principals from 51 school districts that applied to participate in the program were surveyed to determine their attitudes toward the concept. The project now involves nine districts containing 49 schools.

Initially, principals perceived empowering teachers to make decisions as a "zero sum" proposition that would threaten their own authority, Mr. Graber said.

Mr. Mitchell, whose firm serves as the primary consultant for the program, said the prevailing attitude was reflected by one principal who said, "I don't have any authority, and I'm not going to share it."

In addition, the principals were frustrated by a sense of isolation within their districts and by the heavy state regulation of schools, the survey found.

One of the greatest obstacles to participatory decisionmaking in schools is the time involved, Mr. Mitchell and several participants at the Phoenix conference noted. Particularly in rural areas, Mr. Mitchell said, principals "complain about a blue-collar mentality" among teachers who are not willing to work beyond school hours.

Even principals and teachers who are in agreement about shared decisionmaking must struggle to find ways to release teachers from the classroom for committee work.

Bruce Goldberg, co-director of the A.F.T.'s Center on Restructuring, told the Phoenix audience that there are no simple answers to that question. Changing the school schedule to create blocks of time in which teachers could meet would be a step toward real restructuring, he suggested.

"When you try to create a center of inquiry, then the different roles and relationships will ensue," Mr. Goldberg said. "If you begin with who has the power in the school now and how can we shift it, there won't be very much done."

TOO MANY TASKS

The educational consulting firm Organizational Analysis and Practice recommends that principals, teachers, and others who will share decisionmaking responsibilities develop a model that identifies their objectives and how to measure them. The survey of principals indicated "a tendency in too many schools to adopt too many things at once," Mr. Mitchell said.

Once a school has set clear goals, he said, the principal should become a coordinator and a source of information about where to find the proper resources, research, and materials to accomplish them.

But even principals who are enthusiastic about the potential of school-based management say delegating responsibility and watching a team make mistakes is difficult.

"My whole problem now is I'm starting to get concerned that if they don't follow through, do they fall on their faces or do I pick them up and scramble?" Mr. Holzmiller said of his school committees.

"It's hard for me, because I don't like to see things moving slowly."

37

School Financing in Texas is Ruled Unconstitutional

Michael Newman

In a decision with national implications, the Texas Supreme Court last week unanimously declared the state's method of funding public education unconstitutional.

The legislature must "take immediate action" to craft a plan to reduce the current wide disparities in funding between rich and poor districts, the court said, setting a May 1 deadline.

In response to the decision, Gov. William P. Clements called for a special session of the legislature to convene next spring.

Prominent school-finance experts said the decision could influence pending and future finance suits in other states and add further momentum to the movement to reduce inequities in school spending.

The Texas ruling comes eight months after Montana's highest court struck down that state's school-finance system, and four months after the Kentucky Supreme Court declared its state's entire system of precollegiate education unconstitutional. The New Jersey Supreme Court, meanwhile, is expected to rule in coming months in a suit challenging the state's school-funding method.

Similar lawsuits also are working their way through the courts in Alaska, Connecticut, Indiana, Michigan, Minnesota, North Dakota, Oregon, and Tennessee.

The Oct. 2 ruling in the Texas case, *Edgewood* v. *Kirby*, was met with a nearly universal welcome from state officials, lawmakers, and education lobbyists.

Those leaders have already begun to disagree, however, on what to do next.

Mr. Clements has called for the creation of a task force, which would hold public hearings and make recommendations to the legislature. But many others involved in the issue argue that it has already been studied more than enough.

Groups such as the Texas Research League, a nonpartisan, business-backed think tank, have begun to put forward their own school-finance proposals in response to the ruling.

MORE THAN A 'BAND-AID'

Although the court's unanimity was a surprise to some observers, the content of the decision had been widely expected.

"We felt we had a very good chance," said Al Kauffman, a lawyer for the 67 property-poor school districts and 14 families who were the plaintiffs in the case. "Still, the unanimous decision was overpowering."

The court found "glaring disparities" among rich and poor districts in terms of their ability to raise and spend funds for education. Because the state constitution requires the legislature to establish, support, and maintain "an efficient system of public free schools," the justices ruled that the current aid system was unconstitutional.

"Property-poor districts are trapped in a cycle of poverty from which there is no opportunity to free themselves," wrote Chief Justice Oscar H. Mauzy in the 15-page opinion.

School districts must have "substantially equal access to similar revenues per pupil at similar levels of tax effort," the court concluded.

While the court emphasized that "a Band-Aid will not suffice" and ordered the legislature to revamp the entire system, it offered no suggestions on how to do so.

"We do not now instruct the legislature as to the specifics of the legislation it should enact," Justice Mauzy wrote. "The legislature has primary responsibility to decide how best to achieve an efficient system."

The justices remanded the case to state District Judge Harley Clark, who will have the authority to determine whether the plan adopted by lawmakers remedies the inequalities among districts.

SPILLOVER EFFECT?

Arthur E. Wise, an expert witness for the plaintiffs in the case and director of the RAND Corporation's Center for the Study of the Teaching Profession, said the Texas ruling could affect the outcome of the handful of school-finance suits now pending in other states.

Other defendants also expressed satisfaction. State Comptroller Bob Bullock called the decision "good news," while Attorney General Jim Mattox said through a spokesman that he was personally pleased with the judgment.

The court has "finally settled this issue," said Craig Foster, executive director of the Equity Center, which represents a group of low-wealth districts in the case. "The 9-to-0 decision says, 'Don't come back to us with this,'" he added.

And spokesmen for such groups as the Texas State Teachers Association, the Texas Association of Community Schools, and the Texas Association of School Boards said they were happy with the ruling.

Source: From Michael Newman, "School Financing in Texas is Ruled Unconstitutional," *Education Week*, Volume IX, Number 6, October 11, 1989, pp. 1, 20. Reprinted with permission from *Education Week*.

"We're elated," said Brad Ritter, director of communications for the teachers' association. "Overall, the impact will be very positive for teachers in the state."

DEBATE BEGINS

Amid so much agreement, however, the beginnings of a debate were emerging last week.

The legislature must now address several vexing questions, including whether the new system will require new taxes, how much time the state will have to implement the new program, and what method of funding will best meet the court's mandate.

Although the court's decision explicitly did not order the state to raise taxes, many in the legislature and education community said they think new levies are a virtual certainty.

Margaret La Montagne, director of governmental relations for the state school boards' association, said "additional revenue from the state" must be "a major part of the response to this decision."

Representative Ernestine Glossbrenner, chairman of the House education committee, said those new revenues would probably have to come from new taxes. "I frankly don't see any other way," she said.

But others did. "I think it can be done without raising taxes," at least on the state level, said Winston Power Jr., superintendent of the affluent Highland Park district in Dallas and a former member of a state task force on school finance.

Mr. Clements was also unwilling to say new taxes were necessary. "Money itself is not the answer to quality education," he said at a press conference after the decision was announced.

The Governor's call for the creation of a task force drew sharp criticism from legislators and others. Mr. Clements asked Lieut. Gov. William P. Hobby and Speaker of the House Gibson Lewis to join him in naming the committee's members.

"Why form another task force?" asked Representative Paul Colbert, chairman of the House subcommittee on school finance. "Why? We've had several statewide task forces already."

"I don't think this problem needs more study," Mr. Kauffman said. "It has been studied tremendously now for the past 20 years."

Another matter of concern to lawmakers and lawyers was whether the court intended to give the state time to "phase in" its solution to the problem. "The court is totally silent" on the issue, Mr. Yudof noted.

Mr. Colbert said he thought the legislature would need several years to implement a plan.

MANY PROPOSALS

When it considers the issue next year, the legislature is not likely to suffer for lack of suggestions on what to do.

The Texas Research League, for example, has suggested redrawing school districts along county lines.

That idea has drawn criticism from rural educators, however. Joe Seale, executive director of the community schools' association, cautioned that such a plan could damage "the roots of communities in this state, which are the local schools."

The Equity Center plans to unveil its plan for school-finance reform next month, Mr. Foster said. The proposal probably will call for a "power equalization" formula, in which the state would set a floor for per-pupil funding and help poorer districts reach it with state funds, he explained.

But Mr. Foster also added that, for such a plan to be successful, it would be "terribly important to get the legislature to set the [minimum] funding at a level that will truly provide a high-quality education."

Another suggestion, mentioned by Richard E. Gray, a lawyer for the plaintiffs, was to "create larger school districts for finance purposes only."

Mr. Colbert said, however, that he thought such a plan could cause "fairly nightmarish logistical and political problems."

There is "a certain spillover effect" among state courts in "important cases," he noted.

"In some ways, this is symbolically more important than the Kentucky case," said Mr. Wise, referring to the June ruling in which that state's supreme court struck down "the whole gamut" of its educational system. (*See Education Week, June 14, 1989.*)

Mr. Wise pointed out that the Texas lawsuit traces its history to *San Antonio Independent School District* v. *Rodriguez,* a case tried in the federal courts that produced one of the seminal rulings in school-finance law.

In *Rodriguez,* the U.S. Supreme Court held in 1973 that disparities in school spending among districts do not violate the 14th Amendment's equal-protection clause because education is not a "fundamental right" guaranteed by the Constitution.

The Texas court's decision "effectively negates *Rodriguez,* at least for Texas," Mr. Wise said.

John E. Coons, a professor of law at the University of California at Berkeley, praised the decision as a "moderate solution."

"It doesn't try to wreck the system," he added, "it tries to perfect it."

Mr. Coons, who participated in *Serrano* v. *Priest,* the ground-breaking 1971 case that overturned California's school-finance system, said the ruling "may set a good example for other states."

"This is a signal to other jurisdictions that this can be done in an intelligent way, without destroying local control and without the judiciary overreaching," he added.

But Mark G. Yudof, dean of the University of Texas School of Law, said it was "hard to predict" what impact the *Edgewood* decision would have on suits in other states.

"It all depends on how the [Texas] legislature responds," he said. "That legislative plan could be a model for other states."

PRAISE FROM DEFENDANTS

The court's ruling was popular not only with the plaintiffs, but also with the defendants.

Commissioner of Education William N. Kirby, the first-named defendant, said in a statement that, although he was "required to defend the constitutionality of the system," he has "always maintained that it is not adequate."

Mr. Kirby added that he was "pleased that we finally have a decision."

38

In Finance Arena, A New Activism Emerges

States Pressed on Equity Amid Complications

Nancy Mathis

Submerged by other education issues for nearly a decade, the equity concerns that fomented a revolution in state spending on public schools are resurfacing across the country in litigation and in vigorous debates over school-finance systems in nearly half the states.

The reasons for the activity vary from state to state. But underlying much of it, school-finance experts say, is the sense that the higher standards and expectations for schools generated by this decade's reform movement have intensified fiscal pressures in many districts—typically those with either little property wealth or concentrations of low-achieving pupils, or both.

In the active states, the questions of what constitutes an equitable distribution system for education funds and how to generate the revenue to support it are being raised anew.

Finance experts note, however, that the revival is taking place in a climate vastly different, both politically and financially, from that of the 1970's, when the issue of school finance was the paramount item on education's agenda.

There are new and powerful competitors—both inside and outside the education community—for state aid, they say, at a time when additional revenue is harder to come by. And the reform era has introduced an important complication—"accountability"—into debates over funding mechanisms.

"The current school-finance pressure is coming right on the heels of quality issues," says Richard F. Elmore, professor of education at Michigan State University. "The political connections between funding and accountability are much more explicit."

"People are willing to provide more money for schools, but that willingness is tempered by a desire to see change," adds John Augenblick, president of Augenblick, Van de Water & Associates, a school-finance consulting firm.

Some contend that the current charged atmosphere may lead to deeper divisions within the education community—between urban and rural districts, for instance—as well as to stronger demands for accountability and a rethinking of state tax policies.

One expert predicts that even the U.S. Supreme Court may revisit the school-finance issue, reviewing a 1973 decision in which it denied education the status of a constitutionally protected right.

But much of the new legislative and judicial activity is still in its early stages. It remains to be seen whether more state aid for schools and/or more-equalized aid formulas will result.

ACTION IN MANY STATES

In recent months, governors, blue-ribbon panels, or legislative committees in 21 states have reviewed school-funding formulas with the idea of making them more fair. Two states, Colorado and Connecticut, substantially altered their funding methods last year.

School-finance lawsuits demanding equity for property-poor districts are pending in Kentucky, Minnesota, New Jersey, Tennessee, and Texas.

And in February, the Montana Supreme Court found the school-finance method to be unconstitutional, while the Wisconsin Supreme Court dismissed a challenge to that state's funding system.

In addition to the new litigation, some of the most venerable and influential of the first generation of finance suits are still working their way to a conclusion. Among the developments:

- The West Virginia Supreme Court, which in a dramatic 1982 ruling overturned that state's funding method, recently set in motion a possible resolution of the case, ordering a lower court to review a property-reappraisal plan.
- In New Jersey, litigation on behalf of the state's most beleaguered urban systems continues in a new phase after more than 15 years of various proceedings, including a finding that the previous finance system was unconstitutional. The state now is attempting to apply an accountability argument, saying it is not the level of funding available to the districts that is the issue but the quality of their management.
- *Serrano* v. *Priest*, the 1971 case that launched the entire finance-reform ef-

Source: From Nancy Mathis, "In Finance Arena, A New Activism Emerges: States Pressed on Equity Amid Complications," *Education Week*, Volume VIII, Number 31, April 26, 1989, pp. 1, 8, 10. Reprinted with permission from *Education Week*.

fort and in which the California Supreme Court determined that the state's school-funding method violated its constitution, may come to an official close this spring as lawyers attempt to settle unresolved questions. The case is credited with pushing California toward its current role—similar only to that of Hawaii—as the dominant provider of funds for local schools.

MORE COMPLICATED PICTURE

Such a spate of finance-reform activity has not been seen since the 1970's, when legal and social-science scholars first suggested that the local wealth of a school district should not be the determining factor in the quality of the education it provided.

The success of that theory, first in state courts and then in legislatures, substantially diminished public schools' historic dependence on local property taxes and forced states to assume a greater funding responsibility.

But the politics of the state role in education have become more complicated since then, lawmakers and finance experts point out.

With the publication of *A Nation At Risk* in 1983, governors demanded and legislatures adopted a number of costly reforms, such as reductions in class size, career ladders, salary increases, and other expensive measures. A number of the items were funded outside the regular equalization formulas, a strategy that some think exacerbated the problem that state equalization was intended to solve.

"There was good progress toward equalization during the 1970's," says Arthur E. Wise, director of the RAND Corporation's Center for the Study of the Teaching Profession. "But after the litigation stopped and people turned their attention to excellence issues, inequity in educational opportunities and expenditures began to grow."

Tennessee, for example, gained wide attention as a reform state when former Gov. Lamar Alexander successfully pushed, among other items, a controversial career-ladder program for teachers. But the 66 rural school districts that have initiated a lawsuit over the state's financing system argue that the reforms failed to take their fiscal constraints into account.

Tennessee counties can earmark a 2-cent sales tax for public schools, a revenue source highly beneficial to urban districts. But Tennessee is among the 10 states that levy no personal income tax and it ranks relatively low among all states in per-pupil spending.

"The upgraded requirements have put a further burden on the schools," says Lewis Donalson, the lawyer for the property-poor districts.

CYCLE OF 'CATEGORICALS'

Some experts also attribute the growing inequities to the cyclical nature of the political process, which apportions funding for schools not only through formula aid but through categorical grants.

As lawmakers come under greater pressure from special-interest groups, says Kent McGuire, senior policy analyst for the Education Commission of the States, they turn to categorical grants to ensure financing for specified programs.

After a few years, the number of categorical grants expands to such an extent that the funding system becomes inequitable, prompting demands from property-poor school districts for more equal funding, Mr. McGuire suggests.

Florida education leaders recently proposed revamping the state-aid formula to eliminate most of the 70 categorical items added over the past decade. The Florida funding system, adopted in 1978, originally had three categorical areas.

"Every time someone had an idea for something, they would tack on a categorical program," says John Gaines, executive director of the Florida Association of School Administrators.

FARM WOES, 'ADEQUACY' ISSUE

Special economic circumstances in other states have brought the equity issue to the fore, according to John L. Myers, the National Conference of State Legislatures' senior program director for education.

In much of the Midwest, for instance, the condition of state economies—still struggling because of the collapse of the farm and mineral markets—have prompted calls for changes in funding formulas.

State Representative Arthur Ollie, chairman of the Iowa House's education committee, says his state's declining population trend, spurred by the agricultural crisis, has prompted lawmakers to try to protect districts with declining enrollments by allowing them to count students no longer enrolled for per-pupil aid purposes.

This so-called phantom-student provision, which tends to favor rural schools, has put urban districts on the offensive. They claim that it unfairly and inequitably directs money to rural districts. The battle in the legislature continues this month.

The reconsideration of how state formulas work also reflects concerns over the "adequacy" of local revenue, not simply whether the state disburses aid on an equitable basis, suggests Michigan State's Mr. Elmore, who has studied the impact of the equity movement.

"Local districts are facing budget increases that cannot be met with local funds," he says.

That issue is underscored in Kentucky, where a state judge, in finding the funding formula unconstitutional last year, held that the state's young suffered from "educational malnutrition."

But the problem of how to feed more money into the state's poorest school systems has no easy solution. Says James Parks, spokesman for State Superintendent John Brock: "In Kentucky's case, if you redivided the existing resources, you would be taking away from the poor to give to the very poor."

'THE NUMBER ONE PROBLEM'

Such comments point to an additional complexity in the current finance debates: tight state budgets and changing demographics.

"The competition for resources is the number one problem," says Richard Salmon, a professor of education at Virginia Polytechnic Institute and State University who recently completed a survey of all 50 state funding formulas.

During the 1970's, when states first began equalizing their formulas, explains the N.C.S.L.'s Mr. Myers, fierce inflation helped pour additional dollars into state coffers. Those dollars not only helped equalize state aid but enabled legislators to "level up"—that is, to raise the per-pupil allocation.

Now, however, state revenues have either stabilized or declined. The National Governors' Association and the National Association of State Budget Officers reported last October that year-end general-fund balances were at their lowest point in 12 years and expenditures for fiscal 1989 were expected to out-pace revenues.

Moreover, as the average age of the population drifts upward, demands are increasing on states to offer expensive social and health services. And the corrections systems of many states, long ignored and politically unpopular, are growing at such rates as to force legislators to take action.

The N.C.S.L. reported last summer that the rate of state-spending increases for education had slowed, although it remained the largest segment of state budgets.

"There's a lot more people asking for a lot more money," says Mr. Salmon. "And the climate makes it difficult to raise taxes. Even if the tax effort has been declining, it's difficult to convince people they are not taxed to death."

'ZERO-SUM' COMPETITION?

And not only is education competing with other agencies for a share of the state coffer, he and others contend, but groups within the education community are competing for the available education dollars.

"I believe in what people in the field call a zero-sum concept," Mr. Salmon explains. "There's a fixed amount of money available for education. So when you start emphasizing one program, you automatically reduce the resources to another."

"We're seeing some interesting tradeoffs," says Deborah A. Verstegen, assistant professor of education at the University of Virginia. Ms. Verstegen and Mr. McGuire of the N.C.S.L. recently surveyed all states about the level of support for programs aimed at youngsters at risk of school failure.

Teachers, who are better organized politically than are groups promoting at-risk programs, are able to get funding for salaries at the expense of funding for at-risk youths, Ms. Verstegen suggests.

"We're seeing a redistribution from disadvantaged, at-risk kids to teachers," she says.

INTERDISTRICT TENSIONS RISING

The increased competition has also reopened old political wounds between urban and rural school districts.

Iowa's current finance battle, for instance, is so heated that transportation lobbyists fear it may spill over into other budget areas, such as highway funding.

In Tennessee, urban districts want to intervene on the state's side in the finance suit brought by rural districts. But the judge has ruled that the urban districts' interest already is being defended by the state.

In Minnesota, wealthy suburban districts are forming their own coalition to intervene, on the state's side also, in the equity lawsuit there.

Tensions between different types of school systems have also been reflected in the New York legislature, which must apportion aid to the nation's largest school district as well as to many suburban and rural systems. The New York City public schools are often a legislative target, since they consume about 33 percent of the state aid to education. But in recent arguments before lawmakers, city officials emphasized that the district enrolls 39 percent of the state's students.

At the same time, seemingly wealthy New York districts are battling for extra benefits in order to give tax breaks to local residents. Districts such as West Islip, on Long Island, are facing "a tax revolt," says a local school official.

There, skyrocketing housing values, coupled with $50,000 salaries for teachers living in one of the nation's highest cost-of-living areas, have raised homeowners' tax bills to $7,000 to $8,000 a year, says William Bernhard, the West Islip superintendent.

CALIFORNIA'S DIFFERENT DIRECTION

California educators are no strangers to the implications of tax revolts on the financing of education. The state, site of the first successful equity lawsuit, also was the first in which voters, whose home values soared with inflation, restricted increases in property taxation.

Voters later approved another measure limiting the amount of state and local budget increases for schools and other political entities.

The limitations on local taxes and budgets forced districts to turn to the state for assistance. The result: California essentially has full state funding of public schools, according to experts.

About 95 percent of its school districts are within a $200 range in per-pupil spending levels.

"No one ever doubted that if you eliminated local control [over property taxes] you would achieve equity," says Stephen M. Barro, a finance expert there.

And last year, California voters approved a proposition supported by educators requiring that 40 percent of the state budget each year be dedicated to public schools.

The state, says Superintendent of Public Instruction Bill Honig, had been gradually "disinvesting" in education, allowing its per-pupil spending level to decline as a combination of competition and state-tax changes left districts unable to keep pace financially with their enrollment growth.

AN UNUSUAL ALLIANCE

If California lies at one end of the school-finance spectrum, Texas would seem to be at the other.

There, the issue of local control has sparked an unusual alliance between four property-rich urban districts and the 200 rural districts that in 1987 won the first round of an equity lawsuit—a ruling recently overturned and now on appeal before the state supreme court.

Whatever the outcome, the property-poor districts represented by their coalition, the Equity Center, and the four urban districts have agreed to avoid two of the most divisive issues that surface in school-finance negotiations: local spending caps and school-district consolidation.

While a spending cap would redistribute money from rich to poor districts, it "would be counterproductive," says Craig Foster, executive director of the Equity Center. "Politically, it would just add to our list of enemies."

As it stands now, both the Equity Center schools and the four property-rich districts—Austin, Dallas, Fort Worth, and Houston—would benefit financially from a formula change that would gear state aid toward children needing special programs. Both kinds of districts have large numbers of economically disadvantaged minority students, many of whom have limited English skills.

Such "weighting factors" in state formulas used to be arcana that few understood. But computer technology has given all lawmakers quick access to the bottom line: the printout that shows what increase or decrease their school districts will receive.

'REVOLUTIONIZED BY COMPUTERS'

The computer printout, education officials say, has become the most important tool, or the worst weapon, in the battles over state-aid formulas.

"The politics of school finance has been revolutionized by computers and it's been pushed in the direction of precise, individual calculation," says Mr. Elmore.

Mr. McGuire calls the problem "printoutitus," saying it can be fatal to some proposals.

Representative Naomi Cohen, House chairman of the Connecticut legislature's joint education committee, recalls that it created the biggest difficulty in passing that state's new formula last year. Everyone, she says, wanted to "see if they were getting their fair share of the pie."

'NOT JUST EQUITY ANYMORE'

Legislators are looking at the bottom line from the productivity angle as well. Pressure for accountability from the public and business interests is growing, lawmakers and educators agree, and the funding formula is seen as a new tool.

"It's not just equity anymore, " says Allan Odden, professor of education at the University of Southern California. "There clearly is the accountability issue. You have to respond to both issues these days."

"More and more people want to link the allocation of money to the performance of pupils," says Mr. Augenblick, the school-finance consultant. No one has yet succeeded at forging that link, he adds, "but the talk about it is phenomenal."

The challenge, Mr. Augenblick suggests, is to develop a totally different funding-measurement system, based not on "inputs" such as books, teachers, and class size but on "outputs" such as student performance. "I'm not so sure people have thought about the equity implications of that," he says, adding that such factors affecting state formulas are likely to be developed in the next several years.

"Then, two or three years after that, we'll come back to the equity issue," he predicts.

So far, Connecticut is the only state that has tried to directly tie state funding to student performance. Districts with students scoring low on the state mastery test are given extra money through a weighted formula; the state will also provide grants to 20 cities where students score the lowest on the tests.

Other finance analysts, such as Michael W. Kirst, professor of education at Stanford University, insist, however, that outcome-based formulas are not a realistic answer and that the focus on financial inputs is appropriate.

ENLISTING A NEW PLAYER

Some policymakers are hoping that the pressure on lawmakers and school officials now being exerted by business interests will also translate into a willingness to support funding for education, even if it means tax increases.

Such is the case in Michigan, where the chiefs of the "big three" auto manufacturers have been complaining so loudly that the legislature may take action this year despite the rancor the issue has created in the past two years.

Legislative leaders, stymied in their efforts to adopt tax and formula changes, recently asked Edgar Harden, former president of Michigan State University and co-chairman of a 1987 school-finance panel, to reconvene the committee and, working with education, business, labor, and legislative groups, to develop a compromise by April 15.

When the panel began its work two years ago, Mr. Harden recalls, education interests reacted negatively to business leaders' demands for school reform. But that attitude has changed, he says, marking a vital step forward "if we're going to get any money."

LOOKING AT PAINFUL MEDICINE

The policy is also an unavoidable issue in Tennessee, says Representative Eugene Davidson, chairman of the legislature's House education committee. "It's the only alternative," says Mr. Davidson, conceding that gaining support for an income tax or other new taxes would be difficult.

In Texas, the lack of a personal or corporate income tax is a matter of pride.

"You can't say Texas has exhausted its tax resources," says Mr. Foster of the Equity Center. Lawmakers "are in a [financial] bind only to the extent of what the leadership wants to deal with in terms of taxes," he says.

Voters and politicians in Oregon and Montana repeatedly have scorned proposals for a sales tax in those states. In Oregon, a blue-ribbon panel last year recommended a tax increase, but declined to specify what type.

In Montana, where property-poor schools have won an equity lawsuit, lawmakers are debating a measure to force wealthy school districts to share their local taxes with poor districts because there is not enough state money to equalize school spending.

Connecticut legislators, comforted by a budget surplus, put $750 million into their new formula last year. But this year they face an $800-million budget deficit, and the governor has proposed slowing down the phase-in of the new formula.

Legislators, Ms. Cohen says, are now faced with the prospect of raising taxes, including implementing a state income tax, a proposal the governor has said he would veto.

But trying to change a state's tax system and its school-funding mechanism at the same time compounds the political difficulties.

Says Mr. Harden of Michigan: "It's a little bit harder than trying to move a graveyard."

Last week in fact, Mr. Harden's committee disbanded, unable to reach agreement on tax and school-finance issues.

WILL MORE 'TAKE THE PLUNGE?'

Mr. Wise of the RAND Corporation, whose legal theories about states' responsibility for school finance helped launch the legal drive for equity in 1968, predicts that the recent rise in litigation over state formulas is not likely to be curbed by the flurry of activity in the legislatures.

"If one or two or three of these [pending] suits are sustained by high courts, then I expect we'll see poor districts in other states ready to take the plunge," he says. "The problems will not go away. The only thing that will change is the willingness of people to file suit."

Mr. Wise also foresees that the U.S. Supreme Court may soon be asked to decide a case similar to the one it ruled on in 1973, *San Antonio Independent School District* v. *Rodriguez*. In that case, the High Court held that education was not a right protected by the Constitution's 14th Amendment and that inequities then existing in the Texas funding system were unfortunate byproducts of local control.

But since the *Rodriguez* decision, Mr. Wise argues, states have enacted many mandates as part of their reform efforts—in effect overriding local control in many instances.

"The very rationale that caused the Supreme Court to sustain the whole school-finance system in Texas is gone," he contends.

A determination that education is a constitutional right would offer students the 14th Amendment's "equal protection of the laws," he says, greatly bolstering contentions that funding disparities violate that clause.

"Ironically, the fact that states have expanded their management of local schools makes them all the more susceptible to this type of lawsuit," Mr. Wise asserts. "It raises the question: If they are exercising control to improve the quality of education, then why are they not distributing their resources accordingly?"

39

Budgeting for the 1990s

Harry J. Hartley

Spring heralds the arrival of another budget season. Once again, school administrators face the challenge of providing sound fiscal stewardship as they justify their budget requests for fiscal year 1990.

Clearly, an education budget is more than the sum of its fiscal parts. In many cases, the annual budget is the best statement of values a school system makes. The expenditure plan reveals exactly how many dollars are allocated to competing programs, while the revenue plan indicates the extent to which local and state tax revenues are earmarked for public education.

W.C. Fields once observed, "The future ain't what it used to be." And perhaps the outlook for school budgeting in the 1990s is not what it used to be either.

For instance, each of the past three decades witnessed the emergence of a major budget innovation in the public sector: planning-programming-budgeting system (PPBS) in the 1960s, zero-base budgeting (ZBB) in the 1970s, and school-site budgeting (SSB) in the 1980s.

As we develop fiscal year 1990 budget requests, no single budget format dominates and no fiscal innovation lies ahead. Many superintendents are wisely incorporating the best elements of recent budget concepts: budgeting by individual programs (PPBS); budgeting by individual schools (SSB); and improving the review of budget options and justification of program funding levels (ZBB).

Both practical and eclectic, this approach often results in a school budget that is more responsive to local needs and does not highlight a particular acronym or fad.

The leadership challenge is to develop the best possible budget process and document that will convey to the board and community what is needed and why. Now is a good time to evaluate your own budget system and make appropriate modifications.

SETTING THE STAGE

In starting the budget process, I suggest an annual checkup or an internal management audit to determine that certain procedures and documents are in place. By setting the stage, we are really describing characteristics of the well-managed organization.

Experience has clearly shown that, even though the superintendent has good intentions and a strong desire to implement budget improvements, success will not be achieved unless sound administrative procedures and good documentation exist. Let's examine the prerequisites to successful budgeting.

EVALUATING YOUR BUDGET

In reviewing a school budget, try to avoid drawing a "bad" overall conclusion simply because the budget does not satisfy certain biases of the reader. Remember that each budget is responsive to distinctive local needs, has its own history, and is the product of some degree of compromise. A number of factors influence the format of a given budget, including:

- tradition/past practice,
- municipal budget regulations,
- state budget policies and regulations,
- board of education's policies and needs,
- superintendent's style and needs,
- availability of computers and fiscal staff,
- auditors' recommendations, and
- local political factors.

In short, a budget is the product of many factors that have shaped its contents and appearance. However, it is also clear that all budgets should meet certain standards of quality and principles of public budgeting. The budget process should provide adequate staff and public involvement. The format of the document should be well-organized, readable, and informative. The contents should be accurate, complete, and timely and satisfy legal compliance requirements.

[The] budget evaluation checklist . . . is one I have developed and used extensively with school administrators, including National Academy for School Executives institutes on resource management. By using this checklist, an administrator can assess a local school budget and determine whether certain changes may be needed.

BUDGET HEARINGS

Budget hearings are essential to a budget's successful adoption and for establishing confidence in the executive. The key to preparing for budget hearings is to anticipate questions and minimize surprises.

A useful approach is for the superintendent and staff to prepare a list of the 10 toughest budget questions and develop appropriate responses. One might hope that none of these questions will be raised at the public hearing, but if they are raised, credible answers can be provided. Examples include:

- How do you justify a substantial budget increase while student enrollment is declining?
- Why is the budget increase twice the rate of inflation?
- Why does special education get preferential treatment?

Source: From Harry J. Hartley, "Budgeting for the 1990s," *The School Administrator*, Volume 42, Number 4, April 1989, pp. 31, 34, 36.

- How do you measure program results and relate them to costs?
- How much is spent on administration and why?
- Why don't you cut costs by increasing pupil-teacher ratios?
- How much will taxes rise?

Preparing budget briefing books is helpful so that administrators can respond quickly and accurately to questions. These loose-leaf, internal documents may contain data on enrollment projections, staffing profiles, class size, fringe benefits, energy costs, labor contracts, capital projects, equipment plans, and special education data.

A final suggestion is for the superintendent to conduct mock hearings with other key administrators. Rehearsals for budget presentations are essential since the best way to make a positive impression at a hearing is to know the budget. Credibility is a hallmark of leadership.

Prerequisites to Successful Budgeting

Documents that should be readily available:

Board Policies—current and comprehensive financial policies

Educational Goals—organizational values linked to budgets

Table of Organization—up-to-date administrative structure

Role Descriptions—functional management responsibilities

Budget Procedures Manual—calendar, instructions, codes, forms

Financial Reports—accurate, timely expenditure control data

Annual Report—expenditures and results of past year

Procedures that should be easily observable:

Executive Leadership high profile of superintendent in fiscal matters

Organizational Stability low turnover of superintendent and board

Team Management individual and group values integrated

Business Management competent business office staff

Budget Workshops staff training on budget procedures

Public Hearings open discussions on budget issues

Community Support local schools viewed as community asset

Checklist for Evaluating Local School Budgets

By Harry J. Hartley

	Yes	No
PROCESS: Conducting the Hearings		
1. Roles of board and superintendent clearly defined	□	□
2. Board financial policies updated regularly	□	□
3. Accuracy and timeliness of all financial data	□	□
4. Adequate staff involvement in budget request	□	□
5. Adequate public hearings and citizen participation	□	□
6. Budget document (or summary) widely distributed	□	□
7. Compliance with legal requirements	□	□
8. Community/political support generated for budget	□	□
9. Contingency strategy for cuts (budget options)	□	□
10. Efficient accounting/financial reporting system	□	□
FORMAT: Organizing the Document		
11. Attractive cover, title page, overall appearance	□	□
12. Table of contents or index; numbered pages	□	□
13. Names of board members, officers listed	□	□
14. Table of organization, administrators listed	□	□
15. Budget message or letter of transmittal	□	□
16. Graphics/artwork charts, figures, tables	□	□
17. Clarity of style; avoidance of technical jargon	□	□
18. Manageable size and shape of document	□	□
19. Glossary of key financial terms	□	□
20. Concise executive summary ("budget-in-brief")	□	□
CONTENTS: Compiling the Data		
21. Political feasibility of "bottom-line" request	□	□
22. School system goals and objectives	□	□
23. Budget assumptions, guidelines, or priorities	□	□
24. Object budget summary (e.g., salaries, supplies)	□	□
25. Program budget summary (e.g., reading, math)	□	□
26. Site budget summary (e.g., individual schools)	□	□
27. Budget history (expenditures for past 5 years)	□	□
28. Unit cost analysis (per pupil expenditures)	□	□
29. Summary of estimated revenues (all sources)	□	□
30. Explanation of impact on tax rates	□	□
31. Explanation of major cost factors (contracts, inflation)	□	□
32. Budget coding system explained (chart of accounts)	□	□
33. Performance measures program outcomes; test data	□	□
34. Pupil enrollment projections by grade	□	□
35. Staffing history and projections	□	□
36. Long-range plans (five years) for the school system	□	□
37. Justification for major decisions (layoffs, school closing)	□	□
38. Comparisons with other districts (or with state averages)	□	□
39. Capital budget summary (capital improvement projects)	□	□
40. Budget detail (line-item expenditure data)	□	□

PART FOUR

Historical Foundations of Education

A study of educational foundations would not be complete without an examination of the history of American education. Teachers must know the history of our educational system in order to appreciate the proud heritage of the teaching profession. A knowledge of the history of education also helps educators to better understand contemporary educational problems and to make wiser decisions regarding these problems. The articles in this chapter have been carefully selected to provide the reader with some of the highlights of the history of American education.

The very earliest schools that have been discovered thus far were found in ancient Sumer, which existed over 4,000 years ago. The first essay, "The More Things Change . . . ," by Christopher J. Lucas, provides an interesting look at these ancient Sumarian schools. These schools were better developed than one might expect. Since paper did not exist, students did their writing on wet clay tablets which became hardened as they dried; many of the early clay tablets still exist today.

In "Greek Education," Francesco Cordasco discusses the historical background of education in Greece. As you will see from this article, the Greek educational system was very well developed for its time nearly 4,000 years ago.

The third selection is from "The Great Didactic," written by John Amos Comenius. Comenius lived in the seventeenth century and developed an entire system of education, from primary schools through universities. He authored many school books and was the first to routinely include pictures to help the reader better understand the concepts that he was writing about. This selection outlines many of Comenius's educational views, which were very progressive for his time.

Many of the first teachers in the United States learned to be teachers by serving an apprenticeship or indentureship with an experienced teacher. The next selection is an indenture for teacher training from 1722. These early apprenticeships were the forerunners of contemporary student teaching and internships. Colonial education in America spanned 180 years and, as one might expect, a good deal of educational activity took place during that long period of time. In his essay, "Education in Colonial America," Robert Middlekauff discusses the highlights of education during that 180-year colonial period. This article, of necessity, does not delve deeply into each aspect of colonial education, but rather attempts to capsulize the essence of its history.

Catherine E. Beecher was a pioneer in the development of education for women in the United States. She founded the Hartford Female, Seminary which trained many teachers. The essay "Suggestions Respecting Improvements in Education" represents Beecher's views on the need for educating women for their roles as teachers and as mothers.

Booker T. Washington was one of the most important black educators during the Reconstruction Period after the abolishment of slavery in the United States. Educational opportunities for blacks were very limited during this period of time. Washington advocated an industrial education to help blacks develop the necessary skills for a better life. "Negro Education Not a Failure" represents a defense of this approach to education of blacks.

For a period of time after winning her independence from England, the United States was so preoccupied with settling the pressing affairs of a newly formed nation that relatively little time was devoted to education. Beginning about 1820, however, there was a great deal of educational activity. About this time many states established statewide public school systems. Governors, legislators, and town councils started earnestly discussing the subject of education; many additional elementary schools were established; educational journals were published; more and improved textbooks were published; educational societies and institutes were organized; schools for the deaf and blind were established; Troy Seminary was established, providing the first higher education for women in this country; state school boards were organized; and special teacher-training schools called *normal schools* were established.

During this period of increasing educational activity, there were a number of people who made substantial contributions to educational progress. Men such as Samuel Hall, Henry Barnard, Horace Mann, and Cyrus Peirce, among others, kept the issue of education before the public and led the fight for a universal free educational system. Space does not permit the inclusion of articles on all of these important educators, although each of their contributions was indeed great. However, the next essay elaborates on some of these events, especially education's role in the development of the American society. In "Education's Evolving Role," Wendell Pierce documents three major forces that have historically shaped the development of American education.

Women have not historically been afforded equal educational opportunities in America. Recently, a great deal has been written about this inequity and significant efforts are being made on many fronts to provide equal opportunities for American women. "Historical Notes on the Growth of the Women's Movement," from the Report of the National Commission on the Observance of International Women's Year, provides an interesting history of this area.

The last selection in this section of the book is the "Universal Declaration of Human Rights" of the United Nations. This document consists of a preamble and thirty articles, which, perhaps better than anything else ever written, portray the importance of education in developing human rights throughout the world. As you read this selection, compare your own educational views with those represented in this historic statement by the United Nations.

It is hoped that when you have finished these selections you will realize that although the roots of American education can be traced to Europe, the values, concepts, and organizational patterns of education in the United States today are unique in the world. You should also realize that, as our nation developed from the first thirteen states to the present fifty states, education changed from that for an elite few to education for all. In the current nuclear age, when the world is changing more in decades than it formerly did in centuries, educators should be familiar with, and appreciative of, the historical role that education has played in our ever-changing society. Despite some of the shortcomings of the current American educational system and despite the efforts of a few critics who advocate that we should return to European educational standards, history reveals that no other nation has accomplished what the United States has done through mass education. It is important that we strive for educational improvements, but it is also important to remember that the United States produces more goods and services, provides better opportunity for individual advancement, and enjoys a higher standard of living than most other nations in the world. A study of educational history helps us to realize that much of the credit for these achievements must be given to the educational system which has been developed in this country.

40

The More Things Change . . .

Christopher J. Lucas

The French (who seem to have a saying for practically everything) phrase it best: *"Plus ça change, plus la même chose"* —or, roughly, "The more it changes, the more it remains the same." The aphorism might have been coined expressly to describe the school.

The following story provides a case in point:

A young boy goes off to school. He is called on for an oral recitation covering his written assignment. He breaks for lunch. In the afternoon his class practices writing exercises. At the close of the day he returns home and is greeted by his father, who inquires how he did in school. The boy proudly recites what he has learned and shows off samples of his work. The father is pleased. Later that evening the youth leaves a reminder that he be awakened early in the morning. He is anxious about getting to school on time.

The next day, so the account continues, the boy's mother hands him two rolls for his lunch and he hurries off to the schoolhouse. But, for reasons unexplained, he is delayed en route and arrives late for his first class. The attendance monitor waiting at the door issues a stern reprimand and orders the boy to report to the principal. Heart pounding in fear, the youth complies. As it turns out, besides being tardy, he has failed to complete his homework. The irate principal administers a sound thrashing.

Thereafter matters go from bad to worse. The rest of the day is given over mainly to beatings for still other infractions: for slovenly appearance in violation of the school's dress code, for speaking out of turn, for standing at ease and leaving his assigned seat without permission, for lapsing into the vernacular during a foreign language class, and finally, for loitering about on school grounds after hours.

The boy now dreads school and begins neglecting his lessons. His teacher, thoroughly disgusted, eventually abandons all pretense of trying to teach the youth anything and threatens his dismissal. The boy's father is distraught; his son is on the verge of becoming a school dropout. In a last desperate effort to settle matters, he hits upon the idea of inviting the principal home for a conference.

The schoolmaster is treated royally upon his arrival. He is led to the seat of honor and wined and dined. Gifts are pressed upon him. On cue, the lad begins to recount all he has learned in school. Then the father joins in, lavishing praise on the teacher for his unsparing efforts on the boy's behalf. This stratagem proves successful. By now greatly mollified and in a mellowed mood, the principal launches into a long, windy speech, thanking his host for his generosity and parental concern. In a paroxysm of enthusiasm, he winds up with words of praise for the young student's supposed academic accomplishments. Everyone is greatly relieved and a crisis is averted.

As it happens, this tale does not describe a contemporary "fundamental" school where basics are stressed and strict discipline is the rule. Nor does it date back, say, to the era of the one-room country schoolhouse. Its lineage is much older—by over 40 centuries. The so-called "schooldays" composition, meticulously assembled and restored from about 20 separate cuneiform-tablet fragments, dates back some 4,300 years or more, to the very dawn of recorded civilization.

Composed by some anonymous scribe of ancient Sumer, somewhere in the late 3000s B.C., this rough equivalent of a McGuffey's Reader or a blue-backed speller was probably already hoary with age when it found application as a copy piece for schoolchildren learning to read and write. Its age is difficult to grasp. At the time pupils first began laboriously incising copies of the essay on their clay tablets, the advent of the Christian era still lay over 20 centuries ahead. Phrasing it another way, the birth of Christ was *more* distant in time from the Sumerians than that same event is removed from us in our own remote past.

Clearly, schools have been around for an incredibly long time. The Greeks, for example, were strictly latecomers. A full thousand years or more before Homer—as culture sites in the Near East unmistakably attest—formal institutions of teaching and learning were already flourishing in Mesopotamia, throughout the length and breadth of the Tigris-Euphrates basin.

Moreover, despite their awesome antiquity, much is known about these archetypal educational institutions. Archaeological records uncovered from the archaic city-states of Sumer and Akkad reveal in graphic detail how the earliest known schools in history were conducted. The parallels they afford with present-day education are both startling and instructive.

Discipline problems, for instance, are hardly new. Nor are unruly, obstreperous students. Sumerian pedagogues also had their hands full with disrespectful and disruptive pupils. Maintaining order in the classroom was a constant struggle. "Why is it you behave this way?" demands one exasperated teacher, trying to separate two fighting students. "One knocks down the other, 'grinding the grain, threshing the straw' [a metaphor obviously suggestive of a remorseless assault], forever brawling in school."

Source: From Christopher J. Lucas, "The More Things Change . . . ," *Phi Delta Kappa*, February 1980, pp. 413, 415–416.

Having restored peace for the moment, the harried teacher threatens one offender with dire punishment. "There is only a stick awaiting you!" he exclaims disgustedly. "I will beat you with it, wrap a chain around your feet, and keep you confined within the school for a full two months and not let you out!"

A contemporary advocate of corporal punishment might very well applaud the suggestion, even if no school board would agree.

Parents with wayward children also had their problems. Not unlike today's mothers and fathers who wonder what the younger generation is coming to, a Sumerian father portrayed in a school essay titled "A Scribe and His Perverse Sone" berates his offspring. "Where did you go today?" he asks his son. "I didn't go anywhere," the boy replies sullenly. "If you didn't go anywhere," the parent explodes, "then tell me, why do you idle about?"

The father lays down the law. The son is ordered to go to school, to follow the teacher's directions, to complete his assignments diligently, and to return home promptly without hanging around on some street corner. "Come now, be a man," he concludes. "Do not loiter about in the public square or wander along the boulevard. As you walk through the streets, do not gawk at everything around you." The father adds a piece of advice about how to succeed in school: "Be humble and show humility before your teacher. When you make a show of modesty, the teacher will like you."

The son appears not to listen. In growing anger, the father has the boy repeat his instructions verbatim. One can almost hear the teenager responding with exaggerated, weary impatience.

The remainder of the essay consists of a lengthy diatribe on the father's part, a more or less standard speech easily recognizable to today's youth. The parent reproaches his son for his discourtesy, his constant complaining, his indolence. Turning bitter as he speaks, he reminds the boy that unlike many other adolescents his age, he was never forced to work. Other children, the father points out, willingly take jobs to help support the family. "Night and day," he complains, "am I tortured because of you. Night and day you waste in pleasure."

"You are full-grown now and filled with your own sense of self-importance," the father continues. But, he warns, pride goes before a fall. The boy is assured he will come to a bad end unless he straightens out. Maybe it would be a good thing if some calamity befell him, if it would help bring him to his senses. The boy is urged to begin thinking seriously about what he wants to make of himself. The parent advises his son to follow in his father's footsteps and prepare for a career as a scribe.

Other surviving fragments of Sumero-Akkadian schoolhouse literature preserve vignettes of educational routine that sound equally modern. A solicitous parent requests the teacher's help: "Instruct my son while in school," directs a father. "Watch over his handwriting and assist him."

Students poke fun at a classmate who cannot wait for lunch: "He attends more to his stomach than to his lessons."

A teacher cautions a lazy student with an old saying about what happens to boys who do not apply themselves: "A disgraced scribe becomes a man of spells" (i.e., a failing scribal student will be forced to take up a more lowly occupation as a writer of magical incantations.)

Foreign language requirements are unpopular with many youngsters today. It was no different 4,000 years ago when apprentice scribes, besides having to learn to read and write in the vernacular Akkadian, were required to master the intricacies of Sumerian (like Latin, a dead language no longer commonly spoken). Apparently many students needed encouragement. For some, learning a second language was an insuperable task.

"A scribe who does not know Sumerian," one saying asks rhetorically, "where will he expect to obtain a translation of a Sumerian text?" Or, again, a taunt: "If there is a translation to be made from the Sumerian, it is hidden from you!" Scribal students lacking proficiency in both languages were disdained: "A scribe who doesn't know Sumerian, what kind of a scribe is he?"

Schoolchildren, then as now, could be cruel in their gibes at classmates. Two students, Enkimansi and Girnishag, are trading insults. One alleges of the other, "He is a deaf fool when it comes to the scribal art, a silent idiot when it comes to Sumerian." The other disputant hurls a charge of his own: "You have written a tablet, but you cannot decipher its meaning; you can write a letter but nothing else."

The accused retorts sarcastically for a bystander's benefit, "Even if he had a *zami*-instrument, he could not learn the art of singing—he, the most backward among his classmates; he has not been able to make a beautiful tremolo and sound. He cannot chant a song, cannot open his mouth." The student whose musical abilities have been called into question responds: "You are supposedly a scribe and you don't even know your own name! You should slap your face!"

An older student criticizing his junior delivers the ultimate insult: "You're a bungler, a braggart. You cannot shape a tablet properly; you cannot even handle the clay. You cannot write your own name! Your hand is unfit for tablet writing . . . . Clever fool [*galam huru*—literally, 'sophomore'], cover up your ears!"

Similar epithets were reserved for unpopular teachers. On the other hand, a truly inspired instructor might win high accolades. "Master, god, who shapes humanity," runs one typically extravagant panegyric, "my god you truly are. Like a puppy, you have formed 'humanity' in me." Elsewhere, a school graduate's eulogy of his former professor is unstinting in its praise: "He guided my hand on the clay, showed me how to behave properly, opened my mouth with words, uttered good counsel, focused my eyes on the rules that guide the person of achievement."

Judging from recent reports, the mysteries of grammar confound a good number of students. A youth in a Mesopotamian school had the same problem. The teacher's aide, called an "elder brother," is tutoring the boy. "What shall we concentrate on today?" asks the tutor. The student responds with the unheard-of proposal that the day's usual grammar lesson be discarded. "I am resolved to work on something of my own," he declares. "I myself will decide the subject."

The elder brother is shocked by this display of youthful independence. Obviously unaccustomed to the motion of "student-initiated inquiry," the tutor asks defensively, "If *you* are to decide the subject matter for yourself, then how can *I* serve as your 'elder brother'? In what, pray tell, does my 'big brotherhood' consist?" The boy's suggestion is rejected out of hand, at which point the two begin to quarrel.

Rare is the modern doctoral student who does not approach the final oral examination with trepidation. Everyone has heard of the overconfident student humiliated at the hands of an unforgiving examiner. A Sumero-Babylonian text labeled "Examination Text A," dating to the period 1720–1625 B.C., depicts an analogous situation.

The scene is the school courtyard where the head teacher is preparing to examine a student scribe before the assembly of masters. He queries the candidate: "From your earliest years to adulthood you have been reposing in the tablethouse [i.e., the school]. Do you know the scribal art that you have pursued?"

The candidate responds confidently, "What would I not know? Ask me, and I will supply the answers." The professor is dubious. He predicts—correctly, as it turns out—that the boastful young man will fail. There follows a barrage of difficult and involved problems. The interrogation is a lengthy one and inevitably the student falters. In self-defense, he blames his teachers for not having taught him sufficiently. In modern parlance, the faculty members are incompetent and the degree program itself is at fault.

The chief examiner is incensed. His sharp rejoinder: "And what have *you* done, what good came of you sitting here? You are already a ripe man and close to being aged! Like an old ass, you are not teachable anymore. Like withered grain, you have passed the season!.How much longer," he demands angrily, "do you intend to play around?"

His irritation subsiding at last, the interrogator then concludes on a more optimistic note. "But, it is still not too late," he tells the candidate. "If you study night and day and work ceaselessly, modestly, and without arrogance, if you attend to your colleagues and teachers, you still may become a scribe!" A latter-day scribal student in a contemporary university would find the advice familiar.

Countless other examples might be adduced to show how little school life has changed from thousands of years ago. Functioning within role models established by the institution of schooling itself, students and teachers behave pretty much as they always have, responding to problems and situations that are timeless. The general impression conveyed by Sumerian schoolhouse literature is that specific institutional conventions may vary, depending on time, place, and cultural context, but the more fundamental features of school interaction endure basically unaltered. All things considered, there is not much new under the sun.

In an often-quoted dictum, George Santayana warned that the person who cannot remember the past is doomed to repeat it. Had he been speaking to teachers and students in school, he might more aptly have observed, "Whether you remember the past or not, you will probably repeat it anyway."

41

Greek Education

Francesco Cordasco

Historical background. The people who called themselves *Hellenes* came into the Greek peninsula sometime soon after 2,000 B.C. They were united by language, religion, and a common civilization, but there was no Greek government or nation. The settlements on the mainland were separated by steep valleys and tall mountains. Each large settlement formed a *polis*, or city-state. The Doric Age (*ca.* 1200 B.C.) began with the movement of primitive tribes called Dorians from northern Greece into the Peloponnesus. Migrations forced Hellenic peoples in Peloponnesus to cross the Aegean Sea to Asia Minor where they established Greek colonies. The chief Dorian tribe, the Spartans, developed the city-state of Sparta into one of two great powers of Greece; in this period the city-state of Athens in Attica took form. The Doric Age lasted several hundred years. The struggle of the Greek city-states and the Persian Empire culminated in 479 B.C. with a Greek victory at Plataea. Rivalry between Sparta and Athens caused the Peloponnesian War, with the final defeat of Athens in 404 B.C. Spartan leadership passed to Thebes in 371 B.C. Greece was finally overrun by Macedon and made part of its empire in 338 B.C. The period of Hellenistic civilization ended with the Roman conquest of Greece in 146 B.C.[1]

Periods of Greek education. The division of Greek education is into the Old and the New Greek periods, with the division point at the Periclean Age (459–431 B.C.). The Old Greek period is divided into (1) the Homeric Age; (2) the historic period, including both Spartan and Athenian types. In the Old Greek education the emphasis was on the social and institutional rather than on the individualistic aspect of education. The New Greek period includes (1) a period of transition in the educational, religious, and moral ideas following the Age of Pericles; (2) a period from the Macedonian conquest until Greek civilization is thoroughly incorporated with Roman life. By the time of the end of the New Greek period, the philosophical schools had been formed and were finally organized into the University of Athens.

The education of the Homeric period was best exemplified in the great epic poems, *The Iliad* and *The Odyssey* (*ca.* 900–800 B.C.). It included the two fold ideal of the man of action and the man of wisdom, typified by Achilles and Odysseus. Both ideals were to be attained by each free Greek. Bravery was to be tempered by reverence; the primary virtue of the man of wisdom was good practical judgment.

The Old Greek education of the historic period was determined, in its character and its organization, by the dominant social institution, the polis, or city-state. The city-state was the outgrowth of the tribe and council of the Homeric period, and furnished the basis and ideals of education.

1. **Spartan education** was typical of the Old Greek education in its most pronounced form. Definite formulation of this system of education was consolidated in the constitution of Lycurgus (*ca.* 850–800 B.C.). It resulted in a socialistic state with governmental control of education with emphasis upon the educational function of various social institutions.

a) **The aim of Spartan education** was an extreme paternalistic education, which sought the complete submergence of the individual in the citizen with attributes of courage, complete obedience, and physical perfection.

b) **The organization of Spartan education.** A general superintendent (*paedonomus*) and assistants were in charge of education. The first seven years of the child were spent with its mother; afterwards as wards of the state they were instructed by elder males; from eighteen to twenty they were classed as Irens, and at thirty were classed as warriors completely devoted to the state.

c) **The content of Spartan education** was dominantly physical and moral with very little that was intellectual or aesthetic. Plutarch says, "All the rest of their education was calculated to make them subject to command, to endure labor, to fight, and to conquer." Emphasis on gymnastics made for military resourcefulness. Music and religious dances were used to develop the same quality. Approval or disapproval of the elders was a constant source of discipline. Every Spartan adult was a teacher, and every Spartan boy had a tutor. Women were educated as men, with the purpose of training mothers of warriors.

2. **Athenian education** had little in common with that of Sparta, save in the simplicity of aim and in the means adopted for training. Even in these two general aspects there was wide divergence.

a) **The organization of Athenian education.** While Sparta destroyed the family, Athens preserved it and placed upon it the burden of responsibility for education. All schools were private schools. The state provided only for education between the ages of sixteen and twenty, almost wholly a direct preparation for military service. Until the age of seven, the training of a child was in the hands of its family. For the next eight or nine years, the Athenian boy attended two public schools—the music school, and the *palaestra* (gymnastic school). At about age sixteen, he discontinued all literary and mu-

Source: From Francesco Cordasco, "Greek Education," *A Brief History of Education*, pp. 3–10. Copyright © 1963 by Littlefield, Adams & Co., Inc.: Paterson, NJ. Reprinted with permission from the publisher.

[1] J. C. Stobart, *The Glory That Was Greece: A Survey of Hellenic Culture and Civilization*, 3rd ed., New York, 1962.

sical instruction to attend the gymnasium, where for two years he prepared for the life of an Athenian citizen; the last two years (*ephebic* or cadet education) were under the direct control of state officials.

b) **The content of Athenian education.** Reading, writing, and the literary element of education were included in the work of the music school. Heavy emphasis in palaestra and formal education of the ephebic period was given to gymnastics. Music was understood to mean poetry, drama, history, oratory, and the sciences, as well as music in the more limited sense.

The New Greek education—Transitional period. The Old Greek education culminated in the brilliant Age of Pericles, but this period of fruition was also one of transition. The life of the period made greater demands on the individual and offered greater opportunities. Placement of greater emphasis on the individual, and not on the citizen, led to the New Greek education. Many transitional forces induced change, among which may be numbered (1) political changes; (2) literary development; (3) introspective psychology and philosophy; (4) greater freedom for the individual.

1. **The Sophists.** Agencies of the new education were teachers known as Sophists, peripatetic professors-at-large, who increased in numbers following the Age of Pericles. The Sophists were unorganized and represented no common opinion, but they laid great stress on rhetoric, and were skeptical of old Athenian beliefs and traditions; their educational aims were chiefly utilitarian, and Plato reports one of the Sophists, Protagoras (481–411 B.C.), as saying of an ambitious Athenian youth, "If he comes to me, he will learn that which he comes to learn." The moral teachings of the Sophists placed an unprecedented emphasis on individuality. Consequently, there arose against the Sophists a violent opposition by all the conservatives and those concerned with the most worthy traits of old Greek life. Both in content and method, education was graphically changed by the Sophists, who both modified the old Greek education and contributed to the new. The former home training became milder, intellectual instruction supplanted the process of forming moral habits, a knowledge content was added to gymnastics and music, and the gymnasium tended to substitute beauty for strength. The destructive tendencies and criticism of the Sophists aroused Socrates, and so the movement of Plato and Aristotle was made possible.

2. **The Greek Educational theorists.** The occasion for the work of the theorists was the conflict between the New Greek education and the Old. They held the ideals as well as the process of the Old Greek education to be wholly inadequate; but they rejected the negative attitude of the Sophists and believed that some general moral bonds must be furnished.

a) **Socrates** (469–399 B.C.) first stated the problem of conflict between the Old and the New Greek education, between social and individual interests, and somewhat vaguely suggested the principles of solution. Although he left no writings, Socrates is studied in the writings of Xenophon and Plato. He accepted as his starting point the basal principle of the Sophists, "Man is the measure of all things," but added that the first obligation of man is to know himself. As opposed to the purely individualistic basis of opinion, he held that knowledge possessed universal validity, and from this arrived at the fundamental principle, "Knowledge is virtue." The Socratic Method is a process of obtaining a concept or definition inductively by conversation on moral and philosophic problems. Socrates' method can be studied in the *Dialogues* of Plato (e.g., *Apology, Euthyphro, Lysis, Protagoras, Republic*) and in Xenophon's *Memorabilia*. The contributions of Socrates to education are: (a) knowledge is obtained objectively by conversation, and subjectively by the reflection and classification of one's experiences; (b) knowledge has a moral and therefore universal value; (c) education has for its immediate object the development of the power of thought, not the imparting of knowledge.[2]

b) **Plato** (420–348 B.C.) agreed with Socrates that the great need of the time was the formulation of a new moral bond in life to replace the ancient ideals of old Greek society rejected by the new individualism. In his ideal schemes of education, he formulated an aristocratic government of socialistic nature. *The Republic* is Plato's exposition of an ideal society. There were three classes in this society: the philosophical (to rule); the soldier (to protect); the artisan (to obey and support the first two). The education outlined in *The Republic* is similar to that of the Athens of Plato's day. The substance is formed of gymnastics and music for children and youth; higher education is divided into two phases: scientific and philosophic. The scientific extends from age twenty to thirty and includes arithmetic, geometry, music, and astronomy. The philosophic extends over a period of five years devoted to study of dialectic, i.e., philosophy. The value of Plato's educational writings is in the principles formulated, which suggest that it is the function of education to determine what each individual is most fitted by nature to do, and then to prepare him for this service. This is the formulation of the Greek ideal of a liberal education. Plato allows for the education of women, and gives one of the earliest defenses of women's education. The practical influence of Plato is to be seen in the formation of the philosophical schools of Athens; in the direction he gave these schools; in the determination of a curriculum that remained influential for centuries; and in the final formulation of the Greek idea of a liberal education. Essentially, this last consisted in discarding the practical value of all the subjects of study as subordinate to that which they possess as mental disciplines.[3]

c) **Aristotle** (384–322 B.C.). Aristotle's ideas on education appear in *The Ethics* and *The Politics*. The first describes how the individual should discipline himself in life; the second describes the social and economic conditions in society most favorable for achieving this purpose. Aristotle viewed education as an important branch of practical political science and the means of securing the well-being and well-doing of the citizens of the community. The ultimate function of the state is educational, and the perfection of society depends upon the perfection of its members. The method of the education of Aristotle is objective and scientific, as opposed to the philosophical plan of Plato; the educational scheme is composed of elements drawn chiefly from Athenian education and is similar to that of Plato. The child until six should be trained by the parent; beyond this period education should be controlled by the government. *The Politics,* which is a fragment, says nothing about higher education, although from his other writings we can infer that higher education would include mathematics, physics, and astronomy. Theoretical or intellectual education is followed with practical education in citizenship. The influence of Aristotle was profound; through scholasticism his work became the basis of all studies and of all educational institutions during the Middle Ages.

The Cosmopolitan period of Greek education. Two general characteristics are educational features of this period, extending to the period of the dominance of Christianity: (1) the spread of Greek culture; (2) fusion with Roman education.[4]

1. **Spread of Greek culture.** Through the military and administrative genius of Alexander the Great, the habits and customs of all the East were influenced by Greece. As culture became universal and education individual, new types of educational institutions came into existence. By the latter part of the fourth century B.C., the work of the Sophists resulted in the formation of two types of schools, the rhetorical and the philosophical. The rhetorical schools prepared for the practical activities of life by training in oratory and the new knowledge of the times. A leader in the formation of rhetorical

[2]See further R. W. Livingstone, *Portrait of Socrates*, Oxford University Press, 1938.
[3]See further Richard L. Nettleship, *Lectures on the Republic of Plato*, London, 1936.
[4]W. W. Tarn, *Hellenistic Civilization*, 3rd ed., Cleveland, 1961.

schools was Isocrates (393–338 B.C.); just as Socrates formed a transition from the early Sophists to the philosophical schools whose primary interest lay in speculative questions of metaphysical or ethical import, Plato, Aristotle, and other philosophers gathered students around them that were soon organized into schools (e.g., Zeno and the Stoics; Epicurus and the Epicureans). Eventually, Platonism, Stoicism, and Epicureanism adapted themselves to Roman ideals of life. The philosophical schools became as formal and artificial as the work of the early Sophists, and represented an educational decline.

2. **The Universities** of the Greek world grew out of the rhetorical and philosophical schools. **The University of Athens** represented a combination of three such schools: the Academy; the Peripatetic school (Aristotle's); and the Stoic. Its head was elected by the Athenian senate. In many ways, it had the elaborate structure of a modern university and it continued to function until suppressed by Justinian in 529 A.D. The **University of Alexandria,** during the early Christian centuries, surpassed Athens as the intellectual center of the world. In Alexandria, the Aristotelian method of investigation was employed, and many early scientific theories were formulated (e.g., Archimedes, Euclid, Ptolemaic theory of the universe).[5] With the fall of Alexandria to Islamic power in 640 A.D., all university activity ceased, even though some interest was transferred to the Arabs to be revived later at Baghdad and the Moorish intellectual centers of Spain.

3. **Fusion with Roman education.** After the Roman Conquest of 146 B.C., Greek civilization in general was rapidly appropriated by the Roman conquerors, and Greek education extended its boundaries without changing its character. In a sense, Roman education is but one aspect of the cosmopolitan education of Greece.

[5]For science in ancient times, see S. F. Mason, *A History of the Sciences*, London, 1953.

42

The Great Didactic

John Amos Comenius

1. Our method does not really concern itself with University studies, but there is no reason why we should not state our views and our wishes with regard to them. We have already expressed our opinion that the complete training in any of the sciences or faculties should be reserved for the University.

2. Our ideal scheme is as follows;

(i) The curriculum should be really universal, and provision should be made for the study of every branch of human knowledge.

(ii) The methods adopted should be easy and thorough, that all may receive a sound education.

(iii) Positions of honour should be given only to those who have completed their University course with success, and have shown themselves fit to be entrusted with the management of affairs.

We will briefly give some details on each of these points.

3. If its curriculum is to be universal, the University must possess (1) learned and able professors of all the sciences, arts, faculties, and languages, who can thus impart information to all the students on any subject; (2) a library of well-selected books for the common use of all.

4. The studies will progress with ease and success if, firstly, only select intellects, the flower of mankind, attempt them. The rest had better turn their attention to more suitable occupations, such as agriculture, mechanics, or trade.

5. Secondly, if each student devote his undivided energies to that subject for which he is evidently suited by nature. For some men are more suited than others to be theologians, doctors, or lawyers, just as others have a natural aptitude for and excel in music, poetry, or oratory. This is a matter in which we are apt to make frequent mistakes, trying to carve statues out of every piece of wood, and disregarding the intention of nature. The result is that many enter on branches of study for which they have no vocation, produce no good results in them, and attain to greater success in their subsidiary pursuits than in those that they have chosen.

A public examination, therefore, should be held for the students who leave the Latin-School, and from its results the masters may decide which of them should be sent to the University, and which should enter on the other occupations of life. Those who are selected will pursue their studies, some choosing theology, some politics, and some medicine, in accordance with their natural inclination and with the needs of the Church and of the state.

6. Thirdly, those of quite exceptional talent should be urged to pursue all the branches of study, that there may always be some men whose knowledge is encyclopaedic.

7. Care should be taken to admit to the University only those who are diligent and of good moral character. False students, who waste their patrimony and their time in ease and luxury, and thus set a bad example to others, should not be tolerated. Thus, if there is no disease, there can be no infection, and all will be intent upon their work.

8. We said that every class of author should be read in the University. Now this would be a laborious task, but its use is great, and it is therefore to be hoped that men of learning, philologers, philosophers, theologians, physicians, etc., will render the same service to students as has been rendered to those who study geography by geographers. For these latter make maps of the provinces, kingdoms, and divisions of the world, and thus present to the eye huge tracts of sea and land on a small scale, so that they can be taken in at a glance. Painters, also, produce accurate and life-like representations of countries, cities, houses, and men, no matter of what size the originals may be. Why, therefore, should not Cicero, Livy, Plato, Aristotle, Plutarch, Tacitus, Gellius, Hippocrates, Galen, Celsius, Augustine, Jerome, etc., be treated in the same way and epitomised? By this we do not allude to the collection of extracts and flowers of rhetoric, that are often met with. These epitomes should contain the whole author, only somewhat reduced in bulk.

9. Epitomes of this kind will be of great use. In the first place it will be possible to obtain a general notion of an author when there is no time to read his works at length. Secondly, those who (following Seneca's advice) wish to confine themselves to the works of one writer (for different writers suit different dispositions), will be able to take a rapid survey of all and to make their choice in accordance with their tastes. Thirdly, those who are going to read the authors in their entirety will find that these epitomes enable them to read with greater profit, just as a traveller is able to take in the details of his journey with greater ease, if he have first studied them on a map. Finally, these abstracts will be of great use to those who wish to make a rapid revision of the authors that they have read, as it will help them to remember the chief points, and to master them thoroughly.

Source: From John Amos Comenius, *The Great Didactic*, pp. 433–438. London: Adam and Charles Black, 1896.

10. Summaries of this kind may be issued both separately (for the use of poor students and those who are not in the position to read the complete works) and bound up with the complete works, that those who wish to read them may get an idea of the subject-matter before they begin.

11. As regards academic exercises, I imagine that public debates, on the model of a Gellian society, should be of great assistance. Whenever a professor delivers lectures on any subject, works which treat of that subject, and these the best that exist, should be given to the students for their private reading. Then the morning lecture of the professor should serve as the subject for an afternoon debate, in which the whole class may join. One student may ask a question about some point that he does not understand, and may point out that in the author which he has been studying he has found an opinion, backed by reasonable arguments and opposed to that of the professor. Any other student may then rise (some forms of order being observed), and may answer the question raised; while others may then decide if the point has been properly argued. Finally the professor, as president, may terminate the discussion. In this way, the private reading of each student will be of use to the whole class, and the subject will be so impressed on their minds that they will make real progress in the theory and practice of the sciences.

12. This practice of dissertation may be the means of fulfilling my third wish, that public posts of honour be given to none but the worthy. This result will be obtained if the appointment to these posts depend not on the decision of one man, but on the unanimous opinion of all. Once a year, therefore, the University should be visited by commissioners appointed by the king or by the state, just as the Latin-School is examined by its masters. The industry of the professors and students can thus be tested, and the most diligent of the latter should receive a public recognition of merit by having the degree of doctor or of master conferred upon them.

13. It is most important that everything be conducted with perfect fairness, and therefore, instead of allowing the academic degree to be won by a disputation, the following plan should be adopted. The candidate (or several at once) should be placed in the midst. Then men of the greatest knowledge and experience should question him and do all they can to find out what progress he has made, both in theory and in practice. For example, they may examine him on the text of the Scriptures, of Hippocrates, of the Corpus Juris, etc.; asking him where such and such a passage occurs, and how it agrees with some other passage? if he knows of any writer who holds a different opinion, and who that writer is? What arguments he brings to bear, and how the contradictory views may be reconciled? with other similar questions. A practical examination should then follow. Various cases of conscience, of disease, and of law should be submitted to the candidate, and he should be asked what course of action he would pursue, and why? He should thus be examined with regard to a number of cases, until it is evident that he has an intelligent and thorough grasp of his subject. Surely, students who knew that they were to be publicly examined with such severity, would be stimulated to great industry.

14. There is no need to say anything about travel (to which we assigned a place in this last period of six years, or at its conclusion), except to remark that we are at one with Plato, who forbade the young to travel until the hotheadedness of youth had passed away, and they were sufficiently versed in the ways of the world to do so with advantage.

15. It is scarcely necessary to point out how useful a School of Schools or Didactic College would be, in whatever part of the world it were founded. Even if it be vain to hope for the actual foundation of such a college, the desired result might still be brought about, existing institutions being left as they are, if learned men would work together, and in this way seek to promote the glory of God. These men should make it the object of their associated labours to thoroughly establish the foundations of the sciences, to spread the light of wisdom throughout the human race with greater success than has hitherto been attained, and to benefit humanity by new and useful inventions; for, unless we wish to remain stationary or to lose ground, we must take care that our successful beginnings lead to further advances. For this no single man and no single generation is sufficient, and it is therefore essential that the work be carried on by many, working together and employing the researches of their predecessors as a starting-point. This Universal College, therefore, will bear the same relation to other schools that the belly bears to the other members of the body; since it will be a kind of workshop, supplying blood, life, and strength to all.

43

Education in Colonial America

Robert Middlekauff

When an American colonist discussed a "public school," he was not talking about the institution familiar to us since the nineteenth century; usually he simply meant a school open to anyone who wished to attend. The chances were that the school was privately owned and financed. The designation "public" was given to distinguish it from a school catering exclusively to a special group—usually a religious sect.

Indeed, the modern idea of "public education," implying a state-owned system of schools, supported by taxation, and administered by officials chosen by the community, which compels attendance of all children within a certain age group and which carefully separates itself from the educational efforts of private groups, did not exist in the colonial period. To be sure, the state sometimes participated in organizing and financing schools, but its role (outside of New England) was small. Indeed, several other agencies assumed the burdens of education; chief among them were the family, apprenticeship, and private schools of various sorts.

Of these institutions early in the colonial period, the family carried the greatest burden. In the primitive conditions of settlement, other agencies did not exist. Parents had to give their children education—if any was to be given. Frequently, of course, children went untutored or picked up rudimentary vocational training while they were working.[1]

The family continued to be an important center of training even after colonial society developed. For colonial parents, like their English forefathers, frequently placed their children with other families for rearing and training. They had good reasons for doing so: some did not trust themselves to discipline their own children vigorously enough; others, wishing to see their children acquire certain skills, apprenticed them to masters capable of providing the appropriate knowledge.[2]

Throughout most of the colonial period, indentures, as the apprentice agreements were called, usually enjoined the master to see that his charge was taught the essentials of the Christian religion and to read and write. Apprenticeship, of course, was never simply an educational instrument. A master taking on a young boy or girl expected his charge to work as well as to learn. The indenture always provided that the apprentice would obey and serve his master for a specified time, usually seven years or until the apprentice reached twenty-one. The instruction a boy received was always in return for his service. Sometimes apprenticeship proved to be only an agency of work, as masters refused to teach their boys. In such cases, the apprentice's only protection was his parents—or the local courts.

Schools in the first years of settlement were scarce in all the colonies. Scattered settlement and scant resources discouraged attempts to maintain schools continuously. Thus in the first years education in schools was largely a temporary, even sporadic, affair.

EDUCATION IN THE SOUTH

If education in the first years of settlement was much alike in all the colonies, it took on regional characteristics as colonial society matured. In the southern colonies—Virginia, the Carolinas, Maryland and later Georgia—where population always remained scattered on farms and plantations, geography prevented a neat structure of schools, yet children were educated. A wealthy planter sent his sons to England to sit in one of the great grammar schools, or brought a tutor to the plantation, where he lived with the family. Smaller planters and farmers, especially in Virginia, sometimes combined their resources to build a "field school"—a building in a tobacco field, hence the name—and to hire a teacher to instruct the children living nearby. Boarding schools usually established by an ambitious college graduate or itinerant schoolmaster appeared late in the colonial period and were usually found only in the larger villages like Williamsburg and Charles Town.[3]

Tutors, field schools, boarding schools were all maintained without any reference to public authorities. This was not true of most of the endowed schools of the southern colonies. Founded through the generosity of private donors, these schools were usually managed by county or parish officials—or a combination of both. Such officers found a place for the school's meeting, hired its master, and supervised its operation.

The most renowned of these institutions were the Symmes and Eaton schools. Both were founded around the middle of the seventeenth century from bequests of Virginians. Both were controlled by a board of trustees composed from county and parish officers. Symmes school secured incorporation in 1753; Eaton in 1759. During at least a part of its history each offered instruction in the classical languages as well as in reading, writing and arithmetic.[4]

Altogether nine such schools in Virginia survived at least a part of the colonial period. All in all, they were not of great importance for they took root in only seven parishes; eighty-three parishes had none.[5] In the colonial South only the grammar school at the College of William and Mary consistently received public funds.

THE MIDDLE COLONIES

The southern colonies were not unique; contributions from public treasuries in the middle colonies—New York, Pennsylvania, Delaware, New Jersey—rarely were given. Even Philadelphia and New York, large cities in the eighteenth century by English standards, did not direct municipal revenues into education.

An energetic and self-conscious denominationalism supplied Philadelphia with schools. First on the scene, the Society of Friends established elementary schools and a single grammar school shortly after Pennsylvania was settled. William Penn gave his encouragement by bestowing a charter on the grammar school in 1701. The Friends apparently needed no official endorsement, and throughout the colonial period they gave the schools vigorous support through private subscriptions and legacies.[6]

Other religious groups as eager as the Friends to preserve their identity and to perpetuate themselves maintained schools in Philadelphia. An Anglican parish school was begun in 1698, and the Society for the Propagation of the Gospel supported a charity school for poor children for most of the period before the Revolution. The Lutheran church opened a classical school around the middle of the eighteenth century, and the Baptists followed with the same type in 1755; the Moravians—never a rich group—began an elementary school in 1745.[7]

Besides these efforts—and probably equally important—were the numerous private school masters of Philadelphia. The average private master displayed a variety of skills to Philadelphians. If his newspaper advertisements accurately stated his qualifications, he could teach everything from arithmetic to astronomy—including Latin and Greek, rhetoric, oratory, logic, navigation, surveying, bookkeeping, higher mathematics and natural science. His offerings were necessarily broad; he had to attract students since their tuition provided his sole means of support.[8]

New York, the other city of the middle colonies, could not match Philadelphia's denominational offerings. Still, its religious groups were important agencies of education. Under the Dutch in the first half of the seventeenth century, the Reformed Church maintained a school. After the English took over the colony in 1664, the church, in an attempt to hold its children to the old ways and to the old language, opened several more. Though English culture eventually washed out the results, these attempts helped preserve Dutch homogeneity for years. As in Philadelphia the Society for the Propagation of the Gospel also proved active, sponsoring charity schools for children of the poor.[9]

New York could also boast numerous private schools in the eighteenth century with masters, judging from the claims in the newspapers, no less talented than those of Philadelphia. But on the whole, education was neglected in New York. Perhaps the most auspicious development of the pre-Revolutionary period was the opening of a grammar school by the newly founded Kings College in 1762. The college and its school promised to renew interest in education beyond the elementary level.[10]

Small towns and villages in the middle colonies lagged badly in education. A few parish schools struggled along in several; private masters taught reading, writing, and arithmetic and occasionally vocational subjects like surveying; apprenticeship supplied most of the skilled crafts. If a boy desired advanced training in the languages or higher mathematics, he had to travel to New York or Philadelphia. By the late colonial period, apparently there were many boys who sought such instruction, for the city schools were filled with students from the country.

THE NEW ENGLAND AREA

This brief treatment of the southern and middle colonies suggest, perhaps, that a variety of agencies—each for its own purposes—promoted education. In New England a number of the same forces appeared: the Society for the Propagation of the Gospel sent out masters instructed to bring the dissenters back to the true faith; Baptists, Quakers and other religious groups strove to maintain schools purveying learning and their versions of Christianity; and in large towns and cities, private masters giving classical and vocational training flourished. Although this was in the familiar colonial pattern, New England, in education as in much else, departed from the familiar. The state made the difference by entering the field of education in Massachusetts, Connecticut, New Hampshire, and (before it merged with Massachusetts) in Plymouth.

New England was settled by Puritans who, unlike some of the radical sects they left behind in England, valued education. The Puritans came to the New World imbued with a sense of mission. They had left the Old World to complete the Protestant Reformation, to demonstrate that they held the true conception of church polity and religious doctrine. The success of their task depended in large measure, they were convinced, on an educated community. Hence they wished to erect a system of schools equal to the task.

They wasted no time in getting started. Six years after the Great Migration of the faithful began in 1630, the Massachusetts General Court set Harvard College on its distinguished road. Erecting and financing schools proved a difficult task (as did financing the college for that matter) and after a period in which private contributions were relied upon, the General Court of Massachusetts decided to compel towns to assume the burden.

Towns of at least 50 families, it decreed in 1647, must maintain a reading and writing master, and those of at least 100 families, a grammar master—as one who taught Latin and Greek was often called. Responsibility for enforcement of the law was placed with the county courts which were empowered to fine offending communities.[11]

With the exception of Rhode Island, the other New England colonies followed the Massachusetts example, though requirements and enforcement varied from one to another.

The statutes compelled local authorities to provide education; they did not force parents to send their children. Nor did the laws require communities to support their schools from taxes; finance was left entirely to the community's discretion.

Under the laws a pattern of control and finance appeared among New England villages. In its meeting—the most important institution of local government—the town handled the school in about the same way it did any public business. This was a fact of enormous importance, for, so located, the school could not avoid the impact of local politics and of public financial pressures.

Though the town meeting formulated school policy, it depended upon a committee (chosen in the meeting) or the selectmen (the most important officials chosen by the meeting) to carry it out. School committees and selectmen were usually the best men available—men who had education and political experience.

Committee functions varied little from town to town. Usually the committee hired the schoolmaster, found a place for the school to meet if a regular building was lacking, and handled the finances of the school. In most towns how the committee went about hiring a master was its own business, though it did have to satisfy the meeting. In Massachusetts a statute added another requirement: the local minister with one of his brethren, or any two neighboring ministers together, were supposed to approve the schoolmaster before he was hired. Though evidence is lacking, towns seem to have observed this statute. Only rarely did cases of noncompliance get into the county courts.[12]

SCHOOL EXPENSES

As local taxes on polls and property provided most of the money for ordinary expenses, so also they provided school expenses. Only in Connecticut could towns look to the provincial government for consistent financial help. Connecticut towns received an annual contribution out of provincial taxes, but few, if any, found this subsidy large enough to meet the expenses of their schools.

In every New England colony, there were towns which could rely on public lands for part of their school expenses. Donated by individuals, the colony, or set aside by the towns themselves, these lands could be rented or sold. Shrewdly invested, the income from such lands could often relieve the taxpayers of a large portion of school charges.

One other source of finance for schools existed—the parents of boys who attended. They could be assessed tuition for every child they sent to school and until the middle of the eighteenth century they occasionally were. In Watertown, Massachusetts, in 1700, for example, six pence a week was collected for each Latin scholar, four pence for a "writer," and three for a "reader." Few towns required tuition payments but many insisted that parents provide firewood in the winter. Parents also purchased paper, pens and schoolbooks for their children.

Town growth intensified financial problems and created new difficulties. As its once compact population increased and spread out, a village saw its single school become inadequate. Far from the original settlement, children could not attend the once centrally located school. Nothing, of course, prevented a town from providing a second more accessible school—nothing except money. To soften the clamor for education that arose from remote areas, many towns decided to uproot their schools and send them out on the road. The school might "go round with the Sun" as it did in Duxbury, Massachusetts, for many years, meeting successively in the four quarters of the town for three months at a time.

Putting the school on the move had the obvious disadvantage of spreading learning very thin. A boy who had attended the school for nine or ten months out of a year when it was located in one place might only be able to attend the moving school the three or four months that it was near his house. If he was determined he might follow the school as it traveled from one spot to the next. But this was such a difficult and expensive process that probably few boys did it.

If many towns sent their schools into outlying sections, an equal number divided themselves into districts and established a school in each. Usually citizens in each district elected a committee charged with responsibility for hiring a master and providing a place for the school to meet. The authority of the district, and its committee, rarely included more important matters. Towns continued to hold taxing powers and understandably enough were reluctant to share them. Every town allocated annually a portion of its revenues to districts on the basis of their populations. Such divisions were often contested by jealous districts, but on the whole the system worked well.

The success of the system left Rhode Islanders unimpressed, and their legislature steadfastly refused to establish educational standards for its towns. The results for the colony's intellectual life were obvious: in the seventeenth century only one Rhode Island boy attended college. In the next century more traveled to Harvard and Yale but no college took shape in Rhode Island itself until just before the Revolution.[13]

Yet there were publicly supported schools in Rhode Island, even a few which offered instruction in Latin and Greek. But most of these schools were in towns which had been transferred from Massachusetts to Rhode Island on the settlement of a boundary dispute in 1747. Thoroughly imbued with the educational tradition of Massachusetts, they probably never considered dropping their schools in removal from the Bay Colony's jurisdiction.

For the most part, Rhode Islanders relied upon private sources for the support of schools. Often this means failed them; and their schools, compared to those of the neighboring colonies, enjoyed a precarious existence.

Rhode Island's educational history obviously parallels much of that of the southern and middle colonies, where no public commitment to education existed and no private source of support was ever entirely reliable. In no colony did one group monopolize education. Rather, variety in support, in sponsors, in state participation, and in the forms institutions assumed characterized colonial education. Inevitably educational development followed an uneven course.

It did because it was an expression of a colonial society, which was altering at an uneven pace. Education itself, of course, was a force in this process of change. As it helped shape colonial society, so also was it shaped. What emerged by the end of the colonial period was a peculiar blend of public and private, classical and vocational, religious and secular. Modern "public education" had not yet been conceived.

References

1. Bernard Bailyn, *Education in the Forming of American Society* (Chapel Hill, 1960), pp. 15–16.
2. E. S. Morgan, *The Puritan Family* (Boston, 1956), pp. 37–38; and *Virginians at Home* (Williamsburg, 1952), p. 23.
3. Morgan, *Virginians at Home*, pp. 8–32.
4. G. F. Wells, *Parish Education in Colonial Virginia* (New York, 1923), pp. 32–39.
5. Ibid., p. 48.
6. Carl Bridenbaugh, *Cities in the Wilderness* (New York, 1955), pp. 123–24, 283; and *Cities in Revolt* (New York, 1955), p. 174.
7. Ibid., p. 284; *Cities in Revolt*, p. 174.
8. Bridenbaugh, *Cities in the Wilderness*, pp. 447–48.
9. Ibid., pp. 123–26, 287.
10. Ibid., p. 287; *Cities in Revolt*, p. 174.
11. S. E. Morison, *The Intellectual Life of Colonial New England* (New York, 1956), pp. 65–78.
12. This paragraph is based on an examination of manuscript court and town records.
13. Morison, *Intellectual Life*, p. 70.

44

Suggestions Respecting Improvements in Education

Catherine E. Beecher

It is to *mothers,* and to *teachers,* that the world is to look for the character which is to be enstamped on each succeeding generation, for it is to them that the great business of education is almost exclusively committed. And will it not appear by examination that neither mothers nor teachers have ever been properly educated for their profession. What is *the profession of a Woman*? Is it not to form immortal minds, and to watch, to nurse, and to rear the bodily system, so fearfully and wonderfully made, and upon the order and regulation of which, the health and well-being of the mind so greatly depends?

But let most of our sex upon whom these arduous duties devolve, be asked; have you ever devoted any time and study, in the course of your education, to any preparation for these duties? Have you been taught any thing of the structure, the nature, and the laws of the body, which you inhabit? Were you ever taught to understand the operation of diet, air, exercise and modes of dress upon the human frame? Have the causes which are continually operating to prevent good health, and the modes by which it might be perfected and preserved ever been made the subject of any *instruction*? Perhaps almost every voice would respond, no; we have attended to almost every thing more than to this; we have been taught more concerning the structure of the earth; the laws of the heavenly bodies; the habits and formation of plants; the philosophy of language; more of *almost any thing,* than the structure of the human frame and the laws of health and reason. But is it not the business, the *profession* of a woman to guard the health and form the physical habits of the young? And is not the cradle of infancy and the chamber of sickness sacred to woman alone? And ought she not to know at least some of the *general principles* of that perfect and wonderful piece of mechanism committed to her preservation and care?

The *restoration* of health is the physician's profession, but the *preservation* of it falls to other hands, and it is believed that the time will come, when woman will be taught to understand something respecting the construction of the human frame, the philosophical results which will naturally follow from restricted exercise, unhealthy modes of dress, improper diet, and many other causes, which are continually operating to destroy the health and life of the young.

Again let our sex be asked respecting the instruction they have received in the course of their education, on that still more arduous and difficult department of their profession, which relates to the *intellect* and the *moral susceptibilities.* Have you been taught the powers and faculties of the human mind, and the laws by which it is regulated? Have you studied how to direct its several faculties; how to restore those that are overgrown, and strengthen and mature those that are deficient? Have you been taught the best modes of *communicating* knowledge as well as of *acquiring* it? Have you learned the best mode of correcting bad *moral* habits and forming good ones? Have you made it an object to find how a selfish disposition may be made generous; how a reserved temper may be made open and frank; how pettishness and ill humor may be changed to cheerfulness and kindness? Has any woman studied her profession in this respect? It is feared the same answer must be returned, if not from all, at least from most of our sex. No; we have acquired wisdom from the observation and experience of others, on almost *all other* subjects, but the philosophy of the direction and control of the human mind has not been an object of thought or study. And thus it appears that tho' it is woman's *express business* to rear the body, and form the mind, there is scarcely anything to which her attention has been less directed. . . .

If all females were not only well educated themselves, but were prepared to communicate in an easy manner their stores of knowledge to others; if they not only knew how to regulate their own minds, tempers and habits, but how to effect improvements in those around them, the face of society would speedily be changed. The time *may* come when the world will look back with wonder to behold how much time and effort have been given to the mere cultivation of the memory, and how little mankind have been aware of what every teacher, parent, and friend could accomplish in forming the social, intellectual and moral character of those by whom they are surrounded.

Source: From Catherine E. Beecher, *Suggestions Respecting Improvements in Education,* pp. 7–9, 16. Hartford: Packard & Butler, 1829.

45

Negro Education Not a Failure

Booker T. Washington

Several persons holding high official position have said recently that it does not pay, from any point of view, to educate the Negro; and that all attempts at his education have so far failed to accomplish any good results. The Southern States, which out of their poverty are contributing rather liberally for the education of all the people, as does individual and organised philanthropy throughout the country, have a right to know whether the Negro is responding to the efforts they have made to place him upon a higher plane of civilisation.

Will it pay to invest further money in this direction? In seeking to answer this question, it is hardly fair to compare the progress of the American Negro with that of the American white man, who, in some unexplained way, got thousands of years ahead of the Negro in the arts and sciences of civilisation. But to get at the real facts and the real capability of the black man, compare for a moment the American Negro with the Negro in Africa, or the black man with the black man. In South Africa alone there are five million black people who have never been brought, through school or other agencies, into contact with a higher civilisation in a way to have their minds or their ambitions strengthened or awakened. As a result, the industries of South Africa languish and refuse to prosper for lack of labour. The native black man refused to labour because he has been neglected. He has few wants and little ambition, and these can be satisfied by labouring one or two days out of the seven. In the southern part of the United States there are more than eight millions of my race who, both by contact with the whites and by education in the home, in school, in church, have had their minds awakened and strengthened—have thus had their wants increased and multiplied many times. Hence, instead of a people in idleness, we have in the South a people who are anxious to work because they want education for their children; they want land and houses, and churches, books, and papers. In a word, they want the highest and best in our civilisation. Looked at, then, from the most material and selfish point of view, it has paid to awaken the Negro's mind, and there should be no limit placed upon the development of that mind.

Does the American Negro take advantage of opportunities to secure education? Practically no schoolhouse has been opened for the Negro since the war that has not been filled. Often hungry and in rags, making heroic sacrifices, the Negro youth has been determined to annihilate his mental darkness. With all his disadvantages, the Negro, according to official records, has blotted out 55.5 per cent of his illiteracy since he became a free man, while practically 95 per cent of the native Africans are illiterate. After years of civilization and opportunity, in Spain, 68 per cent of the population are illiterate; in Italy, 38 per cent. In the average South American country about 80 per cent are illiterate, while after forty years the American Negro has only 44.5 per cent of illiteracy to his debit. I have thus compared the progress of my race, not with the highest civilised nations, for the reason that, in passing judgment upon us, the world too often forgets that, either consciously or otherwise, because of geographical or physical proximity to the American white man, we are being compared with the very highest civilisation that exists. But when compared with the most advanced and enlightened white people of the South, we find 12 per cent of illiteracy for them and only 44 per cent for our race . . . .

Years ago some one asked an eminent clergyman in Boston if Christianity is a failure. The Reverend doctor replied that it had never been tried. When people are bold enough to suggest that the education of the Negro is a failure, I reply that it has never been tried. The fact is that 44.5 per cent of the coloured people of this country today are illiterate. A very large proportion of those classed as educated have the merest smattering of knowledge, which means practically no education. Can the Negro child get an education in school four months and out of school eight months? Can the white child of the South who receives $4.92 per capita for education, or the black child who receives $2.21, be said to be given an equal chance in the battle of life, or has education been tried on them? The official records in Louisiana, for instance, show that less than one-fourth of the Negro children of school age attend any school during the year. This one-fourth was in school for a period of less than five months, and each Negro child of school age in the State had spent on him for education last year but $1.89, while each child of school age in the State of New York had spent on him $20.53. In the former slave States ninety per cent of the Negro children of school age did not attend school for six months during the year 1900.

Wherever the race is given an opportunity for education, it takes advantage of that opportunity, and the change can be seen in the improved material, educational, moral and religious condition of the masses. Contrast two townships, one in Louisiana, where the race has had little chance, with one in Farmville, Virginia, by means of the United States Bulletin of the Department of Labour. In the Louisiana township only 10 per cent attend school, and they attend for but four months in a year, and 71 per cent of the people are illiterate. And as a result of this ignorance and neglect, we find that only 50

Source: From Booker T. Washington, "Negro Education Not a Failure," *Working with the Hands*, pp. 231–233, 242–246. New York: Doubleday, Page & Co., 1904.

per cent of the people living together as man and wife are legally married. Largely through the leadership of Hampton graduates, 56 per cent of the black children in Farmville, Virginia, attend either public or private school from six to eight months. There is only 39 per cent of illiteracy. Practically all the people living together as man and wife are legally married, and in the whole community only 15 per cent of the births are illegitimate.

But the vital point which I want to emphasise is the disposition of the Negro to exercise self-help in the building up of his own schools in connection with the State public school system. Wherever we send out from Tuskegee, or any of our Southern colleges, a Negro leader of proper character, he shows the people in most cases how to extend the school term beyond the few months provided for by the State. Out of their poverty the Southern States are making a tremendous effort to extend and improve the school term each year, but while this improvement is taking place, the Negro leaders of the character to which I have referred must be depended upon largely to keep alive the spark of education.

It now seems settled that the great body of our people are to reside for all time in the Southern portion of the United States. Since this is true, there is no more helpful and patriotic service than to help cement a friendship between the two races that shall be manly, honourable, and permanent. In this work of moulding and guiding a public sentiment that shall forever maintain peace and good-will between the races on terms commendable to each, it is on the Negro who comes out of our universities, colleges, and industrial schools that we must largely depend. Few people realise how, under the most difficult and trying circumstances, during the last forty years, it has been the educated Negro who counselled patience and self-control and thus averted a war of races. Every Negro going out from our institutions properly educated becomes a link in the chain that shall forever bind the two races together in all the essentials of life.

Finally, reduced to its last analysis, there are but two questions that constitute the problem of this country so far as the black and white races are concerned. The answer to the one rests with my people, the other with the white race. For my race, one of its dangers is that it may grow impatient and feel that it can get upon its feet by artificial and superficial efforts rather than by the slower but surer process which means one step at a time through all the constructive grades of industrial, mental, moral, and social development which all races have had to follow that have become independent and strong. I would counsel: We must be sure that we shall make our greatest progress by keeping our feet on the earth, and by remembering that an inch of progress is worth a yard of complaint. For the white race, the danger is that in its prosperity and power it may forget the claims of a weaker people; may forget that a strong race, like an individual, should put its hand upon its heart and ask, if it were placed in similar circumstances, how it would like the world to treat it; that the stronger race may forget that, in proportion as it lifts up the poorest and weakest, even by a hair's breadth, it strengthens and ennobles itself.

All the Negro race asks is that the door which rewards industry, thrift, intelligence, and character be left as wide open for him as for the foreigner who constantly comes to our country. More than this, he has no right to request. Less than this, a Republic has no right to vouchsafe.

46

Education's Evolving Role

Wendell Pierce

Since Colonial days, three evolving forces in American life have been influenced, shaped, and in some instances determined by that process of transmitting knowledge, skills, and values known as education.

The first of these has been political, expressed primarily in the creation and preservation of new forms of governance.

The second has been economic, reflected in the Nation's steady growth and its transformation from a primarily agrarian to a predominantly industrial-technological economy.

The third force has been social, initially the blending of disparate elements into a more unified whole and more recently a striving to provide equal opportunities for all.

Woven throughout these three forces, an integral part of each, has been an idealistic and inspirational human quality epitomized by a passion for change, improvement, reform, and renewal.

The indispensable condition, the *sine qua non* of the American experience, has been the first of these forces—the political. Although important economic factors also were involved, it was basically certain deep philosophical and pragmatic differences between England and the American Colonies over the form and function of government that led to the upheaval of the American Revolution and the subsequent creation of an entirely new and unusually dynamic political structure. Similarly, from the beginning of American history, government has been the central force in developing an educational system, and education and politics have been inextricably linked. In the Middle and Southern Colonies, the establishment of education came about when the governing bodies gave permission to various religious groups to establish schools or granted educational charters to businessmen or landowners. In the New England Colonies, the governing bodies used the authority they had received from the crown and parliament themselves to establish, support and administer schools and colleges. Thus colonists setting out to found a new town in Massachusetts were required to reserve one building lot for the support of education.

It is interesting to note that the legislature of the Massachusetts Bay Colony chartered the first college in Colonial America in 1636 (Harvard), that three years later the first pubic school supported by direct taxation was established, and that three years after that the first locally elected school board was formed. Thus, more than 100 years before the American Revolution, were created the basic models for the governance of American education. Two principles had emerged: educational institutions derive their authority to operate from government sanction, and local schools should have some degree of local control. The broad application of those principles, however, was to come about only with the gradual evolution of the Nation itself.

While the Declaration of Independence in 1776 provided a stirring intellectual rationale for what was yet to be, it was the Constitutional Convention 11 years later that produced the cornerstone upon which a nation could be built. When the Founding Fathers met in Philadelphia during that hot summer of 1787 to design a new form of government, schools and colleges were but two of many educational institutions. The family, the farm, the shop, and the churches were of equal if not greater importance.

Few conceived that the aim of formal education should be to give all children an opportunity to develop to their full potential. Common schools for youngsters of differing religions and backgrounds were rare, and the children of the poor usually received no schooling at all. When the Constitution went into effect in 1789, American education served for the most part to maintain the kind of class distinctions characteristic of Europe at that time. Formal educational endeavors were not considered of sufficient national bearing to warrant inclusion among the basic laws establishing the new Federal republic. Instead, education was one of the responsibilities reserved, under the Bill of Rights, to the individual former Colonies that collectively had become the United States of America. Events were in fact to render education the single most important prerogative of the Colonial legislatures that evolved into the governing bodies of the Quasi-independent States of the new Federal union.

Very soon after ratification of the Constitution it became apparent that the new form of government required a new view of education. A government of the people, deriving its powers from the consent of the governed, required an educated populace. President George Washington recognized this proposition in his Farewell Address. "It is essential that public opinion should be enlightened," he said on that occasion, and he went on to urge the people to promote "institutions for the general diffusion of knowledge." Similarly, Thomas Jefferson, the author of the Declaration of Independence, said that "any nation that expects to be ignorant and free . . . expects what never was and never will be"; and James Madison, a prime mover in the development of the Constitution and the Bill of Rights, declared that "knowledge will forever govern ignorance; and a people who mean to be their own governors must arm themselves with the power which knowledge gives."

Source: From Wendell Pierce, "Education's Evolving Role," *American Education,* May 1975, pp. 16–29.

In any case, under the newly developed Federal system of "shared power," responsibility for providing the means by which the people could arm themselves for popular government was retained by the several States. The States thereby found themselves held accountable for the success or failure of popular government itself, both within their own borders and throughout the young republic. Their deliberate but successful response to this challenge was to become the signal feature of American federalism.

By 1827—38 years after the founding of the new Republic—all of the original 13 States and all but two of the 11 that had since joined the union had made some provision for public or popular education, either through their State constitutions or by legislation. The Indiana constitution of 1816, for example, stated: "Knowledge and learning generally diffused through a community being essential to the preservation of a free government, . . . it shall be the duty of the general assembly . . . to provide by law for a system of education, ascending in regular gradation from township schools to a State university, wherein tuition shall be gratis, and equally open to all."

Thus was developed during the early and middle years of the 19th century the structure and substance of a completely new kind of school system, created and sustained by State governments. Given the latter circumstance, it was natural that the impetus, both philosophical and practical, should come not from professional educators but from persons active in the political arena. It was the politicians who took the lead in institutionalizing the educational component essential to the success of the new Constitution. The philosophical foundations had been provided earlier by such national statesmen as Thomas Jefferson, James Madison, and Benjamin Franklin. The practical process of implementation was led by State legislators, notably Henry Barnard of Connecticut and Horace Mann of Massachusetts.

Jefferson and Madison, although agreeing on the need for some kind of basic education for all, were from a classical tradition that considered Latin and Greek as the cornerstones of Western civilization. It was Franklin who provided the motivating principles for a more utilitarian approach. In his "Proposals Relating to the Education of Youth in Pennsylvania," he recommended three innovations: First, emphasis on English and modern languages; second, emphasis on mathematics and science; and third, emphasis on experimentation and practical application. ("While they are reading natural history," Franklin wrote, "might not a little gardening, grafting, modulating, etc., be taught and practiced; and now and then excursions made to the neighboring plantations of the best farmers, their methods observed and reasoned upon for the information of youth?")

Whatever their differences of approach, however, Jefferson, Madison, and Franklin were agreed on the critical importance of an educated populace. And so, spurred by the principles enunciated by such revered leaders as these, the State legislatures set out to fulfill their education responsibilities. The Virginia Legislature, for example, finally enacted in 1796 a bill "for the More General Diffusion of Knowledge" that Jefferson had introduced in 1779, although amendments giving great power to local communities served to block effective implementation until the passage of new legislation in 1829. In 1812, the New York Legislature created the first statewide public school organization in the young Nation, providing a State Department of Public Instruction headed by a State Superintendent of Schools. In the 1830s and 40s, two New England legislators—Henry Barnard and Horace Mann—played prominent roles in a sweeping reform movement that was to spread, State-by-State, across the Nation. Out of that movement came a concept of education that was not only to serve the overall needs of the society but to respond to such special circumstances as the onset of massive waves of immigrants and a shift from an agrarian to an industrial economy.

In 1837, Mann gave up the presidency of the Massachusetts Senate to become the first secretary of a new State board of education. As a 26-year-old member of the Connecticut Assembly, Barnard introduced "An Act for the Better Supervision of Common Schools," and upon its passage in 1838 he followed Mann's example and became the State's first Commissioner of Education. These two politicians-turned-educators personified the drive toward a uniquely American form of education—the character, financing, and control of which was to prove as revolutionary in its way as the Constitution it was created to preserve.

To support that Constitution by ensuring an educated electorate, the State legislatures were confronted by issues that remain familiar today: religion, finance, and governance. The adroit though usually slow and sometimes painful manner in which these issues were resolved during the first half of the 19th century largely determined education's role in the Republic's subsequent development.

Although silent as regards education the Federal Constitution did provide guidance on the religion issue. One of many experimental elements in that experimental document linked freedom of religion to the principle of separation of church and state. Neither the Federal nor state governments could interfere in religious affairs or provide public funds to support churches or church-related activities. Proponents of a universal system of public elementary schools took this thesis a step further by arguing that nonsectarianism would promote a greater sense of national unity, an important consideration in education for citizenship in a republic. While disputes over various forms of public aid to church-related education and over the role of religion in the school program and curriculum continue today, the original principle remains: Schools controlled by churches may not be supported by public funds. This proposition has not been taken as relieving the schools of all responsibility for imparting to their pupils some sense of ethics and morality. Rather, such instruction has increasingly become more generalized, oriented toward standards and aspirations of the society as a whole rather than to the tenets of a particular sect.

If schools were to be nonsectarian, how were they to be supported? Obviously, schools created by religious groups and financially dependent upon donations and the payment of tuition—as most were in Colonial America and during the early years of the Republic—were inherently exclusive and specifically unfair to the children of the poor. One step toward ameliorating this situation was the development of "free schools" where the children of what we now term low-income parents were supported by public funds and all others paid tuition. Advocates of equality argued that such an arrangement continued and in fact fostered class distinctions, and that these distinctions could be reduced only by financing the education of *all* children, regardless of parental means, through public funds raised through public taxation. Free public education limited to the children of poverty, they insisted, was simply an elitist extension of charity and in any event a divisive force in what was supposed to be a free and equitable society. If Jefferson and Franklin and Madison had been correct in holding education to be essential in maintaining the Republic, they reasoned, schooling should be free to all and supported through public taxation. Even those taxpayers who had no children in the schools would benefit from the existence of an educated electorate. Some of the warmest and in any case most decisive advocates of these principles were to be found among the elected officials of the States, and by one State legislature after another the concept of free public education was spelled out in the State constitutions.

As for how the necessary money was to be raised, the early public schools were variously supported by liquor and amusement taxes, land grants, special taxes on parents of students, lotteries, and—stemming from a Massachusetts law of 1647—what became the characteristic method of support, the property tax. The latter was particularly pushed by school districts established in some of the bigger cities under State legislation enacted even before the States themselves began to support education. Moreover, when the States did begin to share the cost, local property taxes continued to be the chief source of school funds, as indeed they are today, amidst much controversy. Among the major elements of this controversy are first, the feeling that local tax rates have been pushed just about to the limit, and second, that wide variances in the wealth of local jurisdictions seriously undermine the principle of equal education opportunity. The school finance issue is, in short, thorny and complex, and as with so many other basic questions in education, political decision-making would appear to be central to its resolution.

In any case, the pattern having been set that the schools would be nonsectarian and publicly supported, the question remained of how they were to be governed. Obviously, if public education were left entirely to the pleasures of local communities, its scope and quality would vary enormously, as in fact was the case in the early years. Thus there evolved the concept of local control under State mandate, with the States, through their constitutions and by legislation, establishing minimum standards and requirements for public schooling. State school superintendents and State boards of education, elected by the people or appointed by the governor, were held responsible for monitoring those standards and requirements. Meanwhile, the day-to-day operation and management of local schools was left to locally appointed teachers, locally selected superintendents, and locally elected school boards. Usually the latter were made independent of other local officials or agencies—kept immune, as agents of the State, from the routine of local politics.

This uniquely American method of shared power in local-State school governance made it possible for American education to be responsive both to specific local needs and, through the broad State mandate, to the greater needs of the larger society. To make sure those needs were met, the States ultimately enacted laws requiring all communities to establish and maintain public schools. And then, led by Massachusetts in 1852, they enacted compulsory school attendance laws. And so by the middle of the 19th century the States had by and large fulfilled the need to provide enough education for enough people to be reasonably certain that there existed a reasonably well-educated electorate—though to be sure, members of racial minorities, females, and the handicapped continued to receive short shrift.

Throughout, the primary motivating force and rationale for education had been education for citizenship. As Horace Mann wrote on his tenth annual report as secretary of the Massachusetts Board of Education: "Since the achievement of American independence, the universal and ever-repeated argument in favor of free schools has been that the general intelligence which they are capable of diffusing, and which can be imparted by no other human instrumentality, is indispensable to the continuance of a republican government."

Then in the middle of the 19th century, certain social and economic forces came to the fore to compel the educational system to expand its base and broaden its horizons, first in secondary schools and later in the colleges and universities. One of the most dramatic of these forces was an industrial revolution that shifted the American economy from an agricultural to an industrial base and displayed an almost insatiable appetite for the Nation's human, physical, and financial resources. Of the three, the human proved the most essential. A small, experimental democracy with a limited population composed primarily of farmers and traders had needed to provide the majority of its citizens with only enough education to enable them to read the Scriptures. Now the demand was for trained people ready to run the factories, build the railroads, staff the businesses, start up the new industries, and handle the financial affairs of an expanding and increasingly complex economy. Meanwhile the Nation itself was expanding, both in geographic size and in population. Schooling no longer was simply a democratic ideal but a practical necessity.

And so, during the latter half of the 19th century, public education increasingly included the availability of free, public high schools in addition to the "common" schools mandated earlier by State law. In the 1870s a number of court cases, particularly the *Kalamazoo* decision of the U.S. Supreme Court, established the principle that the use of tax funds for educational purposes need not be limited to the elementary level. Thus the concept of secondary and postsecondary education as a tuition-paying proposition necessarily reserved to only a few gave way to the goal of providing and even requiring as much education as possible for all. State after State adopted compulsory school attendance laws covering youngsters to at least age 14 or 16.

The enrollment statistics tell the story of what happened thereafter. In 1900, some 70 percent of all children aged six to 13 were in elementary schools, while about ten percent of those 14–17 years of age were attending secondary schools. By 1930, nearly 85 percent of elementary school-age children were enrolled, and the figure for high school-age youngsters had climbed to 50 percent. The current figures are almost 100 percent of all children aged 6–13 and more than 90 percent of those aged 14–17. Even more remarkable has been the growth of enrollment rates in postsecondary education. In 1900, less than five percent of all youth ages 18–21 were attending colleges or universities. By 1930, this proportion had grown to 20 percent. Today it exceeds 50 percent.

This record contribution to the Nation's welfare is no better illustrated than by its economic impact, both on the individual and in the aggregate. Most easily measured is the financial benefit of education to the individual. As analyses by the U.S. Census Bureau show, the more education people have the higher their lifetime earnings are likely to be. For example, the lifetime worth of a 22-year-old male shows the following average variance according to different educational backgrounds: Less than eight years of schooling—$159,000; elementary school graduate—$192,000; one to three years of high school—$216,000; high school graduate—$264,000; one to three years of college—$301,000; college graduate—$388,000; five years or more of college—$443,000. Obviously, one of education's primary contributions has been to provide a greater number of individuals with greater personal income and employment security.

Nor is such private return the only justification for public support of education endeavors that now directly involve nearly 30 percent of the population and consume more than $100 billion annually—almost eight percent of the Gross National Product. As the individual benefits, so does the Nation as a whole. Higher personal incomes provide a direct benefit to local, State, and Federal governments in the form of larger tax returns. Communities in which the median income is high enjoy higher average per capita retail sales. And, harking back to that early American ideal, statistics indicate that the more education a person has, the greater that person's interest in political affairs. The percent of those casting ballots in Presidential elections, for example, increases in direct proportion to the level of education attained.

Beyond these matters, a number of economists in recent years have concluded that education is a far more vital factor in stimulating economic growth than previously had been recognized. Traditionally it had been held that while education produces and reproduces a body of skilled manpower, it had little to do with increased productivity as such. Physical capita and natural resources—these, it was maintained, are the keys to economic development. Economists today respond that such a position ignores the force of human capital—that education not only provides trained workers but carries with it the potential for creating and developing new goods, new technologies, new services. No other kind of capital, they say, combines all these features. Thus a number of economists now believe that the growth in real per capita income in the United States since 1930 has been due far more to advances in knowledge and education than to private capital investments. Moreover, their projections for the future indicate that this effect will be even more powerful in the future.

In any case, it is self-evident that nations with high education attainment levels tend to have higher per capita incomes, regardless of the level of their natural resources, than nations with high levels of natural resources and low education attainment levels. Switzerland and Denmark, with few natural resources, are cases in point. So are Colombia and Brazil, which have high levels of natural resources but low education attainment levels and low per capita incomes. The United States, with high levels of both natural resources and education attainment, has the highest per capita income in the world. The American labor force possesses more educational capital per person than that of any other country, and the result is to be seen in the Nation's extraordinary economic development.

But the Nation's schools and colleges have been expected to make further contributions—to provide more than education for citizenship and education for economic growth. From the beginning they have also been called up to fulfill a variety of social as well as political and economic functions. It was the schools, more than any other institution in American society, that provided the cohesion necessary for the creation of a sense of national unity. It was the schools that bore the prime responsibility for "Americanizing" the millions upon millions of immigrants that poured into the Nation from the middle of the 19th century through the second decade of the 20th. And it has been the schools and colleges of the country that have been in the forefront of more contemporary efforts to provide equal opportunities for those who once had been systematically excluded—women, blacks and other minorities, the mentally or physically handicapped.

Americans have deliberately used their schools and colleges as agents of social change. They have asked more of their education institutions than any people in history. In so doing they have exhibited what has been termed a "consistent, often intense, and sometimes touching faith in the efficacy of popular education." Paradoxically, education is considered so essential a part of the national experience that it frequently leads the list of scapegoats when the Nation suffers a reversal. When the Soviet Union was the first to orbit a man-made satellite, it was American education that was held to have failed. The more furious the debate over desegregation, the more visibly the schools have occupied the center of the storm. Criticism of education is something of a national sport.

Some of this criticism is justified, though it should be noted that there has always been a gap between expectation and performance. In any case, it is apparent that elaborate administrative bureaucracies, deemed essential to the management of mass education enterprises, frequently have proven to be barriers to social and economic mobility. More crucially, significant numbers of young people are not benefiting appropriately from their school experience, for reasons unrelated to native intelligence. According to the National Assessment of Educational Progress, the achievement of young Americans who are poor or black, who live in the inner city or in rural communities or in the Southeast, lags behind national levels in a number of subjects.

And yet, as historian Henry Steele Commager has noted, "No other people ever demanded so much of education . . . . None other was ever served so well by its schools and educators."

There is a story that when an aging Benjamin Franklin was leaving one of the final sessions of the Constitutional Convention, a woman asked what kind of government the fledgling nation was to have. Franklin replied, "A republic, madam. If you can keep it." Thanks in no small part to the role of education, we've kept it.

47

Historical Notes on the Growth of the Women's Movement

Report of the National Commission on the Observance of International Women's Year

Early in 1776, as patriots were demanding a Declaration of Independence, Abigail Adams wrote her husband John:

> . . . in the new Code of laws . . . I desire you would Remember the Ladies, and be more generous and favourable to them than your ancestors. Do not put such unlimited power into the hands of the Husbands. Remember all Men would be tyrants if they could. If particuliar care and attention is not paid to the Ladies we are determined to foment a Rebellion, and will not hold ourselves bound by any Laws in which we have no voice, or Representation.
>
> That your Sex are Naturally Tyrannical is a Truth so thoroughly established as to admit of no dispute, but such of you as wish to be happy willingly give up the harsh title of Master for the more tender and endearing one of Friend. Why then, not put it out of the power of the vicious and the Lawless to use us with cruelty and indignity with impunity. Men of Sense in all Ages abhor those customs which treat us only as the vassals of your Sex. Regard us then as Beings . . .

John's bantering reply called his wife "saucy." "Depend upon it," he wrote her, "we know better than to repeal our Masculine systems."

Abigail Adams' letter spoke for those colonial women who wove cloth, preserved food, farmed, butchered, and often worked side by side with their husbands in trade. Even though these women were subordinate, they were highly valued for skills they performed in the labor-short economy. By contrast, a wellborn woman's worth was measured by the prestige she could bring her husband through her birth and family connections.

The Revolution and, a few decades later, Jacksonian democracy unleashed ideas that gave ordinary people a new view of their own potential. Small shops expanded into great stores; industry grew; the manufacture of cloth moved out of the home. Men moved from a home-oriented, stable culture into an expanding world of educational, business, and financial opportunity.

Women, on the other hand, found their spheres had narrowed; they were now less important to men. Their sense of self-worth suffered. Shut out of the larger world, many began to find that the qualities that counted most were piety, purity, submissiveness, and domesticity.

A few women found expression for their non-conformist intellectual drives in the reform movements which were surging through the churches. They became this nation's crusaders in missionary work; education societies; and the movement for antislavery, temperance, and eventually women's rights.

The Seneca Falls convention of 1848, the first women's rights meeting in America, drew more than 250 women and about 40 men, who arrived in buggies and wagons drawn by farm horses. They met for 2 days and demanded opportunities for women in education; trade; commerce; the professions; and rights in property, free speech, and the guardianship of their children. After much controversy, they took the daring step and asked for suffrage.

But many setbacks marked the struggled that followed. In particular women's hopes were dashed when the 14th amendment extended the right to vote only to all *male* citizens.[1] Two years later, in 1870, black males achieved suffrage through the 15th amendment. But it took 50 more long years before all women won the right to vote.

Some historians say that feminism died after the woman's suffrage amendment (the 19th) was passed in 1920. Actually there were new forces at work which were reordering and extending women's interests in relation to socioeconomic events.

Prime among them were the women's organizations, some of which had their beginning in the 19th century.

In 1882 a group of women who had obtained college degrees despite great obstacles came together to see how they could make education useful. Their first study was of women's health and physical education. They sought to counter the attitude that young women could not undergo the intellectual strain of schooling without damaging their health. This group later became the American Association of University Women.

Churchwomen founded the Young Woman's Christian Association out of concern for the plight of women flocking to eastern city factory jobs where they endured sweatshop conditions.

The General Federation of Women's Clubs, formed in 1890, was the outgrowth of the Sorosis Club organized 21 years earlier by a newspaper woman, Mrs. Jane C. Crolly, because the all-male New York Press Club would not admit her to a dinner honoring Charles Dickens.

Source: From Report of the National Commission on the Observance of International Women's Year, "Historical Notes on the Growth of the Women's Movement," *Justice for American Women*, 1987, pp. 3–9. Washington, D.C.: U.S. Government Printing Office.

Early 20th century organizations also laid much of the groundwork for the women's movement of the 1960's. The National Women's Party, founded in 1913 to advance the suffrage movement, also spearheaded the introduction of the first Equal Rights Amendment in Congress in 1923.

In 1920, The League of Women Voters was formed by former suffrage workers to educate the new women electorate.

The National Federation of Business and Professional Women's Clubs, one of the strongest forces behind the drive for ERA ratification today, was formed in 1919. Its roots go back to World War I when the U.S. War Department organized a Woman's War Council to mobilize business and professional women to support the war effort.

All of these groups gained strength and status throughout the twenties and thirties when millions of American women came together in weekly or monthly meetings to discuss civic, business, cultural, and personal problems and their solutions. While those meetings were nothing like the consciousness-raising sessions of the sixties, these organizations built a broadbased constituency and leadership for later action.

At the same time, many American women were applying the feminist momentum to their private lives.

The family sociologist Alice S. Rossi describes the thirties as a time when "women earned the highest proportion of advanced degrees in the history of American higher education. So too, the proportion of women in the labor force continued to climb dramatically throughout the 1940's and 1950's. . . . Strong-minded descendants of the suffragists between 1920 and 1960 were pouring much of their energy into education and employment, and if they were married they did double duty at work and at home, such a profile leaves little time and energy for political involvement."[2]

Women went into the labor market as never before during World War II. When the war was over, however, Rosie the Riveter was urged to go home. Many Rosies did. Women's focus was once again on homemaking and babies.

Eleanor Roosevelt, who had been speaking to readers in a daily newspaper column ever since 1935, became an inspiration and role model to thousands of women.

Other elements entered the American scene. Black Americans were protesting their second-class citizenship. Women, who had long recognized the parallel between injustice to blacks and injustice to women, were encouraged by the success of the civil rights movement.

Advances in contraceptive technology gave women a chance to space their children. Better family planning resulted in better health and allowed women to participate more fully in public life.

Women were beginning to recognize that full-time homemaking was not the best of all possible worlds for everyone, especially after children went off to school. And women alone—divorced, widowed, or separated—found it hard to support themselves in society where businesses, industries, and universities often did not regard women as full partners.

Authors such as Margaret Mead, Virginia Woolf, Simone de Beauvoir, Jessie Bernard, and others began to examine the conflicts and injustices. Betty Friedan's *Feminine Mystique* captured a popular audience. And the drive for self-fulfillment and equal justice was launched with new vigor.

In 1963 the President's Commission on the Status of Women, which had been chaired by Eleanor Roosevelt until her death in 1962, documented many inequalities, especially in education, employment, legal status, and politics.[3]

The demand for justice grew. New and powerful women's rights groups were formed, and the older, established women's organizations renewed their interest in the movement for equality. Among the powerful new women's groups were the National Organization for Women, the Women's Equity Action League, the National Women's Political Caucus, and the National Association of Commissions for Women.

Under pressure from women's groups, Congress enacted a series of laws beneficial to women. Among them were the Equal Pay Act. Title VII of the Civil Rights Act of 1964, passage of the Equal Rights Amendment and subsequent submittal to the States for ratification, and Title IX of the Education Amendment of 1972 banning sex discrimination in education.

Status of Women Commissions were established by practically all governors, and the Federal Interdepartmental Committee and Citizens Advisory Council on the Status of Women provided leadership and held conferences of the State Commissions.

The Federal Government began expanding its antidiscrimination orders involving Federal contracts, so that women were included. In one landmark case, American Telephone and Telegraph Company (AT&T) agreed in 1973 to provide goals and timetables for increased utilization of women and racial/ethnic minorities. The agreement reached by AT&T, the Equal Employment Opportunity Commission, the Labor Department, and the Justice Department awarded $15 million in back pay to some 15,000 employees.

Meanwhile, the momentum continued on a worldwide basis and culminated with a U.N. conference in Mexico.

The World Conference held in Mexico City in the summer of 1975 drew 1,300 delegates from 130 countries and 7,000 persons, mostly women who came at their own expense, to the unofficial Tribune. Both of these bodies got mixed reviews. There was inadequate funding and a lack of serious commitment from the governments of member countries, lack of adequate space and technical assistance, and lack of power on the part of women attending.

It is important to realize, however, that these large bodies of diverse women did unite on goals. The unofficial Tribune debated various women's issues, and the Conference produced the World Plan of Action, many points of which were endorsed in December 1975 by the U.N. General Assembly.

Senator Charles H. Percy of Illinois, a Congressional adviser to the U.S. delegation, has pointed out that

> the Conference was an opportunity for women to meet, find reassurance in each other's experiences and gain new challenges in each other's ideas. The Conference toughened and matured the international women's movement. Women . . . began . . . building the informal associations and networks so important in the exercise of influence and power.

U.S. participation in International Women's year got underway in 1972 when the U.S. Department of State set up an informal interagency group to plan for U.S. Government observance of IWY. This group made a number of proposals including suggested IWY activity for U.N. member states, creation of the U.S. Center for IWY, and establishment of the National Commission.

Things now began to move quickly.

A Presidential proclamation called upon the country to take stock of women's roles and "to provide for the observance of International Women's Year with practical and constructive measures for the advancement of the status of women.[4]

The Department of State established the IWY Secretariat, responsible to Deputy Secretary Robert S. Ingersoll, to assist in preparing materials for the U.S. delegation to Mexico City and to act as staff for the National Commission. The U.S. Center for IWY at Meridian House was established to share information and to be a bridge between government and many nongovernmental organizations. Before 1975 was over, thousands of IWY programs had taken place throughout America.[5]

Early in the year, President Ford created the National Commission, saying "Americans must now deal with those inequities that still linger as barriers to the full participation of women in our Nation's life . . . ."

Thirty-five members were appointed from the private sector and four from Congress. Jill Ruckelshaus was named presiding officer. Funding came in the form of staff services or money contributed by Executive Branch agencies as their share in the government's observance of IWY.

Two hundred nongovernmental organizations concerned with women were asked to suggest areas the Commission should deal with, and as a result the Commission set up 13 work committees. An Interdepartmental Task Force to implement IWY projects within government departments was created.

The committees then went to work, broadening their expertise by adding public members and by holding many long, concentrated sessions. They called in expert witnesses, authorized certain original research and participated in a number of public hearings, under various auspices.

Among the larger hearings were:

- The Southwest Indian Women's Conference in Window Rock, Arizona. Annie Dodge Wauneka, Commission member and member of the Navajo Tribal Council, was the keynote speaker.
- Massachusetts public hearings for IWY held in Boston through the efforts of Representative Margaret Heckler, Congressional Commission member, and in Norton, Massachusetts, with the added sponsorship of Wheaton College.
- The Conference on Women in Public Life, sponsored by the Lyndon B. Johnson School of Public Affairs and the Lyndon Baines Johnson Library at the University of Texas in Austin. The Commission's Women in Power Committee participated extensively.

By early 1976 the Commission had adopted recommendations as those most imperative to eliminating the "barriers" to full justice.

But as one public Commission member said: "Sexism is still so rampant throughout our country, we could not possibly address ourselves to all the areas that need action in the few short months the Commission has had."

Two hundred years ago the Declaration of Independence said: "We hold these truths to be self-evident, that all men are created equal . . . ." Commission members believe that women and men together will strive earnestly to make that principle a reality. They also believe it is urgent to extend full justice to American women in order "to form a more perfect union," as the Constitution promises.

References

1. The second section of the 14th amendment placed in the Constitution for the first time the word "male." Three times the word "male" was used in conjunction with the term "citizens." In 1874 the U.S. Supreme Court, in the case of *Minor* v. *Happersett*, held that the Constitution did not confer the right of suffrage on those who were citizens at the time it was adopted, and that the States, having withheld voting rights from certain classes of males, were equally within their rights in withholding suffrage from all women.
2. Alice S. Rossi, *The Feminist Papers* (N.Y.: Columbia University Press, 1973), p. 617.
3. President Nixon's 1969 Task Force on Women's Rights and Responsibilities also summarized progress and outlines the job ahead.
4. President Nixon issued his proclamation on January 30, 1974.
5. Some of these programs were given in connection with U.N. Day, since the United Nations Association of the United States stressed IWY as a theme of the 1975 observance.

48

Universal Declaration of Human Rights

United Nations

PREAMBLE

Whereas recognition of the inherent dignity and of the equal and inalienable rights of all members of the human family is the foundation of freedom, justice and peace in the world,

Whereas disregard and contempt for human rights have resulted in barbarous acts which have outraged the conscience of mankind, and the advent of a world in which human beings shall enjoy freedom of speech and belief and freedom from fear and want has been proclaimed as the highest aspiration of the common people,

Whereas it is essential, if man is not to be compelled to have recourse, as a last resort, to rebellion against tyranny and oppression, that human rights should be protected by the rule of law,

Whereas it is essential to promote the development of friendly relations between nations,

Whereas the peoples of the United Nations have in the Charter reaffirmed their faith in fundamental human rights, in the dignity and worth of the human person and in the equal rights of men and women and have determined to promote social progress and better standards of life in larger freedom,

Whereas Member States have pledged themselves to achieve, in cooperation with the United Nations, the promotion of universal respect for and observance of human rights and fundamental freedoms,

Whereas a common understanding of these rights and freedoms is of the greatest importance for the full realisation of this pledge,

Now therefore

THE GENERAL ASSEMBLY

Proclaims this Universal Declaration of Human Rights as a common standard of achievement for all peoples and all nations, to the end that every individual and every organ of society, keeping this declaration constantly in mind, shall strive by teaching and education to promote respect for these rights and freedoms and by progressive measures, national and international, to secure their universal and effective recognition and observance, both among the peoples of Member States themselves and among the peoples of territories under their jurisdiction.

Art. 1. All human beings are born free and equal in dignity and rights. They are endowed with reason and conscience and should act towards one another in a spirit of brotherhood.

Art. 2. Everyone is entitled to all the rights and freedoms set forth in this Declaration, without distinction of any kind, such as race, colour, sex, language, religion, political or other opinion, national or social origin, property, birth, or other status.

Furthermore, no distinction shall be made on the basis of the political, jurisdictional, or international status of the country or territory to which a person belongs, whether it be an independent, trust, or non-self-governing territory or under any limitation of sovereignty.

Art 3. Everyone has the right to life, liberty, and security of person.

Art. 4. No one shall be held in slavery or servitude; slavery and the slave trade shall be prohibited in all their forms.

Art. 5. No one shall be subjected to torture or to cruel, inhuman, or degrading treatment or punishment.

Art. 6. Everyone has the right to recognition everywhere as a person before the law.

Art. 7. All are equal before the law and are entitled without any discrimination to equal protection of the law. All are entitled to equal protection against any discrimination in violation of this Declaration and against any incitement to such discrimination.

Art. 8. Everyone has the right to an effective remedy by the competent national tribunals for acts violating the fundamental rights granted him by the Constitution or by law.

Art. 9. No one shall be subjected to arbitrary arrest, detention, or exile.

Art. 10. Everyone is entitled in full equality to a fair and public hearing by an independent and impartial tribunal, in the determination of his rights and obligations and of any criminal charge against him.

Art. 11. 1. Everyone charges with a penal offence has the right to be presumed innocent until proved guilty according to law in a public trial at which he has had all the guarantees necessary for his defence.

2. No one shall be held guilty of any penal offence on account of any act or omission which did not constitute a penal offence, under national or international law, at the time when it was committed. Nor shall a heavier penalty be imposed than the one that was applicable at the time the penal offence was committed.

Art. 12. No one shall be subjected to arbitrary interference with his privacy, fam-

Source: From United Nations, General Assembly, *Universal Declaration of Human Rights*, Document A/811, December 16, 1948.

ily, home, or correspondence, nor to attacks upon his honour and reputation. Everyone has the right to the protection of the law against such interference or attacks.

Art. 13. 1. Everyone has the right to freedom of movement and residence within the borders of each State.

2. Everyone has the right to leave any country, including his own, and to return to his country.

Art. 14. 1. Everyone has the right to seek and to enjoy in other countries asylum from persecution.

2. This right may not be invoked in the case of prosecutions genuinely arising from non-political crimes or from acts contrary to the purposes and principles of the United Nations.

Art. 15. 1. Everyone has the right to a nationality.

2. No one shall be arbitrarily deprived of his nationality nor denied the right to change his nationality.

Art. 16. 1. Men and women of full age, without any limitation due to race, nationality, or religion, have the right to marry and to found a family. They are entitled to equal rights as to marriage, during marriage, and at its dissolution.

2. Marriage shall be entered into only with the free and full consent of the intending spouses.

3. The family is the natural and fundamental group unit of society and is entitled to protection by society and the State.

Art. 17. 1. Everyone has the right to own property alone as well as in association with others.

2. No one shall be arbitrarily deprived of his property.

Art. 18. Everyone has the right to freedom of thought, conscience, and religion; this right includes freedom to change his religion or belief, and freedom either alone or in community with others and in public or private, to manifest his religion or belief in teaching, practice, worship, and observance.

Art. 19. Everyone has the right to freedom of opinion and expression; this right includes freedom to hold opinions without interference and to seek, receive, and impart information and ideas through any media and regardless of frontiers.

Art. 20. 1. Everyone has the right to freedom of peaceful assembly and association.

2. No one may be compelled to belong to an association.

Art. 21. 1. Everyone has the right to take part in the government of his country, directly or through freely chosen representatives.

2. Everyone has the right of equal access to public service in his country.

3. The will of the people shall be the basis of the authority of Government; this will shall be expressed in periodic and genuine elections which shall be by universal and equal suffrage and shall be held by secret vote or by equivalent free voting procedures.

Art. 22. Everyone, as a member of society, has the right to social security and is entitled to the realisation, through national effort and international co-operation and in accordance with the organisation and resources of each State, of the economic, social, and cultural rights indispensable for his dignity and the free development of his personality.

Art. 23. 1. Everyone has the right to work, to free choice of employment, to just and favourable conditions of work, and to protection against unemployment:

2. Everyone, without any discrimination, has the right to equal pay for equal work.

3. Everyone who works has the right to just and favourable remuneration, insuring for himself and his family an existence worthy of human dignity, and supplemented, if necessary, by other means of social protection.

4. Everyone has the right to form and to join trade unions for the protection of his interests.

Art. 24. Everyone has the right to rest and leisure, including reasonable limitations of working hours and periodic holidays with pay.

Art. 25. Everyone has the right to a standard of living adequate for the health and well-being of himself and of his family, including food, clothing, housing, and medical care and necessary social services, and the right to security in the event of unemployment, sickness, disability, widowhood, old age, or other lack of livelihood in circumstances beyond his control.

2. Motherhood and childhood are entitled to special care and assistance. All children, whether born in or out of wedlock, shall enjoy the same social protection.

Art. 26. 1. Everyone has the right to education. Education shall be free, at least in the elementary and fundamental stages. Elementary education shall be compulsory. Technical and professional education shall be made generally available, and higher education shall be equally accessible to all on the basis of merit.

2. Education shall be directed to the full development of the human personality and to the strengthening of respect for human rights and fundamental freedoms. It shall promote understanding, tolerance, and friendship among all nations, racial or religious groups, and shall further the activities of the United Nations for the maintenance of peace.

3. Parents have a prior right to choose the kind of education that shall be given to their children.

Art. 27. 1. Everyone has the right freely to participate in the cultural life of the community, to enjoy the arts, and to share in scientific advancement and its benefits.

2. Everyone has the right to the protection of the moral and material interests resulting from any scientific, literary, or artistic production of which he is the author.

Art. 28. Everyone is entitled to a social and international order in which the rights and freedoms set forth in this declaration can be fully realised.

Art. 29. 1. Everyone has duties to the community in which alone the free and full development of his personality is possible.

2. In the exercise of his rights and freedoms, everyone shall be subject only to such limitations as are determined by law solely for the purpose of securing due recognition and respect for the rights and freedoms of others and of meeting the just requirements of morality, public order, and the general welfare in a democratic society.

3. These rights and freedoms may in no case be exercised contrary to the purposes and principles of the United Nations.

Art. 30. Nothing in this Declaration may be interpreted as implying for any State, group, or person any right to engage in any activity or to perform any act aimed at the destruction of any of the rights and freedoms set forth herein.

PART FIVE

Philosophical Concepts, Educational Views, and Teaching Styles

The challenge of critical reflective and logical thinking found in the study of philosophy, along with the association with the greatest minds of civilization, seems a sure way to produce the intelligent men and women necessary to insure the growth of democracy. It is suggested that a degree of involvement on the part of all teachers with regard to both classical and contemporary philosophical systems of thought might provide the clues which teachers may best use in helping to develop the minds of their pupils. The growth of the comprehensive American system of education has obviously been aligned with the growth of the American democratic way of life. The American democracy depends upon an educated citizenry functioning within a framework of several simultaneously existing systems of thought. Teachers working within the framework of American democracy usually formulate a philosophy of education which they personally feel best enables them to work with their pupils. While the contemporary American teacher chooses the educational philosophy personally desired, most of the various views regarding education may be identified as having been suggested within the classical philosophies of the historical past.

The relevance of philosophy to successful teaching practice is a loosely grounded notion in the minds of many persons who are preparing for teaching careers. In "The Relevance of Philosophy," George F. Kneller suggests that philosophy is both natural and necessary and that educational philosophy depends on formal philosophy to the extent that the problems of education are of a general philosophical character.

In order to sustain patterns of meaningful actions, teachers need to systematize their beliefs. They also need to be familiar with general terminology of philosophy if they are to order their beliefs under the various branch categories of philosophy. Proper utilization of terminology will enable teachers both to communicate their personal philosophies and to understand the philosophical positions of others. Since much of the vocabulary of philosophy consists of words that have clear, straightforward meanings, lack of clarity arises when terms from our everyday forms of speech are loosely interpreted and/or used when solving problems of a philosophical nature. Linguistic analysis as part of the analytic movement in philosophy stresses clarity and analysis of terms as essential in the approach to educational problems. That part of the introductory terminology of philosophy considered here consists of the basic terms which have commonly accepted philosophical definitions. Familiarity with these terms will provide the reader with an overview of the positions described in the readings in this part.

J. Donald Butler specifies his purpose in the treatment of terminology entitled "The Vocabulary of Philosophy" as twofold: to define terms, and to show, by outline, some of the interrelationships between terms and the problems with which they are commonly associated. Four major categories of philosophy: metaphysics (theories of the nature of reality), epistemology (theories of the nature of knowledge), logic (science of exact thought), and axiology (general theory of values) are discussed. Obviously, no pretense can be made that study of a brief vocabulary outline substitutes for in-depth study of the original works of philosophers. However, since one of the purposes of this section of the book is to view the carry-over influence of the classical philosophical positions to the contemporary American scene, Butler's vocabulary outline serves this purpose well.

Philosophers have not been able to agree upon the number of formal philosophies that exist. Thus, attempts to group schools of philosophy by classification schemes may be viewed as questionable practices. Further confusion may arise when classifications are made under the headings of traditional views, contemporary views, and emergent views since most systems of thought have their origins with the ancient Greeks. As a matter of mere internal consistency, the educational views classified as traditional are drawn heavily from the classical philosophical schools of idealism, realism, and neo-Thomism. Experimentalism and reconstructionism are considered contemporary educational views. Existentialism is considered an emergent approach to education.

In the past few decades, perennialist philosophy has been revived under the heading of neo-Thomism. Growing numbers of intellectuals adhere to the thinking that the basic beliefs and knowledge of ancient cultures apply as well in our lives today. Historically, Thomism has been associated with the Roman Catholic Church, but the revival of perennialism in America is associated mainly with lay educators. Differences among the views of the lay and ecclesiastical neo-Thomists, if judged by religious standards, would be considered vast. Yet, Roman Catholic educators have welcomed the revival of the scholasticism of Thomas Aquinas and share many common educational views with lay perennialists.

In "Dewey's Legacy to Education," Phillip S. Riner emphasizes that Dewey's legacy has created within the educational culture a belief in social amelioration through education. He notes that social amelioration comes not by being educated, but by being empowered with the intellectual and social tools to obtain our ends. Our schools cannot eliminate discrimination and anti-social activity, but they can empower students with rational modes of thinking, reflecting, judging, and acting, which allow each ensuing generation to toil closer and closer toward that ideal. Dewey's legacy, according to Riner, in addition to social amelioration, includes Dewey's beliefs that subject matter comes from the interest of the child, learning is the reconstruction of experience and knowledge, education requires reflection, and education is experimental.

In "The Basis of Education," Robert M. Hutchins outlines what he considers the best kind of education appropriate to free men and women. He asserts that the sole purpose of education is to improve people, stating that the prime object of education is to know what is "good" for people. Teachers should find this selection intriguing because of emphasis on using education to free people and to improve society. Hutchins also believes that peace in the world is unlikely unless there are continuous, unlimited opportunities for learning.

One of the major conflicts in American education exists between the *Traditionalists,* whose primary interests are in the curriculum or in the so-called "subject-centered" activities in the school, and the contemporary *Progressivists,* who stress the importance of the experiences of life or "student-centered" activities as the emphasis in curriculum. The function of progressive schools is to be an active leader in bringing about change. In this context, one can envision the antithetical positions of Traditionalism and Progressivism. John Dewey has been placed at the center of this conflict by many contemporary educators. Many have fallaciously identified Dewey as the father of Progressive education when, in fact, many of the notions of the Progressivists are independent of Dewey. It should also be noted that Dewey was a severe critic of several of the basic assumptions of the Progressive movement. To a large degree, the work of John Dewey has been subjected to attack by many identified with the Traditionalists' positions. Upon careful examination it seems that the meanings in certain of his works indicate that this American philosopher was dedicated to the reconciliation of the split between the Traditionalists and the Progressivists, since he felt that both views were important to education. Among the hundreds of books, essays, and other works Dewey produced in his long career, "My Pedagogic Creed," which he wrote in 1897, is uniquely significant. In its style and content, it may most clearly exemplify the reformist fervor of his Chicago period. Here is Dewey passionately, even flamboyantly, confident of his vision of the nature, purpose, and inevitable progress of education. At once a personal declaration and a revolutionary manifesto, it dispenses with supporting arguments or documentation. The resulting clarity, succinctness, and even eloquence have offered incomparable opportunities for interpretation.

The next selection, "My Idea of Education," is authored by Ashley Montagu. Montagu is a noted anthropologist who has come to the conclusion that humans are distinguished from all other creatures by their ability to love and to be educated. In this article, Montagu discusses the implications for schools and for teachers in light of his conclusion about the distinguishing features of human beings. Future teachers should find his ideas both interesting and useful.

In "Where Has All Our Empathy Gone?" Dea Forney presents an excellent analysis of the transition in values that occurred from 1960 to the present. This shift was fomented by rapidly changing domestic and international issues of the period. She laments the materialistic notions of modern-day students but attempts to explain those attitudes as natural results of the society in which the students live. She develops a thesis for not only accepting the differences in values but searching for the empathy one needs to help students cope with these materialistic notions of value.

In "The Normative and the Possible: Values in the Curriculum," William Ayers and William H. Schubert discuss the fundamental questions of the contemporary curriculum. They ask what knowledge and experiences are most worthwhile and present three curriculum orientations: the intellectual traditionalist, the social behaviorist, and the experientialist.

The next article by Sammie McCormack, "Implementing an Effective Discipline Program" describes the characteristics of good discipline programs. McCormack's recommendations are practical, rational, and effective.

Philosophical involvement on the part of all teachers with regard to both classical and contemporary philosophical systems of thought might provide the clues which teachers may best use in helping to develop the minds of their pupils. The American democracy depends upon an educated citizenry functioning within a framework of several simultaneously existing systems of thought. Teachers operating within the framework of American democracy usually formulate a philosophy of education which they personally feel best enables them to work with their pupils.

49

The Relevance of Philosophy

George F. Kneller

From time to time every teacher and student asks himself questions that are implicitly philosophical. The teacher wonders, "Why am I teaching? Why am I teaching history? What is teaching at its best?" And the student asks, "Why am I studying algebra? What am I going to school for anyway?" Taken far enough, these questions become philosophical. They become questions about the nature of man and the world, about knowledge, value, and the good life.

MODES OF PHILOSOPHY

Unfortunately, nothing illuminating can be said about philosophy with a single definition. Let us therefore think of philosophy as an activity in three modes or styles; the speculative, the prescriptive, and the analytic.

Speculative Philosophy

Speculative philosophy is a way of thinking systematically about everything that exists. Why do philosophers want to do this? Why are they not content, like scientists, to study particular aspects of reality? The answer is that the human mind wishes to see things as a whole. It wishes to understand how all the different things that have been discovered together form some sort of meaningful totality. We are all aware of this tendency in ourselves. When we read a book, look at a painting, or study an assignment, we are concerned not only with particular details but also with the order or pattern that gives these details their significance. Speculative philosophy, then, is a search for order and wholeness, applied not to particular items or experiences but to all knowledge and all experience. In brief, speculative philosophy is the attempt to find a coherence in the whole realm of thought and experience.

Prescriptive Philosophy

Prescriptive philosophy seeks to establish standards for assessing values, judging conduct, and appraising art. It examines what we mean by good and bad, right and wrong, beautiful and ugly. It asks whether these qualities inhere in things themselves or whether they are projections of our own minds. To the experimental psychologist the varieties of human conduct are morally neither good or bad; they are simply forms of behavior to be studied empirically. But to the educator and the prescriptive philosopher some forms of behavior are worthwhile and others are not. The prescriptive philosopher seeks to discover and to recommend principles for deciding what actions and qualities are most worthwhile and why they should be so.

Analytic Philosophy

Analytic philosophy focuses on words and meaning. The analytic philosopher examines such notions as "cause," "mind," "academic freedom," and "equality of opportunity" in order to assess the different meanings they carry in different contexts. He shows how inconsistencies may arise when meanings appropriate in certain contexts are imported into others. The analytic philosopher tends to be skeptical, cautious, and disinclined to build systems of thought.

Today the analytic approach dominates American and British philosophy. On the Continent the speculative tradition prevails. But whichever approach is uppermost at any time, most philosophers agree that all approaches contribute to the health of philosophy. Speculation unaccompanied by analysis soars too easily into a heaven of its own, irrelevant to the world as we know it; analysis without speculation descends to minutiae and becomes sterile. In any case few philosophers are solely speculative, solely prescriptive, or solely analytic. Speculation, prescription, and analysis are all present to some degree in the work of all mature philosophers.

PHILOSOPHY AND SCIENCE

A great deal of information has been gathered by various sciences on subjects treated by philosophy, particularly human nature. But when we look at this information, we find that psychology gives us one picture of man, sociology another, biology another, and so on. What we have after all the sciences have been searched is not a composite picture of man but a series of different pictures. These pictures fail to satisfy because they explain different aspects of man rather than man as a whole. Can we unify our partial pictures of man into one that is single and complete? Yes, but not by using scientific methods alone. It is through philosophy that we unify the separate findings of science and interrelate the fundamental concepts these findings presuppose.

The philosopher considers questions that arise before and after the scientist has done his work. Traditional science presupposes, for example, that every event is caused by other events and in turn causes still other events. Hence, for science no event is uncaused. But how can we be sure of this? Do cause and effect exist in the world itself or are they read into the world by men? These questions cannot be answered scientifically because causality is not a finding but an assumption of science. Unless the scientist assumes that reality is causal in nature, he cannot begin to investigate it. Again, science deals with things as they appear to our senses and to our

Source: From George F. Kneller, "The Relevance of Philosophy," *Foundations of Education*, Third Edition, pp. 199–202. New York: John Wiley & Sons, Inc. Reprinted with permission from the publisher.

instruments. But are things in themselves really the same as they appear to us? The scientist cannot say, because things in themselves, as opposed to their appearances, are by definition beyond empirical verification.

Philosophy, then, is both natural and necessary to man. We are forever seeking some comprehensive framework within which our separate findings may be given a total significance. Not only is philosophy a branch of knowledge along with art, science, and history, but also it actually embraces these disciplines in their theoretical reaches and seeks to establish connections between them. Once again, *philosophy attempts to establish a coherence throughout the whole domain of experience.*

PHILOSOPHY OF EDUCATION

Besides having its own concerns, philosophy considers the fundamental assumptions of other branches of knowledge. When philosophy turns its attention to science, we have philosophy of science; when it examines the basic concepts of the law, we have philosophy of law; and when it deals with education, we have philosophy of education or educational philosophy.

Just as formal philosophy attempts to understand reality as a whole by explaining it in the most general and systematic way, so educational philosophy seeks to comprehend education in its entirety, interpreting it by means of general concepts that will guide our choice of educational ends and policies. In the same way that general philosophy coordinates the findings of the different sciences, educational philosophy interprets these findings as they bear on education. Scientific theories do not carry direct educational implications; they cannot be applied to educational practice without first being examined philosophically.

Educational philosophy depends on general or formal philosophy to the extent that the problems of education are a general philosophical character. We cannot criticize existing educational policies or suggest new ones without considering such general philosophic problems as (a) the nature of the good life, to which education should lead; (b) the nature of man himself, because it is man we are educating; (c) the nature of society, because education is a social process; and (d) the nature of ultimate reality, which all knowledge seeks to penetrate. Educational philosophy, then, involves among other things the application of formal philosophy to the field of education.*

Like general philosophy, educational philosophy is speculative, prescriptive, and analytic. It is speculative when it seeks to establish theories of the nature of man, society, and the world by which to order and interpret the conflicting data of educational research and the behavioral sciences. It is prescriptive when it specifies the ends that education ought to follow and the general means it should use to attain them. It is analytic when it clarifies speculative and prescriptive statements. The analyst, as we shall see, examines the rationality of our educational ideas, their consistency with other ideas, and the way in which they are distorted by loose thinking. He tests the logic of our concepts and their adequacy to the facts they seek to explain. Above all, he attempts to clarify the many different meanings that have been attached to such heavily worked educational terms as "freedom," "adjustment," "growth," "experience," "needs," and "knowledge."

*Educational philosophy derives also from the experiences of education.

50

The Vocabulary of Philosophy

J. Donald Butler

The vocabulary of philosophy, while different from our everyday forms of speech, is not necessarily difficult. Some helpful explanation of meanings plus a bit of patient study will go a long way toward making the student feel at home among philosophers. In the following treatment of terminology the purpose is twofold: to define terms, and to show, by the outline arrangement, some of the interrelationships between terms and the problems with which they are commonly associated.

I. *Metaphysics*. Theories of the nature of reality.
   A. *Cosmology*. Theories of the nature of the cosmos and explanations of its origin and development.
      1. Some considerations in *cosmology* are
         a. *Causality*. The nature of cause and effect relations.
         b. The nature of time.
         c. The nature of space.
      2. Two distinctive views in *cosmology* are
         a. *Evolutionism*. The universe evolved of itself.
         b. *Creationism*. The universe came to be as the result of the working of a Creative Cause or Personality.
   B. The nature of man as one important aspect of reality.
      1. The problem of the essential nature of the self. There are no particular terms but there are divergent answers which can be identified with general viewpoints.
         a. The self is a soul, a spiritual being. A principle of *idealism* and *spiritual realism*.
         b. The self is essentially the same as the body. A principle of *naturalism* and *physical realism*.
         c. The self is a social-vocal phenomenon. A principle held especially by *experimentalists*.
      2. The problem of the relation of body and mind.
         a. *Interactionism*. Mind and body are two different kinds of reality, each of which can affect the other.
         b. *Parallelism*. Mind and body are two different kinds of reality which do not and cannot affect each other. But in some unknown way, every mental event is paralleled by a corresponding physical event.
         c. *Epiphenomenalism*. Mind is merely a function of the brain, an overtone accompanying bodily activity. It is an onlooker at events, never influencing them.
         d. *Double Aspect Theory*. Mind and body are two aspects of a fundamental reality whose nature is unknown.
         e. *Emergence Theory*. Mind is something new which has been produced by Nature in the evolutionary process, neither identical with body, parallel to it, nor wholly dependent upon it.
         f. *Spiritualism*. (A definition common to most *idealists* and *spiritual realists*.) Mind is more fundamental than body. The relation of body and mind is better described as body depending upon mind, as compared to the common-sense description according to which mind depends upon body.
      3. The problem of freedom.
         a. *Determinism*. Man is not free. All of his actions are determined by forces greater than he is.
         b. *Free Will*. Man has the power of choice and is capable of genuine initiative.
         c. There is a third alternative proposed especially by the *experimentalists*, for which there is no name. Man is neither free nor determined; but he can and does delay some of his responses long enough to reconstruct a total response, not completely automatic but not free, which does give a new direction to subsequent activity.
   C. Conceptions of and about God.
      1. *Atheism*. There is no ultimate reality in or behind the cosmos which is Person or Spirit.
      2. *Deism*. God exists quite apart from, and is disinterested in, the physical universe and human beings. But he created both and is the Author of all natural and moral laws.
      3. *Pantheism*. All is God and God is all. The cosmos and God are identical.
      4. The conception of God as emerging, for which there is no common name. God is evolving with the cosmos; He is the end toward

which it is moving, instead of the beginning from which it came.

5. *Polytheism.* Spiritual reality is plural rather than a unity. There is more than one God.
6. *Theism.* Ultimate reality is a personal God who is more than the cosmos but within whom and through whom the cosmos exists.

D. *Teleology.* Considerations as to whether or not there is purpose in the universe.
1. Philosophies holding that the world is what it is because of chance, accident, or blind mechanism are *nonteleological.*
2. Philosophies holding that there has been purpose in the universe from the beginning, and/or purpose can be discerned in history, are *teleological* philosophies.
3. It may be that a special case must be made of the *experimentalists* again on this particular question, as they do not find purpose inherent in the cosmos but by purposeful activity seek to impose purpose upon it.

E. Considerations relating to the constancy, or lack of it, in reality.
1. *Absolutism.* Fundamental reality is constant, unchanging, fixed, and dependable.
2. *Relativism.* Reality is a changing thing. So-called realities are always relative to something or other.

F. Problems of quantity. Consideration of the number of ultimate realities, apart from qualitative aspects.
1. *Monism.* Reality is unified. It is one. It is mind, or matter, or energy, or will—but only one of these.
2. *Dualism.* Reality is two. Usually these realities are antithetical, as spirit and matter, good and evil. Commonly, the antithesis is weighted, so that one of the two is considered more important and more enduring than the other.
3. *Pluralism.* Reality is many. Minds, things, materials, energies, laws, processes, etc., all may be considered equally real and to some degree independent of each other.

G. *Ontology.* The meaning of existence as such. To exist, to have being, means what?
1. Space-time or Nature is identical with existence. To exist means to occupy time and space, to be matter or physical energy (e.g., *naturalism* and *physical realism*).
2. Spirit or God is identical with existence. To exist means to be Mind or Spirit, or to be dependent upon Mind or Spirit. (Especially true of *idealism.*)
3. Existence as a category which is not valid. This is held by those, especially the *pragmatists,* who insist that everything is flux or change and there is nothing which fits into the category of existence in any ultimate sense.

II. *Epistemology.* Theories of the nature of knowledge.

A. The possibility of knowledge.
1. *Agnosticism.* The position that conclusive knowledge of ultimate reality is an impossibility.
2. *Skepticism.* A questioning attitude toward the possibility of having any knowledge.
3. The affirmation of knowledge. The position that true knowledge of ultimate reality is possible.
4. The affirmation of functional knowledge. The position that knowledge is always fractional, never total, and functions in a present field or situation where it is needed, and that we can appropriate such fractional and functional knowledge (especially true of *experimentalists*).

B. The kinds of knowledge.
1. *A posteriori.* Knowledge which is based upon experience and observation.
2. Experimental knowledge. Not exactly the same as *a posteriori* knowledge because it is not regarded as something finally to be concluded from experience or observation, by induction. Rather, it is something to be put to work in experience as a function which carries experience forward satisfactorily.
3. *A priori.* Knowledge which is self-evident. Principles which, when once understood, are recognized to be true and do not require proof through observation, experience, or experiment.

C. The instrument of knowledge.
1. *Empiricism.* The position that sensation, or sense-perceptual experience, is the medium through which knowledge is gained.
2. *Rationalism.* The position that reason is the chief source of knowledge.
3. *Intuitionism.* A position that knowledge is gained through immediate insight and awareness.
4. *Authoritarianism.* The position that much important knowledge is certified to us by an indisputable authority, such as the Bible, the Church, or the State.
5. *Revelation.* The position that God presently reveals Himself in the Bible and the Church.

III. *Logic.* The science of exact thought. The systematic treatment of the relation of ideas. A study of methods distinguishing valid thinking from thinking which is fallacious.

A. *Induction.* Reasoning from particulars to a general conclusion.

B. *Deduction.* Reasoning from a general principle to particulars included within the scope of that principle.

C. The *Syllogism.* A form in which to cast deductive reasoning. It is comprised of three propositions: The major premise, the minor premise, and the conclusion.

D. Experimental reasoning or problem-solving. A form of reasoning, largely *inductive* but using *deduction* as well, which begins with a problem, observes all the data relating to the problem, formulates hypotheses, and tests them to reach a workable solution of the problem.

E. *Dialectic.* A method of reasoning in which the conflict or contrast of ideas is utilized as a means of detecting the truth. In Hegel's formulation of it there are three stages: *thesis, antithesis,* and *synthesis.*

IV. *Axiology.* The general theory of value. The nature of values, the different kinds of value, specific values worthy of possession.

A. The nature of value.
1. The interest theory. Values depend upon the interest of the person who enjoys them. Strictly speaking, they do not exist but are supported by the interest of the valuer. According to this theory, what is desired has value.
2. The existence theory. Values have an existence in their own right which is independent of the valuer and his interest. Values are not qualities or essences without foundation in existence: They are essence plus existence.
3. The experimentalist theory. That is of value which yields a greater sense of happiness in the present and at the same time opens the way to further goods in future experiences.
4. The part-whole theory. The key to realizing and enjoying value is the effective relating of parts to wholes.

B. Realms of value.
1. *Ethics.* The nature of good and evil. The problems of conduct and ultimate objectives.
   a. The worth of living.
      (1) *Optimism.* Existence is good. Life is worth living.

Our outlook can be hopeful.

(2) *Pessimism. Existence is evil.* Life is not worth the struggle: we should escape it by some means.

(3) *Meliorism.* Conclusions as to the goodness or evil of existence cannot be made final. Human effort may improve the human situation. The final end cannot be assured, but we must face life, not escape it, applying all the effort and resources we can command.

b. The highest good or *summum bonum.* The end, aim, or objective of living which is above all other ends. In absolutist philosophies it is the ultimate end which by its nature cannot be a means to another end.

(1) *Hedonism.* The highest good is pleasure. Hedonist philosophies vary in their conceptions of pleasure, ranging from the intense pleasure of the moment to highly refined and enduring pleasure and contentment. *Utilitarianism* is a form of hedonism having society as its frame of reference. According to it, the greatest happiness of the greatest number is the prime objective.

(2) *Perfectionism.* The highest good is the perfection of the self, or self-realization. Perfectionism may also have its social frame of reference, envisioning an ideal social order as the ultimate objective of society.

c. The criteria of conduct. From one's conception of the highest good there follow logically certain practical principles for everyday living. Some examples are:

(1) Kant's maxim: act only on those principles which you are willing should become universal moral laws.

(2) Spencer's principle: action to be right must be conducive to self-preservation.

(3) Dewey's principle: discover the probable consequences of what you consider doing, by going through an imaginative rehearsal of the possibilities.

(4) The religious principle: obey the will of God; commit yourself completely to the fulfillment of God's purpose for yourself and the world.

d. The motivation of conduct. The kind and scope of the interests which guide conduct.

(1) *Egoism.* The interests of self should be served by an individual's actions.

(2) *Altruism.* The interests of others or of the social group should be served by an individual's actions. One realizes his own fullest selfhood in seeking the best interests of others.

2. *Aesthetics.* The nature of the values which are found in the feeling aspects of experience. The conscious search for the principles governing the creation and appreciation of beautiful things.
3. *Religious Values.* The kind, nature, and worth of values to be possessed in worship, religious experience, and religious service.
4. *Educational Values.* The kind, nature, and worth of values inherent in the educative process.
5. *Social Values.* The kind, nature, and worth of values only realized in community and in the individual's relation to society. Some more specific kinds of social values are the *political* and the *economic.*
6. *Utilitarian Values.* The kind, nature, and worth of values to be realized in harmonious adjustment to or efficient control of the forces of the physical environment.

51

Dewey's Legacy to Education

Phillip S. Riner

Throughout this century periodic examinations of American educational institutions have pointed to perceived weaknesses in the curriculum and academic standards of public schools. Current criticisms have centered around the economic imperative that schools must, first and foremost, attend to societal needs for an educated work force. Educational organizations have responded to this new wave of criticism with raised standards in course requirements for graduation and increased dependence on standardized tests for decision making. However, the road of reform in American education has not been a smooth one. Many educators have been seriously questioning the "pay-off" aims of education and the role of omnibus standards. Particularly, within the classroom teacher ranks, there appears to be an unarticulated curriculum; a curriculum passed into the American subconscious that contends a child's social well-being to be an essential prerequisite for his intellectual development. This desire to promote the affective growth of children is the result of many people who have dedicated their careers to schools. Among the most influential is John Dewey. It is Dewey's legacy to have created within the educational culture a belief in social amelioration through education.

Throughout his life Dewey challenged the complacent curriculum of his day with ideas that were powerful in their appeal but elusive in their realization. Dewey's challenge for fellow educators to escape the psychology of entrenchment is as poignant today as it was to his contemporaries. It continues to haunt the essentialist curriculum reformers in their efforts to confine curriculum to traditional subject matters, as well as the defenders of the status quo.

> Any significant problem involves conditions that for the moment contradict each other. Solution comes only by getting away from the meaning of terms that is already fixed upon and coming to see the conditions from another point of view, and hence in a fresh light. But this reconstruction means travail of thought. Easier than thinking with surrender of already formed ideas and detachment from facts already learned, is just to stick by what is already said, looking about for something with which to buttress it against attack.[1]

Dewey knew most intimately the bitter attacks on his experimental Laboratory School by the "old" school of subject-centered educators, and understood the inevitability of criticism. Likewise, Dewey understood that the "new" child-centered approach and its concomitant extremes were gleaning only, at best, a misunderstanding of the meanings of "education as living." In scarcely more than a decade from the publication of his first article on education in 1885, Dewey had come to grips with the greatest problem he faced in his lifelong promotion of school reform—if education is to promote an evolutionary improvement in society, particularly in a democratic society, it must free the individual's capacity for growth toward social aims.

The recognition of the social aim of education being paramount in a democratic society precluded any dogmatic or "practical" plan of action developed as an omnibus approach to social amelioration. Because of the fluidity of social problems, no a priori plan of action can be substituted for the experimentalist spirit. Education was condemned, so to speak, to solve the recurring problems, which were stifling the American dreams for social justice and equity, piecemeal, bit by bit. Education faced a virtual Hydra where one injustice removed brought to light two more social imperatives.

Not having prescriptions for these complex problems, Dewey argued for a democratic ideal to guide education that was very similar to Henry Barnard's statement, "What we want of the common schools . . . is enough education to educate ourselves."[2] Dewey attempted to focus this liberating educational attitude by insisting on a freeing of individual capacity to solve problems uniquely. The freeing of capacity, however, must not be turned inward; it must be directed toward social relationships. Dewey explained:

> A society which makes provision for participation in its good of all its members on equal terms and which secures flexible readjustments of its institutions through interaction of the different forms of associated life is in so far democratic. *Such a society must have a type of education which gives individuals a personal interest in social relationships and control, and the habits of mind which secure social changes without introducing disorder.*[3]

How could schools possibly accomplish such an exacting task? Perhaps from a more practical view, what is to be the proper balance among individual freedom, readjustment of social aims, and order?

Dewey's solution is a difficult and unwieldy one at best. His philosophy had continually stressed "the conceptions of process, the continuity of nature, and the method of inductive science. . . . "[4] By this view, pat and specific answers cannot be given to educators. They must develop answers by *education in action.* This is a difficult position to present to a goal-oriented

Source: From Phillip S. Riner, "Dewey's Legacy to Education," *The Educational Forum*, Volume 53, Number 2, Winter 1989, pp. 183–190. Printed by permission of Kappa Delta Pi, An International Honor Society in Education.

society that measures success in the tangible terms of milepost *attainment*. American society has historically paid little homage to the philosophical orientations of ***becoming***, preferring instead a vision of success as *having*.

Dewey, however, was not the only person grappling with the emerging role of education in those formative years following the Civil War and lasting well into the twentieth century. Although he did have key interest in the Laboratory School, Dewey was viewed primarily as a philosopher and only secondarily as a school administrator.[5] In Benjamin's words, "John Dewey was not so much a combat commander as he was a banner around which the troops rallied."[6] There were other, more visible realizations of the liberal experimentalist perspective, for example, the jurist, Oliver Wendell Holmes. Dewey acknowledged that Holmes expressed the three ideas that were the essence of liberalism.

1. A belief in the intelligence of humankind as *the* directive force in life.
2. A belief that this intelligence can be directed and powered only under the conditions of freedom of thought and expression.
3. A belief in the experimental character of life and thought.[7]

Similarly, Dewey was not the only believer in the value of an emerging social life as a source of educational goals, Colonel Francis Wayland Parker being another. A man of action, Parker administered the Quincy, Massachusetts, school system in the belief that the social spirit of the classroom had a far greater impact on what children learn than did the formal lectures and lessons presented to them. At a time when Dewey was still an undergraduate at the University of Vermont, Colonel Parker was putting into practice the view "that the climate of the school must be one of freedom, and that the greatest educational resources were those of mutual aid, sympathy, and love."[8]

Dewey's enduring legacy hinges on his prolific articulation and constant promotion of the liberal democratic ideal in American education. Dewey attempted, time and again, to promote an understanding of some of the most difficult ideals of his era. Never having shown a great deal of affection for the Progressive Education Association (PEA), Dewey later relented in his separation from PEA, agreeing to serve as its president in its ninth year. He used the opportunity to impress upon educators the necessity of the intellectual rigor required to promote the science of education, rigor that had been neglected in the attempts to oppose formalism.

> An illustration may help make clearer what is meant. Progressive schools set store by individuality, and sometimes it seems to be thought that orderly organization of subject-matter is hostile to the needs of students in their individual character. But individuality is something developing and to be continuously attained, not something given all at once and ready-made. It is found only in life-history, in its continuing growth; it is, so to say, a career and not just discoverable at a particular cross section of life. It is quite possible for teachers to make such a fuss over individual children, worrying about their peculiarities, their likes and dislikes, their weaknesses and failures, so that they miss perception of real individuality. A child's individuality cannot be found in what he does or in what he consciously likes at a given moment; it can be found only in the connected course of his actions. Consciousness of desire and purpose can be genuinely attained only toward the close of some fairly prolonged sequence of activities.[9]

Dewey did influence the progressive school movement's attempts at reform but the movement was always beyond his control. It is an ironic twist that the freeing of individual capacity can make consensus on social action even more difficult. This perhaps is a key element in understanding Dewey's legacy; the *process* of social action, even with all its diversions and mislaid plans, is perhaps more meaningful than the eventual outcome.

While it would be unfair to characterize Dewey as being constantly on the defensive and in opposition to his followers, it must be acknowledged that Dewey had great difficulty embodying his ideas into educational practice, particularly in directing the reformist movement toward a scientific experimentalist posture. The progressive movement was never an embodiment of Dewey's ideal or the source of his legacy. Some individuals in the progressive movement and many of Dewey's students made influential contributions to education. Yet, none was true to the Dewey philosophy. Each chose to interpret Dewey's teachings in his or her own unique way. Each of Dewey's followers accepted Dewey's ideas and acted on them in a personal way, creating educational ideals both congruent and divergent to Dewey's ideals. Here, however, is perhaps the best place to look for the Dewey legacy. While the experimentalist ideal and social reconstruction were often accepted in general terms, the application, import, and practice of these ideals have been subject to grossly varying opinions. Many of these attempts, such as the Eight Year Study, ended in apparent failures because of an inability to instigate major revisions in school curricula. Nevertheless, the themes themselves have never died. It is this perennial refrain of social aims and democratic attainment through education that shoulders the Dewey legacy.

Somehow, Dewey, with his pragmatic outlook, has pierced the American facade and discovered those ideals that are true to the American experiment in democracy. These ideals Dewey elucidated and examined. Even if they were elusive in a changing society, these ideals nevertheless have proven worthy of continued consideration in spite of unfavorable odds of attainment. Dewey perceived this dilemma in the pursuit of social aims and gave rise to the branch of pragmatic philosophy called Experimentalism to deal with social flux. Within this framework we are forced into the plight of Sisyphus. Although the goal of social equality and justice may be unattainable, we are forced by our own aspirations to trudge up the hill escaping, if only temporarily, the abyss of discrimination and favoritism. In our efforts to obtain our social ideals, we must seek them in whatever pervasive situation is manifest at that time, knowing that the likelihood of success is limited. Our efforts must mirror this situation; hence, there can be no steadfast and unwavering way to obtain our ideas, and no ideals can remain unchanged by our social condition. In a society in flux, a method of obtaining goals must be a process and not a prescription. That process, according to Dewey, must be a combination of reflection and experience that encourages the reconstruction of our thinking.

The foregoing discussion contains all the elements of what this author feels is the core of John Dewey's legacy to American education. The legacy includes five philosophical postulates:

1) *Social amelioration comes through education;* not by being educated, but by being empowered with the intellectual and social tools to obtain our ends. Hence, education is life *and* living. Our schools cannot eliminate discrimination and anti-social activity, but they can empower students with rational modes of thinking, reflecting, judging, and acting, which allow each ensuing generation to toil closer and closer toward that ideal.

2) *Subject matter comes from the interest of the child.* In determining which is most educative, the nature of that interest and its role in guiding the learner is vital. Listing of culture is not possible. Culture is a living heritage of action, the social group's hopes and dreams cast against the realities of its time. To transmit the culture and knowledge of our society, the subject matter of schooling must attach itself to the living.

3) *Learning is the reconstruction of experience and knowledge.* This requires learner contact with the world, hence the school is a stylized version of the world where people learn primarily and most effectively by direct experience (learning by doing). Children must learn of their world and gain knowledge of the past in contrast to the present. Schooling must be more than preparation for some later day; it must be a part of living now.

4) *Education requires reflection.* The reconstruction of experience requires an attitude of thinking and effective thinking requires a complete act of thought, thus giving rise to the process of reflection. Since experience is personal, reflection must be personal and will vary, yet will contain some form of:

> a) a situation in which one's habitual modes of activity are challenged, thus producing confusion, doubt, concern; b) an impulsive, anticipatory assessment of what the system seems to forebode; c) a critical consideration of relevant data . . .; d) the formation of hypotheses [leading to] action which removes the problem; and e) reflection on whether any hypothesis and action could have resolved the situation more effectively.[10]

Knowledge and social aims can be shared, but are owned collectively and kept alive by the individual.

5) *Education is experimental.* If education is to be useful to the individual it must also attend to the variations among society, learners, schools, and environment. Therefore, education will be experimental in finding the best techniques for the situation at hand. Education cannot be dictated. Excellence in education originates within the teacher-student interaction with the teacher functioning as guide as the student explores ever-increasing bits of reality.

While the Dewey legacy is far greater than these five points, they are the distinguishing attributes that point us to the core of his philosophy. As Berger put it:

> Here is the soul of Dewey's entire philosophy: a system of education that best recognized the dignity and worth of all individuals, that allows every individual to develop to his fullest, and that teaches the virtues of democracy by establishing a democratic atmosphere.[11]

It must be remembered that Dewey held an unwavering belief in change and opportunity to aid the emergence of democratic individuals in a democratic society. He, undoubtedly, would have us reflect and critically examine all ideas in light of current conditions. Dewey believed that there cannot be one method that will resolve the problems of education, and his efforts were directed toward enabling us to comprehend the problem, to orient our senses and intellect toward the amelioration of an emerging democratic society, and to bring democracy and education into a systematic unity. Educators must add a personal commitment and a reexamination of beliefs if the incredibly complex ideals espoused by Dewey are to be realized. Certainly the embodiment of his ideals will take the dedication of generations.

There is ample evidence that Dewey's work is now a point of division rather than unification. One can, however, safely conclude that Dewey has led us toward a renunciation of any expectation of easy or permanent solution to educational dilemmas. The thread running through Dewey's ideas in regard to a philosophy of experience, the scientific method, the guidance of learning, the nature of democracy, and the social role of the school is that the only true answers in education must come through the process itself, and that that will require continuous experimental participation.

References

1. John Dewey, "My Pedagogic Creed" [1897], in *Dewey on Education: Selections*, ed. Martin S. Dworkin (New York: Columbia University Press, 1959), p. 91.
2. Harold Benjamin, "John Dewey's Influence on Educational Practice," in *John Dewey and the World View*, eds. Douglas Lawson and Arthur Lean (Carbondale, Illinois: Southern Illinois University Press, 1964), p. 16.
3. John Dewey, *Democracy and Education* [1916], as cited in *Curriculum Development: Theory into Practice*, 4th ed., eds. Daniel Tanner and Laurel Tanner (New York: MacMillan, 1980), p. 266.
4. William Kilpatrick, "Reminiscences of Dewey and His Influence," in *John Dewey: Master Educator*, eds. William W. Brickman and Stanley Lehrer (New York: Society for the Advancement of Education, 1959), p. 59.
5. Julius L. Meriam, "John Dewey in History," in *John Dewey: Master Educator*, eds. William W. Brickman and Stanley Lehrer (New York: Society for the Advancement of Education, 1959).
6. Benjamin, "John Dewey's Influence," p. 16.
7. Ibid.
8. Ibid., p. 21.
9. John Dewey, *The Sources of a Science Education* (New York: Horace Liveright, 1928), p. 121.
10. George E. Axtelle and Joe R. Burnett, "Dewey on Education and Schooling," in *Guide to the Works of John Dewey*, ed. Jo Ann Boydston (Carbondale, Illinois: Southern Illinois University Press, 1970).
11. M.I. Berger, "John Dewey's Influence on Educational Practice," in *John Dewey: Master Educator*, eds. William W. Brickman and Stanley Lehrer (New York: Society for the Advancement of Education, 1959), p. 88.

52

The Basis of Education

Robert M. Hutchins

The obvious failures of the doctrines of adaptation, immediate needs, social reform, and of the doctrine that we need no doctrine at all may suggest to us that we require a better definition of education. Let us concede that every society must have some system that attempts to adapt the young to their social and political environment. If the society is bad, in the sense, for example, in which the Nazi state was bad, the system will aim at the same bad ends. To the extent that it makes men bad in order that they may be tractable subjects of a bad state, the system may help to achieve the social ideals of the society. It may be what the society wants; it may even be what the society needs, if it is to perpetuate its form and accomplish its aims. In pragmatic terms, in terms of success in the society, it may be a "good" system.

But it seems to me clearer to say that, though it may be a system of training, or instruction, or adaptation, or meeting immediate needs, it is not a system of education. It seems clearer to say that the purpose of education is to improve men. Any system that tries to make them bad is not education, but something else. If, for example, democracy is the best form of society, a system that adapts the young to it will be an educational system. If despotism is a bad form of society, a system that adapts the young to it will not be an educational system, and the better it succeeds in adapting them the less educational it will be.

Every man has a function as a man. The function of a citizen or a subject may vary from society to society, and the system of training, or adaptation, or instruction, or meeting immediate needs may vary with it. But the function of a man as man is the same in every age and in every society, since it results from his nature as a man. The aim of an educational system is the same in every age and in every society where such a system can exist: it is to improve man as man.

If we are going to talk about improving men and societies, we have to believe that there is some difference between good and bad. This difference must not be, as the positivists think it is, merely conventional. We cannot tell this difference by an examination of the effectiveness of a given program as the pragmatists propose: the time required to estimate these effects is usually too long and the complexity of society is always too great for us to say that the consequences of a given program are altogether clear. We cannot discover the difference between good and bad by going to the laboratory animals. If we believe that there is no truth, there is no knowledge, and there are no values except those which are validated by laboratory experiment, we cannot talk about the improvement of men and societies, for we can have no standard of judging anything that takes place among men or in societies.

Society is to be improved, not by forcing a program of social reform down its throat, through the schools or otherwise, but by the improvement of the individuals who compose it. As Plato said, "Governments reflect human nature. States are not made out of stone or wood, but out of the characters of their citizens: these turn the scale and draw everything after them." The individual is the heart of society.

To talk about making men better we must have some idea of what men are, because if we have none, we can have no idea of what is good or bad for them. If men are brutes like other animals, then there is no reason why they should not be treated like brutes by anybody who can gain power over them. And there is no reason why they should not be trained as brutes are trained. A sound philosophy in general suggests that men are rational, moral, and spiritual beings and that the improvement of men means the fullest development of their rational, moral, and spiritual powers. All men have these powers, and all men should develop them to the fullest extent.

Man is by nature free, and he is by nature social. To use his freedom rightly he needs discipline. To live in society he needs the moral virtues. Good moral and intellectual habits are required for the fullest development of the nature of man.

To develop fully as a social, political animal man needs participation in his own government. A benevolent despotism will not do. You cannot expect the slave to show the virtues of the free man unless you first set him free. Only democracy, in which all men rule and are ruled in turn for the good life of the whole community, can be an absolutely good form of government.

The community rests on the social nature of men. It requires communication among its members. They do not have to agree with one another; but they must be able to understand one another. And their philosophy in general must supply them with a common purpose and a common concept of man and society adequate to hold the community together. Civilization is the deliberate pursuit of a common ideal. The good society is not just a society we happen to like or to be used to. It is a community of good men.

Education deals with the development of the intellectual powers of men. Their moral and spiritual powers are the sphere of the family and the church. All three agencies must work in harmony; for, though a man has three aspects, he is still one man. But the schools cannot take over the role of the family and the church without promoting the atrophy of those institutions and failing in the task that is proper to the schools.

We cannot talk about the intellectual powers of men, though we can talk about training them, or amusing them, or adapting them, and meeting their immediate needs, unless our philosophy in general tells us that there is knowledge and that there is a difference between true and false. We must believe, too, that there are no other means of obtaining knowledge than scientific experimentation. If knowledge can be sought only in the laboratory, many fields in which we thought we had knowledge will offer us nothing but opinion or superstition, and we shall be forced to conclude that we cannot know anything about the most important aspects of man and society. If we are to set about developing the intellectual powers of men through having them acquire knowledge of the most important subjects, we have to begin with the proposition that experimentation and empirical data will be of only limited use to us, contrary to the convictions of many American social scientists, and that philosophy, history, literature, and art give us knowledge, and significant knowledge, on the most significant issues.

If the object of education is the improvement of men, then any system of education that is without values is a contradiction in terms. A system that seeks bad values is bad. A system that denies the existence of values denies the possibility of education. Relativism, scientism, skepticism, and anti-intellectualism, the four horsemen of the philosophical apocalypse, have produced that chaos in education which will end in the disintegration of the West.

The prime object of education is to know what is good for man. It is to know the goods in their order. There is a hierarchy of values. The task of education is to help us understand it, establish it, and live by it. This Aristotle had in mind when he said: "It is not the possessions but the desires of men that must be equalized, and this is impossible unless they have a sufficient education according to the nature of things."

Such an education is far removed from the triviality of that produced by the doctrines of adaptation, of immediate needs, of social reform, or of the doctrine of no doctrine at all. Such an education will not adapt the young to a bad environment, but it will encourage them to make good. It will not overlook immediate needs, but it will place these needs in their proper relationship to more distant, less tangible, and more important goods. It will be the only effective means of reforming society.

This is the education appropriate to free men. It is liberal education. If all men are to be free, all men must have this education. It makes no difference how they are to earn their living or what their special interests and aptitudes may be. They can learn to make a living, and they can develop their special interests and aptitudes, after they have laid the foundation of free and responsible manhood through liberal education. It will not do to say that they are incapable of such education. This claim is made by those who are too indolent or unconvinced to make the effort to give such education to the masses.

Nor will it do to say that there is not enough time to give everybody a liberal education before he becomes a specialist. In America, at least, the waste and frivolity of the educational system are so great that it would be possible through getting rid of them to give every citizen a liberal education and make him a qualified specialist, too, in less time than is now consumed in turning out uneducated specialists.

A liberal education aims to develop the powers of understanding and judgment. It is impossible that too many people can be educated in this sense, because there cannot be too many people with understanding and judgment. We hear a great deal today about the dangers that will come upon us through the frustration of educated people who have got educated in the expectation that education will get them a better job, and who then fail to get it. But surely this depends on the representations that are made to the young about what education is. If we allow them to believe that education will get them better jobs and encourage them to get educated with this end in view, they are entitled to a sense of frustration if, when they have got the education, they do not get the jobs. But, if we say that they should be educated in order to be men, and that everybody, whether he is a ditchdigger or a bank president, should have this education because he is a man, then the ditchdigger may still feel frustrated, but not because of his education.

Nor is it possible for a person to have too much liberal education, because it is impossible to have too much understanding and judgment. But it is possible to undertake too much in the name of liberal education in youth. The object of liberal education in youth is not to teach the young all they will ever need to know. It is to give them the habits, ideas, and techniques that they need to continue to educate themselves. Thus the object of formal institutional liberal education in youth is to prepare the young to educate themselves throughout their lives.

I would remind you of the impossibility of learning to understand and judge many of the most important things in youth. The judgment and understanding of practical affairs can amount to little in the absence of experience with practical affairs. Subjects that cannot be understood without experience should not be taught to those who are without experience. Or, if these subjects are taught to those who are without experience, it should be clear that these subjects can be taught only by way of introduction and that their value to the student depends on his continuing to study them as he acquires experience. The tragedy of America is that economics, ethics, politics, history, and literature are studied in youth, and seldom studied again. Therefore the graduates of American universities seldom understand them.

This pedagogical principle, that subjects requiring experience can be learned only by the experienced, leads to the conclusion that the most important branch of education is the education of adults. We sometimes seem to think of education as something like the mumps, measles, whooping-cough, or chicken-pox. If a person has had education in childhood, he need not, in fact he cannot, have it again. But the pedagogical principle that the most important things can be learned only in mature life is supported by a sound philosophy in general. Men are rational animals. They achieve their terrestrial felicity by the use of reason. And this means that they have to use it for their entire lives. To say that they should learn only in childhood would mean that they were human only in childhood.

And it would mean that they were unfit to be citizens of a republic. A republic, a true *res publica,* can maintain justice, peace, freedom, and order only by the exercise of intelligence. When we speak of the consent of the governed, we mean, since men are not angels who seek the truth intuitively and do not have to learn it, that every act of assent on the part of the governed is a product of learning. A republic is really a common educational life in process. So Montesquieu said that, whereas the principle of a monarchy was honor, and the principle of tyranny was fear, the principle of a republic was education.

Hence the ideal republic is the republic of learning. It is the utopia by which all actual political republics are measured. The goal toward which we started with the Athenians twenty-five centuries ago is an unlimited republic of learning and a world-wide political republic mutually supporting each other.

All men are capable of learning. Learning does not stop as long as a man lives, unless his learning power atrophies because he does not use it. Political freedom cannot endure unless it is accompanied by provision for the unlimited acquisition of knowledge. Truth is not long retained in human affairs without continual learning and relearning. Peace is unlikely unless there are continuous, unlimited opportunities for learning and unless men continuously avail themselves of them. The world of law and justice for which we yearn, the world-wide political republic, cannot be realized without the world-wide republic of learning. The civilization we seek will be achieved when all men are citizens of the world republic of law and justice and of the republic of learning all their lives long.*

*I owe this discussion to the suggestions of Scott Buchanan.

53

My Pedagogic Creed

John Dewey

ARTICLE I—WHAT EDUCATION IS

I believe that all education proceeds by the participation of the individual in the social consciousness of the race. The process begins unconsciously almost at birth, and is continually shaping the individual's powers, saturating his consciousness, forming his habits, training his ideas, and arousing his feelings and emotions. Through this unconscious education the individual gradually comes to share in the intellectual and moral resources which humanity has succeeded in getting together. He becomes an inheritor of the funded capital of civilization. The most formal and technical education in the world cannot safely depart from this general process. It can only organize it or differentiate it in some particular direction.

I believe that the only true education comes through the stimulation of the child's powers by the demands of the social situations in which he finds himself. Through these demands he is stimulated to act as a member of a unity, to emerge from his original narrowness of action and feeling, and to conceive of himself from the standpoint of the welfare of the group to which he belongs. Through the responses which others make to his own activities he comes to know what these mean in social terms. The value which they have is reflected back into them. For instance, through the response which is made to the child's instinctive babblings the child comes to know what those babblings mean; they are transformed into articulate language and thus the child is introduced into the consolidated wealth of ideas and emotions which are now summed up in language.

I believe that this educational process has two sides—one psychological and one sociological; and that neither can be subordinated to the other or neglected without evil results following. Of these two sides, the psychological is the basis. The child's own instincts and powers furnish the material and give the starting point for all education. Save as the efforts of the educator connect with some activity which the child is carrying on of his own initiative independent of the educator, education becomes reduced to a pressure from without. It may, indeed, give certain external results, but cannot truly be called educative. Without insight into the psychological structure and activities of the individual, the educative process will, therefore, be haphazard and arbitrary. If it chances to coincide with the child's activity it will get a leverage; if it does not, it will result in friction, or disintegration, or arrest of the child's nature.

I believe that knowledge of social conditions, of the present state of civilization, is necessary in order properly to interpret the child's powers. The child has his own instincts and tendencies, but we do not know what these mean until we can translate them into their social equivalents. We must be able to carry them back into a social past and see them as the inheritance of previous race activities. We must also be able to project them into the future to see what their outcome and end will be. In the illustration just used, it is the ability to see in the child's babblings the promise and potency of a future social intercourse and conversation which enables one to deal in the proper way with that instinct.

I believe that the psychological and social sides are organically related and that education cannot be regarded as a compromise between the two, or a superimposition of one upon the other. We are told that the psychological definition of education is barren and formal—that it gives us only the idea of a development of all the mental powers without giving us any idea of the use to which these powers are put. On the other hand, it is urged that the social definition of education, as getting adjusted to civilization, makes of it a forced and external process, and results in subordinating the freedom of the individual to a preconceived political status.

I believe that each of these objections is true when urged against one side isolated from the other. In order to know what a power really is we must know what its end, use, or function is; and this we cannot know save as we conceive of the individual as active in social relationships. But, on the other hand, the only possible adjustment which we can give to the child under existing conditions, is that which arises through putting him in complete possession of all his powers. With the advent of democracy and modern industrial conditions, it is impossible to foretell definitely just what civilization will be twenty years from now. Hence it is impossible to prepare the child for any precise set of conditions. To prepare him for the future life means to give him command of himself; it means so to train him that he will have the full and ready use of all his capacities; that his eye and ear and hand may be tools ready to command, that his judgment may be capable of grasping the conditions under which it has to work, and the executive forces be trained to act economically and efficiently. It is impossible to reach this sort of adjustment save as constant regard is had to the individual's own powers, tastes, and interests—say, that is, as education is continually converted into psychological terms.

In sum, I believe that the individual who is to be educated is a social individual and that society is an organic union of individuals. If we eliminate the social factor from the

Source: From John Dewey, "My Pedagogic Creed," Number IX in a series under this title, in *The Second Journal* LIV, Number 3, January 16, 1897, pp. 77–80.

child we are left only with an abstraction; if we eliminate the individual factor from society, we are left only with an inert and lifeless mass. Education, therefore, must begin with a psychological insight into the child's capacities, interests, and habits. It must be controlled at every point by reference to these same considerations. These powers, interests, and habits must be continually interpreted—we must know what they mean. They must be translated into terms of their social equivalents—into terms of what they are capable of in the way of social service.

ARTICLE II—WHAT THE SCHOOL IS

I believe that the school is primarily a social institution. Education being a social process, the school is simply that form of community life in which all those agencies are concentrated that will be most effective in bringing the child to share in the inherited resources of the race, and to use his own powers for social ends.

I believe that education, therefore, is a process of living and not a preparation for future living.

I believe that the school must represent present life—life as real and vital to the child as that which he carries on in the home, in the neighborhood, or on the playground.

I believe that education which does not occur through forms of life, or that are worth living for their own sake, is always a poor substitute for the genuine reality and tends to cramp and to deaden.

I believe that the school, as an institution, should simplify existing social life; should reduce it, as it were, to an embryonic form. Existing life is so complex that the child cannot be brought into contact with it without either confusion or distraction; he is either overwhelmed by the multiplicity of activities which are going on, so that he loses his own power of orderly reaction, or he is so stimulated by these various activities that his powers are prematurely called into play and he becomes unduly specialized or else disintegrated.

I believe that as such simplified social life, the school life should grow gradually out of the home life; that it should take up and continue the activities with which the child is already familiar in the home.

I believe that it should exhibit these activities to the child, and reproduce them in such ways that the child will gradually learn the meaning of them, and be capable of playing his own part in relation to them.

I believe that this is a psychological necessity, because it is the only way of securing continuity in the child's growth, the only way of giving a background of past experience to the new ideas given in school.

I believe that it is also a social necessity because the home is the form of social life in which the child has been nurtured and in connection with which he has had his moral training. It is the business of the school to deepen and extend his sense of the values bound up in his home life.

I believe that much of present education fails because it neglects this fundamental principle of the school as a form of community life. It conceives the school as a place where certain information is to be given, where certain lessons are to be learned, or where certain habits are to be formed. The value of these is conceived as lying largely in the remote future; the child must do these things for the sake of something else he is to do; they are mere preparation. As a result they do not become a part of the life experience of the child and so are not truly educative.

I believe that the moral education centers upon this conception of the school as a mode of social life, that the best and deepest moral training is precisely that which one gets through having to enter into proper relations with others in a unity of work and thought. The present educational systems, so far as they destroy or neglect this unity, render it difficult or impossible to get any genuine, regular moral training.

I believe that the child should be stimulated and controlled in his work through the life of the community.

I believe that under existing conditions far too much of the stimulus and control proceeds from the teacher, because of neglect of the idea of the school as a form of social life.

I believe that the teacher's place and work in the school is to be interpreted from this same basis. The teacher is not in the school to impose certain ideas or to form certain habits in the child, but is there as a member of the community to select the influences which shall affect the child and to assist him in properly responding to these influences.

I believe that the discipline of the school should proceed from the life of the school as a whole and not directly from the teacher.

I believe that the teacher's business is simply to determine on the basis of larger experience and riper wisdom, how the discipline of life shall come to the child.

I believe that all questions of the grading of the child and his promotion should be determined by reference to the same standard. Examinations are of use only so far as they test the child's fitness for social life and reveal the place in which he can be of the most service and where he can receive the most help.

ARTICLE III—THE SUBJECT-MATTER OF EDUCATION

I believe that the social life of the child is the basis of concentration, or correlation, in all his training or growth. The social life gives the unconscious unit and the background of all his efforts and of all his attainments.

I believe that the subject-matter of the school curriculum should mark a gradual differentiation out of the primitive unconscious unity of social life.

I believe that we violate the child's nature and render difficult the best ethical results, by introducing the child too abruptly to a number of special studies, of reading, writing, geography, etc., out of relation to this social life.

I believe, therefore, that the true center of correlation on the school subjects is not science, nor literature, nor history, nor geography, but the child's own social activities.

I believe that education cannot be unified in the study of science, or so called nature study, because apart from human activity, nature itself is not a unity; nature in itself is a number of diverse objects in space and time, and to attempt to make it the center of work by itself, is to introduce a principle of radiation rather than one of concentration.

I believe that literature is the reflex expression and interpretation of social experience; that hence it must follow upon and not precede such experience. It, therefore, cannot be made the basis, although it may be made the summary of unification.

I believe once more that history is of educative value in so far as it presents phases of social life and growth. It must be controlled by reference to social life. When taken simply as history it is thrown into the distant past and becomes dead and inert. Taken as the record of man's social life and progress it becomes full of meaning. I believe, however, that it cannot be so taken excepting as the child is also introduced directly into social life.

I believe accordingly that the primary basis of education is in the child's powers at work along the same general constructive lines as those which have brought civilization into being.

I believe that the only way to make the child conscious of his social heritage is to enable him to perform those fundamental types of activity which make civilization what it is.

I believe, therefore, in the so-called expressive or constructive activities as the center of correlation.

I believe that this gives the standard for the place of cooking, sewing, manual training, etc., in the school.

I believe that they are not special studies which are to be introduced over and above a lot of others in the way of relaxation or relief, or as additional accomplishments. I believe rather that they represent, as types, fundamental forms of social activity; and that it is possible and desirable that the child's introduction into the more formal subjects of the curriculum be through the medium of these activities.

I believe that the study of science is educational in so far as it brings out the materials and processes which make social life what it is.

I believe that one of the greatest difficulties in the present teaching of science is that the material is presented in purely objective form, or is treated as a new peculiar kind of experience which the child can add to that which he has already had. In reality, science is of value because it gives the ability to interpret and control the experience already had. It should be introduced, not as so much new subject-matter, but as showing the factors already involved in previous experience and as furnishing tools by which that experience can be more easily and effectively regulated.

I believe that at present we lost much of the value of literature and language studies because of our elimination of the social element. Language is almost always treated in the books of pedagogy simply as the expression of thought. It is true that language is a logical instrument, but it is fundamentally and primarily a social instrument. Language is the device for communication; it is the tool through which one individual comes to share the ideas and feelings of others. When treated simply as a way of getting individual information, or as a means of showing off what one has learned, it loses its social motive and end.

I believe that there is, therefore, no succession of studies in the ideal school curriculum. If education is life, all life has, from the outset, a scientific aspect, an aspect of art and culture, and an aspect of communication. It cannot, therefore, be true that the proper studies for one grade are mere reading and writing, and that at a later grade, reading, or literature, or science, may be introduced. The progress is not in the succession of studies but in the development of new attitudes towards, and new interests in, experience.

I believe finally, that education must be conceived as a continuing reconstruction of experience; that the process and the goal of education are one and the same thing.

I believe that to set up any end outside of education, as furnishing its goal and standard, is to deprive the educational process of much of its meaning and tends to make us rely upon false and external stimuli in dealing with the child.

ARTICLE IV—THE NATURE OF METHOD

I believe that the question of method is ultimately reducible to the question of the order of development of the child's powers and interests. The law for presenting and treating material is the law implicit with the child's own nature. Because this is so I believe the following statements are of supreme importance as determining the spirit in which education is carried on:

1. I believe that the active side precedes the passive in the development of the child's nature; that expression comes before conscious impression; that the muscular development precedes the sensory; that movements come before conscious sensations; I believe that consciousness is essentially motor or impulsive; that conscious states tend to project themselves in action.

I believe that the neglect of this principle is the cause of a large part of the waste of time and strength in school work. The child is thrown into a passive, receptive, or absorbing attitude. The conditions are such that he is not permitted to follow the law of his nature; the result is friction and waste.

I believe that ideas (intellectual and rational processes) also result from action and devolve for the sake of the better control of action. What we term reason is primarily the law of orderly or effective action. To attempt to develop the reasoning powers, the powers of judgment, without reference to the selection and arrangement of means in action, is the fundamental fallacy in our present methods of dealing with this matter. As a result we present the child with arbitrary symbols. Symbols are a necessity in mental development, but they have their place as tools for economizing effort; presented by themselves they are a mass of meaningless and arbitrary ideas imposed from without.

2. I believe that the image is the great instrument of instruction. What a child gets out of any subject presented to him is simply the images which he himself forms with regard to it.

I believe that if nine tenths of the energy at present directed towards making the child learn certain things, were spent in seeing to it that the child was forming proper images, the work of instruction would be indefinitely facilitated.

I believe that much of the time and attention now given to the preparation and presentation of lessons might be more wisely and profitably expended in training the child's power of imagery and in seeing to it that he was continually forming definite, vivid, and growing images of the various subjects with which he comes in contact in his experience.

3. I believe that interests are the signs and symptoms of growing power. I believe that they represent dawning capacities. Accordingly the constant and careful observation of interests is of the utmost importance for the educator.

I believe that these interests are to be observed as showing the state of development which the child has reached.

I believe that they prophesy the stage upon which he is about to enter.

I believe that only through the continual and sympathetic observation of childhood's interests can the adult enter into the child's life and see what it is ready for, and upon what material it could work most readily and fruitfully.

I believe that these interests are neither to be humored nor repressed. To repress interest is to substitute the adult for the child, and so to weaken intellectual curiosity and alertness, to suppress initiative, and to deaden interest. To humor the interests is to substitute the transient for the permanent. The interest is always the sign of some power below; the important thing is to discover this power. To humor the interest is to fail to penetrate below the surface and its sure result is to substitute caprice and whim for genuine interest.

4. I believe that the emotions are the reflex of actions.

I believe that to endeavor to stimulate or arouse the emotions apart from their corresponding activities, is to introduce an unhealthy and morbid state of mind.

I believe that if we can only secure right habits of action and thought, with reference to the good, the true, and the beautiful, the emotions will for the most part take care of themselves.

I believe that next to deadness and dullness, formalism and routine, our education is threatened with no greater evil than sentimentalism.

I believe that this sentimentalism is the necessary result of the attempt to divorce feeling from action.

ARTICLE V—THE SCHOOL AND SOCIAL PROGRESS

I believe that education is the fundamental method of social progress and reform.

I believe that all reforms which rest simply upon the enactment of law, or the threatening of certain penalties, or upon changes in mechanical or outward arrangements, are transitory and futile.

I believe that education is a regulation of the process of coming to share in the social consciousness; and that the adjustment of individual activity on the basis of this social consciousness is the only sure method of social reconstruction.

I believe that this conception has due regard for both the individualistic and socialistic ideals. It is duly individual because it recognizes the formation of a certain character as the only genuine basis of right living. It is socialistic because it recognizes that this right character is not to be formed by merely individual precept, example, or exhortation, but rather by the influence of a certain form of institutional or community life upon the individual, and that the social organism through the school, as its organ, may determine ethical results.

I believe that in the ideal school we have the reconciliation of the individualistic and the institutional ideals.

I believe that the community's duty to education is, therefore, its paramount moral duty. By law and punishment, by social agitation and discussion, society can regulate and form itself in a more or less haphazard and chance way. But through education society can formulate its own purposes, can organize its own means and resources, and thus shape itself with definiteness and economy in the direction in which it wishes to move.

I believe that when society once recognizes the possibilities in this direction, and the obligations which these possibilities impose, it is impossible to conceive of the resources of time, attention, and money which will be put at the disposal of the educator.

I believe that it is the business of every one interested in education to insist upon the school as a primary and most effective interest of social progress and reform in order that society may be awakened to realize what the school stands for, and aroused to the necessity of endowing the educator with sufficient equipment properly to perform his task.

I believe that education thus conceived marks the most perfect and intimate union of science and art conceivable in human experience.

I believe that the art of thus giving shape to human powers and adapting them to social service, is the supreme art; one calling into its service the best of artists; that no insight, sympathy, tact, executive power, is too great for such service.

I believe that with the growth of psychological service, giving added insight into individual structure and laws of growth; and with growth of social science, adding to our knowledge of the right organization of individuals, all scientific resources can be utilized for the purposes of education.

I believe that when science and art thus join hands the most commanding motive for human action will be reached; the most genuine springs of human conduct aroused and the best service that human nature is capable of guaranteed.

I believe, finally, that the teacher is engaged, not simply in the training of individuals, but in the formation of the proper social life.

I believe that every teacher should realize the dignity of his calling; that he is a social servant set apart for the maintenance of proper social order and the securing of the right social growth.

I believe that in this way the teacher always is the prophet of the true God and the usherer in the true kingdom of God.

54

My Idea of Education

Ashley Montagu

As an anthropologist who has been studying the 6-million-year course of human evolution for nearly 60 years, I have become convinced that the characteristic that distinguishes humans from all other creatures is educability and that the most important of all basic human psychological needs is the need for love. Both of these findings have profound implications for schools and teachers.

The human is capable of learning anything, under the appropriate environmental conditions. The human brain is an organ of the assimilation of diverse kinds of experiences and for turning accidents into opportunities. It is the most flexible, the most malleable, and the most educable of all the brains in the world.

It is capable of making the most of the improbable. Some people use their brains to arrive at truth and conclusions that others might conceive as utterly impossible. For example, at the very time the flying machine was invented, leading experts of the world said it was a physical impossibility.

We must recognize the educability of the human brain, particularly in dealing with children, who are the most educable of all human beings.

One thing most of us don't understand is the nature of the child and his or her extraordinary educability. Furthermore, we don't understand that we need to grow up into children and not adults. By this I mean that we should preserve some of the traits that the child so conspicuously exhibits.

What are these traits? Beside educability, they are the need to love, sensitivity, the need to think soundly, the need to learn, the need to work, the need to organize, curiosity and wonder, open mindedness, experimental mindedness, imagination, creativity, playfulness, sense of humor, joyfulness, laughter, optimism, honesty, trust, compassionate intelligence, and the desire to grow and develop in all these traits. Frequently, we feel we ought to limit this desire to grow to certain stages that we arbitrarily designate as infancy, childhood, and adolescence or to this one stage or another. Then we treat children of the same chronological age as if they were developmentally of the same age, too.

This is a damaging idea, and it has done an enormous amount of harm to children. Every child has his or her own developmental rate. To treat children, even children the same age, as if they were all equal is to commit a biological and social absurdity. The equal treatment of unequals is the most unequal way of dealing with human beings ever devised. We're all very different, and because we're all very different, we require individual attention. We should not be treated as if we were an agglutinated mass affixed to one another on the basis of our particular age level.

Even though many teachers recognize the great differences among children, they are not in a position to do anything about them because of the way school systems are organized and the inadequacy of those who are presiding at their top levels. These top-level officials are usually unequipped to understand what the child is, what the teacher's needs are, and what education is all about.

What education is all about is being human, in other words, developing those traits that are uniquely human for the benefit of the individual, the family, the community, the society, and the world. Eventually what teachers do in the classroom is going to determine what the world is going to be like; for it is there that children learn all about being human if they have not learned it in the home.

Unfortunately, the probabilities are that children have not learned this in the home, because most parents are not equipped to do the job of parenting. Why? Simply because they have lived in a society that has not recognized the nature of the child, the nature of the human being, and the nature of what the child ought to be.

We now know what human beings ought to be because we understand for the first time in the history of our species that the most important of all human basic psychological needs is the need for love. It stands at the center of all human needs just as our sun stands at the center of our solar system with the planets orbiting around it. So the basic needs, the need for oxygen, food, liquid, rest, for activity, and so on, these revolve around the need for love—the sun of the human being.

It is this need for love that nature designates the mother to satisfy and that we have interfered with for a very long time by having mothers give birth to babies in hospitals, by taking babies away from their mothers in hospitals, by bottle-feeding babies, and by committing many other frightful offenses against babies at the very beginnings of their lives. These are offenses not only against the baby but against the mother and the family. The family should be involved in the ceremony and the celebration of welcoming a new member into the family. It is the family's job to turn this educable creature into the kind of human being that he or she is striving to be from the moment of birth.

Now that's quite a statement for a scientist to make. How do I know what this baby is striving to be? Well, I have discussed this with hundreds of babies. I've observed them, and I've talked with them. So have a good many other people. What they and I have observed is that the baby wants more than

Source: From Ashley Montagu, "My Idea of Education," *Today's Education*, February–March 1980, pp. 48–49. Reprinted with permission from the publisher and from Patricia Gannon.

anything else to learn to love. Not only to be loved, but to love, because if the baby fails in this, then he or she fails to grow up as a warm, loving human being.

It's as simple as that. Nothing very complicated, but it's taken a long time for us to understand this.

The child who has not been loved is biochemically, physiologically, and psychologically very different from the one who has been loved. The former even grows differently from the latter. What we now know is that the human being is born to live as if to live and love were one.

This is not, of course, new. This is a validation of the Sermon on the Mount. I who am not a Christian and who am not a member of any religious affiliation say this.

The only religion I believe in is goodness and love. This is what we should be teaching in our schools. The greatest gift a teacher has to give a student is his or her love.

A teacher can recognize that the biggest behavior problems in the classroom are the ones who have been failed in their need for love and that what their need is is not to be sent to the principal but to be loved by the teacher. They will try the teacher again and again because they have been failed so many times and they don't trust anyone.

Every time the teacher offers them love, they may not improve their behavior, but if the teacher persists, then the teacher will win the children over. I speak from experience as an old teacher. I know very well how this works, because I've frequently done it myself.

I know this is very difficult in many cases—and it's extremely difficult in certain parts of America where teachers face behavior problems of the worst kind and where violence and vandalism are increasing at an accelerating rate in the schools. Even in those places, however, I think each teacher can make a difference by doing what he or she ought to do: behaving as a warm, loving human being.

How do we become warm, loving human beings? We act *as if* we were warm, loving human beings. If we act as if we were, someday we may find we've become what we've been trying to be, because what we are is not what we say but what we do.

I have been discussing love, but I have not defined it yet for the simple reason that a definition isn't meaningful at the beginning of an inquiry. It can be so only at the end of one.

Love is the ability to communicate by demonstrative acts to others our profound involvement in their welfare. We communicate our deep interest in them because we are aware that to be born human is to be born in danger, and therefore we will never commit the supreme treason against others of not helping them when they are most in need of us. We will minister to their needs and give them all the supports, all the stimulation, all the succor that they need or want.

That's love, and that's what we should be teaching in the schools, and everything else should be secondary to that. Reading, writing, and arithmetic, yes—but not of primary importance, of secondary importance in the development of a warm, loving human being.

This is my idea of education. If we put this into action, we stand a chance of solving most of the problems that bedevil the world at the present time, for teachers are the unacknowledged legislators of the world.

55

Where Has All Our Empathy Gone?

Dea Forney

Approximately two years ago, Skip Sturman, career director at Dartmouth College, wrote a very thought-provoking article, "Where Have All Our Values Gone?," which appeared in the *Journal*. Since that time, I have often reflected on this piece, and I have referred to it in presentations and informal discussions with colleagues. I think the time has finally come for me, as another product of the '60s, to offer my formal response to Skip's well-written commentary and to introduce some new dimensions to the values issues and controversies which surround career development professionals working in college and university settings.

Skip Sturman challenged us to re-examine the nature of our interactions with students who seem to lack an understanding of the term "commitment" and who "want it all" (typically defined in financial terms). Certainly, acts of avoidance on our part—e.g., failing to question student values and refusing to offer alternative perspectives—deserve to be regarded as irresponsible. Both as professional counselors and advisers and as members of society, we must own our responsibility to challenge students. As William Perry has noted, commitment is genuine only when choices have been made with an awareness of other possibilities. Choices and values "swallowed whole" without active thought are not really commitments at all but passive absorptions. Moreover, there is a greater good, and humanity is dependent upon our efforts to help students keep sight of the larger community.

On the other hand, I believe that it is easier to promote the common good in some contexts than in others. Maslow's hierarchy of needs, a mainstay in introductory psychology courses, asserts that lower-level needs associated with basic survival—e.g. food, clothing, and shelter—must be satisfied before higher-order needs—e.g. self-actualization—can be acted upon. For many of today's and tomorrow's students, satisfaction of lower-order needs has consumed and will no doubt continue to consume more time and energy than has necessarily been the case in the past. Let's consider what our current context really looks like, how it has evolved, and what some of the implications are for our students and ourselves as career counselors.

THE SOCIAL CONTEXT

Levine, in *When Dreams and Heroes Died*, has given us a sensitive and honest depiction of students of the '60s and '70s. Both generations are portrayed has having virtues and blemishes. In reality, the '60s generation may have been the last our country will see for some time for whom success was almost assured and a life style equal to or better than one's parents could be assumed. In such a social context, it could be comparatively easy to turn away from financial security and opt for alternative life styles, for the traditional options would be waiting if the yippies chose to return to the mainstream. Relatedly, the challenging of societal values, though never easy, was buoyed by a romanticism that Reich, in *The Greening of America*, and others presented to a well-fed youth for whom anything was still possible.

For students of the '70s, social forces included Vietnam, Watergate, and a more competitive job market. The "meism" label was applied to a student generation which simply mirrored the growing pessimism in the country as a whole. Most of these students entered adolescence "between the time Lyndon Johnson's dream of a great society faded and Gerald Ford promised to end a long national nightmare" (Levine, p. 13). Levine describes these students as being optimistic about their own futures despite their pessimism about the country in general. He portrays them as wanting to ride first-class on the Titanic. Such an image vividly captures the extent to which their dreams had been dashed. Creature comforts on the inevitable route to disaster were all that seemed within reach. Given the social context during the '70s, might not some of our criticism of this student group seem unduly harsh?

Moving to students of the '80s, Levine has noted, "Today's students are just turning the corner on a decade that brought unchecked inflation, three recessions, and intermittent crises of unemployment" (p. 65). Concern about survival would seem easy to understand, considering such economic realities.

Looking at the contemporary social context, one continues to find much that contributes to the formation of materialistic, survival-oriented values. The July 6, 1987, issue of *Fortune* featured as its cover story "The Money Society." Its author, Myron Magnet, presents an interesting analysis, which includes quotes from university scholars, of why money seems to be the only thing that counts today. Discussing inflation, he argues that not only economic values but also moral ones were turned upside down by this phenomenon in the '70s.

Source: From Dea Forney, "Where Has All Our Empathy Gone?," *T.H.E. Journal*, Volume 49, Winter 1989, pp. 30–33. Reprinted with permission from the publisher.

Magnet also asserts that what inflation began in the '70s, corporate restructuring completed in the '80s by implicitly reinforcing the message of "every man for himself" (p. 28). Since Levine had already placed us on the Titanic as a society, it seems no surprise that the lifeboat mentality of looking out for Number One described by Magnet would soon follow. Moreover, students learned this lesson well. Living on the "edge of anxiety," they advocate getting *what* you can *while* you can (p. 28).

This corporate restructuring is described as resulting in more than just economic change. Sociological outcomes are also evident as the relationship between employers and employees has been transformed. Organizations can no longer offer long-term commitments to their workers, nor can they very readily inspire loyalty.

Perhaps the most caustic critic of the impact of current work environments on the individual is Douglas LaBier. His book *Modern Madness* is subtitled, "The Emotional Fallout of Success." Looking at what he considers to be the highly competitive and power-driven nature of large organizations, LaBier views work as having the potential to rob individuals of their sanity. Organizational values which promote the good of the company, often at the expense of the individual, induce values conflicts and emotional difficulties for workers.

Ultimately, LaBier maintains that sometimes the individuals who appear most adjusted to the work environment may, in reality, be most unbalanced. By displaying pathological attitudes, they are able to adjust to an inherently unhealthy environment, while those whom LaBier classifies as "the working wounded," those who are unable to adjust, are often healthier people in psychological terms. Certainly, LaBier's work can be considered controversial. However, given the nature of the challenges that he raises, I believe all of us in the career development field who have some responsibility for helping individuals choose careers and employing organizations should have some exposure to LaBier's concerns.

Meanwhile, we continue to see social forces exerting an influence on student values. What feelings of financial insecurity was last fall's stock market plunge likely to have generated or reinforced? And how are students expected to interpret messages such as Gordon Gekko's advocacy of greed in the film *Wall Street*, and the valuing of William Hurt's pretty boy image over Albert Brooks' professional competency in *Broadcast News*?

A NEW QUESTION

Skip Sturman asked, "Where have all our values gone?" Now, as I look at us as career development professionals, my new question is more likely to be, "Where has all our empathy gone?" While I take no personal joy in the values of the student who is out to make a fast buck, I think I understand something about how he may have come to be that way. And I also see many students around me who struggle with challenges that our social context has presented to them.

A couple of years ago, I was facilitating a "transition" group for seniors about to graduate from college. One of the students, a bit of a throwback to the '60s with his Grateful Dead jacket and his work with the street people, lamented the concern for money which he felt he had to have in order to survive. He commented, "Money really doesn't matter . . . unless you don't have any." For me, he captured succinctly and with good humor a reality that many of our students face. It may be easy for us to forget what it is like to be unemployed, from less than well-to-do families, etc. In fact, some of us may never have had such experiences.

I'm also inclined to remember a student who had a genuine interest in public school teaching. He really wanted to pursue a career in education, but the low income and the potential burden that would place on the family he planned to have induced a painful conflict regarding career choice. As I now find myself employed by a public institution in a state whose legislature recently voted to spend millions of dollars to retain a baseball team while simultaneously failing to increase funds for education for the past two years, I identify with the student's plight. Who truly bears the responsibility if he forsakes his interest in teaching in order to support his family? And who truly suffers the loss?

I suspect Magnet might say that we are all responsible and that, in turn, we all lose. He states, "Editorialists who recently have been haranguing the young to give up all this soulless materialism and return to the commitment of the sixties have got it exactly wrong. That 'commitment,' with its heavy charge of destructive anger and protest, ultimately helped bleed the value out of existing institutions, giving them their present zombielike character" (p. 31).

WHAT WE DO NOW

As students of the '60s, we may have done some good and we may have done some harm. More important to me is what we do now. First, I think we need to never lose sight of the fact that our students do not come to us "vacuum-packed." They have learned much from society as a whole and from their immediate environments. For example, a freshman student enrolled in the career and personal development course that I teach was having difficulty understanding the emphasis given to self-exploration and individual choice. She was certain that she would not succeed academically in college and that even if somehow she did, she would still be destined to return to the same metropolitan area where she was born and to work in the same factory where her mother was currently employed.

The diversity which the students enrolled in our academic institutions represent has never been greater, and as Hodgkinson has noted, this diversity will increase even more in the future. We will need, more than ever before, to be able to understand and deal constructively with what this diversity will mean in terms of life experiences, values, and goals.

Second, I think we need to come to terms with ourselves. While I doubt that any of us in the career development field are likely to be profiled on *Lifestyles of the Rich and Famous*, I do expect that we are all living in a reasonably comfortable fashion. In the same way that I hope we can accept diversity in student values, I also hope that we can honor our own desires to be comfortable without experiencing guilt. In addition, I think we need to recognize that money remains a symbol of how we are valued by those who employ us. Because we are in the field of education, we are likely to experience some dissonance over whether we think we're being paid what we are worth. If the answer is "no," let's try to avoid letting that perception make us miserable, cranky, and old before our time.

Lastly, I think we need to expand our focus in regard to our responsibility to challenge values. The topic of challenging student values is often addressed in writing and in discussions among colleagues. So be it, provided that we challenge without losing our ability to empathize. By contrast, what rarely seems to be addressed is the issue of challenging organizational and societal views. I maintain that if we are going to enter into the values fray, we do a disservice to students, ourselves, and society if we are willing to risk challenging only our student clients.

Certainly, many of our academic institutions operate with a bottom-line mentality. Fund raising has become a revered function at many institutions, while public image is also held dear to the hearts of ranking administrators. While external support is undeniably important to the survival of our institutions, I think we run a risk of letting the tail wag the dog if the bottom-line mentality is permitted to dominate, unchecked, the nature of our relationships with alumni, parents, corporations, and others. It seems to me that we relinquish our right to challenge student values if the role model we present institutionally is one that is more corporate than academic.

Relatedly, are we willing to challenge those organizations that employ our students to examine the degree to which they provide healthy work environments? And, finally, are we willing to tackle broader social issues, such as apartheid and nuclear disarmament, that threaten humanity?

Am I trying to make career development professionals responsible for the world?

Truthfully, yes and no. While I am not advocating that our professional groups launch "save the whales" campaigns, I do consider us each partially responsible for that small corner of the universe which we inhabit. To what extent do we each consider ourselves satisfactory role models for students? I think students are desperate for positive examples to follow. How we choose to demonstrate our definition of "commitment" has the potential to make a tremendous difference, for we are linked to the various components of our institutions and our society in a way that no other function within higher education shares. We know yesterday's and today's students, our academic institutions, and the world of work. I believe we can use this knowledge and these connections for the good of all.

56

The Normative and the Possible

Values in the Curriculum

William Ayers
William H. Schubert

Over a century ago Herbert Spencer asked a question that captured the dimensions of curriculum thought and deliberation through the ages, and focused curriculum debate for theorists and practitioners in modern times: "What knowledge is of most worth?"[1] It is an elegant question, its contours being seemingly clear and evident, and yet it is a difficult question as well, one that becomes thicker and thornier as one attends to its deeper meanings and enters its open spaces. Spencer's own answer to the question set him on the path of social Darwinism, and was not of lasting value. But the question remains, and it is a question that fascinates, troubles, and excites.

What knowledge and experiences are most worthwhile? This fundamental curriculum question resonates in contemporary curriculum debates, and provides a useful frame for the present discussion. It must be noted at the outset that this question is not essentially a question of fact, of externally-generated conventions or law-like propositions, of rules or even of preferences. Considered consciously and seriously, this question points in the direction of moral reflection: What constitutes the good life? What action is right and what action is wrong? Who is a good person and how do we know? And in schools, at least, it is linked to a fundamental pedagogical question: What are the means to strengthen, invigorate, and enable people to take full advantage of those worthwhile experiences and that valuable knowledge?

Current debates about values too often overlook that Spencer's question is present in explicit or implicit form in every classroom and is at bottom a moral question. Values interpenetrate knowledge in all kinds of ways, and values can never really be left behind, or suspended for later consideration. For example, focus on who should teach values, the school or the home, misses the point that both do teach values at all times and in a variety of ways. Similarly a concern for "higher-order thinking skills" in the curriculum often assumes a value-free stance, as if one can learn to weigh ideas, tell fact from opinion, identify assumptions, assess the soundness of logic, and the like, without full consideration of moral choice. Such a perspective ignores the fact that this kind of choice making, this selection of critical thinking as a curricular emphasis, is itself based on assumptions that value that sort of thinking, that accept the separation of process and content of thought, that assume a conception of critical thinking disembodied from politics, lived experience, and emotion. Perhaps the biggest fallacy in current curriculum discourse is the assumption that we can avoid the troubling and difficult world of moral choice by labeling an issue controversial ("creationism" versus evolution) or by having a separate curriculum offering on ethics (values clarification, for example) — in short, the assumption that we can separate the normative from the everyday. Knowledge is social and culturally created, and there is, therefore, no knowledge devoid of value.

Thus, curriculum itself is a value offered to (sometimes imposed upon) learners by educators and by the social and cultural milieu in which education takes place. From the ancients among curriculum theorists (e.g. Plato, Aristotle, Confucius, Lao Tse) through scholars such as Augustine, Erasmus, Luther, Montaigne, Locke, and Rousseau, to those of the past and present centuries (Pestalozzi, Herbart, Froebel, Dewey, and Whitehead), this indivisible remnant of knowledge and value in the learning process has been obvious. This is evident in the fact that all great treatises that address the question of what education should be like (from Plato's *Republic* to Dewey's *Democracy and Education*) immerse education deeply within an image of society that perceives its own growth and that of its people as rooted in a continuous human quest to understand the fundamental curriculum question: What knowledge and experiences are most worthwhile? Flowing from such a question are issues of the nature of the good life, right conduct, and the just society. With such issues at stake the significance of curriculum ascends to immeasurable magnitude. Rather than accepting a simplistic either-or answer to the question of parental and school responsibility, it becomes clear that both must realize that not only *what* they advocate (the traditional image of curriculum) but also *who* they are and what they do, simultaneously convey knowledge *and* value.

Because knowledge and values are inseparable in human action (though they may

Source: From William Ayers and William H. Schubert, "The Normative and the Possible: Values in the Curriculum," *The Educational Forum*, Volume 53, Summer 1989, pp. 355–365. Printed by permission of Kappa Delta Pi, An International Honor Society in Education.

be separable for purposes of analysis and discussion), and because the educative process is a form of human action, it is clear that anyone who teaches addresses values. Sometimes the values taught are explicit, but more often they are implicit; sometimes moral deliberation is engaged intentionally and vigorously, other times morality is embodied in a kind of hidden curriculum. In either case, educators in both families and schools teach values. Sometimes they teach by precept and instruction; always they teach by example, personality, social context, and the life they create as educators or parents or, simply, persons. Thus, the central question that emerges is: On what basis are the knowledge and values we deem worthwhile for students selected? In other words, where do educators look for advice about what should be taught? One response to this question is to turn to those who have grappled with this central curriculum problem before. While curriculum history reveals several alternative themes, three long-standing orientations to curriculum theorizing may be particularly useful to this discussion: the intellectual traditionalist, the social behaviorist, and the experientialist.[2] What do these three perennial stances toward curriculum offer schools and families in the way of precedent?

THREE CURRICULUM ORIENTATIONS

Intellectual traditionalist. From antiquity onward, one finds educators who think of themselves as intellectual traditionalists, and who promote the teaching of great ideas (from the great books) as the most worthwhile educational enterprise. Most valued in this position is acquainting young persons with the insights and observations of the greatest minds throughout history. The great poems, plays, novels, paintings, philosophical treatises, musical compositions, mathematical formulae, scientific explanations, social science theories, and the like embody the wisdom of the ages in this view. They reveal human connectedness to life's great mysteries and events: e.g., birth, death, love, salvation, society and the crowd, success and failure, anxiety, and tradition.[3] They demonstrate the deep human interest in what Adler called the six great ideas: truth, beauty, goodness, liberty, equality, and justice.[4] Like his intellectual mentor, Hutchins at the University of Chicago, Adler calls for a return to the great books and the great ideas. A century ago William Torrey Harris elegantly promoted the subject areas that now dominate the curriculum of schools, calling them the "five windows on the soul": (1) mathematics; (2) biology; (3) art and literature; (4) grammar, which included psychology and logic; and (5) history, which involved socio-political theory. To use a metaphor identified by Kliebard, curriculum for the intellectual traditionalist is a *journey* through a world of great works that reveals the best thoughts and values that humanity has created.[5]

Social behaviorist. In contrast to the intellectual traditionalist who values ideas thought to span the boundaries of culture, history, place, class, and idiosyncratic preference, the social behaviorist is more deeply concerned with techniques of curriculum delivery. Such techniques involve broader questions of teaching methods, organizational patterns, and instructional materials that have the warrant of scientific investigation. While the current character of social behaviorist curriculum development puts great stock in the positivist research tradition of the twentieth century, its origins stretch back to crafts and trades training in ancient Egypt and the promotion of craft knowledge in every historical period. In the twentieth century, the position has emerged with great power and authority as educational theorists and researchers have increasingly identified themselves as scientists. Foremost among these curricularists was Bobbitt who utilized a method of curriculum-making called "activity analysis."[6] He advocated study of what successful adults do in a culture or community, and the concomitant translation of adult activities into behavioral objectives and learning activities. Charters offered a revision by suggesting that curricularists begin with the ideals of a culture rather than concrete activities.[7] This position was, of course, reactivated by Mager and others who advocated behavioral objectives precisely stated in terms of observable and measurable student outcomes.[8] Moreover, a sizeable proportion of the research on teaching literature, so highly touted in the promotion of "effective schools" and "teaching effectiveness," similarly emphasizes technique more than the precise knowledge and values to be taught. The social behaviorist is characterized by a *production* metaphor. Thus, in teaching of values as in anything else, the delivery of values is considered more centrally curricular than the selection of values to be promoted. Selection is not the business of educators—schools, teachers, and families alike are merely required to deliver the selected material efficiently and effectively.

Experientialist. A *growth* metaphor, rather than either a production or a journey metaphor, best characterizes the experientialist position. Drawn from the kind and quality of reflective thinking that persons use in everyday life as they encounter and deal with the continuous flow of problems, the experientialist posture also has a long history. The adage that we learn from experience has been central to practical, common-sense language on education in every era. This viewpoint was given its most serious intellectual formulation in the philosophy of Dewey who observed that learning begins with the psychological and moves to the logical, which is the sequence almost completely opposite to most formal instruction in schools or families.[9] By *psychological* Dewey meant interests, and by *logical* he referred to the disciplines of knowledge. His argument was that effective learning and teaching must begin with a serious respect for the momentary occupations of student interests, because these interests symbolize deeper interests shared by the human community (not unlike the intellectual traditionalist's mysteries and events of life or great ideas). As students begin to see a community of interest evolve around the deeper manifestations of momentary whim, they learn to value together common ideas, commitments, and practices. Seemingly idiosyncratic problems can then be realized as common human problems. At this point learners are in a position to benefit eclectically from the storehouses known as disciplines of knowledge. Knowledge-in-use can speak to and inform deeper human interests and momentary concerns alike. Values, then, are not known in advance, only needing to be bestowed on students; they are created through community deliberation in light of problems experienced and shared. They are refined and made sophisticated by the informing power of the disciplines of knowledge. Both families and schools must collaborate if this movement from the psychological to the logical is to be realized in the lives of students in and out of school.

INTERPRETIVE APPLICATIONS

How can knowledge of these three orientations to curriculum be used to provide greater historical awareness? One clear way is to be in a better position to interpret contemporary proposals, practices, and trends through the lenses of each orientation. A second way is to be able to notice similarities among episodes and events that occurred at different times. To illustrate these applications, we briefly interpret four curriculum emphases of the past thirty years. How are values taught in each event or episode? Our interpretation focuses on relative emphasis of the three curriculum orientations in each, and on precedent in previous episodes and events.

Example 1: Cultural literacy. The current calls for greater student knowledge of the hallmarks of liberal education[10] represent a strange blend of intellectual traditionalist and social behaviorist positions. They are the former in their emphasis on knowledge of the classics of Western civilization, but they are the latter in the excited mixing of a classical education with a rigid and uniform basic skills approach to education replete with testing and minimum standards. Missing in the emphasis on symbols of cultural literacy (memorized information) is the deeper rationale, implicit in the experientialist, for experiencing the great mysteries and for the liberating power of great ideas. The great works' emancipatory power to free people from the intellectual fetters of their day seems to be lost by many proponents of cultural literacy in the acceptance of tradition for its own sake. Similar calls, also condemning schools for intellectual softness and ignorance of the "great conversation" surfaced after World War I, during the Great Depression, and again after World War II.[11] In each instance the milieu of the day can be examined productively for similarities with the current emphasis on cultural literacy.

In all of these situations, worthwhile values are sought in an attempt to assert a tighter grip on that which seems long-lasting. Once grasped, the task becomes to deliver it to the young.

Example II: Standards as reform. Spurred by *A Nation at Risk*[12] and a host of related reform reports, initiatives, and proposals, most states in the 1980s embarked on a mass movement to enhance the quality of education.[13] Discontent with student performance in schools, coupled with worries that the United States was losing preeminence among world economies, moved state legislatures to begin to set curricular aims. As legislatures elected representatives from different spheres to sit on various "blue ribbon commissions," the reform of the 1980s appeared to exhibit an experientialist interest in democracy. In most cases, however, the dominant concern has become less an exercise in democratic empowerment and more a social behaviorist delivery of predetermined ends to school districts, classrooms, and students who have little or nothing to say about the central curricular question of what is worthwhile to know and experience in their own lives. The precedent of post-Sputnik curriculum reform, along with the laments of reformers,[14] reminds us that failure to reform is often due to lack of creative involvement on the part of those in schools who are most familiar with local needs. Frequently neglected in major reform initiatives historically has been the practical wisdom of participants at the situationally specific level.

Values in this case are not considered as problematic as the delivery system that conveys them. Proponents of rigid, uniform standards assume that values are given, immutable, and obvious. Schools have merely to orchestrate the delivery of values to inert students.

Example III: Behavioral objectives. Similar, though not as charged with large scale political efforts as the reform of the 1980s, was the behavioral objectives thrust of the late 1960s and 1970s. Teachers were expected to reduce the sense of purpose that guided their teaching to a set of statements indicating the observable behavior that would provide evidence for attaining precisely stated purposes. Moreover, such evidence was to be set forth in measurable terms whenever possible.[15] Of course, this emphasis on social and psychological efficiency was not without precedent. Its roots run at least back to the 1920s and the works of Bobbitt[16] and Charters,[17] who recommended great precision in the itemization of objectives. Still farther back, this kind of curriculum management thrust can be traced to the call by Joseph Mayer Rice at the turn of the century as he implored schools to be more accountable.[18] Fueled by the behavioristic psychology of Skinner and others, behavioral objectives can be found reconstituted in the Individual Educational Program (IEP) that influences so much of special education today. It might prove useful for those who are involved in promoting the IEP to assess the strengths and criticisms of previous incarnations of behavioral objectives. Such assessment would help clarify the relative extent to which IEPs used in specific situations facilitate management (social behaviorist orientation) versus curricula tailored to individual needs and interests (experientialist orientation).

Again, values are seen as secondary, or perhaps more accurately, as given. Values are taken for granted, something to be received and accepted. Schools and parents are responsible to convey and inculcate values in children and youth, who are expected to receive but not develop those things which will give their lives greater meaning and direction.

Example IV: Open education. "Open education" emerged in the late 1960s and emphasized the student as a creator of knowledge and a moral agent.[19] Roots of open education can be traced to the philosophy, theory, and practice of the British primary schools in the 1960s and to the idea of the integrated day.[20] Neglected in much of the open education literature was the deep kinship its practitioners and theorists had with Dewey and his closest followers and allies such as Harold Rugg, William H. Kilpatrick, L. Thomas Hopkins, George S. Counts, Boyd Bode, and others throughout the first half of the twentieth century. Some of the conflicts and contradictions of open education may well have been resolved if more attention had been given to these early theorists and practitioners of progressive education. For instance, a careful reading of Dewey's *Experience and Education* might have offset the tendency in open education to diminish the teacher's role in classroom decision making, as Dewey demonstrated that such withdrawal by the teacher is a detriment to democratic deliberation where all members of a group genuinely contribute according to their expertise.[21] Emphasis on student caprice tended to debilitate both progressive education and open education, and careful study of precedent in progressive education by open educators may have prevented undue rediscovery. Similarly, the fact that both progressive education and British primary education occurred in a variety of physical settings highlights the fact that experientialist education is more of an ideology than a place. Recognition of this may have prevented the infatuation with open-space architecture, and the wide experimentation in the 1970s with wall-less spaces. Some open educators and many public school leaders were unwittingly convinced that values like open communication among persons, each person being the agent of his or her own morality and people being the creators of knowledge, could be enhanced markedly by learning in buildings with fewer walls. Many of these wall-less buildings now contain makeshift walls, and the values of open education became associated in the minds of many people with superficial elements of form devoid of substance.

The central values of open education (that everyone is capable of creating knowledge, that students have the wherewithal to create their own lives, and that educational growth occurs when all involved address the question of what is worth knowing) were less effective due to a lack of connectedness to precedent.

The questions of values and how values should be taught emerges as quite complex within the countenance of historical perspective. The issue of whether values should be taught by school or family becomes superficial when one comes to grips with the pervasiveness of values deeply embedded in all curriculum, teaching, and learning. Curriculum innovation can be considered in light of three orientations or perspectives that have informed curriculum deliberation since time immemorial. Indeed, if we want to imbue students with a sense of value that can carry them through unpredictable lives, if we want to prepare them for a world that does not yet exist, we must move beyond the tendency to fill them with one or another value or even set of values. Parents and educators alike can heed the technology of the social behaviorist, but cannot accept as unproblematic the dominant values of any society. They can also move beyond the technical to embrace the quest for excellence implicit in the intellectual traditionalist position. Because excellence must be developed and not bestowed, those who seek to enhance the values of children and youth—of students of all ages for that matter—must place the basic curriculum question (What is worthwhile to know and experience?) at the center of inquiry. This simple step requires time and space, most of all, but it also creates the possibility for wonder, appreciation, perspective, and discipline to occur.

Finally, the question of worth is one that students, not only professional educators and parents, should address. Students should be allowed to move beyond the self-involved pursuit of preference and pleasure, beyond, too, the sense of values as a distinct product or script to follow or a set of laws. Students should continually return to the questions of what is moral action in each situation encountered: What is right? What is good? What is worthwhile? This allows classrooms and families really to become sites of moral action, places where people, adults and children alike, are immersed in the wholehearted quest for a moral life, a life lived within a community where shared values and individual values are honored, a life of cooperation, harmony with nature, improvement, and possibility. It allows people to search for a world that is more caring, more peaceful, more meaningful, more beautiful, and more fair, and it creates a space for people to act on behalf of that search. It should become the organizing center of the curriculum itself, and so is in the best of both the experientialist and intellectual traditionalist positions. The essence, then, of teaching values does not lie in which value in a competing set should be conveyed. Rather, it resides in enabling and inspiring students to ask continuously: What is worthwhile? What is valuable to think about, study, do, be, and become?

References

1. Herbert Spencer, *Education: Intellectual, Moral, and Physical* (New York: D. Appleton, 1861).
2. William H. Schubert, *Curriculum: Perspective, Paradigm, and Possibility* (New York: Macmillan, 1986).
3. Robert Ulich, "Comments on Ralph Harper's Essay," in *Modern Philosophies of Education*, ed. N. B. Henry (Chicago: University of Chicago Press, 1955) pp. 254–257.
4. Mortimer Adler, *Six Great Ideas* (New York: Macmillan, 1981).
5. Herbert Kliebard, "Metaphorical Roots of Curriculum Design," *Teachers College Record* 74 (February 1972): 403–404.
6. Franklin Bobbitt, *The Curriculum* (Boston: Houghton Mifflin, 1918); *How to Make a Curriculum* (Boston, Houghton Mifflin, 1924).
7. W. W. Charters, *Curriculum Construction* (New York, Macmillan, 1923).
8. Robert F. Mager, *Preparing Instructional Objectives* (Palo Alto, California: Fearon, 1962).
9. See, for example, John Dewey, *Democracy and Education* (New York: Macmillan, 1916); *How We Think* (New York: D. C. Heath, 1933); *Logic, The Theory of Inquiry* (New York: Holt, 1938).
10. E.g., Allan Bloom, *The Closing of the American Mind* (New York: Simon and Schuster, 1986); E. D. Hirsch, *Cultural Literacy* (Boston: Houghton Mifflin, 1987); Dianne Ravitch and Chester Finn, *What Do Our 17-Year-Olds Know?* (New York: Harper and Row, 1987).
11. E.g., William C. Bagley, *Education and Emergent Man* (New York: Macmillan, 1934); Arthur Bestor, *The Restoration of Learning* (New York: Knopf, 1956).
12. The National Commission on Excellence in Education, *A Nation at Risk: The Imperative for Education Reform* (Washington, D.C.: U.S. Government Printing Office, 1983).
13. For an overview of these reports and an analysis of their similarities and differences with earlier reform efforts, see, Harry Passow, "Tackling the Reform Report of the 1980's," *Phi Delta Kappa* 65 (June 1984): 674–683.
14. Ford Foundation, *A Foundation Goes to School* (New York: Author, 1972).
15. E.g., W. James Popham and Eva Baker, *Establishing Instructional Goals* (Englewood Cliffs, N.J.: Prentice-Hall, 1970).
16. Bobbitt, *The Curriculum; How To Make a Curriculum.*
17. Charters, *Curriculum Construction.*
18. J. M. Rice, *The Public School System of the United States* (New York: The Century Company, 1893); *Scientific Management in Education* (New York: Nobel and Eldridge, 1913).
19. E.g., Herbert Kohl, *36 Children* (New York: Signet, 1968); George Dennison, *The Lives of Children* (New York: Random House, 1969); James Herndon, *How to Survive in Your Native Land* (New York: Simon and Schuster, 1971); John Holt, *How Children Fail* (New York: Delta, 1964); Paul Goodman, *Growing Up Absurd* (New York: Random House, 1960); Charles Silberman, *Crisis in the Classroom* (New York: Random House, 1970).
20. R. F. Dearden, *The Philosophy of Primary Education* (London: Routledge and Kegan Paul, 1968); J. Walton, *The Integrated Day in Theory and Practice* (London: Ward Lock Educational, 1972).
21. John Dewey, *Experience and Education* (New York: Macmillan, 1938).

57

Implementing an Effective Discipline Program

Sammie McCormack

Students at Twin Peaks Middle School in Poway find their school a good place to study and a pleasant place to be. They take great pride in their school as evidenced by: minimal vandalism, high school-spirit, and academic and athletic achievement. Several programs have been implemented to encourage self-discipline and achieve a balance between positive and negative incentives. Twin Peaks is just one of San Diego County's effective schools.

Do all effective schools have effective discipline? Does a school with effective discipline also exhibit other characteristics of effective schools? In San Diego County, the answer to both questions is yes. Is good discipline a coincidence? Absolutely not!

To the staff members of effective schools, good discipline is a conscious and ongoing process. A student-oriented self-discipline program instituted by the school is a solid foundation on which to build an effective school because the characteristics of both are similar.

CHARACTERISTICS OF GOOD DISCIPLINE PROGRAMS

High Expectations. *"Students here follow the rules because we helped write them, we even suggested rewards."* (Tina, sixth grade student body president). Teachers believe students will behave. They convey and acknowledge that expectation to students and parents at all times. A variety of school-wide methods are used in San Diego County, as elsewhere, to recognize and reinforce appropriate behavior. These include (but are not limited to) honor days, positive letters and notes to parents, commendation cards, awards, praise, publicity, photographs, special lunches, privileges, assemblies, bumper stickers ["My child is citizen of the month at Sycamore Canyon Elementary School"], and ice cream socials.

In addition, staff members individually reinforce good behavior. Elementary teachers award certificates, stars, stickers, and special privileges. Secondary teachers use computer time, choice of activities, no homework days, "walk-man" time, dances, field trips, and a variety of other methods to reward good behavior. Recognition is used regularly rather than occasionally.

Prevention of behavior problems is more widely used than punitive action. "I use a 'buddy system' to insure that each new student has a successful first week both behaviorally and academically," reports Jon, a fourth grade teacher. Even schools with very strict discipline codes project an atmosphere of caring and concern for students. The self-esteem of students is positive and the needs of at-risk students are addressed.

Safe and Orderly Environment. *"We know what our school expects."* (Carole and Rex, parents of a second grade student). Successful school programs focus on a positive environment and include regular school newsletters that inform parents and community members of school activities and student achievements; evening workshops for parents and students about effective discipline at school and home; and projects that physically improve the looks of the school. These include students painting the exterior or interior of the buildings, beautification projects, and arbor day activities. Minimal vandalism and graffiti occur. The cafeteria has a restaurant-like atmosphere and the playground or campus is a place for pleasant socialization.

Frequent Monitoring. Elementary all-school discipline plans include monitoring and rewards for appropriate behavior. A student discipline code, developed with input and support of students, parents and staff members, is evident at schools such as San Pasqual School (Escondido). Oceanside School District uses the "No Bad Kids" program. In every school where a positive code exists, students are taught the code, and staff members are consistent in monitoring and enforcing it. Warner Springs Elementary School, like other effective discipline schools, now posts copies of its positive behavior expectations in all school locations. The code is reviewed annually to assure that it is updated and appropriately implemented. Students are rewarded for positive behavior.

Both elementary and secondary staff members focus their energy on the growth of students and the positive image of their school. Staff members are seen as advocates for students. "Is this good for children?" is a question asked before changes are considered. All school personnel believe all children can learn, all children have talent, and success influences behavior and commitment to the school program.

Opportunity to Learn. *"This school is a place where students and staff members come to work and experience success,"* Finney Elementary School (Chula Vista) teachers report. Students in effective discipline schools are constantly reminded in

Source: From Sammie McCormack, "Implementing an Effective Discipline Program," *Thrust,* Volume 18, February/March 1989, pp. 43–44.

class, in bulletins, over the public address system, and by other methods that staff members and parents expect excellence in all things. Students' successes are shared with the entire student body and with the public. A school "reader board" at Southwest High School (Sweetwater) praises student success. The marquee at Del Dios Middle School (Escondido) announces the "citizen of the month" each month. Elsewhere, a local newspaper runs a periodic feature about students' achievement and behavior. Positive behavior occurs in each school and there is no shortcutting of academic studies.

Instructional Leadership and Shared Leadership. The building principal is the primary key to effective discipline. When the impact is positive, the learning environment is positively affected. The outcomes are seen in high expectations of staff, high expectations of students, personal interest in people, and behavior modeling. By example, the principal shares leadership and all staff members participate in the decision-making process.

"In summary then, we've agreed that our cafeteria manner of the week is 'please will you pass the . . .,' " is an example of the way one elementary school principal brings faculty members to consensus at a staff meeting. Current student behavior patterns, the success of rewards and consequences and ideas for continued student responsibility are regular staff meeting agenda items.

Staff members also communicate regularly about the curriculum. At Lauderbach Elementary (Chula Vista), for example, if two teachers attend a math conference, they meet with the building math curriculum committee to share what they learned. They then prepare an inservice session for the entire staff and focus efforts toward interdisciplinary uses of materials. All teachers serve on at least one curricular area committee. At other schools, teachers from different grade levels and teaching disciplines team-teach. They describe the experience as a period of intense creative growth. A "family" attitude permeates the entire school.

"Of course I know what other teachers in this school do. We observe one another regularly" (Alberto, eighth grade math teacher). Staff members work together in each effective discipline school to improve the school; no one works in isolation. Special programs and policies are known by all. Volunteers in the building are recognized by name and face. For example, at one school I recently visited, every teacher knows how many parent volunteers (41) come to the building each week, even though several teachers have no direct contact with volunteers. Another school's teachers report that the TESA (Teacher Expectations and Student Achievement) training is one of the most effective and long lasting programs in their school environment, although not all teachers participated in the original training.

The principal encourages teachers to handle all or most of the routine discipline problems, and to send only the most severe to the principal's office. At the same time, the principal's office is the scene of rewards for both students' academic achievement and students' behavior. Being "sent to the office" no longer always implies misbehavior.

Clear School Mission. *"Students are responsible for their own actions and can accept the consequences of their choices, be they positive or negative"* (Positive Action Plan, Sunnyside Elementary School, Chula Vista). Schools with effective programs emphasize appropriate behavior just as they emphasize a clear academic mission. Causes of misbehavior are addressed as soon as the symptoms are identified. Staff members at Dewey Elementary School (San Diego) work together to develop activities that relate to the causes of behavior problems. These activities involve both the school and the community, and include policy writing, sharing power and authority, retreats, and student leadership training. When misbehavior is reduced, progress toward the mutually agreed upon academic goal is uninterrupted.

Home-School Relations. In an effective school, a strong communication system and support network exists among parents, community, and school. At Chaparrel Elementary (Poway), community members have input in decision-making, goal-setting, budget decisions, discipline procedures, scholarship awards, and policy-making. They are encouraged to drop in at school, and to volunteer in the classrooms. Naval personnel stationed in San Diego cooperatively established a voluntary reading tutorial program (for both adults and students) with the elementary schools in Chula Vista. All tutoring occurs on Saturday mornings. Reading scores already reflect the impact of this partnership.

Frequently, parents are included as members of curriculum committees, and serve on interview committees for prospective hiring. South Bay School District (Imperial Beach) has committed to the "Partners in Learning" concept that unites students, teachers, parents, and administrators in teaching and learning. At Tierra del Sol Middle School (Lakeside), parents are informed weekly of student progress and homework. Many schools use not only the traditional report card process but also phone calls, and weekly or bi-weekly up-dates to parents.

"Our student success program started six years ago and it gets better every year." (Tron, parent of fifth grade student). Although many effective schools began their discipline programs with training from one of the more widely publicized approaches (Lee Canter, Fred Jones, Madeline Hunter, William Glasser, etc.), they have adapted the programs to their local needs. The modifications usually add appropriate reward techniques.

Effective schools build on successful programs rather than always looking for new ones. The programs develop, in students, teachers, and community, a sense of personal pride and of being a valued school participant. Students' achievements go up, and dropout rates go down.

Effective discipline schools truly are good places to study and learn, pleasant places to be. *"This is a great school. My teacher treats me more like an adult than a kid. He says we're the best students he has ever had, . . . and we are!"* (Teddy, fifth grade student).

PART SIX

Program Design, Experiences, and Instructional Practices

The decade of the 1990s has ushered in new problems and changing needs in school programs. To begin with, enrollment increases, as expressed by the baby boomlet, have begun to be felt at all levels of elementary education and soon will descend upon the high school. Accountability problems for programs have become even greater in this decade as education has assumed a significant priority status on the national scene. The not-so-subtle comparisons with other nation states have increased the accountability pressures on the common school. Added to these two program problems is the growing diversity in the clientele of schools. So, in addition to the continuing program problems of the past three decades, schools now are challenged to accommodate new issues for program design, experiences, and instructional practices.

While attempting to address these additional educational needs, schools must continue to revise their programs, retrain their teachers through staff development programs, and attend to the public's demands for "basics" accountability, due process for exceptional learners, individualization for special needs and groups, and an overall societal demand for excellence. This latter societal demand impacts the beginning teacher from day one in the classroom. Program development requires a teacher to be competent in the use of the knowledge of educational foundations as it impacts school programs. This section of the text offers some different perspectives on the issues faced by the teachers in the decade of the nineties.

Thinking skills for learning have become a hot topic for the curriculum. In "Teaching Thinking Skills: State Mandates and the K–12 Curriculum," George L. Grice and M. Anway Jones offer a classification of thinking skills as they are needed in the K–12 program. Although there is a lack of universal agreement concerning the content of the program, or what is to be taught, there is a developing consensus about the need for thinking skills. In particular, these authors have suggested the list of Chuska, which includes creative or inventive skills, logical skills, experimental or investigative skills, analytical or critical skills, and reflective skills. The latter skill also dominates the current literature for teachers' need of skills.

Technology and its use in schools have dominated the current thinking in school program design. Christopher Dede talks of empowering the learning environment with the computer in his essay "The Evolution of Information Technology: Implications for Curriculum." He refers to this empowerment as *hypermedia,* with its multi-symbolic approaches with the use of text, graphics, visuals, images, and codes. These uses lead to greater use of simulations for the learner in an interactive environment. Not only is this environment enriching in the preparation of school programs, but also it has significant meaning because of its current applicability in the workplace.

Censorship continues to rear its ugly head in the curriculum. In the article "Curriculum Censorship: Values in Conflict," Martha M. McCarthy discusses this issue. Censorship is manifested in the selection of text materials for literature study, values materials in social studies, and scientific theories proposed for science study. It is led by many of the conservative members of society who fear elements of knowledge that may challenge their personal beliefs. This value issue now addresses the national examination of diversity issues in the school program.

Patricia Cordeiro presents a whole language approach to be used with sixth graders in the elementary school in "Structuring for Success." This whole language approach includes the use of verbal displays for learning, artifacts as exemplified by journals, posters, books, and data bases that encourage learners to establish assertions that can be explored for learning. She concludes with four goals that can be used in establishing a whole language approach in the classroom. The beginning teacher should reflect upon how these goals affect the teaching assignment they are about to receive.

The success of a well-developed curriculum is wholly dependent upon the classroom management program of the teacher. A model worth examining is proposed by Thomas J. Lasley in "A Teacher Development Model for Classroom Management." Since one of the ultimate goals of the curriculum is to enhance a student's development as a self-directed learner, classroom management strategies that direct learners toward self-direction of their learning efforts become most important. Teacher growth in classroom management techniques should be geared toward moving above mere survival strategies in the classroom to effective teaching.

Charlie Reed cautions the dangers of current attempts at censorship of reading materials for adolescents in "The Back Door: Are We Censoring Adolescence?" In particular, he suggests that in effect the school may actually be censoring the adolescent because many of the materials reviewed for censoring are those that contain adolescent characters in the material. He believes that adolescents need all the help they can get in understanding themselves as they mirror their peers in the materials they read.

The debate over right brain and left brain performance of students usually gets examined through some examination of achievement test performances of these different types of learners. One such examination of those differences is offered by Michael L. Bell and Darrell L. Roubinek in "A Comparison of Standardized Achievement Test Scores on Right and Left Brain Dominant Fourth-Grade Students." Their study concludes that the performance of young learners on different batteries of standardized tests yields, different results as to the variations in achievement between right and left brained children. This suggests that the curriculum program should be clear about its expectations for its learners and plan accordingly in selecting the kind of standardized normative tests to be used in measuring student performance.

Effective instruction is the successful key to learning in the classroom. One of the more effective instructional models has been developed by Madeline Hunter. Lisa A. Freund and Sidney A. Freund discuss the uses of the Hunter model with the mainstreaming of exceptional learners in "Effective Instruction: Application of the Hunter Instructional Skills Model to Staff Development for Mainstreaming." They propose that the same kind of effectiveness of the model that is used in regular classrooms can be achieved with the classrooms having mainstreamed learners. Their list for effective teaching of exceptional children is equally applicable to the regular classroom. The article also offers a review of the Hunter model and its application to classroom lesson planning.

In addition to instructional delivery of planned learning for students, the use of computers offers sophisticated management of instructional and management systems for schools. In "Integrated Instructional Management Systems and Outcome Based Education," Mark Whitman and Phil Lambert share the use of computers for management purposes in their school district. They outline the internal uses of such a management system as well as the external uses with computer connections to their state department of education. Additionally, they point to the computer uses for curriculum building and assessment of the program. Since their programs are capable of being stored en masse, they can be examined as to the interactions of curriculum development, curriculum assessment, and student assessment.

The twenty-first century will witness extensive use of prototypes of "California's Smart Classroom." As described by Charles H. Slaughter, this science classroom delivers a variety of technological instructional activities and is controlled by a computer. It is important to note that the teachers' main responsibilities are to continue to develop new software and to upgrade existent software. Their remaining time is used more effectively with individual and group activities for learning. This smart classroom has led to significant learner gains in achievement and serves as a model for other California schools to emulate.

58

Teaching Thinking Skills

State Mandates and the K–12 Curriculum

George L. Grice
M. Anway Jones

Bruce Romanish (1986) argues that critical thinking programs in education are important in a society in transition. The "American society," he observes, "has been in such a state ever since its inception, . . . the quantitative and qualitative differences marked by modern forces of change demand that the populace be equipped to understand, analyze, and respond in ways that are positive and productive on both individual and societal levels" (45–46). Wales, Nardi and Stager (1986) support thinking skills programs on similar grounds. Norris (1985) calls critical thinking an indispensable part of education.

Although many might argue that a primary goal of education is the development of thinking skills, a 1979–80 report entitled *Reading, Thinking and Writing,* published by the National Assessment of Educational Progress (1981), concluded,

> The most significant finding . . . is that while students learn to read a wide range of material, they develop very few skills for examining the nature of ideas that they take away from their reading; . . . what the majority seem to lack is experience in undertaking such explanatory tasks and the problem-solving strategies and critical-thinking that would develop through such experience. (2)

Furthermore, Nathan (1986), coordinator for *Time for Results: The Governors' 1991 Report on Education,* summarized a key position advanced in that document that corroborates these findings. "Students need much more than basic skills; they must also become thoughtful, responsible problem-solvers" (198).

If the findings of the reports are valid, we can only conclude that many students lack the skills to respond to their changing environments. Thus the need for instruction in thinking skills is one that generates much support. At least thirteen organizations have endorsed its inclusion at all levels of education (Ruggiero 1988). Twenty-eight organizations have formed the Association Collaborative for Teaching Thinking (Marzano et al. 1988), and many scholarly articles have assessed the need for, and strategies of, thinking instruction (Paul 1985b). This essay examines the issues surrounding the implementation of thinking skills programs in public school curricula. It seeks to classify thinking skills, to provide options for selection of an instructional framework, and to suggest guidelines for teacher training in thinking skills curricula.

CLASSIFICATION OF THINKING SKILLS

Beyer (1987b) defines thinking in its broadest sense as "the search for meaning, . . . the mental process by which individuals make sense out of experience" (16). LaCounte (1987) notes that thinking is "'abstract mental manipulation'; . . . [it] is not reading, writing, speaking, acting, listening, sensing, etc., which are concrete or physical acts. Thinking processes enable the acts" (250). While the product of thinking may be concrete, the process of thinking is necessarily abstract. Therein lies much of the difficulty in approaching the subject of thinking instruction.

Much of the literature classifies thinking into two general types: critical thinking and creative thinking. Ruggiero (1988) posits that the disciplines of philosophy and psychology account for this distinction. He says that thinking as taught by philosophy departments can be labeled critical thinking, explained as, teaching students how to construct arguments and to apply logic and avoid fallacies in their reasoning. Ennis (cited in Marzano 1988, 146) defines critical thinking as "reasonable, reflective thinking that is focused on deciding what to believe or do."

Cognitive psychologists, argues Ruggiero (1988), focus more on creative thinking. Halpern (cited in Marzano 1988, 146) calls it "the ability to form new combinations of ideas to fulfill a need." DeBono (1986), an advocate of creative thinking, uses terms such as "generative thinking," and "lateral thinking" (16). Creative thinking is proactive and lateral, he contends, as opposed to critical thinking, which is reactive and vertical (deBono 1984; 1970).

Distinguishing between critical and creative thinking may be constructive, but viewing the thinking instruction debate in the context of one method versus another does a disservice to the goal of producing better students. If creative thinking is the production of ideas and critical thinking is the evaluation of ideas (Ruggiero 1988),

Source: From George L. Grice and M. Anway Jones, "Teaching Thinking Skills: State Mandates and the K–12 Curriculum," *The Clearing House,* Volume 62, April 1989, pp. 337–342. Reprinted with permission from the author.

then we should be teaching both. The goal, according to Perkins (1986) is to improve intelligence, and that can be done only if we improve thinking. Perhaps the best advice is provided by Marzano et al. (1988): "The terms 'critical' and 'creative' are ways of describing the way we go about thinking. The two are not opposite ends of a single continuum but are complementary" (146). To argue that we should teach critical thinking should not imply that we are not concerned with teaching creative thinking. Ruggiero (1988) concludes,

> The larger truths lost in this squabble are that both creative thinking and critical thinking have been neglected, that both are needed for solving problems and resolving issues, and that each benefits from the other—critical thinking saves creative from pursuing novelty for its own sake; creative thinking prevents critical from being merely reactive and negative. (18)

The appropriate question for educators to ask is, What thinking skills should be taught in the educational curriculum?

The most widely accepted subset of thinking skills is identified by Bloom and his associates (1956). This classification of educational objectives has become known as "Bloom's taxonomy." The hierarchy includes six thinking skills: knowledge, comprehension, application, analysis, synthesis, and evaluation. Skills of analysis, synthesis, and evaluation are often referred to as higher-order skills and considered essential for critical thinking (Ennis 1985; Paul 1985a).

Other scholars offer competing frameworks that detail the skills they believe should be taught. For example, Marzano et al. (1988) list twenty-one core skills organized into eight generalized skills: focusing, information gathering, remembering, organizing, analyzing, generating, integrating, and evaluating. But perhaps the most practical approach to classifying thinking skills is that provided by Chuska (1986). Chuska discovered what he believed to be twenty-seven of the most commonly identified skills in the thinking skills literature. The list includes the following:

> Comparing, classifying, estimating, summarizing, hypothesizing, synthesizing, sequencing, predicting, evaluating, translating, reorganizing, prioritizing, setting criteria, goal setting, problem solving, decision making, justifying, making assumptions, using analogies, imagining, logical deducing, identifying pros/cons, identifying propaganda, identifying consequences, observing, creating/designing, and interpreting. (11)

Adler (1986), Norris (1985), and Wales et al. (1986) have offered similar operational definitions of thinking skills.

Chuska organized his list of skills into five more manageable categories that include both creative and critical thinking. *Creative or inventive* skills enable students to produce original ideas, processes, and products. According to Chuska, "Synthesis is a major method in this category." *Logical* skills enable students to follow steps in thinking, to justify if-then relationships, and to solve problems using deductive reasoning. *Experimental or investigation* skills enable students to test hypotheses, to conduct surveys in order to learn about issues and opinions, and to understand the use of control of variables in scientific investigations. *Analytical or critical* skills enable students to use whole-to-part and part-to-whole thinking, to learn methods of inquiry common to the social studies and science, and make good decisions. *Reflective* skills enable students to wait to make decisions until information is gathered and alternatives are explored (19).

The first step in designing an instructional strategy to enhance the development of thinking skills is to determine what should be taught. Chuska's lists encompass a broad spectrum of skills organized into five skill clusters. In reviewing the literature regarding thinking skills, we discover much overlap. This is a healthy sign. It suggests that there is substantial agreement on what should be taught. If the focus is on teaching thinking skills, not just critical or creative thinking skills, educators may discover that they have complementary missions.

OPTIONS FOR INSTRUCTIONAL FRAMEWORKS

Although there is strong support for implementation of thinking skills curricula, evidence suggests that schools are not successful in doing so. After reviewing research on critical thinking, Norris (1985) concluded that "critical thinking is not widespread. Most students do not score well on tests that measure ability to recognize assumptions, evaluate arguments, and appraise inferences" (44). Perkins (1986), codirector of Harvard Project Zero at Harvard University's Graduate School of Education, concurs: "I have found that conventional education at high school, college, and graduate school level has hardly any effect on the development of general reasoning abilities" (6). Goodlad (1984), who collected data from 38 schools, 8,634 parents, 1,350 teachers, 17,163 students, and over 1,000 classrooms, found that although junior and senior high school teachers desired student involvement in the scientific processes and thinking, their teaching and testing still emphasized recall rather than the exercise of higher intellectual functions. Paul (1985) notes that such practice undermines independent thought. His observation is validated by Young (1988), who says that "the perlocutionary pedagogy, however well intentioned, is self-defeating—its content goals are not reached in any sustained way, and it fails to provide opportunities for students to develop the critical interlocutionary capacities that would enable them to develop a mature ability to continue to learn" (57). Hart (1986) concludes that schools actively *discourage* thinking.

Two primary reasons that thinking skills programs have received low priority are "the abstract nature of thinking," and "the confusing array of proposed approaches to teaching thinking" (LaCounte, 1987, 250). Hart (1986) points out a third reason for the skepticism toward thinking skills programs: "We are far from having any agreement, or any substantive evidence, to support a program for training in thinking skills. I would go further and say that we do not know that such skills (as distinct from some moderately useful strategies) even exist" (45–46). Adler (1986) agrees with Hart in principle. He says that devising a program to produce critical thinking on the part of students is impossible. Perhaps these are valid reasons, especially in light of the results of a recent survey we conducted of all fifty states to determine the status of thinking skills curricula. Of the forty-three departments of education that responded, only ten (approximately 23%) reported that thinking skills are mandated in their school curricula. Those states are Florida, Georgia, New Mexico, North Carolina, Rhode Island, South Carolina, Tennessee, Texas, Vermont, and Virginia. Only one state, Iowa, has a proposal under consideration to mandate the teaching of thinking skills (see table 1).

TABLE 1
States That Have Mandated Thinking Skills

State	*Year*
Florida	1986
Georgia	1976
New Mexico	1974
North Carolina	1985
Rhode Island	1985
South Carolina	1984
Tennessee	Not recorded
Texas	1984
Vermont	1975
Virginia	Not recorded
Iowa	Under consideration

Although most scholars would not argue against the teaching of thinking skills as Hart and Adler do, they would agree with LaCounte (1987), who points out the problems in selecting the best approach to developing a thinking skills curriculum. LaCounte says, "Beware of one who travels from town to town with an entertaining show and purports to have the single, simple answer on teaching people to be effective thinkers . . . there is not a single, simple way to do it" (250).

Teaching thinking skills may take three forms: (1) the subject-matter-free course approach, (2) the integrated approach, or (3) the separate and integrated approach (Beyer 1987a). The first of these, the subject-matter-free course, defined by others as the "subject approach," (Joyce 1985), or the "isolated skills model" (LaCounte 1987), is not as prevalent in the United States as in some other countries. This approach emphasizes acquiring skills in thinking without relying on specific course content.

DeBono (1986), who strongly advocates the subject approach, argues for the program from many angles: Thinking would not receive adequate attention if it were part of other courses; if it were part of other courses, it would be closely bound to the subject matter of those courses; a specialized course in thinking would allow students, teachers, and parents to focus more directly on acquiring a specific skill; students who do not normally do well in other subject areas would have the opportunity to excel if thinking were taught separately.

Though there are distinct advantages to a subject approach, Beyer (1987a), as well as LaCounte (1987), argue against a single course on the grounds that thinking skills should be taught continuously, across disciplines, and that one-shot teaching is insufficient (Beyer 1987a).

The second approach can be labeled the "integrated content course" (Beyer 1987a) or pervasive model. The advocates of this approach argue that the teaching of thinking is an important component of every school activity (Joyce 1985). The approach assumes that instruction in content and intellectual process are mutually reinforcing. Thinking skills are not taught in isolation but are applied to a variety of contexts.

Advocates of the pervasive approach support their position with four arguments. First, exposure to thinking instruction must be broadly, rather than narrowly, based. Higher-order thinking must be an expectation in every course, not positioned as adjunct to the curriculum.

Second, advocates of the pervasive approach contend that thinking skills are shaped by subject matter or context. "These operations, it seems, do not automatically transfer to other contexts, nor do students seem inclined to make such transfer" (Beyer, 1987b, 7). The teacher of the specific content area is best able to guide the transfer.

Proponents claim a third benefit of teaching thinking skills across the curriculum. It better motivates the student to learn and produces better learning of the subject (Beyer 1987b). Ruggiero (1988) suggests that "teaching thinking in a course emphasizes the processes that give every subject its vitality—hypothesizing, interpreting, seeking alternative views, raising questions, evaluating, discovering. That emphasis creates excitement and encourages involvement" (12).

A final justification is the message conveyed by the pervasive approach: Thinking instruction should not appear to be the province of a few. A total commitment of all teachers at all levels is necessary if students are to become effective thinkers. All of the ten states that incorporate thinking skills into their curricula use the integrated approach.

The third approach is the separate and integrated, which is a combination of the two. Beyer (1987a) notes that the approach "consists of sequencing thinking skills across a number of courses and years, first introducing them in subject-matter-free courses or units within subject matter courses and then integrating them into subsequent study of subject matter" (106). The key to the success of this approach, according to Beyer, is the introductory, "content-free" thinking skills course, because it provides for the concentration of skills acquisition without the added burden of specific content areas. The premise on which this approach rests is that students need first to acquire skills that enable them to think. Once the students have learned the process, they are then introduced to specific course content that allows for the transfer of the skills acquired.

The three programs, the subject-matter-free course, the integrated approach, and the separate-and-integrated approach, all have advantages and disadvantages. The most feasible of these three is the integrated approach, because it not only enables students to acquire thinking skills but enables them to transfer those skills to other courses as well. This approach fits most easily into existing curriculum programs. However, in spite of some apparent disadvantages, we argue that schools should implement the separate-and-integrated approach because (1) a subject-matter-free course would provide students specialized training in thinking and (2) an integrated approach would ensure that the skills are transferred to other course content.

Opposition to a separate-and-integrated approach is grounded in three disadvantages. According to Beyer (1987a), this kind of program would be quite difficult to fit into a full curriculum. The training would be expensive, time-consuming, and sometimes unproductive, and the transfer of skills from the separate course to other courses would often be ignored. The last two disadvantages would most certainly be common to the other two approaches as well. In order to have an integrated approach, teachers in all subject areas would have to be trained. All teachers would have to be committed to implementing thinking skills in their respective courses. To argue that the transfer of skills from a separate course may not occur assumes a lack of commitment to the development of thinking skills on behalf of the other teachers.

The only significant argument against a separate-and-integrated approach is the problem of fitting a new course into a full curriculum. When school communities find that thinking skills are necessary to the development of their students, and when educators alter their attitudes toward teaching, then such an approach will be welcomed into the curriculum. Perhaps educators should not worry about specific content areas, but about the process of learning. As Romanish (1986) notes:

> The literature is almost silent on the idea that critical thinking in the curriculum is substantially affected by the way schools are organized, by our basic beliefs regarding the nature of human beings, by the way power is distributed within the school hierarchy, by the obligation schools must meet in terms of socializing the young, and so on . . . unless a number of profound changes take place in school organization, even good programs for critical thinking will fall short. (52)

GUIDELINES FOR TEACHER TRAINING IN THINKING SKILLS CURRICULA

The literature illustrates that there is increased recognition of the importance of teaching thinking skills. In order to provide this instruction, educators must determine what skills should be taught and the most appropriate framework for this teaching. Although all teachers can work individually to stimulate thinking in their students (Auten 1985; Barell 1985; Beyer 1987a; Beyer 1987b; Dirkes 1985; Duck 1985; Marzano et al. 1988; Miles 1985a; Miles 1985b; Miles 1985c; Ruggiero 1988; Strahan 1986; Strong, Silver, and Hanson 1985; Wassermann 1987), the challenge also requires training and institutional commitment.

Several scholars have recommended particular skills for teachers who plan to introduce a thinking skills program into their classrooms. For example, Paul (1985) recommends (1) that teachers have a clear insight into the cognitive processes of learning, (2) that Bloom's taxonomy become "two-sided," and (3) that teachers understand that learning is a *process*, not a *product*.

More specifically, Romanish (1986) suggests that teachers improve their questioning skills, become facilitators of critical thinking, and focus on the classroom climate to ensure trust and openness. Beyer (1987a) also provides guidelines for teachers: In particular, teachers should develop competencies to minimize subject matter in the early stages of skill learning, acquire a common instructional language for the skills being taught, and finally, develop appropriate assessments of the skills taught and of their teaching of these skills.

Of course, the most obvious and most important skills needed are the abilities to think and to communicate thinking in order to facilitate learning. Of the ten states that mandate thinking skills curricula, only six require teacher training. Of those six, Texas limits the requirements to those who seek certification after 1986 (table 2). To fail to require that teachers be competent in thinking skills strategies can only undermine the outcomes of these programs for students. Furthermore, to ignore such a mandate only perpetuates the tradition of downplaying thinking skills.

TABLE 2
Teacher Competencies In Thinking Skills

State	*Required*
Florida	Yes
Georgia	Yes
New Mexico	Yes
North Carolina	No
Rhode Island	No
South Carolina	Yes
Tennessee	No
Texas	Yes*
Vermont	No
Virginia	Yes

*Only required of those certified after 1986.

Not only should teachers be trained adequately, they also should be committed to the development of thinking skills in their students. The importance of this commitment is highlighted in the conclusion of the *National Assessment of Educational Progress Report* (1981):

> In a world overloaded with information, both a business and a personal advantage will go to those individuals who can sort the wheat from the chaff, the important information from the trivial. . . . Quality of life is directly tied to our ability to think clearly amid the noise of modern life, to sift through all that competes for our attention until we find what we value, what will make our lives worth living. (5)

Norris (1985) is more succinct. Critical thinking, he argues, "is not an educational option. Students have a moral right to be taught how to think critically" (44).

Because thinking skills are a valuable component in the development of our students, it is time that we implement those skills into our teaching as well as into our curriculum. We should be the spokespersons for the "opening of minds, or better yet, the prevention of their closing" (Romanish 1986, 49).

References

Adler, M. J. 1986. "Critical thinking" programs: Why they won't work. *Education Week* 7(Sept. 17): 28.

Auten, A. 1985. ERIC/RCS: Focus on thinking instruction. *Reading Teacher* 38:454–56.

Barell, J. 1985. You ask the wrong questions! *Educational Leadership* 42:18–23.

Beyer, B. K. 1987a. Planning a thinking skills curriculum—Key questions for principals to consider. *NASSP Bulletin* 71:101–112.

———. 1987b. *Practical strategies for the teaching of thinking*. Boston: Allyn and Bacon.

Bloom, B. S., ed. 1956. *Taxonomy of educational objectives: Handbook I: Cognitive domain*. New York: David McKay.

Bransford, J. D., M. S. Burns, V. R. Delclos, and N. J. Vye. 1986. Teaching thinking: Evaluating evaluators and broadening the data base. *Educational Leadership* 44:68–70.

Chuska, K. R. 1986. Teaching the process of thinking, K–12. *Phi Delta Kappa Fastback Series, no. 244*. Bloomington, Indiana: Phi Delta Kappa Educational Foundation.

deBono, E. 1970. *Lateral thinking: Creativity step by step*. New York: Harper and Row.

———. 1984. Critical thinking is not enough. *Educational Leadership* 42:16–17.

———. 1986. Beyond critical thinking. *Curriculum Review* 25:12–16.

Dirkes, M. A. 1985. Metacognition: Students in charge of their thinking. *Roeper Review* 8:96.

Duck, L. E. 1985. Seven cardinal principles for teaching higher-order thinking. *Social Studies* 76:129–33.

Ennis, R. H. 1985. A logical basis for measuring critical thinking skills. *Educational Leadership* 42:44–48.

Goodlad, J. I. 1984. *A place called school*. New York: McGraw-Hill.

Hart, L. A. 1986. A response: All "thinking" paths lead to the brain. *Educational Leadership* 43:45–48.

Joyce, B. 1985. Models for teaching thinking. *Educational Leadership* 42:4–7.

LaCounte, M. F. 1987. Teaching thinking: Snake oil, medicine shows, and nostrums. *Clearing House* 60:250–51.

Marzano, R. J., R. S. Brandt, C. S. Hughes, B. F. Jones, B. Z. Presseisen, S. C. Rankin, and C. Suhor. 1988. *Dimensions of thinking: A framework for curriculum and instruction*. Alexandria, Virginia: Association for Supervision and Curriculum Development.

Miles, C. 1985a. The fourth R: Basic thinking tools. *Journal of Developmental Education* 8:24–25.

———. 1985b. The fourth R: Active reactors and passive defenders. *Journal of Developmental Education* 9:24–25.

———. 1985c. The fourth R: Modeling the thinking process. *Journal of Developmental Education* 9:26.

Nathan, J. 1986. Implications for educators of Time for Results. *Phi Delta Kappan* 68:197–201.

National Assessment of Educational Progress. 1981. *Reading, thinking and writing: Results from the 1979–80 National Assessment of Reading and Literature, Report No. 11-L-01*, October.

Norris, S. P. 1985. Synthesis of research on critical thinking. *Educational Leadership* 42:40–45.

Paul, R. W. 1985a. Bloom's taxonomy and critical thinking instruction. *Educational Leadership* 42:36–39.

———. 1985b. Critical thinking research: A response to Stephen Norris. *Educational Leadership* 42:46.

Perkins, D. N. 1986. Thinking frames. *Educational Leadership* 43:4–10.

Romanish, B. 1986. Critical thinking and the curriculum: A critique. *Educational Forum* 51:45–56.

Ruggiero, V. R. 1988. *Teaching thinking across the curriculum*. New York: Harper and Row.

Strahan, D. B. 1986. Guided thinking: A research-based approach to effective middle grades instruction. *Clearing House* 60:149–55.

Strong, R. W., H. F. Silver, and R. Hanson. 1985. Integrating teaching strategies and thinking styles with the elements of effective instruction. *Educational Leadership* 42:9–15.

Wales, C. E., A. H. Nardi, and R. A. Stager. 1986. Decision making: Paradigm for education. *Educational Leadership* 43:37–41.

Wasserman, S. 1987. Teaching for thinking: Louis E. Raths revisited. *Phi Delta Kappan* 68:460–65.

59

The Evolution of Information Technology

Implications for Curriculum

Christopher Dede

During the next two decades, major changes in the technological base of American society will alter the knowledge, skills, and values we need to be capable workers and citizens. Evolving information technologies will transform the nature of work, and this transformation will in turn affect the design and content of the school curriculum. As jobs change, schools must shift in response.

TECHNOLOGICAL EVOLUTION

Since World War II, the performance capabilities of computers and telecommunications have been doubling every few years at constant cost. For example, a decade ago $3,500 could buy a new Apple II microcomputer. Today, $6,800—the same amount of purchasing power (adjusted for 10 years of inflation)—can buy a new Macintosh II microcomputer. The Macintosh handles 4 times the information at 16 times the speed, preprogrammed and reprogrammable memory are both about 20 times larger, disk storage is about 90 times larger, and the display has 7 times the resolution and 16 times the number of colors. Comparable figures could be cited for other brands of machines. Equally impressive, users' demands for this power have increased as rapidly as it has become available.

Over the next two decades, data processing and information systems will probably be replaced by sophisticated devices for knowledge creation, capture, transfer, and use. A similar evolution can be forecast for telecommunications: personal videorecorders, optical fiber networks, intelligent telephones, information utilities such as videotex, and digital discs will change the nature of media.

COGNITION ENHANCERS

The concept of "cognition enhancers" can help us understand how we can use these emerging technologies (Dede 1987b). A cognition enhancer combines the complementary strengths of a person and an information technology. Two categories of cognition enhancers will have considerable impact on the workplace: empowering environments and hypermedia.

Empowering Environments

Empowering environments enhance human accomplishment by a division of labor: the machine handles the routine mechanics of a task, while the person is immersed in its higher-order meanings. For example, I once took an oil painting course. My goal was to transfer my mental images to canvas so that viewers could share my experiences and emotions. However, rather than pondering form and composition and aesthetics, I had to spend my time trying to mix colors that remotely resembled my visualizations, trying to keep the paint from running all over the canvas, trying to keep the turpentine out of my hair. Now, I can use a graphics construction set to choose from a huge palette of colors; to alter, pixel by pixel, the contour of an image; to instantly "undo" my mistakes. Now I am involved with the creative aspects of art, while the empowering environment handles the mechanics. (However, my accomplishments as an artist are still ultimately limited by my own talents and knowledge.)

The workplace is adopting many empowering environments: databases for information management, spreadsheets for modeling, computer-aided design systems for manufacturing. And word processors with embedded spelling checkers, thesauruses, outliners, text analyzers, and graphics tools are driving the evolution of a new field: desktop publishing.

Hypermedia

Even with a sophisticated empowering environment for desktop publishing, I can still get writer's block. I can know everything I want to write yet not have my ideas in the linear "stream" required for written or oral communication. I need an "idea processor," a way of creating an external structure that mirrors the concepts and links in my memory. I need a second type of cognition enhancer: hypermedia.

Hypermedia is a framework for creating an interconnected, web-like representation of symbols (text, graphics, images, software codes) in the computer. This representation is similar to human long-term memory: people store information in networks of symbolic, temporal, and visual images related by associ-

Source: Dede, Christopher (1989). "The Evolution of Information Technology: Implications for Curriculum," *Educational Leadership*, 47 1:23–27. Reprinted with permission of the Association for Supervision and Curriculum Development.

ation. For example, in my memory the word *apple* conjures up religious, corporate, computational, botanic, and gustatory associations.

With my knowledge externalized in a hypermedia system, I can traverse this network along alternative paths through nodes and links, seeking the right sequential stream for my intended content, audience, and goals. The computer allows me to avoid overload in transferring long-term to short-term memory. Also, my access to long-term memory may be enhanced be the process of building and using hypermedia.

Hypermedia documents are beginning to appear in the workplace. For example, automobile mechanics will soon be using hypermedia repair manuals to diagnose problems. The mechanic will trace initial symptoms through a series of linked tests to reach final judgment on what is wrong, then follow a web of nodes that map the different steps of the repair. An educational version of such a manual would incorporate "trails" through the hypermedia network that guide the user through a series of structured, sequenced learning experiences.

The emergence of primitive hypermedia systems on personal computers is inspiring new ideas for their use. For example, a hypermedia version of this paper would place each fundamental concept in a separate node; links would tie related concepts together. Chunking and juxtaposing ideas in this way increases comprehension over the forced linearity of textual presentations. Perhaps different styles of remembering and learning will evolve!

Using cognition enhancers, however, requires more than learning how to activate the machine and issue commands; the style of working must change. For example, as a result of using a word processor, I can no longer write well with paper and pencil. I used to compose a sentence by thinking for a couple of minutes and then setting down a near-final version, because making changes meant cutting and pasting; now, I think for half a minute and type in a sentence, think for another 15 seconds and make a change, make another change a few seconds later, and so on. Now I can concentrate on revision and polishing, without the pressure of having to create a finished product. However, when I try to write with a pencil using this new superior style—disaster! The eraser wears out long before the pencil needs sharpening. Most people who use cognition enhancers experience the same unconscious shift of style.

SHIFTS IN OCCUPATIONAL SKILLS

In a world of empowering environments, the ways we accomplish tasks will alter. The global marketplace will drive this evolution; in this new economic "ecology," each nation is seeking a specialized niche based on its financial, human, and natural resources. Developed countries, which no longer have easily available natural resources and cheap labor, cannot compete with developing nations in manufacturing industrial commodities (President's Commission on Industrial Competitiveness 1985). Instead, nations with technological expertise, an advanced industrial base, and an educated citizenry are developing economies that use sophisticated workers and information tools to create products tailored to individual consumers' needs (Reich 1988). For example, we now try to match our stylistic preferences and the shape of our feet to the prepackaged shoes in a store; in a decade, a shoe store may have lasers to measure our feet, videodisc images from which to select styles and colors, and assembly machines to make customized shoes while we wait.

One way of understanding the impact of these changes on occupational skills is to contrast how information technology has changed the job roles of the supermarket checker and the typist. Many supermarkets now have bar code readers; rather than finding the price on each item and punching it into the register, the checker need only pass the goods over the scanner. Efficiency and productivity have increased, and the job requires fewer skills.

In contrast, substituting a word processor/information networking device for a typewriter completely alters a secretary's function. To use the information tool to its full capability, the clerical role must shift from "keyboarding" to using database, desktop publishing, communications, and graphics applications. The job now demands higher-order cognitive skills to extract and tailor knowledge from the huge information capacity of the tool, and the occupational role shifts to the new profession of "information manager."

As workstations become more intelligent through embedded coaches and expert decision-aids, the thinking skills required of the human role in the partnership become more sophisticated. Creativity and flexibility become vital, because the standardized aspects of problem-solving skills are absorbed by the machine. However, technology is no panacea; overautomation and excessive reliance on assembly-line metaphors can deskill work and produce job dissatisfaction (Kraft 1987). Moreover, as the routine parts of work are automated, a greater proportion of decisions will require stressful ethical choices.

Computers and people have complementary intellectual strengths; each can supply what the other lacks. However, the possible future described above is not meant to imply that this transformation of work will be inevitable or universal. On the contrary, advanced technology eliminates jobs as well as creating them; and, in an automated workplace, many of the occupations that survive may require only low-level skills (Rumberger 1987). In every developed nation, significant uncertainty exists about fundamental questions such as:

- How many jobs will be available in the early part of the next century?
- What will be the mix of skilled and unskilled positions?
- Will sufficient "middle class" occupations be available to prevent a polarization of wealth in society, or will most such jobs be deskilled by intelligent machines?
- How will these technological and economic shifts affect equity?

A reasonable assumption is that, during the next decade, developed countries' economies will evolve so as to generate some knowledge-added occupational roles and many lower-skill jobs. Eventually, however, if the majority of the population is to have interesting, well-paid work roles, educators must help shape the needs of the emerging workplace rather than merely respond to present trends (Levin and Rumberger 1987).

IMPLICATIONS FOR CURRICULUM DESIGN AND CONTENT

As the American workplace begins to use intelligent devices, the goals, content, and clients of education will alter (Office of Technology Assessment 1988a). The impact of knowledge bases on the content and design of the school curriculum will be profound. To illustrate, here are some potential effects of the widespread use of cognition enhancers (Dede 1988b):

- Human strengths in partnerships between people and cognition enhancers include skills such as creativity, flexibility, decision making with incomplete data, complex pattern recognition, information evaluation/synthesis, and holistic thinking. These higher-order mental attributes might become our new definition of human intelligence, as basic cognitive skills increasingly shift to the tool's portion of the partnership.

- Methods of assessment will alter from measuring mastery of descriptive knowledge to evaluating attainment of higher-order skills. Developing technological methods for collecting and analyzing detailed performance data could greatly improve the assessment of individual learning needs (Office of Technology Assessment 1988b). For example, we could easily collect the exact hesitation time a student took before each problem-solving step in learning subtraction; this could be valuable diagnostic information.

- "Learning-while-doing" will become a more significant component of occupation education, as combined computer and telecommunications technologies allow delivery of instructional services in a decentralized manner. To allow credit for job-based learning, workers' tools may include intelligent devices that act as job performance aids while simultaneously collecting a cognitive audit trail of user skill improvements. For example, a student in a technical writing course could write all week at work on a word processor, then bring a record of his or her performance to class. The instructor could monitor how the student was writing by scanning his or her actions (deletions, revisions, resequencing), looking for patterns of suboptimal performance and evaluating the learner's writing process.

- As the workplace shifts to an emphasis on group task performance and problem solving, collaborative learning will become more important. Information technology tools may increasingly be designed for use by teams rather than individuals working in isolation (Gorry et al. 1988), and new types of interpersonal skills will be needed for occupational roles in which computer-mediated communication is important (Kiesler et al. 1984). In such an economic environment, adults who lack sophisticated experiences in shared machine-enhanced interaction may be at a disadvantage (Reder and Schwab 1988). Students in conventional classroom settings have few opportunities to build skills of cooperation, compromise, and group decision making; shifts in teaching must occur so that computer-supported collaborative learning becomes a major type of student interaction.

- Interlinked "educational information utilities" that supply access to a variety of data, tools, and training might emerge (Dede 1985). For example, a device may soon be marketed that combines the attributes of the telephone, radio, television, videotape, computer, copier, and printing press. If I heard an item of interest while watching the nightly news, pushing a function key could output articles on that topic from major newspapers. Scanning those might produce keywords of interest; another keystroke would trigger a knowledge base search. From the list of articles that resulted, I might identify the name of a researcher active in this field; yet another command would dial that person's work number. If no one answered, a final keystroke could send an electronic mail message. All this integration may seem merely a gain in speed, but from that perspective the airplane is "just" a faster version of the automobile. Such a device could be inexpensively accessible to a wide range of users, altering the curriculum by shifting emphasis from acquiring data to discussing and synthesizing ideas.

- As discussed earlier, hypermedia would enable a long-standing instructional goal: an integrated curriculum. In a hypertextbook series, the math "book" would contain links to materials in social studies, biology, history, language arts, and physical education. The important interrelationships among different subject areas could be explicitly represented through concept maps; students could modify these webs of linkages to help them learn (Yankelovitch et al. 1985). The curriculum could shift from a subject-centered, disciplinary emphasis to a focus on real-world problem solving using perspectives and tools from multiple fields.

USING TOOLS WISELY

Some claim that technological advances are driving the emergence of a new era: industrial society is being replaced by a civilization based on knowledge processing. Others disagree that the industrial economy is ending but do see many occupational shifts as people implement new information technologies to aid in their work.

The implications for the school curriculum and instructional practice could be profound: a new definition of human intelligence, more sophisticated methods of assessment, decentralization of teaching into workplace settings, a greater emphasis on collaborative learning, a curricular shift from presenting data to evaluating and synthesizing ideas, a focus on solving real-world problems using concepts and skills from multiple subject areas. The most important barriers to this evolution will not be technical or economic but conceptual and organizational; and, unless controlled, the outcome of these changes may be undesirable. We must begin shaping the use of these emerging tools now if we are to have a bright educational future.

References

Dede, C. J. (1985). "Assessing the Potential of Educational Information Utilities." *Library Hi Tech* 3, 4: 115–119.

Dede, C. J. (1987a). "Artificial Intelligence Applications to High Technology Training." *Journal of Educational Communications and Technology* 35, 3: 163–181.

Dede, C. J. (1987b). "Empowering Environments, Hypermedia, and Microworlds." *The Computing Teacher* 15, 3: 20–25.

Dede, C. J. (1988a). "Emerging Information Technologies of Interest for Postsecondary Occupational Education." In *Education Planning for Economic Development*, vol. II, by K. M. Back, C. J. Dede, P. R. Fama, and O. W. Markley, pp. 1–68. Austin, Tex.: Coordinating Board. Texas College and University System.

Dede, C. J. (1988b). "The Probable Evolution of Artificial Intelligence Based Educational Devices." *Technological Forecasting and Social Change* 34: 115–133.

Gorry, G. A., A. M. Burger, R. J. Chaney, K. B. Long, and C. M. Tausk. (1988). "Computer Support for Biomedical Work Groups." Proceedings of the Conference on Computer-Supported Cooperative Work (September 26–28, 1988; Portland, Oreg.), pp. 39–51. New York: Association for Computing Machinery.

Kiesler, S., J. Siegel, and T. W. McGuire. (1984). "Social Psychological Aspects of Computer-Mediated Communication." *American Psychologist* 39: 1123–1134.

Kraft, P. (1987). "Computers and the Automation of Work." In *Technology and the Transformation of White Collar Work*, edited by R. E. Kraut, pp. 99–112. Hillsdale, N.J.: Lawrence Erlbaum Associates.

Levin, H. M., and R. W. Rumberger. (1987). "Educational Requirements for New Technologies: Visions, Possibilities, and Current Realities." *Educational Policy* 1, 3: 333–354.

Office of Technology Assessment, U.S. Congress. (1988a). *Technology and the American Economic Transition: Choices for the Future*. Washington, D.C.: U.S. Government Printing Office.

Office of Technology Assessment, U.S. Congress. (1988b). *Power On: New Tools for Teaching and Learning*. Washington, D.C.: U.S. Government Printing Office.

President's Commission on Industrial Competitiveness. (1985). *Global Competition: The New Reality*, vol. 2. Washington, D.C.: U.S. Government Printing Office.

Reder, S., and R. G. Schwab. (1988). "The Communicative Economy of the Workgroup: Multi-Channel Genres of Communication." Proceedings of the Conference on Computer-Supported Cooperative Work (September 26–28, 1988; Portland, Oreg.), pp. 354–368. New York: Association for Computing Machinery.

Reich, R. B. (1988). *Education and the Next Economy*. Washington, D.C.: National Education Association.

Rumberger, R. W. (1987). "The Potential Impact of Technology on the Skill Requirements of Future Jobs in the United States." In *The Future Impact of Technology on Work and Education*, edited by G. Burke and R. W. Rumberger, pp. 174–192. New York: Falmer Press.

Yankelovitch, N., N. Meyrowitz, and A. van Dam. (October 1985). "Reading and Writing the Electronic Book." *Computer* 18, 10: 15–30.

60

Curriculum Censorship

Values in Conflict

Martha M. McCarthy

Censorship cases are increasing dramatically, and the censor's success rate is rising. Although challenges to the public school curriculum have emanated from groups spanning the political spectrum, most of the cases are brought by groups representing the religious or political right. As legal decisions are made, precedents are set, and the roles and rights of the groups, the schools, and the students are determined . . . until the next challenge.

Curriculum censorship in a sense has always been present in public schools. Decisions must be made regarding what materials to purchase for school libraries and the instructional program. Some materials are not selected because of budget limitations; others are rejected for educational reasons. Traditionally, such determinations made by local school boards were seldom challenged.

Recently, however, curriculum censorship has attracted national attention because of escalating claims that courses and materials *already* selected should be *removed* from the schools to shield students from exposure to "objectionable" content. Although accurate figures on the number of curriculum challenges have been difficult to compile because numerous incidents are not reported, groups that track curriculum controversies have reported a steady increase in public school censorship activity during the past decade. For example, People for the American Way reported a 168% increase in reported censorship cases from 1982 until 1987.[1] During this period the censors' success rate increased from about 26% to approximately 37%. A higher success rate of about 50% has been estimated when also considering complaints informally accommodated by school authorities.[2]

Given the various actors and interests involved in censorship controversies, there are no simple solutions. Parents' rights to direct the religious and moral upbringing of their children, school boards' rights to determine what materials should be included in the curriculum, and students' rights to express their views are often in conflict. This article addresses the nature of the current attacks on the public school curriculum and the actors involved, judicial interpretations of the First Amendment rights at stake, and implications of the censorship activity for the integrity of the public school program.

THE ACTORS AND ALLEGATIONS

Those attacking the public school curriculum and seeking to tailor the curriculum to their view of appropriate American values are well organized and extremely vocal. The most widely publicized challenges to the curriculum have been raised by religious fundamentalists and conservative parent groups. Jenkinson has estimated that over 2,000 national, state, and local groups are involved in efforts to restrict the public school curriculum.[3] Pat Robertson's National Legal Foundation, Phyllis Schlafly's Eagle Forum, Beverly LaHaye's Concerned Women for America, and Mel and Norma Gabler's Educational Research Analysts are among groups that have received substantial national publicity. Other well-known groups involved in the curriculum protests include the Concerned Coalition of Parents, the Liberty Foundation, the Free Congress, the Pro-Family Forum, the American Education Coalition, the Heritage Foundation, the National Association of Christian Educators, and Citizens for Excellence in Education.

These groups that are attacking materials in public schools reject the assertion that they are "censors." Indeed, they claim that they are merely trying to correct censorship that has already taken place in that everything moral has been eliminated from curriculum materials used in public education. Despite their rejection of the label, "censors" will often be used in this paper to refer to the groups—primarily conservative parent groups—that are protesting instructional materials and course content.

Few aspects of the curriculum have remained unchallenged. Some conservative parent groups claim that specific instructional materials are immoral because they include profanity or references to sexual activity. Other materials are attacked as anti-American because they allegedly promote Soviet propaganda or disrespect for traditional American values, such as a domestic role for women.

One of the censors' central charges is that particular materials and course offerings in public schools promote "secular humanism," an allegedly antitheistic creed that disavows God and exalts human nature.[4] Some fundamentalist groups contend that *all* instruction promotes either a strict biblical interpretation of Christianity or an alternative godless faith. According to this reasoning, *no* instruction is religiously neutral. Fundamentalist critics of the public school

Source: From Martha M. McCarthy, "Curriculum Censorship: Values in Conflict," *Educational Horizons*, Volume 67, Fall/Winter 1989, pp. 26–35. Reprinted with permission of *Educational Horizons* quarterly journal published by Pi Lambda Theta national honor and professional association, Bloomington, IN 47407–6626. Reprinted with permission from Martha M. McCarthy.

curriculum have used "secular humanism" as a catchall phrase to refer to any instruction that is considered a threat to Christian tenets.

Illustrative of the materials attacked are *The Diary of Anne Frank* because a passage indicates that all religions are equal; *Cinderella, Macbeth,* and *The Wizard of Oz* because they include references to the supernatural; and *Romeo and Juliet* because it romanticizes teenage suicide. The lengthy list of challenged books includes such well-known selections as *The Catcher in the Rye, The Adventures of Huckleberry Finn, The Scarlet Letter, Soul on Ice, Of Mice and Men, To Kill a Mockingbird,* and *The Color Purple.* Course content has also been challenged, such as instruction in evolution because it conflicts with the biblical account of creation, sex education because it allegedly encourages students to become sexually active, and values clarification because values are not presented as moral absolutes.

Some organizations are combatting the censors. The central mission of both the National Coalition Against Censorship and People for the American Way is to protect the free flow of information. Several education associations as well as organizations that traditionally have defended free speech rights have also become involved in fighting curriculum censorship. For example, the Association for Supervision and Curriculum Development, the National Council of Teachers of English, the American Library Association, and the American Civil Liberties Union have adopted statements condemning public school censorship activity.

It would be incorrect to give the impression that all challenges to the public school curriculum have emanated from the religious or political right. In fact, challenges have been made by groups spanning the political spectrum. For example, several Massachusetts parents recently challenged an eighth-grade history text for allegedly indoctrinating students toward a conservative, status quo world view rather than presenting history accurately and developing critical thinking skills.[5] The National Organization for Women and the Council on Interracial Books for Children have faulted curriculum materials because of their sexist or racist language or their biased presentation of women and minorities.[6] Some consumer protection groups have contested content that allegedly promotes bad health habits for students, such as eating junk food.

With the increasing number of challenges to curriculum materials and the range of actors, textbook publishers are often caught in the middle. In their efforts to respond to the demands of special interest groups, publishers have felt pressure to avoid controversial topics in textbooks. Substantial recent attention has focused on allegations that textbook publishers omit selected religious, historical, and scientific facts in an effort to present "safe" content that will not alienate major textbook purchasers. For example, recent studies conducted by People for the American Way, the U.S. Department of Education, and several independent researchers have documented that the role of religion in American life has been given insufficient attention in books currently used in public schools.[7]

THE CENSORS' TACTICS

The tactics used by individuals and groups attacking the curriculum are as varied as the actors. Often the protesters initially appeal to the school administration or to the school board, requesting that particular courses or materials be removed from the school. If relief is granted at this level, the controversial materials or courses may simply be deleted from the curriculum with little publicity. However, if the administrators or board deny the requests or refer the complaints to review committees that reject the claims, other strategies are usually employed.

Increasingly, conservative groups have attempted to secure state and even federal legislation that restricts the curriculum or guarantees parents the right to have their children excused from activities considered offensive. In 1984 a controversial provision was added to the federal Education for Economic Security Act that provides federal grants for magnet schools. The provision prohibited school districts from using the federal aid to teach "secular humanism."[8] Neither the statute nor its regulations, issued by the Department of Education, defined what constitutes "secular humanism." A group of prominent authors initiated a suit challenging the provision under the First Amendment, but the prohibition on "secular humanism" was removed from the law in 1985 before the suit came to trial.

Controversy has also surrounded the 1978 amendment to the General Education Provision Act (commonly called the Hatch Amendment after its sponsor, Senator Orrin Hatch).[9] This law requires parental consent before students participate in federally supported programs involving psychiatric or psychological examination, testing or treatment designed to reveal information in specified sensitive areas (e.g., religious or political affiliations, potentially embarrassing mental or psychological problems, sexual behavior and attitudes, illegal or antisocial behavior, privileged relationships, and family matters). Although the law applies only to federally funded activities in very limited domains, some conservative parent organizations have broadly interpreted the law's application and have urged parents to rely on the Hatch Amendment to seek exemptions for their children from a variety of public school activities (e.g., role playing, instruction in critical thinking, values clarification, and keeping log books or personal journals). Sample letters for parents to use in demanding exemptions for their children have been distributed nationally in several mass mailings.

Parent groups also have sought state legislation to require parental permission for children to participate in the state-funded curriculum. Such "pupil protection" laws, modeled after the Hatch Amendment, have been introduced in a number of states and enacted in Arizona, California, Missouri, and Oklahoma.[10] Although these laws are couched in terms of individual exemptions, the ultimate goal of the sponsors of such measures is to bring about changes in the curriculum itself.

Other legislation has been sought to conform the public school curriculum to particular belief systems. While a state law barring instruction in evolution was struck down by the Supreme Court in 1968, a few states (Tennessee, Arkansas, and Louisiana) more recently passed laws requiring instruction in the biblical version of creation if evolution is taught.[11] Such measures, however, have not withstood judicial scrutiny when challenged under the First Amendment.[12] In 1987 the Supreme Court settled the constitutional issue by ruling that Louisiana's "balanced treatment" law, calling for instruction in creation science whenever evolution is taught, was designed to discredit legitimate scientific information about evolution and give a clear preference to the biblical account, which advances religion in violation of the First Amendment.[13]

In an effort to promote patriotism, some states have passed statutes that place constraints on how political ideologies, such as communism, are presented. For example, identical wording is used in Alabama and Florida statutes, stipulating that instruction contrasting communism with the free-enterprise economy "shall lay particular emphasis upon the dangers of communism, the ways to fight communism, and the false doctrines of communism."[14] The Alabama statute further stipulates:

> In addition to all other laws which forbid the use of textbooks in the public school of the state by authors who are members of the communist party or members of communist front organizations, all contracts with publishers for furnished state-owned textbooks shall stipulate that the author or authors of such book or books is not a member of the communist party or known advocate of communism or Marxist socialism.[15]

Because laws requiring teachers to disavow membership in the Communist party have been struck down as an unconstitutional invasion of privacy rights,[16] the second Alabama provision would appear vulnerable to constitutional attack.

The censors' lobbying efforts have not been confined to the legislative process; the conservative parent groups have also attempted to influence the textbook adoption process and publishers. As noted previously, the textbook industry is a business enterprise dependent on the marketplace. Because California and Texas are the two largest purchasers of textbooks, censors have concentrated their efforts on the textbook adoption processes in these states.

Texas has statewide textbook adoption, and until 1983 only those objecting to books were allowed to speak at hearings held by the State Textbook Committee, which is an arm of the Texas Education Agency. This committee provides publishers with a list of changes that must be made before books will be adopted in the state. The content of numerous books, including school dictionaries, has been affected by this committee's recommendations. Particularly controversial have been science textbooks. In 1974, advocates of creationism were successful in getting the Texas Education Agency and subsequently the Texas Board of Education to stipulate that biology materials must be edited to carry a disclaimer that evolution is only one of competing theories and is not factually verifiable. This policy influenced the content of science textbooks until 1984, when the policy was rescinded after considerable public debate and a declaration by the Texas Attorney General that the requirement was unconstitutional.[17]

In 1981 advocates of creationism in California secured a similar mandate that evolution cannot be presented as fact in the state's public schools and that textbooks must be screened accordingly.[18] Responding to this mandate, publishers downplayed or omitted references to evolution in textbooks used in California and elsewhere. Like developments in Texas, however, pressure from the scientific community and education groups built until the California State Board of Education in 1985 refused to approve any of the proposed junior high school science texts because they failed to treat evolution adequately.[19] Despite these recent setbacks in Texas and California, the curriculum censors continue to view the textbook adoption process as an important vehicle to realize their objectives.

When other tactics have failed, some individuals and groups have sought judicial support in their efforts to alter the public school curriculum. Courts have been called on to interpret statutory enactments and, as discussed below, to apply constitutional protections to disputes involving the public school curriculum.

FIRST AMENDMENT RIGHTS AT STAKE

Most of the legal challenges to censorship activity have been grounded in the First Amendment to the U.S. Constitution. This amendment stipulates that

> Congress shall make no law respecting an establishment of religion, or prohibiting the free exercise thereof; or abridging the freedom of speech, or of the press, or the right of the people peaceably to assemble, and to petition the Government for a redress of grievances.[20]

While the First Amendment was designed to impose restrictions on Congress, the Supreme Court has subsequently applied these restrictions to state governments as well. The Court has interpreted the Fourteenth Amendment's protection of individual liberties as incorporating the rights specified in the First Amendment. This concept of incorporation has been severely criticized,[21] but Supreme Court precedent supports the application of First Amendment restrictions to the states.

Both those protesting the curriculum and those fighting the censors have attempted to rely on First Amendment guarantees. For example, critics of censorship assert that students have a free speech right to receive information and be exposed to new ideas and that censorship unconstitutionally restricts these rights. Critics also argue that efforts to conform the curriculum to particular religious creeds unconstitutionally advance religion in violation of the establishment clause. The counter argument made by those attempting to restrict the curriculum is that certain materials and subjects unconstitutionally promote an antitheistic faith or interfere with the free exercise of religious beliefs. Thus, both sides claim First Amendment support for their positions.

Courts traditionally have been reluctant to interfere with curriculum decisions made by local school boards unless First Amendment rights have been directly implicated. The Supreme Court has recognized on numerous occasions that the federal judiciary should not interfere in the internal operations of public schools unless constitutional rights clearly hang in the balance.[22] Thus, parents have a heavy burden of proof when challenging decisions of local school boards.

For example, in one of the first widely publicized censorship cases, parents were unsuccessful in challenging the school board's adoption of a series of English materials in Kanawha County, Virginia.[23] The parents considered the materials to be godless, communistic, profane, and otherwise inappropriate for use in the schools. Although the federal district court upheld the school board's authority to determine curricular materials, the controversy did not end with the judicial ruling. There were school boycotts, a strike by coal miners, bombing of the courthouse, and even public prayer calling for the death of the school board members. Eventually, the conservative parent coalition managed to elect a majority of the school board, so the controversial materials ultimately were eliminated from the curriculum despite the judicial ruling.

Also reflecting judicial deference to the school board's authority in curriculum matters, a Michigan appeals court rejected a parental challenge to the use of Kurt Vonnegut's *Slaughterhouse Five* in English classes.[24] Similarly, the Ninth Circuit Court of Appeals rejected a parental attack on the school board's use of Gordon Park's *The Learning Tree* in the high school curriculum.[25] Finding that the book about the struggles of a black youth did not unconstitutionally promote secular humanism, the court ruled that the book was religiously neutral and related to legitimate educational objectives.

In a 1987 case, *Smith* v. *Board of School Commissioners of Mobile County*, the Eleventh Circuit Court of Appeals similarly rejected a claim that several dozen textbooks promoted secular humanism.[26] The lower court had banned 44 books from the Mobile County, Alabama, public schools, concluding that the books promoted an antitheistic creed. Reversing this decision, the appeals court held that the home economics, history, and social studies books in question were religiously neutral and did not serve to advance or inhibit any religious beliefs. While recognizing that the omission of certain religious facts from the textbooks is unfortunate, the court held that such omissions do not constitute a First Amendment infringement. The court noted that the trial judge had erroneously changed the constitutional mandate of governmental neutrality toward religion "into an affirmative obligation to speak about religion."[27]

In an interesting Tennessee case, *Mozert* v. *Hawkins County School District*, parents initially were successful in securing an exemption for their children from exposure to the Holt, Rinehart, and Winston reading series used in grades one through eight in the school district.[28] The parents asserted that exposure to the books violated their fundamentalist religious beliefs, and they sought an alternative reading program for their children. The federal district court concluded that the provision of an alternative reading program for the offended children would abridge the establishment clause by advancing particular religious beliefs. But the district court ruled that to protect the children's free exercise of their beliefs, they were entitled to "opt out" of reading instruction and study this subject at home with their parents as long as they made satisfactory progress on standardized reading tests. On appeal, however, the Sixth Circuit Court of Appeals reversed the lower court's conclusion that the fundamentalist children were entitled to be excused from reading instruction in the public school. Finding nothing in the contested readers that required students to profess an antitheistic belief, the court upheld the school board's authority to compel all students to use the adopted readers.

This case differs from the *Smith* case discussed above because the parents in *Mozert* were seeking a religious accommodation for their own children in contrast to the removal of materials available to *all* students. Courts traditionally have been more receptive to parental requests for individual accommodations (i.e., exemptions from instruction that interferes with religious beliefs) than they have been to requests for the curriculum itself to be altered. Students have been excused from participating in the pledge of allegiance, coeducational physical education classes, sex education classes, and officers' training courses because such activities interfered with their religious beliefs.[29] Despite the judiciary's traditional support for such exemptions, the appeals court in *Mozert* concluded that the request to be excused from the entire reading series went too far and would set a dangerous precedent that could threaten the management of public schools.

Courts have not been receptive to parental challenges to school board decisions, but they have been far more supportive when the school board backs the censorship activity. For example, in upholding the school board's authority to remove books and courses from the curriculum, the Seventh Circuit Court of Appeals endorsed an Indiana federal district court's conclusion that

> it is legitimate for school officials to develop an opinion about what type of citizens are good citizens, to determine what curriculum and materials will best develop good citizens, and to prohibit the use of textbooks, remove library books, and delete courses from the curriculum as a part of the effort to shape students into good citizens.[30]

The court recognized that challenges by secondary school students to educational decisions must "cross a relatively high threshold" before implicating First Amendment rights to justify judicial intervention.

In the Supreme Court's first decision involving curriculum censorship, *Board of Education, Island Trees Union Free School District No. 26* v. *Pico* (1982), the Court did not provide definitive guidance.[31] Seven different opinions were written, showing a range of interpretations. Five of the justices joined to affirm the appellate court's remand of the case for a trial to ascertain whether the students' First Amendment rights had been violated by the school board's removal of several contested books from the school library. A majority of the justices reasoned that a trial was warranted because of the procedural irregularities in the school board's application of its own procedures and questions regarding the motivation for the censorship activity. However, only three of the justices agreed that students have a protected right to receive information, and even those justices recognized the broad authority of school boards to remove materials that are "pervasively vulgar" or educationally unsuitable. The justices were in general agreement that the board's motivation is a key consideration. While political motivation will not be tolerated as grounds for censorship, the school board retains broad discretion in making decisions regarding the educational suitability of materials.

In two recent cases dealing with student expression rights, the Supreme Court strongly supported the school board's discretion in restricting student expression that may carry the imprimatur of the school. These decisions have significant implications for the school board's authority to censor course content and materials as well as student expression. In *Bethel School District No. 403* v. *Fraser*, the Court upheld disciplinary action imposed on a student for using a sexual metaphor in a nominating speech during a student government assembly.[32] Recognizing the school's legitimate interest in protecting minors from exposure to vulgar and offensive speech, the Court declared that the school board is authorized to determine what manner of speech is inappropriate in classes or assemblies. The Court noted that in a public school, where "habits and manners of civility" must be taught, the "sensibilities of others" must be considered in assessing the appropriateness of student expression.[33]

In a subsequent decision involving a principal's censorship of a school-sponsored student publication, *Hazelwood School District* v. *Kuhlmeier*, the Supreme Court reiterated that the school board and school authorities have broad latitude in determining what content is appropriate for high school students.[34] In this case, two articles dealing with students' views toward their parents' divorces and teenage pregnancy were deleted from the school paper because of the potential invasion of privacy rights. The Court reasoned that school authorities can censor the content of newspapers, drama productions, and similar activities carrying the imprimatur of the school, as long as the restrictions on student expression are "reasonably related to legitimate pedagogical concerns."[35] The Court distinguished student expression that merely occurs at school and is constitutionally protected from school-sponsored expression that is subject to restrictions. In both of these cases the Court recognized that the public school is not a traditional open forum for expression: thus, school officials may reasonably regulate expression to ensure that school activities advance educational goals.

The Supreme Court's pronouncements in the *Fraser* and *Hazelwood* cases have already influenced censorship controversies. A recent Florida decision is illustrative. In this case, the federal district court allowed a school board to bar use of Volume I of *The Humanities: Cultural Roots and Continuities* in the first semester of a high school humanities course.[36] Initially, a fundamentalist minister and some parents challenged two selections in the volume (Aristophanes' *Lysistrata* and Chaucer's *The Miller's Tale*) as vulgar and immoral. A review committee recommended that the volume be retained in the curriculum, but that *Lysistrata* and *The Miller's Tale* not be required reading. The superintendent, however, disagreed with the committee and recommended that the two "offensive" selections be removed from the volume or that an alternative text be used. The board voted to discontinue use of the controversial volume in the curriculum, and subsequently offered the rationale that the two selections were inappropriate because of their excessive vulgarity, immorality, and sexuality that violated conservative community norms.

The federal district court recognized the undisputed literary value of the selections in question, but held that the school board is authorized to determine which materials are unsuitable for its students. Relying on the *Hazelwood* decision, the court found that the board was empowered to determine curriculum materials as long as its decisions were reasonably related to educational concerns. Conceding that the school board's decision in this case reflected its restrictive (fundamentalist) views of appropriate values to which students should be exposed, the court nonetheless held that such content-based restrictions regarding the curriculum were permissible under the Supreme Court's *Hazelwood* standard:

> Although the court wishes that the board had imposed its standards in a manner less restrictive of speech, the court recognizes that the board retains broad discretion in dealing with potentially sensitive topics.[37]

The court further declared that a school board's censorship activity will be upheld if reasonable, even though less restrictive means may be available for the board to achieve its goals.

Whether other courts will show such deference to school boards in censorship matters remains to be seen. In light of recent Supreme Court decisions, there is some sentiment that school boards may feel more confident than they did a decade ago in imposing curriculum restrictions as long as their actions are based on pedagogical concerns. It appears that the judiciary will not interfere with a school board's broad discretion in making curricular determinations unless there is a flagrant abuse of that discretion.

IMPLICATIONS

While few would question the public school's legitimate role in transmitting societal values, controversy surrounds *what* those values should be and *who* should make such decisions. The various groups with a stake in the public school curriculum are not in agreement on the means to achieve the goals of public schooling or even on what those goals should be. Many issues remain unsolved. For example, are there basic values, fundamental to our democratic nation, that are constitutionally protected against state interference (e.g., respect for ethnic and racial diversity, protection of free speech)? Or should each school board determine which values to promote? If local school boards are granted considerable latitude in determining what is pedagogically appropriate, might problems arise when students are subjected to statewide assessment programs?

The Supreme Court has not provided clear guidance regarding constitutional constraints, if any, on school board prerogatives in curriculum matters. Although the Supreme Court stated in 1969 that "in our system, students may not be regarded as closed-circuit recipients of only that which the State chooses to communicate," one must wonder whether the current Court is still committed to this sentiment, at least in connection with activities that are sponsored by the school.[38] The Court in *Pico* indicated that the removal of books based solely on the "educational suitability . . . would be 'perfectly permissible'."[39] In subsequent decisions the Court has shown considerable deference to school board judgments in instructional matters, even actions that restrict free expression. Laurence Tribe, constitutional law professor at Harvard University, has asserted that the Supreme Court's recent Hazelwood decision gives school boards "a virtual blank check for censorship in public high schools."[40]

In the abstract, broad discretion for school boards in pedagogical matters may appear appropriate, but concerns have been raised when local boards have attempted to restrict students' access to particular viewpoints. The public school has a legitimate role in transmitting community values, but it also has an important role in developing individual autonomy and preparing future citizens to engage in open and informed inquiry and debate.[41] Justice Brennan, dissenting in the Hazelwood decision, observed that educators' ". . . undeniably vital mandate to inculcate moral and political values is not a general warrant to act as 'thought police' stifling discussion of all but state-approved topics and advocacy of all but the official position."[42] Are we fulfilling our duty to educate students for participation in American life if they are denied exposure to ideas and philosophies found distasteful by a majority of the school board members?

It would appear that judgments regarding "educational suitability" could be used by school boards to justify a range of censorship activity. If a board is allowed to impose its values, no matter how restrictive, the implications for our society could be far reaching. Indeed, some school districts no doubt would be operating under racially discriminatory policies today without judicial intervention to protect constitutional rights.

There are no more emotionally charged issues than those dealing with instructional censorship. They evoke strong sentiments and have resulted in polarized groups that appear to be more interested in making their positions known than in listening to each other. These groups are confident that they are correct and that they know what is appropriate for *everyone*. The basic notion of the school serving as a marketplace of ideas is objectionable to some groups who view critical thinking per se as offensive. This sentiment is difficult to confront and, if it becomes dominant, can threaten the academic integrity of the school program, not to mention the rights of minority groups who do not share those beliefs.

Educators need to be proactive, rather than reactive in curriculum matters. They need to educate the public regarding the difference between encouraging students to accept ideas that conflict with their values and exposing students to a body of new knowledge. School boards also would be well advised to have policies in place to handle curriculum challenges and to establish review committees with broad representation for the selection of instructional materials. Written rationales should be provided for the materials selected. Several educational organizations have issued model policies in this regard, which advise school districts to include in their written procedures explicit criteria for judging the merits of curriculum materials.[43] With such procedures and better communication regarding the justification for instructional decisions, perhaps some curriculum controversies can be defused. But more importantly, such efforts may protect free inquiry in our schools which is crucial to the survival of our democratic nation. As James Madison observed in 1882:

> Knowledge will forever govern ignorance; and a people who mean to be their governors must arm themselves with the power which knowledge gives.[44]

References

1. "Censorship Attempts and Victories on the Rise, Civil Liberties Group Says," *Education Daily*, 28 August 1987, pp. 5–6; *see also* Edward Jenkinson, *The Schoolbook Protest Movement* (Bloomington, IN: Phi Delta Kappa, 1986), pp. 14–16.
2. Caroline Cody, "Can We Have Freedom to Read in American Schools?" (Paper presented at the annual meeting of the American Educational Research Association, New Orleans, LA, April 1988). The estimated 50 percent success rate for curriculum challenges was based on a 1981 survey of school administrators and librarians conducted by the Association of American Publishers, the American Library Association, and the Association for Supervision and Curriculum Development.
3. Jenkinson, *The Schoolbook Protest Movement*, p. 70.
4. *See* Paul Kurtz, "Who Are the Secular Humanists?" *Free Inquiry*, 2(1) (1981): 1, 48. Those who profess to be secular humanists (about 3,000 belong to the American Humanist Association) reject the contention that humanism has the characteristics of an antitheistic religious creed.
5. "Massachusetts Superintendent Upholds Use of 'Conservative' Textbooks," *Education Daily*, 23 November 1987, pp. 3–4.
6. Ken Donelson, "Six Statements/Questions From the Censors," *Phi Delta KAPPAN* (November 1987): 208–214.
7. O. L. Davis, "Another Walk Along the Razor's Edge: Teaching about the Roles of Religion in American Life," Kappa Delta Pi *Record*, *24* (1988): 122.
8. 20 U.S.C. § 4059; 34 C.F.R., Part 280.
9. 20 U.S.C. § 1232h; 34 C.F.R., Parts 75, 76, and 98.
10. *See* Martha McCarthy, *Religious Challenges to the Public School Curriculum* (Bloomington, IN: Consortium on Educational Policy Studies, 1988).
11. Epperson v. Arkansas, 393 U.S. 97 (1968).
12. For a discussion of these cases, *see* McCarthy, *Religious Challenges to the Public School Curriculum*.
13. Edwards v. Aguillard, 107 S. Ct. 2573 (1987).
14. Alabama Code § 16–40–3 (c); Florida Statutes Annotated § 233.064 (5).
15. Alabama Code § 16–36–10.
16. *See* Keyishian v. Board of Educ., 385 U.S. 589 (1967).
17. Anne Brigman, "Texas Board Votes to Change Rule on Tests' Treatment of Evolution," *Education Week*, 25 April 1984, p. 8; Jenkinson, *The Schoolbook Protest Movement*, pp. 61–63.
18. Seagraves v. California, No. 278978 (Cal. Super. 1981).
19. Franklyn Haiman, "School Censors and the Law," *Communication Education, 36* (1987): 337.
20. U.S. Constitution, Amendment 1.
21. *See* James McClellan, *Joseph Story and the American Constitution* (Norman, OK: University of Oklahoma Press, 1971), pp. 144–145; Felix Morley, *Freedom and Federalism* (Chicago: Regnery, 1959).
22. *See*, for example, Epperson v. Arkansas, 393 U.S. 97, 104 (1968); San Antonio Independent School Dist. v. Rodriguez, 411 U.S. 1, 40–44 (1973).
23. Williams v. Board of Educ. of County of Kanawha, 388 F. Supp. 93 (S.D. W. Va. 1975), *aff'd*, 530 F.2d 972 (4th Cir. 1975).
24. Todd v. Rochester Community Schools, 200 N.W.2d 90, 93–94 (Mich. App. 1972).
25. Grove v. Mead School Dist., 753 F.2d 1528 (9th Cir. 1985), *cert. denied*, 106 S. Ct. 85 (1985).
26. Smith v. Board of School Commissioners of Mobile County, 655 F. Supp. 939 (S.D. Ala. 1987), *rev'd*, 827 F. 2d 684 (11th Cir. 1987).
27. *Id.*, 827 F.2d at 695.
28. Mozert v. Hawkins County Public Schools, 647 F. Supp. 1194 (E.D. Tenn. 1986), *rev'd*, 827 F.2d 1058 (6th Cir. 1987), *cert. denied*, 108 S. Ct. 1029 (1988).
29. *See* Martha McCarthy and Nelda Cambron-McCabe, *Public School Law: Teachers' and Students' Rights* (Boston: Allyn & Bacon, 1987), pp. 39–42.

30. Zykan v. Warsaw Community School Corp., 631 F.2d 1300, 1303 (7th Cir. 1980).
31. Board of Educ., Island Trees Union Free School Dist. No. 26 v. Pico, 457 U.S. 853 (1982).
32. 478 U.S. 675 (1986).
33. *Id.* at 681, citing Charles Beard and Mary Beard, *New Basic History of the United States* 228 (1968).
34. Hazelwood School Dist. v. Kuhlmeier, 108 S. Ct. 562 (1988).
35. *Id.* at 571.
36. Virgil v. School Bd. of Columbia County, Florida, 677 F. Supp. 1547 (M.D. Fla. 1988).
37. *Id.* at 1554.
38. Tinker v. Des Moines Independent School Dist. 393 U.S. 503, 511 (1969).
39. Board of Educ., Island Trees Union Free School Dist. No. 26 v. Pico, 457 U.S. 853, 871–872 (1982).
40. Laurence Tribe, quoted in "Constitutional Law Conference," *United States Law Week, 57*, 18 October 1988: 2226.
41. *See* Mark G. Yudof, "Library Book Selection and the Public Schools: The Quest for the Archimedean Point," *Indiana Law Journal, 59* (1984): 528.
42. Hazelwood School Dist. v. Kuhlmeier, 108 S. Ct. 562, 577 (1988) (Brennan, J., dissenting).
43. *See* Haiman, "School Censors and the Law," p. 335.
44. James Madison, quoted in "Has the Pen of the Press Been Turned into a Weapon?" *Law Studies, 10*(2) (1985): 33.

61

Structuring for Success

Setting Up a Whole Language Sixth Grade

Patricia Cordeiro

When I went to school, the first day was like no other. It was a day apart. All dressed up in shoes that didn't fit and clothes that were too hot for the last days of summer, we sat in rows, looking around at each other, without talking. We got new books, we took a math test and a spelling test, and we got THE RULES—lots of very specific rules with penalties clearly spelled out in advance.

For years as a teacher, I started my sixth graders off on their first day just the way I had started. That was the best way to get things done, I thought. The first day always went like clockwork. Until recently.

Recently, I got excited about going back to school in the fall. I wanted to get started on so many projects at once that, without even realizing it, we just started school right off. The first day was like other days—we learned things.

Now, my first day starts with me handing notebooks to the kids as they walk in the door. "It's writing time," I say. We learn about the processes of writing, and since it takes time to do it right, we have to get started first thing. As the kids settle down to writing time, I give them writing plans so they can let me know how they'll spend this time. I also invite them to find a desk that they like.

I arrange our desks in a circle. (I use a student desk in the circle because I find it helps me work better in the classroom community.) I also arrange basic supplies—pencils, notebooks, erasers, folders—on each desktop.

I used to walk around the room the first day and tell the students about the different areas of the room—what they were for, what materials were there, what THE RULES were. Now I put up signs. I count on the kids' involvement with print.

Classics on display. Trade books are laid out on a table in the center of the room. There's always a great variety of books: fiction, nonfiction, small, big, *National Geographics,* books for readers of all kinds and abilities.

I put out some classics, too: *Make Way for Ducklings, Winnie the Pooh, Are You My Mother?* I've found that sixth graders enjoy these classics. Some have never read them; others were struggling with print when they first read them; and still others know them well and have always loved them.

Sometime during the day, we'll begin a Readers' Workshop. We'll use special journals to share our reflections on books read individually. Later in the year, we'll read other books together and discuss how authors accomplish their purposes. By the end of the year, reading and writing will blend into one as authors consult with each other and with books about readers' expectations.

Message from the mummy. This fall, our schoolwide social studies theme is ancient Egypt, so there are many artifacts, posters and books about Egypt in the room. We'll make use of the *National Geographic* index database, which is part of the classroom library. I had a lot of fun putting up a large bulletin board, "The Mummy's Message," to get us started on the Interact simulation. Part of our first day will be spent pretending, role playing, and starting an archaeologist's journal about the Egypt of the mind.

Our simulation will provide incentive to create and solve math problems. As much as possible, math learning, drill and practice, along with all word problems, will be derived from real needs, those generated during simulation and science work.

I'll help my students this first day to learn how to do "correcting by consensus." Those finished first will compare answers. If three agree, they're on to something. If four or five agree, we'll begin to create answer sheets. I've found that students who correct by consensus don't want to cheat, perhaps because the peer relationship fosters honesty.

Students will then do an error analysis. Answers which don't agree will be analyzed. The student will then write what went wrong next to the problem. This simple error analysis helps my students eventually to be able to explain in writing the thinking that went into solving a problem.

On each desk, I've attached a pad of paper. This is for jotting down ideas. I'm interested in improving students' ability to make use of informal strategies for writing. This is writing which helps them to organize and clarify thinking, and which helps them to remember.

I want thinking to be an ongoing activity in my room. I ask all students to jot down an idea before such activities as brainstorming so that they can organize their thoughts before contributing. I often ask students to jot down their interpretation of current lessons. I want to know as soon as possible what they are making of what we are learning.

On the magnetic chalkboard, I have put up the Problem-Solving Framework we use

Source: From Patricia Cordeiro, "Structuring for Success: Setting Up a Whole Language Sixth Grade," *Teaching K–8,* Volume 20, August/September 1989, pp. 83–87. Reprinted with permission of the publisher, Early Years Inc., Norwalk, Connecticut 06854. From the August/September 1989 issue of *Teaching/K–8* magazine.

to infuse critical and creative thinking in all our curricular areas. This particular model has separate parts, and we pull each part out of the framework and study it. Problem solving thus becomes an active and guiding aid to organizing thinking. This first day we'll begin to solve the problem of how to organize our time, so I'll pull down the first section of the framework, "Stating the Situation," and we'll begin to plan.

Moonwatching. Our first science work is always "moonwatching." This study is just what it sounds like: We watch the moon. We keep track of when we see it, how it looks, where it's seen. We keep a large calendar chart on the wall, recording information about the moon.

My goal here is twofold: to provide concrete, observable information about the world around us, and to practice basic processes of the scientific method. We collect data from direct observation. Hypotheses are formed and tested, based on direct experience. Conclusions result from actual observation and experience. I have a large collection of fiction and nonfiction books relating to the moon. We use these in two ways: We analyze the science information presented for accuracy in light of our own observations, and we study them as models for presenting content material.

We chart information from the first day of school. Students decide how to set up the chart and how to collect information. Some of the data we use is firsthand from moon and weather watching; some is secondhand from the almanac section of the local newspaper. Sometimes our charts go from one end of the hall to the other. We do a lot of writing from what develops.

Four goals. The activities and structure of my classroom result from beliefs I hold about how people learn and what students need to know to enter the 21st century. I have certain goals which are cross-grade, cross-ability and cross-cultural. I would hold these same goals, no matter what the age or composition of the learning community I was working with. They are:

- To enable learners to see themselves in real, significant and authentic learning situations. Thus, my learners (and I) participate in meaningful interactions with subject material. School becomes an environment where real people learn and rehearse real things.
- To foster a community of learners (and this includes me). We all participate in conferencing, sharing, teaching and learning. We grow together.
- To provide my students with an integrated day. Since I want to help children become well-integrated adults, it's essential that we work within a well-integrated framework, and that means working with subject matter areas in a creative, contingent way. No more of what Don Graves called the "cha-cha-cha" curriculum, no hopping from this to that, here to there. Learning throughout the day must be woven into an organized fabric—related, interactive and meaningful. I call this "The Whole Learning Concept."
- To provide frameworks through which all members of the classroom community participate in decision making about learning, the classroom climate and environment. I believe that in the long run the most important thing my students learn is decision making, how to maintain control of themselves and their lives.

I aim high for myself and my students. I always did, but now I structure for success. I try to make everything from the physical plant to my classroom role support my goals for my sixth graders.

And when will they learn THE RULES? Sometime along the way, we'll all learn each other's rules. I'll learn what each child needs and how the students order their worlds. They'll learn how I order mine. Together, we'll share a desire to learn new things. Together, we'll participate in Whole Learning.

62

A Teacher Development Model for Classroom Management

Thomas J. Lasley

Concerns about discipline and classroom management continue to dominate the thinking of teachers. Lack of discipline is consistently cited in the annual Gallup education poll as one of the most serious problems confronting the public schools, and a variety of "solutions" to discipline problems have been proposed in recent years.[1] Some of these approaches synthesize management techniques that have been prevalent in classroom practice;[2] others suggest techniques that are packaged as new.[3]

School faculties must determine which, if any, of these approaches to try. But the abundance of articles and books on discipline provides staff developers and teachers with more information than they can possibly assimilate. Thus they tend to select strategies not because they are inherently better, but simply because the materials or the "experts" are available for inservice training. Unfortunately, most "experts" fail to mention that the efficacy of any approach to classroom management depends on the classroom context: on who is being taught and who is doing the teaching.

WHO IS BEING TAUGHT?

The developmental level of the students should influence the type of management technique a teacher uses.[4] For example, young children are developmentally immature and undisciplined. They learn "right" behavior by engaging in "wrong" behavior. Such youngsters require interventionist techniques, which emphasize teacher power and control.[5] In other words, the teacher structures and directs the classroom environment. Such approaches as behavior modification and assertive discipline would appear to be useful in these circumstances.

As students mature and as their cognitive processing becomes more sophisticated, teachers should begin to use strategies that enhance student involvement and self-discipline.[6] Cognitive behavior modification,[7] anecdotal monitoring,[8] and logical consequences[9] are good examples of such approaches. They place more of the burden on students for controlling their own behaviors, but the teacher still sets and guards the boundaries beyond which students may not transgress.

Most students in elementary and secondary schools require teachers who use techniques geared to these first two developmental levels. A few students move to a third level—a self-directive stage in which they profit from teachers who provide opportunities for free expression. Students at this stage require only limited amounts of adult monitoring, but they need more support and encouragement from adults. Such students direct their own behavior; if they do misbehave, teachers can deal with the problem by talking to them, using teacher effectiveness training or transactional analysis.

WHO IS TEACHING?

The type of management strategy a teacher uses also depends on that teacher's predispositions and skills. Every teacher is predisposed to act in certain ways when confronted with misbehavior. Charles Wolfgang and Carl Glickman[10] have developed a rudimentary instrument to help teachers understand their personal approaches to disciplinary problems. Wolfgang and Glickman classified teachers as interventionist (oriented toward power), interactionalist (oriented toward problem solving), or noninterventionist (nondirective). If you were to ask a teacher at each of these levels to deal with chronic disruptive behavior (e.g., talking out of turn), the response would vary according to each teacher's basic predisposition. The interventionist would argue that clear punishment procedures, such as checks on the chalkboard or detention, ought to be established. The interactionalist might seek to work with the student to solve the problem—perhaps by setting up a contract for improved behavior. The noninterventionist might attempt to discuss the problem with the student.

Difficulties arise when the predisposition of teachers clash with the developmental levels of students. Noninterventionist teachers are likely to be ineffective with students who understand only power—who function at Lawrence Kohlberg's first or second level of moral development.[11] Similarly, interventionist high school teachers may prove ineffective in disciplining students who are advanced in their cognitive and moral levels of reasoning.

Teachers should identify their own predispositions, and they should understand that a match ought to exist between their own predispositions and their students' developmental levels and needs. Ideally, teachers should use a classroom management technique that is slightly above the developmental level of their students. When the match is exact (e.g., power-oriented student with power-oriented teacher), the learner's

Source: From Thomas J. Lasley, "A Teacher Development Model for Classroom Management," *Phi Delta Kappa*, Volume 71, September 1989, pp. 36–39. Reprinted with permission from the publisher and from Thomas J. Lasley.

growth is arrested.[12] Therefore, teachers who work with power-oriented students should use interventionist techniques (the "ideal" match) but should occasionally turn to interactionalist approaches that give students more responsibility for controlling their own behavior.

In addition to their personal predispositions to particular styles of classroom management, teachers vary in their pedagogical competence—their capacity to prevent, anticipate, and deal with management problems. There are three levels of pedagogical competence: survival, task, and impact.[13]

Teachers operating at a survival level worry about making it through the day. They tend to be preoccupied with who they are and how they respond in the classroom, and they interpret misbehavior as a threat to their authority. Task-oriented teachers focus on management and organization of the classroom environment; their teaching emphasizes isolated skills, ditto sheets, or activities. Teachers who wish to make an impact, by contrast, are concerned with whether and how students learn.

Novices (student teachers and first-year teachers) tend to worry about survival. They have learned a variety of disciplinary techniques and usually *know* more than they can *do*. They commonly establish clear rules, for example, but fail to enforce them. Regrettably, teacher educators often exacerbate the problem by providing novices with too broad a repertoire of classroom management strategies. Indeed, some writers have suggested that teacher educators teach students all the techniques and then require each student to adopt the technique that best suits him or her.[14]

I would argue for the opposite approach. New teachers should be taught a minimum number of strategies, but they should be required to demonstrate a high level of competence in using them. New teachers tend to feel a strong need for classroom control. They should know how to use assertive discipline, and they must have a clear understanding of the principles and techniques recommended in the applied science literature on teacher control of classrooms, i.e., the teacher starts the year with chairs in rows, with rules clearly stated, and with consequences spelled out.[15] As they learn new skills, novice teachers can encourage greater self-discipline in their students.

The approach I am advocating is aggregative. Teachers begin with a highly select set of skills—those skills that are sufficient to insure survival. Once teachers begin to gain confidence in their ability to control their classrooms, they can add other techniques to their repertoires and strive to match those techniques to the unique needs of each student.

IMPLICATIONS

This aggregative approach suggests, first, that staff development activities in the area of classroom management should be better matched to the level at which teacher participants are functioning. Inservice training for new teachers should emphasize techniques of teacher control, with substantial attention to the strengths and weaknesses of assertive discipline and to the principles of effective classroom management.[16] New teachers might be required to develop and defend classroom rules, and their effectiveness in enforcing those rules could be judged through classroom observations. As teachers' goals shift from merely surviving to teaching effectively, they should be encouraged how (and which) techniques can be used to foster self-discipline in their students.

Moreover, staff development activities that deal with classroom management should be matched to the types of students with whom teacher participants work. Primary teachers will rely more heavily on "control" strategies, such as assertive discipline; they should also know which techniques can be used to wean students from dependence on teacher control. Secondary teachers, by contrast, should understand and use a variety of interactional and noninterventionist approaches (e.g., anecdotal monitoring), with primary emphasis on the former. Most important, teachers at both levels should attempt to create a classroom environment that is slightly ahead of the developmental needs of the learners.[17]

Clearly, teachers will need coaching to see the possibilities inherent in new techniques. Explanations of theory by skilled presenters are an appropriate first step, but teachers who have relied on a repertoire of "personally tested" approaches will no doubt question or be uncomfortable with the introduction of alternative approaches to classroom management. Such teachers should be shown videotapes of teachers who have succeeded (or failed) with various management strategies. They could also talk with other teachers or with experts about specific discipline problems and how well the "new" technique serves as a way of dealing with those problems.

Classroom management is a complex phenomenon. No single approach fits the needs of all students and teachers. The aggregative approach to staff development that I am suggesting here provides a way of addressing this complexity. Indeed, if any single generalization holds for disciplining students, it is this: the greater the repertoire of management techniques that a teacher knows and can effectively use, the fewer *recurrences* of problem behaviors there will be. An aggregative approach gives practicing teachers continuing opportunities to acquire that repertoire of techniques.

References

1 *See*, for example, John S. Cangelosi, *Classroom Management Strategies* (New York: Longman, 1988); Vernon F. Jones and Louise S. Jones, *Comprehensive Classroom Management* (Boston: Allyn and Bacon, 1986); C. M. Charles, *Building Classroom Discipline: From Models to Practice* (New York: Longman, 1985); and Delwyn P. Tatum, *Management of Disruptive Pupil Behavior in Schools* (Chichester: John Wiley, 1986).
2. Norris Haring, *Assessing and Managing Behavior Problems* (Seattle: University of Washington Press, 1987); Edmund T. Emmer et al., *Classroom Management for Secondary Teachers* (Englewood Cliffs, N.J.: Prentice-Hall, 1984); and Charles H. Wolfgang and Carl D. Glickman, *Solving Discipline Problems* (Boston: Allyn and Bacon, 1980, 1986).
3. Lee Canter and Marlene Canter, *Assertive Discipline: A Take-Charge Approach for Today's Educator* (Seal Beach, Calif.: Canter and Associates, 1976); William Glasser, *Schools Without Failure* (New York: Harper & Row, 1965); idem, "Ten Steps to Good Discipline," *Today's Education*, vol. 66, 1977, pp. 60–63; Thomas Gordon, *TET: Teacher Effectiveness Training* (New York: Peter H. Wyden, 1974); and Thomas A. Harris, *I'm OK–You're OK* (New York: Harper & Row, 1969).
4. Paul George, "Discipline and Moral Development," *Educational Forum*, November 1980, pp. 57–68.
5. Wolfgang and Glickman, 1980.
6. George, op. cit.
7. Donald Meichenbaum, *Cognitive Behavior Modification: An Integrative Approach* (New York: Plenum, 1977).
8. James Levin, James Nolan, and Nancy Hoffman, "A Strategy for Classroom Resolution of Chronic Discipline Problems," *NASSP Bulletin*, vol. 69, 1985, pp. 11–18.
9. Rudolf Dreikurs and Loren Grey, *Logical Consequences* (New York: Meredith Press, 1968).
10. Wolfgang and Glickman, 1980.
11. Lawrence Kohlberg, "The Cognitive-Developmental Approach to Moral Education," *Phi Delta Kappan*, June 1975, pp. 670–77.
12. Bruce Joyce and Marsha Weil, *Models of Teaching* (Englewood Cliffs, N.J.: Prentice-Hall, 1986).
13. Frances F. Fuller, "Concerns of Teachers: A Developmental Conceptualization," *American Educational Research Journal*, vol. 6, 1969, pp. 207–66.
14. Daniel Duke and Adrienne Meckel, *Classroom Management* (New York: Random House, 1984).
15. Emmer et al., op. cit.; Carolyn Evertson, "Managing Classrooms: A Framework for Teachers," in David Berliner and Barak V. Rosenshine, eds., *Talks to Teachers* (New York: Random House, 1987), pp. 54–74; and Thomas J. Lasley, "Classroom Management: A Curricular View," *Educational Forum*, vol. 51, 1987, pp. 285–98.
16. Evertson, op. cit.
17. Joyce and Weil, op. cit.

63

The Back Door

Are We Censoring Adolescence?

Charlie Reed

Several weeks ago this list of books most often challenged in the courts to be banned from public schools appeared in a local newspaper. Though there were no surprises on the list, I clipped it from the paper and put it in a file labeled "censorship." Even though the list was safely deposited in a metal file cabinet, I found myself thinking about it. What makes these particular books most objectionable? Why are they being challenged? By whom? I tried to remember all the titles on the list, searching for common elements in these most frequently challenged books. Finally, I took the list out of the file and spent several minutes simply staring at it, remembering scenes and characters from each of the books. I had found many of them memorable; some of them pure fun, some thought-provoking, some disturbing. Characters like Huck and Jerry and Holden are a part of my life; they are my friends. A few of the books I would not use in my own classroom. But, objectionable—in what way? Suddenly a common element came to mind. ALL OF THESE BOOKS HAVE ADOLESCENT CHARACTERS. Are book banners banning books or are they banning adolescence?

Certainly, it is logical that many of the books used in public school classrooms and placed in public school libraries have adolescent characters. Those of us who know about the reading interests of the young know that adolescents are most interested in reading about themselves, most interested in exploring their own world. In 1960 Margaret Early established that most adolescents are at a stage of reading development she labeled "egocentric." Anyone who has worked with adolescents is not surprised by this, for the adolescent is him/herself egocentric. Therefore, when we select books to use in classrooms, frequently we attempt to select books that will appeal to adolescent readers, hence, adolescent characters.

However, many books read regularly in the schools have adult characters: *The Old Man and the Sea, The Scarlet Letter, Jane Eyre, Moby Dick, Julius Caesar, Macbeth* and *Frankenstein.* Surely these books are just as disturbing; surely much in them might be objectionable to some people. They are read just as often, perhaps more often, than the books that appear on the "most challenged list." Of course, all of these books have been challenged at some time in some place, but not as frequently as those that appear on the "list." Why?

I remember listening to a lecture on discipline a number of years ago, back in the days when we talked about student-centered discipline rather than the assertive discipline we speak of today. I can't remember to whom I was listening, but I remember a comment made by the speaker.

"When we speak of adults, we speak of their behavior. When we speak of adolescents, we speak of their misbehavior."

"Yes, indeed," I thought, "we never talk of an adult misbehaving."

We might conclude that Jim Bakker's behavior was inappropriate, but we don't say, "Jim, you misbehaved." However, we frequently tell the young that they misbehave. "Why do we consider so much of the behavior of the adolescent misbehavior?" I wondered.

Even in this age when we require teachers to learn about assertive discipline, I still wonder. Is it because we are censoring the behavior of the adolescent?

The behavior of Jerry in *The Chocolate War,* Huck in *The Adventures of Huckleberry Finn* and Katherine in *Forever* is normal adolescent behavior. In fact, all three characters, as well as those in several other books on the "most often challenged list," rise above their peers and, in the end, behave in a more "mature" manner.

Even the language we use shows our distaste for the behavior of the young. We talk about "mature" behavior, and, by that we mean "good" or "appropriate" behavior, rather than the misbehavior of the adolescent. We tell our adolescents to "act like adults," at the same time our schools adopt discipline procedures that encourage them to act like children.

We encourage our adolescents to be more adultlike while we protect them from a perceived danger in books. Perhaps the banners of these books are attempting to protect adolescents from themselves.

George Bernard Shaw has said, "No child should be shielded from mischief and danger, either physical or moral, in the library or out of it. Such protection leaves them incapable of resistance when they are exposed as they finally must be, to all the mischief and danger of the world." Adolescence is a time when the young discover much of the mischief and danger that exists in the world. If we ban books about young people who have faced the challenges of mischief and danger, the only way the adolescent will learn of these things is from first hand experience, and learn of them they will. We can ban adolescent books, but we cannot ban adolescence. With or without our help, our young people will face the mischief and danger that exists in our world. I, for one, vote to give them all the help we can provide through books, discussions and an understanding of what it is to be an adolescent.

Source: From Arthea J.S. Reed, "The Back Door: Are We Censoring Adolescence?," *The ALAN Review*, Volume 16, Winter 1989, pp. 47–48. Reprinted with permission from the publisher.

A Comparison of Standardized Achievement Test Scores on Right and Left Brain Dominant Fourth-Grade Students

Michael L. Bell
Darrell L. Roubinek
Southwest Missouri State University

This study was conducted to determine if there were differences in achievement of right brain dominant and left brain dominant fourth-grade students on the Stanford Achievement Test, SAT, the Iowa Test of Basic Skills, ITBS, and the Metropolitan Achievement Test, MAT.

Subtest scores on each achievement test were compared for right and left brain dominant students using an independent t-test. The right brain dominant students scored significantly greater on four subtests of the SAT. The left brain dominant students scored significantly greater on four subtests of the ITBS and on two subtests of the MAT.

The business of schools is learning. Attempting to discover how children learn continues as a primary goal of educators. Recent research on how the brain functions has stimulated the interest of many educators. This interest has centered not only on how the brain functions but also on how the learning environment can best be structured to insure maximum learning.

In the area of brain functioning, hemisphericity has received a great deal of attention. Considerable research has been done to determine what, if any, relationship exists between hemispheric dominance and achievement (Dean, 1980; Oexle and Zenhausern, 1980; Jarsonbeck, 1984; Roubinek and Bell, 1985). In these studies children were assessed to determine whether they exhibited a preferred right, left or integrated brain dominance. The achievement test scores of each of these dominance groups were then compared. In general it was found that the group who exhibited a right dominance preference frequently did not score as high on achievement tests as children who exhibited a left dominance preference. These research studies and others have led some to suggest that our schools tend to favor those children who exhibit a preferred left dominance.

The above mentioned research studies had several limitations. Among these limitations was the issue of determining dominance with a paper and pencil assessment instrument. This is, of course, a limitation which cannot be corrected easily when investigating large numbers of subjects with limited resources. Other limitations were the relatively small number of subjects in many of these studies and the fact that in most of these studies only one achievement test was utilized to determine which dominance group tended to score higher.

In the study reported in this article the investigators attempted to minimize two of these limitations. Significantly more subjects were utilized in this study than in other similar studies and more than one achievement test was utilized to determine the effect of dominance on achievement test scores. Increasing the number of achievement tests appeared to have a most interesting effect on the results of this study.

PROCEDURES

The children's version of the *Hemispheric Cognitive Style* (HCS) developed by Zenhausern was administered to 405 fourth-grade students from six elementary schools in Southwest Missouri. The *Hemispheric Cognitive Style* has been developed by Zenhausern, based on Torrence's *Your Style of Learning and Thinking*. It provides a measure of relative hemispheric activation. According to Zenhausern, HCS has test/retest reliability for college students of .72 for right score, .86 for left score, and .82 for the difference score. The test has evidenced construct validity, based on the construct that if persons prefer a hemisphere, they will do better on tasks for which that hemisphere is more specialized than someone who prefers

Source: From Michael L. Bell and Darell L. Roubinek, "A Comparison of Standardized Achievement Test Scores on Right and Left Brain Dominant Fourth-Grade Students," ***Reading Improvement***, Volume 26, Spring 1989, pp. 7–11. Reprinted with permission from the publisher.

the less specialized hemisphere (Zenhausern et al., 1981).

The HCS was scored so that left brain scores were recorded as negative scores and right brain scores were recorded as positive scores. A score of zero on the HCS would theoretically indicate that the subject was neither left brain oriented nor right brain oriented, but was integrated.

In the absence of norms on the HCS, a mean and a standard deviation for the 405 subjects were calculated. Those subjects whose scores were greater than on standard deviation above the mean were identified as right brain dominant subjects. Those whose scores were greater than one standard deviation below the mean were identified as left brain dominant subjects.

Of the 405 subjects, 127 had taken the *Stanford Achievement Test* (SAT) as a part of their school testing program at the end of the fourth-grade year. Of the 127 who had taken the SAT, 25 were identified as left brain dominant subjects while 19 were identified as right brain dominant subjects.

Of the 405 subjects, 125 had taken the *Iowa Test of Basic Skills* (ITBS) as a part of their school testing program at the end of the fourth-grade year. Of the 125 who had taken the ITBS, 25 were identified as left brain dominant subjects while 15 were identified as right brain dominant subjects.

Of the 405 subjects, 153 had taken the *Metropolitan Achievement Test* (MAT) as a part of their school testing program at the end of the fourth-grade year. Of the 153 who had taken the MAT, 29 were identified as left brain dominant subjects while 19 were identified as right brain dominant subjects.

The achievement of the right brain dominant and the left brain dominant subjects were compared on each subtest of the SAT, the ITBS, and the MAT. Raw score achievement data were used on each of the tests.

ANALYSIS

The mean and standard deviation of the 405 subjects on the HCS are shown in Table 1. Theoretically, the mean of the group should have been zero. The actual mean was 2.5. Of the 405 subjects, 273 (67.4%) of them were within one standard deviation of the mean, indicating a somewhat normal distribution of scores on the HCS.

The right brain dominant subjects scored greater on every subtest of the SAT as shown in Table 2. The differences were significant (p.05) on Reading Comprehension, Vocabulary, Math Concepts, and Math Application. The difference approached significance at the .05 level on the subtest of Language.

The left brain dominant subjects scored greater on every subtest of the ITBS as shown in Table 3. The differences were significant (p.05) on Vocabulary, Reading, Usage, and Math Concepts.

The left brain dominant subjects scored greater on every subtest of the MAT as

TABLE 1
Mean and Standard Deviation of Student Scores on HCS

N	*X*	*S.D.*
405	2.5	16.5

TABLE 2
A Comparison of Stanford Achievement Test Subtest Scores Between Right Brain Dominant and Left Brain Dominant Fourth Grade Students

Subtest	X_l	SD_l	N_l	X_r	SD_r	N_r	*t*	*P*
Reading Comprehension	37.55	9.96	25	45.53	9.19	19	2.71	.0094
Vocabulary	25.44	6.40	25	29.05	3.32	19	2.23	.0288
Spelling	29.48	7.60	25	30.47	7.16	19	0.44	.6660
Language	37.60	8.08	25	41.95	6.66	19	1.90	.0606
Math Concepts	20.24	6.66	25	25.79	4.86	19	3.06	.0040
Math Computation	28.80	9.08	25	33.16	8.45	19	1.62	.1080
Math Application	24.76	6.97	25	30.95	6.09	19	3.07	.0040
Science	40.12	11.99	25	44.84	9.20	19	1.42	.1478

TABLE 3
A Comparison of Iowa Test of Basic Skills Subtest Scores Between Right Brain Dominant and Left Brain Dominant Fourth Grade Students

Subtest	X_l	SD_l	N_l	X_r	SD_r	N_r	*t*	*P*
Vocabulary	67.72	24.55	25	50.47	24.59	15	2.15	.0358
Reading	71.28	25.09	25	51.40	27.68	15	2.33	.0236
Spelling	61.76	27.03	25	48.47	27.86	15	1.48	.1412
Usage	70.08	24.27	25	50.67	23.24	15	2.48	.0166
Math Concepts	70.04	23.54	25	53.47	26.20	15	2.06	.0430
Math Problem Solving	64.92	26.12	25	50.73	28.55	15	1.60	.1126
Math Computation	67.76	26.41	25	58.27	29.37	15	1.05	.2982
Science	71.56	23.26	25	59.40	22.41	15	1.62	.1092

TABLE 4
A Comparison of Metropolitan Achievement Test Subtest Scores Between Right Brain Dominant and Left Brain Dominant Fourth Grade Students

Subtest	X_l	SD_l	N_l	X_r	SD_r	N_r	*t*	*P*
Vocabulary	20.59	1.57	29	18.84	4.31	19	1.99	.0492
Reading Comprehension	46.42	9.67	29	42.11	10.14	19	1.33	.1840
Spelling	16.31	3.67	29	15.47	3.10	19	0.82	.4244
Language	32.14	6.27	29	29.37	6.56	19	1.47	.1446
Math Concepts	26.07	3.96	29	23.89	4.69	19	1.72	.0870
Math Problem Solving	22.62	5.19	29	20.59	5.50	19	1.30	.1964
Math Computation	24.93	2.59	29	22.89	3.77	19	2.22	.0294
Science	32.41	6.65	29	30.53	7.40	19	0.91	.3762

shown in Table 4. The differences were significant (p.05) on Vocabulary and Math Computation. The difference approached significance at the .05 level on the subtest of Math Concepts.

CONCLUSIONS

Whereas many similar studies have shown that children with a right brain dominance preference frequently do not score as high on achievement tests as children who exhibited a left brain dominance preference, the results of this study suggest that this may not be true when children take the *Stanford Achievement Test*. Right brain dominant preference children scored higher on the SAT than did children with left brain dominance preference.

However, children with a left brain dominance preference did score higher than children with a right dominance preference on the *Iowa Test of Basic Skills* and the *Metropolitan Achievement Test*. This is consistent with other studies of achievement of left and right brain dominant students (Marcel, Katz, and Smith, 1974; Zenhausern, Dunn, Cavonaugh, and Eberle, 1981; Roubinek and Bell, 1986).

It is likely that the main purposes for which the schools used the three tests in this study were for measuring achievement levels of the students and to get some indication of achievement gains from previous years. There is evidence, however, that the three tests (SAT, ITBS, and MAT) differ in the content which they emphasize as well as in format.

Mehrens and Lehman (1987) cited specific concerns about the SAT. They said that children at lower age levels have to depend too much on memory in completing the Listening Comprehension Test. They also expressed several concerns regarding the way in which examiners time the test and also the ability of the average fourth or fifth grade student to complete the Language section in the allotted time. Analysis of the ITBS included the concern that the Vocabulary test purports to test basic skills, but emphasizes word knowledge. Also, the tests on Work-Study Skills and Mathematics Problem-Solving are said to be overly verbal. With regard to the MAT, it is indicated that factual recall rather than problem solving is overemphasized (Mehrens and Lehman, 1987).

The results of this study seem to suggest that the specific achievement test utilized to assess achievement may have some effect on how children with different dominance preferences score on an achievement test. Perhaps educators are doing children an injustice when they focus on just one measure of achievement for all children. When making an assessment about a child's achievement level perhaps children should be allowed to demonstrate what they know in a variety of ways.

The results of this study might also serve as a caution sign when educators have the desire to suggest that right or left preference children achieve higher scores on achievement tests. At least, educators might want to specify which achievement test was utilized in making that statement.

65

Effective Instruction

Application of the Hunter Instructional Skills Model to Staff Development for Mainstreaming

Lisa A. Freund
Sidney A. Freund

Research on effective instruction in both regular and special education has demonstrated that the way teachers deliver and monitor instruction affects student achievement in basic academic skills. Current research on this topic has consistently identified certain teacher behaviors that are associated with increased levels of academic learning time, or time spent by students actively engaged in academic tasks completed with high success rates, as well as with other measures of student achievement.[1]

Although it has primarily been used in inservice training programs for teachers of normally achieving students, the Instructional Skills Model developed by Hunter[2] incorporates many of the teacher behaviors that have been demonstrated to be effective with mildly handicapped students. The instructional skills and lesson plan designs which make up this model closely parallel those advocated by researchers in effective teaching. For this reason, it is important to consider the value of adapting the Hunter Model for use in the preparation of regular classroom teachers who must address the needs of the mildly handicapped, mainstreamed student.

This article summarizes the findings of recent research on effective instructional practice, and describes the Madeline Hunter Instructional Skills Model and its relationship to the findings of effective instruction research. Finally, the article discusses some cautions and caveats concerning rigid adherence to or misuse of this model at the expense of sound instructional decision making.

EFFECTIVE INSTRUCTIONAL PRACTICE

Much research has pointed to the presence of specific teaching behaviors associated with increased academic success for mildly handicapped students.[3] These teaching behaviors can be outlined as follows:

- *Effective teachers take responsibility for teaching*. Rather than placing the onus of failure on the child, these teachers take responsibility for varying and modifying their strategies, materials, and classroom structure to improve their students' learning. They view student learning as the result of the interaction of the learner, the task, the teacher, and the setting.[4]
- *Effective teachers organize and manage their classrooms efficiently*. A larger percentage of time is devoted to instruction, with less time spent on transitions between lessons. Basically, effective teachers establish routines and schedules and plan efficiently so that they can *teach* more.
- *Effective teachers gear the curriculum for success*. Effective teachers make use of task analysis to insure that their objectives are on the correct level of difficulty for individual students, making extensive use of curriculum-based and other informal methods of assessment.[5]
- *Effective teachers clearly communicate their learning goals to the students as well as their rationale for selecting certain academic tasks*. This improves both attention rates and academic achievement.[6]
- *Effective teachers direct the learning experience*. Effective teachers model, demonstrate, explain, and provide more examples, particularly when teaching new information or skills.
- *Effective teachers teach students to mastery levels*. They provide for overlearning, set high mastery criteria, and require mastery of foundation skills before allowing students to move on to the next level of difficulty.
- *Effective teachers provide students with maximum opportunities to actively respond to instruction*. Effective teachers provide cues, prompts, and signals; ask more questions; and maximize active participation.
- *Effective teachers monitor student learning at all stages of the learning process*. Student progress and accuracy are continuously checked by eliciting overt, active signs of learning. Effective teachers respond to their students' difficulties by providing feedback or offering assistance.[7]

Source: From Lisa A. Freund and Sidney A. Freund, "Effective Instruction: Application of the Hunter Instructional Skills Model to Staff Development for Mainstreaming," *ERS Spectrum*, Volume 7, Spring 1989, pp. 28–33. Reprinted with permission from the publisher.

- *Effective teachers provide for high rates of corrective academic feedback.* Both basic and elaborated feedback are provided. In studies comparing the two types of feedback, elaborated feedback produced the greatest skill acquisitions.[8]
- *Effective teachers are aware of the impact of the emotional climate of the classroom on student learning, and adjust their behavior accordingly.* They use positive affect expression and avoid the use of criticism and humiliation.[9]

While there appears to be general agreement about what constitutes effective teacher behavior, recent studies reveal little application of these behaviors to classroom instruction. Graden, Thurlow, Ysseldyke, and Algozzine report that in second grade regular and special classes, children's opportunities for direct academic responding (as opposed to waiting or "appearing to attend") can average as little as 45 minutes per school day.[10] Morsink found major discrepancies between so-called "best practice" and actual practice with mildly handicapped students including: a) minimal time spent in activities that could be considered direct instruction with active learner response; and b) little direct feedback from the teacher.[11] Finally, Pugach reported that many mainstream teachers did not consistently implement the effective practices listed above. Her findings indicated that mainstream teachers usually failed to: a) establish a positive classroom environment; b) clearly articulate instructional goals; c) use efficient organizational and time management strategies; and d) provide systematic corrective feedback.[12]

THE HUNTER INSTRUCTIONAL SKILLS MODEL

The Hunter Model incorporates many of the teacher behaviors which have been shown to be effective with mildly handicapped students. The core of the model is expressed through Hunter's definition of instruction as "a process of deliberate decision making and action that makes learning more probable and more predictably successful than it would be without teaching."[13] This defines the role of the teacher as an active one—taking responsibility for teaching and directing the learning experience. This role is also emphasized in the effective instruction literature.

The essence of the Hunter Model is summarized in her four Essential Elements of Instruction:

- *Select the learning objective at the correct level of difficulty and complexity.* Informal diagnostic testing based on careful task analyses of the desired learning outcomes helps to determine the correct level of difficulty of content for individual students. Hunter used Bloom's Taxonomy of Educational Objectives[14] to help the teacher categorize the level of complexity, or degree of abstractness, of the thinking skills required to perform the task. These processes allow the classroom teacher to gear the curriculum for success, as well as to teach to mastery levels, both of which are effective instructional practices.
- *Teach to the objective.* To teach to an intended objective, the majority of teacher and student activities must relate to and contribute to the learning as stated in the instructional objective. Teaching to an objective includes four types of teacher actions:
    1. Giving information—Students learning to perform new academic tasks normally lack basic information essential to performing the task correctly. The teacher must provide specific information including definitions, descriptions, examples, or sets of procedures that enable students to perform the task stated in the objective.[15] Effective instruction research has also emphasized the need for teachers to model, demonstrate, and provide sufficient examples for skill acquisition.
    2. Asking questions—Teachers should ask questions that serve a diagnostic purpose. Questions should elicit examples to bring students back to the definition or concept being taught.
    3. Making specific responses to student efforts—Direct and frequent feedback is essential.
    4. Designing student activities—Student activities must include relevant practice of the exact task or tasks stated in the learning objective.
- *Monitor learning and adjust teaching.* As in the effective instruction literature, the Hunter Model places great emphasis on the need for continuous monitoring of student performance at all stages of the learning process. First, students must be given varied and numerous opportunities for overt active participation, either verbal, written, or through movement. Second, teachers must check, interpret, and act on their interpretation of these behaviors. This continuous "dip-sticking" should lead to adjustments in instruction including additional practice, reteaching, or moving up or down the hierarchy of skills.
- *Use principles of learning.* According to the Hunter Model, teachers must be aware of and control the variables that affect the rate, transfer, and maintenance of student learning. For example, most students will be more motivated to learn and will better retain new material if given prompt corrective feedback, or "knowledge of results" in Hunter terminology. As in the effective instruction research, Hunter acknowledges the role that "feeling tone" or emotional climate can have on student motivation and retention of learned material.

LESSON DESIGN

Lesson design, based on the Hunter Model, closely parallels that advocated by researchers in effective teaching. For teaching new material, recent research has identified the lesson structure that will lead to increases in student learning.[16] Briefly, lessons should be divided into three phases:

- *Phase 1: Structuring*—Effective teachers prepare children in advance by stating the lesson objective, describing the activities to follow (including their relevance to the objective), and relating the new material or concept to previous learnings. This phase is particularly valuable for mildly handicapped students, as it provides for review and revisualization of prior knowledge.

- *Phase 2: Presentation and practice*—During this phase, the teacher must explain or define rules or word meanings, provide varied and numerous examples of new concepts, and model procedures or strategies. Students, in turn, should respond overtly to teacher questions and practice items. The teacher needs to provide cues and prompts and corrective feedback to better ensure correct practice.

- *Phase 3: Closure*—Lesson closure must be more than a simple verbal review of concepts by the teacher. Students must practice one or two firm-up examples of the key concept or skill for better retention.

Hunter's lesson design includes the following seven instructional processes. The three phases discussed above are included in parentheses to show the relationship of both lesson paradigms:

(Structuring)

- Anticipatory set: The teacher provides verbal cues or activities to help students focus their attention as well as brief practice of prior related learnings.
- Statement of objective: The teacher lets students know what will be taught and why it is important for them to learn this.

(Presentation and practice)

- Input: When teaching new material, the teacher must model the first examples to avoid error at the beginning of the lesson. Whatever knowledge or skill is needed to achieve the objective is presented at this stage.

• Checking for understanding: The teacher determines, by eliciting overt responses, whether or not students possess the necessary information or skills to reach the objective. To best ensure that all students "have it," the teacher can ask for signaled responses from the entire group ("thumbs up, thumbs down" or "clap if you hear . . .") or individual private responses (whispered or written from each group member).

• Guided practice: Students practice the new learning task with guidance and monitoring from the teacher.

• Closure: In the Hunter Model, closure has a special meaning. It is not summarizing by the teacher. Rather, it allows the learner to summarize for himself/herself what has been learned, and can actually be activated at any time during the lesson. Teachers can activate closure by asking students to summarize what they have learned, or by using a number of other cues or signals.

• Independent practice: Once the teacher is certain that students can perform the learned task, they may continue to practice on their own in class or for homework.

CAUTIONS AND CAVEATS

It is important to caution against rigid adherence to the procedures indicated above, since effective instruction models stress the importance of the decision-making role of the teacher. To hold inflexibly to one set of procedures would violate the "spirit" of effective instructional practice.

In particular, the Hunter Model should be viewed as a means of encouraging independent thinking on the part of teachers. Once teachers understand the purpose of each part of the lesson design, they can make informed decisions about which sections to augment, and which to omit. For example, a teacher may design a lesson to teach new material, but discover that her students have mastered most of the material. In this lesson, then, teacher input would be minimized, with the focus on guided and independent practice. Staff development personnel must emphasize the need for flexibility as well as the difference in purpose between informational, review, diagnostic, and more open-ended or "discovery" lessons.

Finally, it is important to address two common concerns of experienced teachers who are first exposed to this model. First, teachers often view the lesson procedures as didactic and as a threat to their creativity. It is important to stress that while lesson structure, when presenting new basic skills material, should be relatively stable, the activities themselves can vary enormously depending on the students' needs and the teacher's talents. Second, when initially exposed to the Hunter Model, many experienced teachers feel that they must completely overhaul their teaching methods to fit the model. Staff development personnel can alleviate this problem by highlighting and reinforcing each teacher's existing strengths through the use of clinical supervision observation and conferences.

1. J. Brophy and T. Good, "Teacher Behavior and Student Achievement," in M. C. Wittrock (editor) *Handbook of Research on Teaching* (New York: Macmillan, 1985); C. S. Englert, "Effective Direct Instruction Practices in Special Education Settings," *Remedial and Special Education* 5 (1984): 38–47; B. Larrivee, "Effective Teaching for Mainstreamed Students is Effective Teaching for All Students," *Teacher Education and Special Education* 9 (1986): 173–179; and B. Rosenshine, "Teaching Functions in Instructional Programs," *Elementary School Journal* 83 (1983): 335–352.
2. M. Hunter, *Mastery Teaching* (El Segundo, CA: TIP Publications, 1982).
3. D. C. Berliner, "The Half-Full Glass: A Review of Research on Teaching," in P. L. Hosford (editor) *Using What We Know About Teaching* (Alexandria, VA: Association for Supervision and Curriculum Development, 1984); J. Brophy, "Classroom Management and Learning," *American Education* 18 (1982): 20–23; J. Brophy and T. Good, 1985, op cit.; T. B. Corcoran and B. J. Hansen, *The Quest for Excellence: Making Public Schools More Effective* (Trenton, NJ: New Jersey School Board Association, 1983); C. S. Englert, 1984, op cit.; C. R. Greenwood, J. Delquadri, and R. V. Hall, "Opportunity to Respond and Student Academic Performance," in W. Heward, et al., (editors) *Focus on Behavior Analysis in Education* (Columbus, OH: Merrill, 1984); B. Rosenshine and R. Stevens, "Teaching Functions," in M. D. Mittrock (editor) *Handbook of Research on Teaching* (New York: Macmillan, 1986).
4. C. R. Smith, *Learning Disabilities: The Interaction of Learner, Task and Setting* (Boston: Little, Brown and Co., 1983).
5. L. S. Fuchs and D. Fuchs, "The Effects of Systematic Formative Evaluation on Student Achievement, *Exceptional Children* 53 (1986): 199–208.
6. D. C. Berliner, 1984, op cit.
7. H. J. Rieth and T. Frick, *An Analysis of the Impact of Instructional Time With Different Delivery Systems on the Achievement of Mildly Handicapped Students* (Final Grant Research Report) (Bloomington: Indiana University, Center for Innovation in Teaching the Handicapped, 1983).
8. M. Collins, D. Carnine, and R. Gersten, "Elaborated Corrective Feedback and the Acquisition of Reasoning Skills: A Study of Computer Assisted Instruction," *Exceptional Children* 54 (1987): 254–262.
9. D. M. Medley, *Teacher Competence and Teacher Effectiveness: A Review of Process Product Research* (Washington, DC: American Association of Colleges for Teacher Education, 1977).
10. J. Graden, J. Thurlow, J. Ysseldyke, and B. Algozzine, *Instructional Ecology and Academic Responding Time for Students in Different Reading Groups* (Research Report #79) (Minneapolis: University of Minnesota IRLD, 1982).
11. C. Morsink, R. S. Soar, R. M. Soar, and R. Thomas, "Research on Teaching: Opening the Door to Special Education Classrooms," *Exceptional Children* 53 (1986): 32–40.
12. M. Pugach, "The National Education Reports and Special Education: Implications for Teacher Preparation," *Exceptional Children* 53 (1987): 308–314.
13. C. Cummings, *Teaching Makes a Difference* (Edmonds, WA: Teaching, Inc., 1983).
14. B. Bloom (editor), *Taxonomy of Educational Objectives, Handbook I: Cognitive Domain* (New York: Longman, 1956).
15. N. Higgins and H. Sullivan, *Teaching for Competence* (New York: Teachers College Press, 1983).
16. Brophy and Goode, 1985, op cit.; and Englert, 1984, op cit.

66

Integrated Instructional Management Systems and Outcome-Based Education

Mark Whitman, Ph.D.
Asst. Superintendent for Program Development
Phil Lambert, Ed.D.
Asst. Superintendent for Instruction
Tippecanoe School Corp., Lafayette, Ind.

We educators prefer to focus on people; but we can no longer ignore the school's function as an information enterprise.

Each day, in classrooms around the world, teachers immerse students in vast streams of information and, in turn, receive rivers of data whose purpose is to assess student progress. These same teachers continually analyze and organize this data to channel it for distribution to parents, the community, the school administration and the students themselves.

Whatever else they do, educators process and assess information. And, as our society has become increasingly analytical, assessment philosophies and technologically dependent assessment tools have developed in parallel. But it was not until the post-World War II advent of the computer that schools could even remotely consider using the comprehensive and standardized testing that is now so widespread.

Confronted by the irksome fact that they possessed no definable outcomes toward which students were being educated, curriculum leaders of the 1970s attempted to establish instructional objectives in line with the management-by-objective model from industry. However, objective-based curricular development met with limited success. Educators found it difficult to articulate classroom goals and lacked the tools required to meaningfully measure student achievement vis-a-vis these goals.

The inability to write instructional objectives is slowly being overcome; university preparation and the persistence of district-level curriculum directors are seeing to that. However, the quality of assessment has been dependent on the evolution of computer-related technology. As recently as the end of the '70s, only a few well-to-do school districts were able to use regional timesharing or local midsize processors to begin to make inroads into the problem of assessment through districtwide, criterion-referenced testing. It is only now, with the co-emergence of outcome-based education and affordable technology, that we are on the verge of realizing the potential of comprehensive student assessment against local instructional goals.

Our society is habituated to expect accurate, meaningful and instantaneous information. We are seldom willing to hold on for videotapes of events on the other side of the globe; hardly willing to accept weather forecasts, however accurate, fewer than five days in advance; and scarcely willing to wait until the end of a semester for a measurement of our child's performance. So the concept of outcome-based education—the assessment of educational success based upon performance rather than inputs—flows logically from our expectations. But it also has another source: the development of technology.

It may come as a surprise to many educators that vendors of textbooks, supplies, furniture and test materials have been spending the 1980s working in concert with developers of technology. These partners are now ready to make the 1990s the decade of instructional management (or instructional support) systems. Although we lacked the technological foresight to anticipate instructional management (IM), we educators have unknowingly been aspiring toward it since our initial development of instructional objectives. However, it is only just now that a remarkable convergence of technology and educational needs is turning instructional management from idea into practice.

THE APPROACH

In the past, the perception of a school's quality has been based upon its floor space, pupil/teacher ratios, percentage of teachers with master's degrees, and number of vol-

Source: From Mark Whitman and Phil Lambert, "Integrated Instructional Management Systems and Outcome-Based Education," *T.H.E. Journal*, Volume 17, September 1989, pp. 53–60. Reprinted with permission from the publisher.

umes in the library. Today, the trend is to evaluate quality based upon a school's graduation percentage, and its students' reading scores, verbal abilities and computation skills. Our assessment criteria are rapidly shifting from inputs to outputs.

However, without the emergence of a conceptual framework such as instructional management, we would remain critically handicapped by our inability to measure and act on these outputs.

At first glance, the concept of instructional management may seem little more than a reworking of traditional criterion-referenced evaluation. But while IM is definitely a delivery system for criterion-referenced evaluation, it is far from traditional. It combines a clearly defined curriculum made up of uniquely assessable instructional objectives with computer processing to provide the outputs required for the implementation of true outcome-based education.

After four years of development we have produced for the Tippecanoe School Corp. a working IM model directly transferable to school districts of any size. Using IBM System/36 technology and two J&K software products (the CIMS comprehensive information management system, and the ISS instructional support system), we have constructed a cluster of databases capable of delivering the information required for true outcome-based assessment.

Those databases include:

1. All student demographic and traditional classroom performance data, maintained through CIMS.
2. All K–12 core curricula (language arts, mathematics, science and social studies) delineated into uniquely assessable instructional objectives and maintained through ISS.
3. All Indiana state instructional proficiencies, maintained through ISS.
4. All student standardized testing information, stored on the system via a tape dump from the vendor.

With this information, and using the IBM Query and Displaywrite utility software, we have been able to develop the outputs described below.

CURRICULUM DEVELOPMENT

Curriculum guides have traditionally been static documents developed to define what is being taught as well as provide staff members assistance in developing specific course content. However, most curriculum guides have been so poorly developed that they have little or no application to day-to-day classroom activities. More likely than not, they are left to languish in a dark corner of a bottom drawer. Further, the curriculum-revision process has been very labor-intensive; as a result, curriculum revision has historically been a periodic, infrequent process that normally accompanies textbook adoption.

We can now produce a curriculum composed of discrete objectives, each unique, and place those objectives into a relational database. This transforms the curriculum guide into a dynamic document germane to the classroom and capable of being continually revised and updated. For example, curriculum guides need no longer be in a single format to be shared by all. Tippecanoe schools currently have one curriculum guide for the school board and administration with local objectives referenced to state proficiencies and a second curriculum guide for teachers, sequenced by grade level and unit. A fourth-grade teacher may prefer to see the scope and sequence of the elementary mathematics curriculum or may prefer to have the entire fourth-grade curriculum in all subject areas. Either request can be met on demand.

In addition, concept-scope and sequence charts can be produced from the same database. Given the request for a particular concept, such as fractions, maps or capitalization, a departmental chairperson can acquire an entire K–12 scope and sequence listing of the objectives related to a single concept. A one-page identification is also available for each instructional objective. This gives the primary curriculum area, its referenced state proficiency, associated keywords, prerequisite objectives and the instructional units in which it is taught.

The dynamism of the process comes through the fact that revision is now ongoing. A departmental chairperson can hold a curriculum meeting and the department can modify or rearrange objectives at will. With only a few keystrokes, the revised version of a guide can be produced in minutes.

CURRICULUM ASSESSMENT

Traditionally, curriculum assessment and revision has been driven by intuition and textbook publishers. The result: dramatic swings and reversals from one year to the next. Educators have rightly been accused of embracing first one hot topic, then another, as trends have appeared and disappeared. However, the capabilities of instructional management provide an opportunity for local curriculum developers to achieve a measure of freedom to design a curriculum conforming to local needs rather than external forces.

By linking the objectives in the local curriculum database with those in a standardized testing database, the results of standardized tests can be transferred to local objectives. This provides a path for using test results to evaluate districtwide performance versus local objectives. In addition, teachers can now grade electronically and link grade-entries to specific curriculum objectives to obtain a classroom-level assessment of student performance versus local objectives.

Such information should greatly expand the knowledge source from which local curriculum decisions flow. This should be a big step toward freeing local curriculum development from the dictates of textbook publishers. Further, such assessment information is almost certain to elevate the professional level of local decisions and should provide helpful insights for the sequencing of local instructional outcomes.

The same vehicles described above can also be used in a number of ways to support the individual assessment of students. Some ways are mentioned below:

1. Instructional management provides a means to articulate classroom performance well beyond the traditional letter grade. Through IM, performance in terms of specific skills can be conveyed to students, parents and professional staff.
2. Instructional management enables a sophistication previously attainable only through the most laborious and time-consuming of efforts. Individual student performance and development can now be easily tracked and maintained by comparing historical databases.
3. Student groupings can easily be generated, given the proper set of local parameters. Be they both gifted and talented; at-risk, Chapter I, summer-school remediation candidates; overachievers or underachievers—any groupings of students can be quickly and clearly identified.

These areas—curriculum development, curriculum assessment and student assessment—are just three of the more obvious results of IM. However, as it becomes more widespread, its utility is almost limitless. We are not advocating IM as an educational elixir of life; it is a professional tool rather than an end in itself. However, its power warrants close and serious attention by educators. The philosophical and economic commitments associated with instructional management represent one giant step for any school district but only one small step in a direction that will carry instructional decision-making into the 21st century.

67

California's Smart Classroom

Charles H. Slaughter

Nearly a generation ago, futurists were saying that high-tech education would teach students more, and faster, than traditional methods ever had. Convinced that technology will deliver that promise, the administrators and educators of Hueneme School District in Port Hueneme, Calif., have installed a junior high school science room whose delivery of computer-assisted instruction (CAI) is electronically sophisticated to such a degree that it is called a "smart classroom."

An outspoken critic of educational spending, California Assemblyman Tom McClintock, agrees with their decision. He gives the smart classroom a rave review: "Haven't seen anything like it, except at Cal Tech." He points out that California already spends more than $100,000 per 30-student classroom, and he thinks people should get more for their money. McClintock is a conservative Republican who listens to those who complain about graduates passing school tests without learning to think and reason. He likes the smart classroom focus on higher-order thinking skills. What he saw in Port Hueneme seems to be an example of what he wants.

The Hueneme smart classroom focuses on the basic teaching act: student-teacher interaction. Simply stated, its implementers feel the smart classroom demonstrates that the intelligent use of technology significantly improves both the quality and quantity of student-teacher interaction. For them, improved quality means interaction involving higher-order thinking skills and, most often, interaction that motivates learners.

Irving E. Sigel, a senior research scientist for Educational Testing Services, says his research clearly demonstrates that when teachers engage children in thought-provoking dialogues, rather than merely present them with facts, they stimulate student thinking and enhance learning. The smart classroom is a medium for just such an approach.

THE SMART PROCESS

Chris LaRose, now an assistant principal in the district, was the teacher who developed and executed the initial project. She describes the smart-classroom process this way: "The first day, all 196 students are pre-tested. That pretty much tells the teachers where in the learning process to start each of them. One large presentation to the whole roomful of students is made once every two weeks. The unit is introduced and students are told what will be covered and what is expected of them. The rest of the teachers' in-class time is spent with individuals and small groups, sometimes just asking questions and at other times tutoring, much of which entails problem-solving discussions.

"The basic science curriculum is installed on the classroom's main computer. That software teaches basic objectives and covers the seventh-grade content prescribed by the California Science Framework. The content and reading levels range from Grade 4 to Grade 12. The computer-assisted instruction given in the smart classroom is completely interactive. Each student moves at his or her own pace.

"We back all this up with an assortment of presentations and problem-solving activities: laserdisc interactive programs, an entire encyclopedia on CD-ROM, a robotics system, videotapes and programs we pick up with our satellite dish. Some programs go to the entire class, but most go to individual students or small groups.

"For example, students learn abut forecasting weather. Then they go to a Dog Sled Race program that poses questions like: 'The relative humidity is 80 percent; the temperature is minus 40 degrees. Do you want to go on with your race today, or do you want to hold back because you think it may rain?' They apply what they've learned in a fun way. They spend the next two days applying those concepts. Then they're tested again to see how much of what they have been taught they have really understood.

"Then they go to the next level. This could take them up through the 12th grade, depending on how fast each student can cover the material. They start where they want and go just as far as they can."

When asked about those youngsters that might not be ready for higher-level material, LaRose says: "At every stage the teachers look to see what they need. They might separate those students out to work in groups. They hold small-group discussions with them. They can put them to work at a laserdisc holding the same information and the same objectives presented in a slightly different way.

"The computer-based testing programs we use are excellent," she says. "Teachers find out each student's learning modality. They know which students are visual or auditory learners. Maybe a student is a visual learner but has been on a VCR program that gives many verbal explanations with few graphic demonstrations. The teachers then change the approach. When they see a student with a problem they look at all the information and decide what to do.

"We try to know as much about students as we can," continues LaRose. "We want to recognize, and improve on, their strengths. Still, we must build up their weak areas and do it in a way they can follow to success. For example, a not-so-practical student might be assigned to watch a practically minded stu-

Source: From Charles H. Slaughter, "California's Smart Classroom," *T.H.E. Journal*, Volume 17, August 1989, pp. 59–61. Reprinted with permission from the publisher.

dent build a traffic signal to see how the latter goes about piecing the parts together."

How does the teacher keep track of all these activities and all the information?

"A computer-managed instruction system," LaRose explains, "ties everything together. It is essential to our success. It gives a snapshot of individuals, groups and the whole class as often as the teacher wants it. We have a detailed record of what every student has completed, how it was completed, how well each task was performed and how long it took to complete."

THE AMPLIFIER

She points out that smart-classroom teachers basically do the things good teachers have known about for ages. However, knowing what needs to be done, and doing it, isn't always possible. Smart-classroom teachers can more expeditiously do the job because a complex, interactive, high-technology instructional delivery system amplifies their technique and talent. LaRose was a good teacher before her smart classroom opened, and now she is proof of what a good teacher can accomplish with students through using superior tools. Although she had to spend several months preparing the smart-classroom, she has found that only two weeks of training prepares any competent teacher to work there.

Clearly, smart-classroom teachers have more time available for individualized instruction and counseling than do traditional teachers. Eighty percent more, according to LaRose. Of course, there is a limit to how many students a single teacher can handle and still have time for meaningful dialogues. LaRose points out that, physically, the smart classroom only accommodates 36 students. Some classes fill up all 36 student stations in the classroom.

Visitors from throughout California, across the nation and around the world come to see the smart classroom. Australia, Canada, Japan, Russia and Bulgaria are a few of the countries that have sent specialist observers.

Most visitors fall into one of three groups: educator, electronic specialist or politician. One local administrator comments, "The politicians are obviously anxious to find solutions to education's problems. Right now, technology seems to have their complete attention."

But technology isn't the solution every educator is looking for. When Hueneme opened the smart-classroom doors for visits from surrounding districts, some educators stayed away. A few had their hands full dealing with serious problems they had to solve first. The indifference of others sprang from not having the money to buy the technology. Regrettably, skepticism alone kept some away. Those who came were impressed. The result is that several districts in the area have initiated similar large-scale technology development projects.

California's Gov. Deukmejian specifically mentioned the Hueneme smart-classroom project in his 1988 State of the State address and added $1 million to the California Model Technology Schools Project for the Hueneme School District.

Hueneme District has 7,000 K–8 students in 11 schools. More than half the students come from minority groups, predominantly Hispanic. It is, according to California standards, a low-wealth school system. Yet, even before the smart classroom was installed, the district had invested more than $1 million in high-tech education. Each school has a state-of-the-art CAI/CMI computer lab that helps teachers and students in reading, language arts, writing, typing, math and computer literacy. Thus the way to the smart classroom had already been paved.

Student, parent and teacher enthusiasm for CAI is high. Some parents go so far as to reschedule dental and doctor appointments to ensure their children don't miss time in the lab. Such support is essential to student success. After all, computers, laserdiscs and robot systems are machines that accomplish little or nothing when people don't use them well.

Increases in school CAP scores correlate well with how long the labs have been installed. However, Dr. Don Cody, district testing coordinator, speaks cautiously about district test results. No perfect correlation exists between high-tech installations and test scores. "CAP scores do reflect a pattern of continuous improvement since we began installing computer labs," he says. "The greatest gains, 20 percent over four years, occurred in the elementary school with the longest installation time. That school just happens to have the highest Hispanic enrollment in the district." This observation gives encouragement to the expectations that the administrators and educators of Hueneme district have of the smart classroom.

SUPPORT IS GROWING

The smart classroom includes the products of 19 different companies. Staff members waded through a swamp of source material before selecting software and hardware.

"I don't know how many hours we spent previewing software," Chris LaRose says. "There is a great deal of software out there. Some is very good, some is just junk, and some doesn't meet our needs. One major company had excellent software for the applications but said it would be up to the teacher to cover the basic concepts. They aren't dealing with reality. Teachers, in the past, spent all their time in explaining concepts and making sure students had grasped them, so they had no time left over to get on to higher-level thinking skills."

Smart classrooms are expensive, even with private industry helping pay the initial technology costs of $140,518. Still, Hueneme has already added another one. Its educational technology project is long-range. The plan calls for similar classrooms for Grade 8 reading/language arts/literature, math, social studies and industrial arts. Next, these courses will be extended into Grade 7 and then into the elementary and secondary schools. Hueneme district has a reasonable confidence that it will find the money: some of it in the private sector, some in special grants and some in state lottery funds.

The local teachers' union hasn't taken a formal position regarding the smart classroom. Its president says his closest advisors are divided, some for, some against. The "con" fear is that computer labs will lead to doubled class sizes, with teachers still accountable for teaching all the skills computers can't.

Another prominent The Hueneme union leader, John O'Looney, says Hueneme teachers are proud of the district's courage in taking bold steps in using technology. "Existing labs are well-regarded," he says, " and we hope the smart classroom will be equally successful. The union is for technology, but we expect results that would justify expansion." He says the union wasn't involved in developing the smart classroom and most district teachers would like to know more about it. The union is concerned that people may begin to think that teachers can be replaced by a monitor and a machine.

O'Looney says, "We don't want to see computers take the passion out of teaching. We don't want it [the smart classroom] to turn into another boring language lab. Students will always need good teachers to make the subject come alive."

Dr. Richard Miller, assistant superintendent of educational services, one of the key individuals who pioneered Hueneme's entire technology development efforts, agrees with the point. He believes the intelligent use of technology makes good teachers better, makes them more powerful as teachers and makes teaching itself more rewarding.

PART SEVEN

American Education and the Future

Historically, American education has been oriented to the past and present, transmitting culture and responding to social needs. In recent years, deliberate and concerted efforts have been made to study and relate the past and the present to potential futures. This emerging discipline has been referred to as futuristics, futures research, policies research, and future studies. In general, the discipline deals with forecasting potential futures, and hopefully determining desirable futures. Questions addressed by futurists include: What will the future be like if there is no change in present trends? What can the future be like? What should the future be like? Can a desirable future be created?

The concept of futurism is applicable to the purposes of American education. As was indicated earlier, there are two very important purposes of American education: transmitting culture(s) and responding to the needs of society. Cultures can be identified by their common customs, attitudes, behaviors and beliefs. Within the American culture, there is a maze of diversity associated with the aforementioned cultural elements. It is clear that the United States is a pluralistic nation. It is also clear that the culture of the United States is changing. How should the culture change? What should the future of our culture be like? Can we create a desirable culture for the future? For the last three decades there has been a debate about whether American public schools should transmit a distinct American culture or encourage that cultural pluralism be taught in the public schools. What kind of culture would you desire for your life in the future?

The other purpose of American education is to respond to the needs of society. Education's response to the social needs has been consistently retrospective, as compared to looking toward planning and creating a preferable society, which is futuristic.

The needs of society emanate from trends. Trends may also emerge from the analysis of statistical data, from the observation of events, or from ideas or imagination. Among the current trends are: the increasing instability in families; more children living in poverty; latchkey children; increasing women in the workforce; the establishment of school-based health clinics to deal with sexually related issues in addition to conventional medical services; increasing diversity of the population; and the strong desires of parents to be able to select the public school of their choice. Futurists identify and study trends, interpret the trends and attempt to forecast their future effects on society, and generate alternative courses of action that may achieve the desirable effects of the future. Interventions are designed to bring about change or changes.

Three trends that relate to the future of education are presented in the following articles. In "Old Baggage, New Visions: Shaping Policy for Early Childhood Programs," Anne Mitchell points out that distinctions between the care and the education of young children have plagued the early childhood field for decades. She notes that programs for young children cannot be one or the other; any early childhood program provides both education and care; children cannot be well cared for without learning, and they cannot be educated well without being properly cared for.

Judith Pearson, in "Myths of Choice: The Governor's New Clothes?" analyzes the open-enrollment plan in Minnesota which permits parental choice of school(s) for their children. Minnesota's open-enrollment program was voluntary for school districts during the 1987–88 and 1988–89 school years. The program will not be fully implemented until the 1990–91 school year. Governor Rudy Perpich is a strong advocate of parental choice. After raising relevant questions, Pearson concludes that Minnesota's open-enrollment plan will soon make choice of any kind a *myth* in many Minnesota communities. She also suggests that a hidden agenda underlying open enrollment is the forced consolidation of school districts.

In "The Future and America's Schools: What Do These Trends Mean for Education?" Dennis R. Clodi and John Jacobsen describe and explore the future for education. They discuss the population explosion expected in the 1990s, reflect on the 1950s through the 1980s, anticipate tough times ahead, speculate about future families and the generation gap, and provide the educational implications for critical educational issues.

The use of the concept of futurism is applicable to the purposes of American education: namely, transmitting of culture(s) and responding to the needs of society. The articles by Mitchell and by Clodi and Jacobsen illustrate the use of futuristic planning, and the article by Pearson addresses an emerging trend that is still somewhat controversial.

We believe that these essays dealing with American education in the future will help future teachers better understand the challenges they will face in the classroom.

68

Old Baggage, New Visions

Shaping Policy for Early Childhood Programs

Anne Mitchell

Distinctions between the care and the education of young children have plagued the early childhood field for decades. Intense interest in both have fueled the development of state policy during the 1980s and have increased the likelihood of federal action. In this article I wish to discuss principles to guide the development of policy for early childhood programs and to present a view of the early childhood system that will help move us toward an integrated view of early childhood.

The misperception that early childhood education and child care can be discrete services is fast becoming a thing of the past. Programs for young children cannot be one or the other; any early childhood program provides both education and care. These two functions are inextricably bound together; children cannot be well cared for without learning, and they cannot be educated well without being properly cared for.

Probably the most prevalent form of early childhood education experienced by children today is called child care. Parents judge programs for their young children in terms of both their present and their future value—how much their children enjoy the program right now and whether it will help them get off to a good start in their school careers. Parents don't generally separate their demands for care and education. They want both in the same program, in a convenient location, and at a price they can afford. As parents well know and policy makers are beginning to understand, the old distinctions between child care and early education have become so blurred as to be meaningless.

THE LAST DECADE

Ten years ago, the care and education of young children was not the major political issue it is today. Throughout the 1970s repeated attempts to pass federal child-care legislation failed. The care of children was regarded as a service distinctly different from their early childhood education.

Child care, publicly funded through social service agencies, was viewed either as a protective service for children at risk of abuse and neglect or as an employment support service for very poor families. Other families in need of child care to allow parents to work or to pursue their education were to purchase that care privately. The commitment of pubic funds for early education was focused primarily on Head Start programs. In the general population, early education was viewed as the private decision of parents who could afford to send their children to nursery school or preschool.

With the exceptions of some large urban school districts, Title I (later Chapter 1) funds were not often spent on prekindergarten children. The preschool provisions of the Education for the Handicapped Act (earlier through P.L. 94-142 and more recently through P.L. 99-457) were in the early stages of planning and implementation. By 1979 only seven states had appropriated funds for prekindergarten programs in their public schools, and only four states contributed state funds to Head Start programs.

Over the last decade, federal support for early childhood programs has declined in real dollars. Direct federal funding for child care has been reduced and consolidated into the Social Services Block Grant. With the exception of Head Start, which has continued to be funded with modest annual increases, the only federal expenditures for early childhood services that have increased since 1980 are provisions of the tax code that most benefit middle-class families—the Dependent Care Tax Credit and employer-sponsored Dependent Care Assistance plans. The tax credit expenditure, which amounted to about $1 billion in 1980, is now estimated to be more than $4 billion annually.

While the federal government has generally reduced its support for young children living in poor families, the states have become the initiators and funders of programs for young children—especially children who are at risk. Some states have begun to improve their child-care infrastructure by developing and funding resource and referral services and by increasing appropriations for the development of new child-care services. In the wake of serious federal cuts in the early 1980s, a few states increased their overall funding for child care to more than compensate for the loss of federal funds; others were able only to replace the lost federal dollars with state funds, and some managed to make up only partially the loss of federal funds. In the latter half of the decade, states have begun to make greater commitments to child care. For example, Gov. Madeleine Kunin notes that Vermont "has made an unprecedented commitment to affordable child care. . . . Between fiscal

Source: From Anne Mitchell, "Old Baggage, New Visions: Shaping Policy for Early Childhood Programs," *Phi Delta Kappa*, May 1989, pp. 665–672. Reprinted with permission from the publisher and from Anne Mitchell.

[years] 1985 and 1990, Vermont's financial support for subsidized child care will have nearly tripled. At the same time, the state's share of the expense will have risen from 40% to 60%—while the federal government has largely walked away from this challenge."[1]

Along with state efforts to fund child care, the number of states that fund prekindergarten programs has increased dramatically—nearly quadrupling in the past decade. By 1989, 31 states had appropriated funds for state-initiated prekindergarten programs and/or direct contributions to Head Start programs. Table 1 lists the states with prekindergarten programs and those that contribute to Head Start as of mid-1989.

These programs are mainly part-day programs for at-risk 4-year-olds that operate through the school year. They are nearly always administered by state departments of education and provided by public school districts. However, about half of the states permit other community agencies to operate these programs. This is a more common practice in the newer state programs (e.g., New Jersey's two newest programs, both of Florida's programs, and those in Vermont, Massachusetts, and Washington). Together, the state-funded prekindergarten programs and the state contributions to Head Start in these 31 states amount to state investments in young children of more than $300 million annually. Although on a decidedly more modest scale of spending than the federal government, in the 1980s the states have been leading the way in early childhood policy development and new investments in early childhood programs.

Federal legislative interest in early childhood programs has been rekindled in the last year. Numerous early-education/child-care bills—including the Act for Better Child Care, Smart Start, Child Care Choices, and various tax credit proposals—were introduced but not passed. However, two bills that include provisions dealing with early care and education did pass: the Elementary and Secondary School Improvement Amendments of 1988 (reauthorization of Chapter 1) and the Family Support Act of 1988 (so-called welfare reform).

The first created Even Start, a $50 million joint parent-child education program aimed at improving adult literacy and offering early childhood education to children between the ages of 1 and 7, and officially extended the Chapter 1 migrant education program to include 3- and 4-year-olds. The second changed the rules for receipt of Aid to Families with Dependent Children (AFDC) to require parents of children older than 3 to work or to attend job-training programs. It also created an uncapped fund to pay for child care required by AFDC recipients. Federal interest in and support for Head Start remains strong, and the program (currently funded at $1.2 billion annually) is slated to receive a 20% increase in the Bush Administration's proposed budget.

TABLE 1.
State-Funded Prekindergarten Programs and Contributions to Head Start Through Early 1989

States	*Prekindergarten Programs*	*Contributions to Head Start*
Alaska	X	X
California	X	
Colorado	X	
Connecticut		X
Delaware	X	
District of Columbia	X	
Florida	XX*	
Hawaii		X
Illinois	X	X
Iowa	X	
Kentucky	XX	
Louisiana	X	
Maine	XX	X
Maryland	X	
Massachusetts	X	X
Michigan	XX	
Minnesota		X
New Hampshire		X
New Jersey	XXX	
New York	X	
Ohio	X	X
Oklahoma	X	
Oregon	X	
Pennsylvania	X	
Rhode Island	X	X
South Carolina	X	
Texas	X	
Vermont	X	
Washington	X	X
West Virginia	X	
Wisconsin	X	

*States with two or three prekindergarten programs have the appropriate number of X's.

In the 1980s, children under age 5 have clearly made it into the national spotlight. The National Governors' Association Task Force on Children believes that current investment in the health and education of children is linked to the nation's future international competitiveness and calls for a comprehensive approach to child development, beginning with prenatal care and followed by preschool education coordinated with affordable child care.[2] Many governors have put programs serving the needs of children high on the agenda in their state-of-the-state messages—from the Children's Agenda in Oregon to the Decade of the Child in New York. The National Conference of State Legislatures reports that legislators on human services committees rank child care and early childhood education as top issues for the coming year.[3] The major child-care bills that emerged from the last session of Congress have been reintroduced, joined by the Child Development and Education Act sponsored by Rep. Augustus Hawkins (D-Calif.).

The current high level of interest in early childhood programs stems from at least five different sources: 1) the increased demand for child care from the growing numbers of working mothers in all income groups; 2) concern about present and future productivity, international competitiveness, and the changing nature of the work force, which will include more women and be characterized by greater ethnic and racial diversity, as the minority becomes majority; 3) the centrality of child care to efforts to move mothers off AFDC support and into the labor force; 4) a desire to provide a better start for poor children in school and in life; and 5) an accumulating body of evidence that high-quality early childhood programs have long-term positive effects for disadvantaged children and high cost/benefit ratios (on the order of 5 to 1). These varied motivations for interest in programs for young children are strong and intertwined with one another. Alone and in combination, they have already resulted in new policies and programs and will lead to still more.

But where is the system within which to implement these policies? Where can these programs be institutionalized? Unlike other current educational concerns—such as improving math literacy or increasing high school graduation rates, for both of which the clear focal point of public concern and policy action is the public school system—there is no readily apparent early childhood system in which to implement and institutionalize new policies and practices. However, there is a system of sorts, although it is not an intentionally planned one.

THE EARLY CHILDHOOD ECOSYSTEM

Programmatic responses to various interests—child care for all families (or just for welfare recipients), education for poor children, the future of the work force—now emerge from the efforts of many individual early childhood organizations, acting under various auspices (public, private, for-profit, nonprofit, secular, and religious) and funded from public sources at all levels of government and from private sources (mainly parents). In the U.S. today, there are nearly 350,000 early childhood organizations, including the estimated 197,000 private homes offering day-care services.[4]

Examined from an ecological perspective, the current array of providers of early childhood services forms an ecosystem of sorts, sometimes called the early childhood community. The term *ecosystem* implies that the many subsystems of the community are interdependent. If one part changes itself (or is changed by outside forces), the other parts of the ecosystem necessarily change in response.

The early childhood ecosystem has evolved over time and consists of all child-care and early-education services, whether public or private, religious or secular, half-day or full-day; whether called play school, nursery school, or prekindergarten; whether housed in a public school, in a storefront, or in a private home. What the program is called and where it is housed are not indications of its quality. Rather, name and location merely indicate the present purpose or intent of a program (i.e., "nursery school" generally implies part-day, while "day-care center" usually means longer hours) or give clues about its historical origins (e.g., "day nursery" implies origins in the day nursery movement of the early part of the century, while Head Start obviously indicates a more recent program, probably dating from the mid-1960s). Regardless of nomenclature, all these programs serve young children, they are more alike than different, and each has the potential to offer good early childhood services.

However, the components of the existing early childhood system—the child-care centers, the private day-care homes, the nursery schools, and other formal and informal services—are simply too few and too poorly supported to educate and care for all young children. The supply of services must be expanded throughout the ecosystem. Some national education groups, notably the Council of Chief State School Officers and the National Association of State Boards of Education (NASBE), have recognized the need for equity among the many parts of the early childhood system. The report of the NASBE Task Force on Early Childhood Education notes:

> We have a diverse, underfunded, and uncoordinated system for delivering programs to young children. Public education leaders can be a powerful and constructive force for strengthening this system. If they act in partnership with other early childhood programs, our chances for increasing and maximizing resources and quality in *all* settings that serve young children will be greatly improved.[5] (Emphasis added)

Public schools have been a part of the early childhood system for years—albeit a small part. Within the last five years, however, their role as providers or programs for prekindergartners has grown and will probably continue to expand. A useful way to look at the situation is this: the early childhood system is not moving into the public schools; rather, the public school system is a part of the early childhood ecosystem whose role is expanding.

Public schools will continue to provide services to young children through the current federal categorical programs, such as special education and Chapter 1 with its new Even Start program. Public schools will continue to offer child-care services funded through state-subsidized child-care programs, as some now do in many states. Public schools will continue to provide a portion of Head Start programs; currently, about one-fifth of all Head Start programs are operated by the public schools. An increasing number of public schools, mainly in large urban school districts, now offer child-care services to students who are parents, and the number will probably increase as a result of provisions of the Family Support Act of 1988 that deal with education for young parents. This population—student/parents and their very young children—can be logically and easily served by the public schools. In fact, the majority of existing programs for these young parents are housed in public schools.[6]

The current array of state-funded prekindergarten programs will continue to expand slowly, as annual appropriations increase and as a few more states create new programs. Some states will expand their programs more rapidly than others, as a few did last year. For example, Florida's program, originally funded at $700,000 in fiscal year 1987, is funded at $22.9 million for fiscal year 1989; Michigan moved from $2.3 million in fiscal year 1987 to $15 million in fiscal year 1988; and Illinois doubled its prekindergarten appropriation from fiscal year 1988 to fiscal year 1989.[7] It seems likely that most prekindergarten programs will continue to focus mainly on poor or at-risk children. Most will be operated by public schools. However, 13 states currently permit agencies other than public schools to operate state-funded prekindergarten programs, and there is a clear trend toward broader definitions of eligible providers.

There will probably be a modest shift away from part-day and toward full-day programs, as the need for longer hours (to meet child-care demands) is recognized. Programs in only five states (Massachusetts, Vermont, Illinois, both of Florida's programs, and New Jersey's two newer ones) now clearly permit the funding of prekindergarten programs that last for the full working day. Some states will emphasize longer hours to cover the full working day in the expansion of their prekindergarten programs, as Gov. Mario Cuomo of New York has recently proposed.

State policy makers are just beginning to perceive child-care programs as educational opportunities for young children and to recognize the child-care function that so-called educational programs fulfill. Based in part on this new awareness, some states will move toward coordinated approaches that unify early education and child care, such as the Child Development Coordinating Council established in Iowa for fiscal year 1989, the Office of Early Childhood Services being discussed among legislators in New York, and Virginia's Council on Child Day Care and Early Childhood Programs, described as "a major new approach linking together the child-care needs of the labor force and the developmental needs of children at risk."[8]

GUIDING PRINCIPLES

The essential question facing policy makers is, How can we improve the quality of and increase access to early childhood programs for all children—but especially those who are disadvantaged? Any answers we come up with must take account of the needs of children and their families and at the same time understand the early childhood system and recognize its ecological nature.

Children: quality, continuity, and comprehensiveness. From the child's perspective the elements necessary to create good policy are the overall quality of the program and the continuity and comprehensiveness of the services. Quality in an early childhood program consists of five essential elements:

- small group size—for 4-year-olds, for example, between 15 and 20 children;
- favorable staff-child ratios—for 4-year-olds, at least one adult for every eight to 10 children;
- well-trained staff—a thorough understanding of theories of child development and of principles of early childhood education, coupled with direct experience working with young children;
- curriculum—a clearly communicated philosophy of education that is based on theories of child development and that is supported by training and good supervision; and
- strong parent participation—frequent communication between parents and teachers, a variety of ways for parents to participate directly in the education of their children, direct parental influence on the governance of the program, and attention to the needs of parents.

Beyond the obvious fiscal resources necessary to implement a good early childhood program, vision and commitment on the part of its leader are required. The quality of leadership—whether from the director of a single center, the principal of an early childhood school, or the coordinator of a school district's early childhood programs—is directly related to the overall quality of the program for young participants.

Continuity and comprehensiveness are also essential aspects of high-quality programs for young children. Continuity has two dimensions: 1) the number and ease of transitions made by children in a given day and during a given year and 2) the compatibility of philosophies and curricula among the different programs that a child takes part in over time. If a child is in a stable group of children, with the same staff members for most of the day in the same location, and with a stable teaching staff throughout the program year, that program has a high degree of continuity. If a child experiences changes from year to year that are smooth and understandable, continuity is also high. However, if changes are abrupt and disturbing during a day, over the course of a year, or between successive years, continuity is low.

A comprehensive early childhood program is one that provides other necessary services in addition to those that are strictly intellectual or academic. At a minimum, such comprehensive services include:

- health services, such as screening for developmental delays and physical examinations (or other direct health services) provided by a doctor, nurse, or dentist;
- social services, usually provided by a social worker, such as referral to community or governmental agencies that can provide needed assistance; and
- nutrition services, which means the provision of meals and snacks during the program's hours that satisfy the major portion of children's daily nutritional requirements.

Finally, transportation can be a critical support service. A child who can't get to any program at all won't derive any benefit even from a good program with comprehensive services.

Parents: quality, participation, affordability, and accessibility. Because parents want the best for their children, good policy from the perspective of parents rests on the overall quality of the program for children. Parents want programs that are good for their children and that respond to their own needs—the need to work or to continue their own education, the need to be good parents, and the need to be involved in their child's education. For most parents, these needs and desires translate into demand for programs that cover enough hours each day, that provide year-round services, and that give parents opportunities to be involved while balancing work and family responsibilities.

Parents also want choices. Not all families need or want the same services for themselves and their children. Parents deserve choices that reflect the cultural diversity of our nation, the full spectrum of family values regarding child rearing, and the differing needs of individual families. In addition, parents want affordable, conveniently located programs that are easy to find, easy to choose, and easy to use. Many parents prefer having all their children in the same location.

For the parents' perspective, early childhood policy is about ways and means: ways to identify good programs, ways to locate the ones that reflect their family values and needs, and ways to choose the best ones for their children—and the means to pay for the good programs of their choice.

Early childhood ecosystem: quality and unity. From the perspective of the early childhood system, public policy must be guided by principles of quality and unity. Delivering good programs to children is the objective. Many members of the early childhood system have demonstrated their ability to provide high-quality early childhood services; others have clear potential to do so, with some help.

There is growing concern about the quality of all programs for young children—both in public schools and in other settings—and a number of questions are being asked frequently. Is the program appropriate to the developmental stages of the children in it? Are staff members well-trained? Are there enough of them? Do they remain on staff long enough to produce a stable program for children? A number of questions about the content of early childhood programs have also been raised, specifically with regard to programs in the public schools. Should the curriculum be academic or cognitive or developmental? Should it be some combination of these? Should it focus on school readiness or on child development?

No single kind of early childhood program has a monopoly on quality. Community-based, nonprofit programs are not inherently better than community-based, for-profit programs. Nor are programs operated by the public schools necessarily better or worse than those operated by other agencies. There is much more variation in quality from state to state or from one version of a program to another than among different programs.

The problem of quality is a systemwide issue. Legislative solutions must recognize this fact and deal with improving the quality of early childhood programs throughout the system. It may be necessary to target a larger-than-proportional share of resources to some individual programs in order to produce reasonably good programs throughout the system. The goal is to insure uniformly high quality for every child—no matter where or by whom or with which funds an early childhood program is provided.

The early childhood system is an ecosystem. Changes in one part of it affect the other parts—particularly on the community level. For example, when a public school district rapidly expands a program for 4-year-olds, qualified teachers are drawn out of other kinds of early childhood programs because the salaries in the public schools are higher. This only exacerbates any existing staffing shortages in the community. For the system to remain in balance, new policies must take into account the entire system and must be implemented slowly and carefully. Broadly conceived coordinating mechanisms that simultaneously operate on and connect with federal, state and local levels of government must combine with maximum local flexibility in planning and implementing early childhood programs. In short, an optimal early childhood policy would respond in the best interests of the child, of the family, and of the ecosystem.

FEDERAL BILLS

American families and the entire early childhood ecosystem, of which the public schools are clearly a part, will be affected by the passage of any federal early childhood legislation. The major bills that have been introduced in the 101st Congress—Smart Start (S. 123/H.R. 1234), the Act for Better Child Care (S.5/H.R. 30, also known as ABC), and the Child Development and Education Act (H.R. 3, popularly known as the Hawkins bill)—represent different approaches to providing direct federal assistance for early care and education.

The various bills proposing tax credits, although presented as child-care bills, are not. As Norton Grubb said in recent testimony before the House, "We can all applaud President Bush's [tax credit] proposal as an income-support program, but we should not pretend that it is a child-care program or that it will address the varied strands of interest that have brought child care to public attention."[9]

President Bush's proposal offers a tax credit of up to $1,000 for a low-income family with preschool children, whether the family uses child care or not. Families could use either this new credit or the existing tax credit for dependent care, but not both. Under the President's proposal, both tax credits would be made refundable. However, the amount available to a family through either of these tax credits is insufficient to purchase child care, which typically costs about $4,000 per year.

Furthermore, the total amount of federal assistance would be far from adequate. For fiscal year 1990, the total cost of the President's proposed tax credit would be about $200 million. By contrast, the direct-assistance bills propose funding levels for fiscal year 1990 that range from $500 million (Smart Start) to $2.5 billion (both ABC and the Hawkins bill).

Each of the three direct-assistance bills focuses funding on low-income children and requires states to match federal funds. Each includes modest provisions for staff training, requires parent involvement, and mandates the use of a sliding fee scale to determine a parent's proportion of payment for services. These bills differ in the ages of the children served, in the types of service providers that would be eligible, in regulatory standards, in the federal agency that would administer the program, and in whether direct payments to parents are permitted.

Smart Start. This bill proposes $500 million in its first year (increasing to $1 billion by the third year) to fund full-working-day, year-round, child development programs primarily for 4-year-olds, provided by public or nonsectarian nonprofit agencies. Requirements for appropriate training, curriculum, child/adult ratios, and group size are included. Programs receiving funds under this legislation would have to meet applicable state and local child-care standards. Coordination and planning at the local level would also be required. The Department of Education (ED) would administer the program, and policy and regulatory decisions would be made jointly with the Department of Health and Human Services (HHS).

ABC. The Act for Better Child Care proposes spending $2.5 billion to expand the supply and improve the quality of child care for children from infancy through early adolescence. Funds would be provided both to parents and to programs. Any licensed or regulated provider would be eligible to participate, including day-care homes, public schools, and for-profit organizations.

The bill would set aside a portion of the funds for expanding Head Start and for expanding part-day public school programs to cover the full working day. It would also provide funds for staff training, for improving staff salaries, for developing child-care resources and referral programs, for recruiting new child-care providers, and for offering grants and loans to upgrade facilities. Minimum national standards of quality would be established by a national advisory committee, and states would have four years to meet the standards. HHS would be the federal administering agency.

Hawkins bill. The Child Development and Education Act has three titles and is really three bills. It proposes to divide $2.5 billion evenly among its three titles. Title I amends the Head Start Act to allow Head Start programs to expand to full-working-day, year-round services and to establish a sliding scale of fees for parents whose incomes place them above the poverty line but who still cannot afford good child care without some assistance. Head Start standards would apply.

Title II amends the Elementary and Secondary Education Act to permit public schools to provide part-day, child development programs to 4-year-olds and to offer before- and after-school programs for these children and for children in kindergarten and in the early elementary grades. Fees would be charged on a sliding scale based on parental income. State and local standards would apply.

Title III is limited to children under age 3. It includes all the provisions of the Act for Better Child Care, with the addition of provisions to encourage employer-assisted child care and the elimination of vouchers. Title I and Title III would be administered by HHS; Title II would be administered by ED.

PRINCIPLES EMBODIED IN FEDERAL BILLS

In part because these bills represent quite different approaches, many national organizations concerned with public policy for children and families (e.g., the National Council for Jewish Women, the National Association for the Education of Young Children, and the Child Welfare League of America) have not endorsed any one of these bills. Instead, they have endorsed principles to guide policy development and the evaluation of proposed legislation. The principles discussed above—quality and continuity for children, sensible and affordable choices for parents, and equitable use of resources within the early childhood ecosystem—are reflected to some degree in each of these three bills.

Basic quality for children—group size, child/adult ratios, staff training, and parent involvement—and the provision of comprehensive services are addressed in Smart Start, in ABC and in Titles I and III of the Hawkins bill. The provisions of Title II are insufficient on this score, because they depend on state regulations that normally exempt programs operated by public schools and because comprehensive services are to be provided "if practicable."[10]

In terms of continuity, Smart Start appears to promote daily continuity for 4-year-olds, as ABC does for all children served. As it stands, the Hawkins bill would create some serious problems of continuity for children and families. The bill proposes programs for 4-year-olds operated by a limited group of providers, child-care programs for school-age youngsters provided only in public schools, no programs for 3-year-olds, and programs for infants and toddlers operated by a wide range of providers. It would be possible for a child to attend one program until age 2, attend no program at age 3, attend a different program at age 4, and attend still another program at age 5. All these programs could be in different parts of the system, and there would be little hope of curricular continuity. In addition, splitting programs in this way would mean that families couldn't use a single program for all their children. Parents could have children in as many as three different locations, which would be a logistical nightmare.

Programs for children have to meet the needs of parents in terms of available hours, affordability, and access. These federal bills reflect the need for full-working-day, year-round programs, and all three bills propose relatively large amounts of new federal funds to help parents pay for early childhood services. Greater access to services and the opportunity for parental choice are supported through funding resource programs and referral programs to help parents locate and assess services (ABC and Title III of the Hawkins bill) and through maximum use of the existing system (ABC, Title III of the Hawkins bill, and Smart Start). Parental choice and breadth of access under the Hawkins bill would be somewhat limited by the lack of vouchers.

New policy, programs, and funding streams (whether state or federal) have the power to carefully weave the parts of the early childhood system into a stronger network of support for children and families—or to further fragment and divide that system. Recognizing distinct parts of the early childhood system—as ABC and the Hawkins bill do—is an important step. However, the Hawkins bill overlooks some essential parts of the system (e.g., nonpublic programs serving children older than 2 and family day-care providers). Moreover, the Hawkins bill has the potential of being divisive: setting up separate funding streams to serve children of different ages and using different criteria of program quality in different settings could further fragment the early childhood system. Many current resources are ignored, and the opportunity for systemwide improvements is lost. Existing organizations that serve 3- and 4-year-olds but are not part of a public school or operating a Head Start program are not eligible for any funds. Such programs make up a very large part of the early childhood system.

ABC recognizes all the various parts of the early childhood system as service providers eligible for funding. Furthermore, some provisions of ABC begin to deal with the needs of the system's infrastructure: for staff training, for expanding the supply of care by developing new resources, and for basic national standards to promote equity and insure uniform quality.

It is important to keep in mind that none of these bills signals a sea change for the early childhood system. Policy is incremental, and changes in policy tend to be more like the slow, continuous action of drops of water than like the drastic effects of a tidal wave. It is seductive, but unproductive, to contemplate washing the slate clean and building an early childhood system from scratch. All changes in social policy are built upon the existing foundation of programs, services, policies, and practices. In the case of early childhood policy, the foundation and current structure are in need of repair and modification—not demolition—before a stable addition can be constructed.

None of these bills offers the "right answers"—yet. Together they contain many of the building blocks necessary to construct a stable early childhood system. As Hawkins aptly put it in his recent memo to colleagues asking for co-sponsors for H.R. 3:

> I plan to utilize H.R. 3 as the legislative vehicle for child care legislation. I remain committed to developing a revised version of H.R. 3, based on a broad consensus of support, for markup by the Committee [on Education and Labor]. It is my intention that the best features of various child care proposals be incorporated in the final legislation. My aim is to craft legislation which would achieve broad bipartisan support. I am confident that a comprehensive child care program can be enacted into law by this Congress.[11]

Ideally, federal early childhood legislation should regard the entire early childhood ecosystem as the appropriate focus for expanding and improving programs, and it should allocate sufficient funds to help families pay for the programs they choose for their children. Such federal legislation should: promote parental choice and support parental desire for high-quality programs, recognize strengths and correct weaknesses in the system, define and require a uniform level of quality, promote continuity, complement existing funds and programs by drawing them thoughtfully together, and encourage planning and coordination at the federal, state, and local levels. Categorical programs and funding streams do not exist in isolation, even though they may have been created in that way.

The ideal federal bill would take the family's perspective. Parents want affordable programs that are compatible with their values and that combine care and education in one convenient location. All families deserve choices among sound alternatives—and enough money to exercise their right to choose what's best for their children.

There is a clear need for federal action, as this nation begins to shape an agenda for early childhood programs. Federal leadership can provide a model for integrating the care and education of young children that states can emulate as they continue to develop their own early childhood policies. Policy makers at all levels will need to craft solutions that take account of the perspectives of the child, of the family, and of the early childhood ecosystem. Community institutions of all sorts will have to shoulder their share of the responsibility for making high-quality early childhood programs widely available and readily accessible. And public schools must be partners in that effort.

1. Testimony of Gov. Madeleine M. Kunin before the U.S. Senate Committee on Labor and Human Resources, Subcommittee on Children, Family, Drugs, and Alcoholism, 24 January 1989, p. 3.
2. *America in Transition: Report of the Task Force on Children* (Washington, D.C.: National Governors' Association, 1989).
3. *State Issues 1989: A Survey of Priority Issues for State Legislatures* (Denver: National Conference of State Legislatures, 1989).
4. Mike Wilson, *A Strategic Overview of the Early Childhood Market* (Los Angeles: Mike Wilson List Counsel, 1989).
5. *Right from the Start* (Alexandria, Va.: National Association of State Boards of Education, 1988), pp. 5–6.
6. Fern Marx, Susan Bailey, and Judith Francis, "Child Care for the Children of Adolescent Parents: Findings from a National Survey and Case Studies," Working Paper No. 184, Wellesley College Center for Research on Women, Wellesley, Mass., 1988.
7. Fern Marx and Michelle Seligson, *The Public School Early Childhood Study: The State Survey* (New York: Bank Street College of Education, 1988).
8. Eva S. Teig, quoted in Mary Jordan, "Child Care Agency Nears Virginia Passage," *Washington Post*, 4 February 1989, p. B-1.
9. Testimony of W. Norton Grubb before the U.S. House of Representatives, Committee on Education and Labor, 9 February 1989.
10. Augustus F. Hawkins, "Child Development and Education Act of 1989 (H.R. 5)," U.S. House of Representatives, Committee on Education and Labor, p. 14.
11. Augustus F. Hawkins, "Invitation to Cosponsor H.R. 3," U.S. House of Representatives, Committee on Education and Labor, 21 February 1989.

69

Myths of Choice

The Governor's New Clothes?

Judith Pearson

President Bush has endorsed choice in public education. Minnesota's Gov. Rudy Perpich, chairman of the Education Commission of the States, is traveling the country praising and promoting Minnesota's statewide experiment in open enrollment. The bandwagon for choice is picking up speed, and few voices are heard in opposition. Why would anyone question such all-American concepts as "freedom of choice" and "competition for excellence"?

It is interesting to note that the major proponents of open enrollment in public education are either politicians or advocates from the private sector. In an era in education in which reform is the watchword and high-quality education is more expensive than ever, the hidden agenda of these advocates of choice is obvious: this new, exciting, almost "patriotic" reform requires no increase in taxes! But isn't this too good to be true?

Minnesota is clearly leading the way in this new aspect of school reform. Yet one wonders how Gov. Perpich can justify his nationwide, unqualified advocacy of open enrollment when the Minnesota program will not be fully implemented until the 1990–91 school year. Participation in Minnesota's open-enrollment program was voluntary for school districts during the 1987–88 and 1988–89 school years. Participation will be required for districts of more than 1,000 students in the 1989–90 school year, but smaller districts will not be required to participate until 1990–91. Not only is the plan two years from full implementation, but several bills have already been introduced in the Minnesota legislature to address problems that have materialized. Gov. Perpich's premature promotional tours lead one to question whether the real benefits of open enrollment are not more political than educational.

A closer examination of the concept of open enrollment and of its consequences raises a number of questions. Which parents and students will choose to leave their resident districts—and why? What happens to the students and the school districts that are left behind? Are the principles of competition that govern private enterprise relevant for education?

The basic assumption of open enrollment is that students and parents will exercise choice in order to gain access to better academic programs or to academic programs that are not available in their own school districts. However, open enrollment in Minnesota is a laissez-faire program; restrictions apply only to three districts operating under desegregation guidelines. Therefore, any student can change schools and districts for any reason, and the reasons do not have to be stated. Families need only provide their own transportation to the boundary of the nonresident district.

Nevertheless, open enrollment is elitist—at least in the sense that only those who have the means to do the driving will be able to choose. Choice will not be available to many low-income or single-parent families. Distance and geography will also determine who can choose, especially when extracurricular activities are added to the schedule.

So who will go? It may be a district's top scholars, looking for expanded curricula. It may be a district's top athletes, looking for better teams and better scholarship opportunities or responding to recruitment by a neighboring coach. Students may also leave to escape high academic standards, stiff graduation requirements, or unpopular disciplinary action. More troubling still, it could be that parents will move their children to avoid close scrutiny regarding child abuse or neglect. Parents may make choices based on the convenience of day care. Or they may exercise choice if they are unhappy with a school board's decision on a controversial issue. While not all of these reasons are inherently wrong, they do not fit the basic assumptions of choice. Moreover, most have absolutely nothing to do with "competition for excellence," and they have some significant destructive potential.

Once open enrollment is in effect, parents can remove their children from districts that have had to close school buildings. In fact, they are already doing just that. In the Mountain Iron-Buhl School District, parents of more than 50% of the district's 550 secondary students have filed the forms necessary to transfer for the 1989–90 school year as a result of a controversial high school closing. In the Mound-Westonka School District, parents of 131 students have done the same because they are dissatisfied with the results of a recent referendum. Open enrollment leaves a school board terribly vulnerable to single-issue pressure groups. Any controversy—from students with AIDS to censor-

Source: From Judith Pearson, "Myths of Choice: The Governor's New Clothes?," *Phi Delta Kappa*, Volume 70, Number 10, June 1989, pp. 821–823. Reprinted with permission from the publisher and from Judith Pearson.

ship to a teacher strike—could potentially decimate a school district.

For school districts in Minnesota, that decimation includes financial penalties because state aid is attached to enrollments. The amount of state aid per pupil-unit for the 1989–90 school year varies from $4,000 to $5,000, depending on the district formula. If 100 secondary students leave a district, with each secondary student calculated at 1.35 pupil-units, the loss in revenue could be $675,000. In the Mountain Iron-Buhl School District, the loss in revenue because of open enrollment is estimated to be $1.2 million for the 1989–90 school year.

Whatever the reasons why students leave a district, what happens to the students and the districts that are left behind? Once a school district loses significant enrollment, an irreversible sequence of events is set in motion. The loss in revenue forces reductions in expenditures, which in turn will force reduction in programs and services. These reductions will probably prompt further enrollment losses, accompanied by revenue losses, and so on. It is only a matter of time before the district collapses. But how much time? How many years of deteriorating quality of education lie ahead for those left behind? What about those students and parents who can't choose to leave and are now trapped in a declining district?

What form will the final collapse take in those school districts that are injured in the first round? Will the winning districts next door be eager—or even willing—to consolidate, pair, or share? Absolutely not! Why should they, when all current Minnesota legislation on school district reorganization includes obligations regarding teacher seniority, assumption of indebtedness, and ownership/maintenance of school facilities? Open enrollment carries no such obligations. The winning districts can simply accept the new students—with no strings attached.

Could the losing districts perhaps raise local property taxes to compensate for the loss in state aid? In the new, competitive environment, this will be difficult, because Minnesota requires any increase in local property taxes for school districts to be approved by the voters in an "excess levy" referendum. Why would parents vote to increase their property taxes for schools when they can simply enroll their children in neighboring districts? Such a step would be particularly prudent if the neighboring district has already passed an excess levy or built a new facility. One can then benefit from the additional programs or new facilities while someone else pays the bill.

The prospect of these kinds of student migrations raises questions abut the effect of open enrollment on school district governance, local control, and grassroots democracy. Tough, courageous decision making by school boards becomes risky and increasingly unlikely. The survival of school districts becomes a matter of "body counts," and all decisions will be made with one eye on the open doors. The issue is further complicated when one realizes that parents who have moved their children out of their home districts will be voting for school boards that no longer educate their children and will *not* be voting for school boards that do. What happens to the concept of accountability to the electorate? Isn't this de facto disenfranchisement? What happens to grassroots democracy in this "like it or leave it" program? Who is left to serve as the loyal opposition?

Thomas Jefferson wrote, "I know of no safe depository of the ultimate powers of the society but the people themselves; and if we think them not enlightened enough to exercise their control with wholesome discretion, the remedy is not to take it from them, but to inform their discretion by education." This imperative relationship between a democratic society and its educational institutions is expanded in the Minnesota Constitution. Article XIII says, "The stability of a republican form of government depending mainly upon the intelligence of the people, it is the duty of the legislature to establish a general and uniform system of public schools."

The key words here are *general* and *uniform*. Open enrollment is an admission that the schools are not uniform. Furthermore, it sets processes and procedures in motion that encourage some districts to become more excellent—at the expense of other districts.

Open enrollment not only fails to live up to the challenge in the Minnesota Constitution, but it may also fail to meet the provisions of the U.S. Constitution. The 14th Amendment declares, "No state shall make or enforce any law . . . nor deny to any person within its jurisdiction the equal protection of the laws." The courts have interpreted this equal protection clause to include "equal benefit." Clearly, educational benefits will be increasingly *unequal* under the open-enrollment plan. If the Minnesota legislature doesn't get busy repairing the damage, it seems probable that the courts will do so.

Granted, the challenge of operating uniform schools is always difficult. Equal dollars do not make equal schools. Equitable programs will always be difficult to achieve in small school districts that have little property of value and that serve sparsely populated rural areas. Open enrollment is a quick fix for a complex and difficult problem. It is a political experiment—with students, school districts, and communities as the guinea pigs. What if the experiment fails?

Open enrollment is an administrative conundrum. Administrators in districts that students leave will be busy cutting programs to make up for lost enrollments and revenues, just when they should be adding programs to attract new enrollments and revenues. Moreover, the tasks of budgeting, staffing, and scheduling become even more difficult, because Minnesota's choice program does not require any commitment on the part of the new enrollees. They must sign up for open enrollment in the nonresident district before January 1 in order to facilitate planning for the following September. However, they are under no legal obligation to actually attend the nonresident district.

I do not wish to suggest that parents and/or students might be fickle, but what if they are? What if 11th hour political compromise is reached in the home district and significant numbers of students choose not to leave? The nonresident district will already have scheduled space and hired staff to make room for these students, and the home district will have laid off staff members and closed course sections. Open enrollment makes "administrative planning" the oxymoron of education. I wonder whether there was *any* professional input in the legislative process that passed open enrollment.

Shifting enrollments, blowing in the winds of day-care convenience, local elections, or political controversy, will result in unpredictable pockets of teacher unemployment. Teachers laid off because of open enrollment will have none of the seniority and licensure protections that are included in every Minnesota law that governs school district cooperation or reorganization. And will the districts to which large numbers of students migrate hire these senior and more expensive teachers to accommodate their expanding enrollments? Why should they, when they can hire two teachers right out of college for the price of one laid-off veteran? Was this failure to address teacher seniority a legislative oversight, or was it deliberate? Why would anyone want to enter the education profession in an environment so fickle and chaotic?

How could such dramatically new and sweeping changes be enacted into law so quickly in Minnesota? The answer is a combination of politics and the private sector. The legislature granted Gov. Perpich the prerogative to directly appoint the commissioner of education, which, in effect, turned the Minnesota State Department of Education into a political arm of the governor's office. When this structural change in the educational bureaucracy was combined with enthusiastic support for open enrollment from the Minnesota business community, the bandwagon was off and running.

The private sector, oversimplifying and overinterpreting declining test scores, naively assumed that the introduction of competition would automatically increase productivity in education. It is bad enough that this assumption is unsupported by any research or reliable data. It is far worse to have forgotten the abuses of competition in business and to have neglected to anticipate similar abuses in education.

How long before we see abuses in the recruitment of high school athletes and scholars? What form will insider trading or industrial sabotage take? What happens when principals and teachers forget the welfare of *all* students in their frantic bidding for those "attractive" scholars and athletes who will provide the school with positive public relations? Who will worry about unattractive students—the handicapped and the emotionally disturbed—who come with high cost and little prospect of a public relations payoff? How soon before high expectations and standards give way to mediocrity as the safest course for insuring high body counts? Do we really want slick and expensive advertising campaigns to direct educational choice? What about the possibility of false advertising? Will we need consumer protection laws to guarantee that basic skills are not neglected? Can we recall a faulty product?

Potential abuses aside, the basic principles of private business and competition simply don't apply to education. Resident districts have no control over the quality of the raw materials that they begin with; they must accept and educate all students, regardless of their capacity to learn. School districts also have very little control over their labor force. State laws, collective bargaining agreements, and court and arbitration decisions dictate who, when, and how district employees can be laid off or terminated. The administrative time, energy, and expense necessary to meet all the tests of law and regulation in a termination case have always baffled those in the private sector. But how can a school district compete, when it cannot fire the incompetent or reward the best?

My point is not to attack these legal constraints, many of which are essential to protect the institution of public education in a democratic society. My point is simply that private businesspeople often oversimplify education in all respects. Such concepts as accountability, productivity, and profitability fail to recognize the less tangible, less measurable purposes and products of our schools: citizenship, leadership, community identity, integration, mainstreaming, nutrition, parenting, discipline, punctuality—the list is endless. A school is a complex social institution and cannot be reduced to a simple balance sheet.

The myths of choice are clear, and Minnesota's open-enrollment plan will soon make choice of any kind a myth in many Minnesota communities. The choice to remain in local schools will be gone, along with some measure of community identity and of quality of life in rural, small-town Minnesota.

Will we have excellence in return? Between a first-round loss of enrollment and the eventual collapse of a district, the quality of education will deteriorate. This is a high price to pay in an effort to answer that question. One thing is certain: changes or modifications in the law will not reopen schools where there are no districts.

However, the political investment has paid off big. Minnesota is on the map again. The *Arizona Republic* has called Gov. Perpich the "Pied Piper of Choice." Meanwhile, Minnesotans need to work to get the lid back on "Pandora's Box," and they need to reread "The Emperor's New Clothes."

70

The Future of America's Schools

What Do These Trends Mean for Education?

Dennis R. Clodi
John Jacobson

Opportunities and challenges. The future holds both for school and private business leaders who recognize the interdependence between education and our economy.

Reflecting on specific trends will help educators develop strategies to meet the opportunities and challenges of the future. Educators, business leaders, and futurists are exploring these ideas through a series of conferences co-sponsored by the American Association of School Administrators and the Allstate Insurance Company.

THE 1990s EXPLOSION

Here is a snapshot of the 1990s:

- The population will grow 1 percent per year.
- The baby boomers will be age 40 or older.
- People over age 85 will outnumber teens.
- The median age of the entire population will climb.
- Life expectancy in the year 2000 will be 77.
- Minority populations will increase rapidly with Hispanics becoming the biggest group.
- The population will shift to the South and Southwest.

Of great importance, a social values revolution will occur that will increase the need for workers with competent vocational skills and continue the increase of service-oriented jobs. The middle class will have less spendable income and many more families will have two wage earners. Women will continue to be drawn into the job market and fewer jobs will require four-year degrees. Only 15 percent of jobs will be filled by white males.

Unfortunately, the trends toward decreased family stability, increased divorce rates, and more childless couples or single parents will continue. Fewer people will be able to obtain upper-middle-class jobs and leisure time will become more scarce.

Simultaneously, we may experience what some have called the "Lite" decade: a period long on image, but short on substance. Fewer people will have time for cultural pursuits and fast foods and "Doc in a Box" health care will be the norm.

A LOOK BACK

To prepare for the future, a look at the past and present can be instructive. During the post-World War II period, an economic agenda predominated the 1950s. The "baby boomers" were about eight years old then.

Society's goals centered on becoming upwardly mobile, acquiring more material possessions, and providing more for one's children. As a country, we tried to move the U.S. in a position of world leadership and dominance.

Life was tranquil and beautiful and people expected the economy to be on automatic pilot and continue to grow with little guidance or intervention. A "psychology of affluence" took over lives and attitudes.

The 1960s and 1970s, however, were dominated by a social agenda that loosened constraints on "me" values. It was a time of "fix-it" social issues and a movement toward spreading middle-class benefits to all via removing inequalities among people (egalitarianism) and providing for all through entitlement.

During the previous decade, people knew more about "how to make a living than they did about living." The 1960s tried to correct this lifestyle.

The 1980s has tried to provide a synthesis of both earlier periods. It has been a time of sorting things out and taking time to cope with realities such as Watergate, Vietnam, oil problems, Iran, and terrorism. The 1980s threatened the upward mobility of people and posed serious questions about the affordability of "fix-it" social values.

Now, the U.S. faces increasing world pressure on the industrial, economic, and political fronts. A longing to return to the basics and the tranquil lifestyles of the 1950s has surfaced. Some movement is occurring away from equality of entitlement for all as we examine which of our traditional values will be maintained.

TOUGH TIMES AHEAD

Experts point to the trends that will shape the social climate of the 1990s and beyond.

The psychology of affluence is eroding. People increasingly feel that the "party is over"; economic limits have been reached; nothing can be taken for granted; decisions

Source: Dennis R. Clodi and John Jacobson, "The Future of America's Schools: What Do These Trends Mean for Education?," *The School Administrator*, Volume 46, Number 4, April 1989, pp. 15–16, 18.

of all types and at almost all levels will be driven by economics; and the future holds only signals for "hunkering down" for some tough times.

Both individuals and institutions are recognizing and accepting that we are becoming a society of "winners and losers," "haves and have nots." Upward mobility for all is being seriously questioned. And a number of people question whether we can afford equality or entitlement or even *if* we should try to afford it. A sharp decline in the progress toward affluence is occurring.

More people are focusing on the future rather than the past and realizing that planning must be done. "Live for today" doesn't feel right anymore. The intense focus on fitness/wellness and personal/family financial planning reflects the fact that fewer people assume previously secure aspects of life.

A recommitment to the idea of the traditional household of one worker, two parents, and 2.7 school-age children is occurring. But the change will be more psychological than demographic.

People will experience increased pressure to return to the serenity and goodness of the 1950s and a resurgence in child-centered attitudes and behaviors will occur. Women will begin to leave corporate jobs as they reach unbreakable plateaus and salaries.

FUTURE FAMILIES

More women will venture into entrepreneurial enterprises operating out of their homes as they try to balance family and career. The family of the future will have fewer children but parents will strive to "give them everything."

A growing movement toward a more rigid morality will occur. People will be more inclined toward "doing what's right" not just "doing what's right for me." The feeling that we have let down our "moral guard" will lead to support for more societal rules for all, accompanied by a declining tolerance for cheating and law breaking.

Society will increase its acceptance of sacrifice as it adjusts to lower wages, fewer jobs, less material possessions, and more economically driven decisions.

GENERATION GAP CLOSES

The focus on older citizens will heighten as the baby boomers age, life expectancy increases, and values of the young and old begin to blend. Both age groups will share more values as we produce "older joggers" and "younger burnouts."

A move toward more formalism will occur. This will be evidenced by more traditional formal experiences such as proms, evening wear, and a return to elegance, manners, and traditionalism.

Such external behavior, outward symbols of "being one of the winners," will reflect the cohesive role rituals and broadly accepted codes of behavior play in our society. Dress codes will begin to return through the realization that standardized dress is cheaper and quicker—evidence of more decisions that are economically driven.

The hunger for "meaning" will increase and some religions will return to fundamentalism; cults will increase; people will need "something" to believe in; and they will need to focus on a goal rather than just "feeling good."

Citizens will increase their interest in local and state politics while they pull back from national political involvement. People will prepare themselves for a smaller pie, or at least a smaller piece of the pie, as they review their acceptance of the rights of passage and tradition. An implication of this trend for schools will be increased expectations to perform and behave well.

Last, and perhaps most crucial to public education, will be an acceptance of competitiveness as a way of life. An accelerated focus on adult literacy, curricular reform, and private sector efforts to retool or remediate the workforce will occur.

As more preschool, senior citizen, and retraining programs are demanded, public education will not automatically be the delivery system used. Rather, public education will have to compete in the open marketplace to deliver these services.

This competitive factor will be magnified by the growing foreign investment in U.S. industry, the role of organized labor, and the impact of Wall Street on decision making. The highest priority identified by business today is the preparation of America's workforce for the future.

EDUCATIONAL IMPLICATIONS

All these factors add up to the following critical educational issues:

- Vocational needs will change.
- Special problems will arise for rural and adult education.
- The home economics curricula will refocus to include child care, total health care, and nutrition.
- Programs will be needed to help students adjust to single-parent and latchkey homes.
- The role of senior citizens as both consumers and resources will need redefining.
- The need for programs for at-risk students and early childhood education programs will increase.
- Programs to increase funding for the arts and cultural education will have to be found.
- Aggressive competition with alternative and parochial schools will occur.
- A large decrease in the people believing they are middle class will occur (the belief may not be true).

THE BOTTOM LINE

Education must project its needs beyond that of just more funding. It must:

- identify its competition in the marketplace,
- identify and enlist potential allies,
- exploit its successes,
- increase the use of technology beyond that of managerial and resource functions,
- analyze demographics of the nation and local areas to adapt to changing needs,
- stop sending good money after bad,
- stop resisting all forms of change or reform,
- understand the values of constituents and integrate them into the decision-making process, and
- adopt strategic planning as one way to succeed in the future.

We must build the "perfect" educational system—one designed without regard for external or internal boundaries or limitations. We, then, must place that perfect system "on hold" and make daily decisions and plans based on reality as we take small steps toward implementing the perfect system.

We can no longer afford to be data rich and information poor. We must learn from where we have been and use the data to move forward on the strategic competitive edge. A quotation from an old slave comes to mind which aptly applies to the public education system: "We ain't where we're gonna be. We ain't where we wanna be. Thank God we ain't where we was!"

John Naisbett said, "Today's capital is the workforce and knowledge." Public education is in the best strategic position to build that capital.

Tim Watson said, "Organizations make mistakes in good times and find out about them in bad times." Consider this: Is public education having a good time?

If we fail to meet the challenges of the 1990s, the reason will not be because we failed to face our problems but because we failed to face the *right* problems.

Now is the time to renew the qualities of American competitiveness to ensure our leadership role in the international marketplace.

The business community stands ready to assist us in this shared agenda. The educational community is responsible for initiating this dialogue.

AASA is developing business supported foundations to promote common agendas between business and education as we prepare for the 21st century.

If you desire more information, please contact Walt Turner, executive director, American Association of Educational Service Agencies, 1801 N. Moore Street, Arlington, VA 22209.

Index